Justice Bertha Wilson

Law and Society Series
W. Wesley Pue, General Editor

The Law and Society Series explores law as a socially embedded phenomenon. It is premised on the understanding that the conventional division of law from society creates false dichotomies in thinking, scholarship, educational practice, and social life. Books in the series treat law and society as mutually constitutive and seek to bridge scholarship emerging from interdisciplinary engagement of law with disciplines such as politics, social theory, history, political economy, and gender studies.

A list of the titles in this series appears at the end of this book.

Edited by Kim Brooks

Justice Bertha Wilson
One Woman's Difference

UBCPress · Vancouver · Toronto

17 16 15 14 13 12 11 10 09   5 4 3 2 1

Printed in Canada on ancient-forest-free paper (100% post-consumer recycled) that is processed chlorine- and acid-free.

Library and Archives Canada Cataloguing in Publication

Justice Bertha Wilson : one woman's difference / edited by Kim Brooks.

(Law and society, 1496-4953)
Includes bibliographical references and index.
ISBN 978-0-7748-1732-5 (bound)
ISBN 978-0-7748-1733-2 (pbk.)
ISBN 978-0-7748-1734-9 (e-book)

1. Wilson, Bertha, 1923-2007. 2. Canada. Supreme Court – Biography. 3. Women judges – Canada – Biography. 4. Judges – Canada – Biography. I. Brooks, Kim II. Series: Law and society series (Vancouver, B.C.)

KE8248.W54J88 2009   347.71'03534   C2009-901348-7
KF345.Z9W54J88 2009

Canadä

UBC Press gratefully acknowledges the financial support for our publishing program of the Government of Canada through the Book Publishing Industry Development Program (BPIDP), and of the Canada Council for the Arts, and the British Columbia Arts Council.

This book has been published with the help of a grant from the Canadian Federation for the Humanities and Social Sciences, through the Aid to Scholarly Publications Programme, using funds provided by the Social Sciences and Humanities Research Council of Canada.

Printed and bound in Canada by Friesens
Set in Stone by Artegraphica Design Co. Ltd.
Copy editor: Deborah Kerr
Proofreader: Stacy Belden

UBC Press
The University of British Columbia
2029 West Mall
Vancouver, BC V6T 1Z2
604-822-5959 / Fax: 604-822-6083
www.ubcpress.ca

This collection is dedicated to the many women who make a difference, including Inez Lillian Henrietta Reid Baines, Ruth Brooks, Marlène Cano, Isabel Grant, Cecilia Johnstone, Lee Lakeman, Claire L'Heureux-Dubé, Doris Milberry, Mary Jane Mossman, Joyce O'Byrne, Sr Pauline O'Regan, Clarissa Otto, Kim Pate, Leona F. Paterson, Toni Pickard, Lynn Smith, Jane Tice, Margaret Van De Pitte, Bertha Wilson, the women who worked together on the China-Canada Young Women's Project (1993-96), the women on the court, and the women on the Eaton's picket line.

Contents

Preface

Justice Claire L'Heureux-Dubé

In a speech on gender equality given at the University of Ottawa Faculty of Law in 1994, Justice Bertha Wilson posed the following question: "[W]here would we be without the strident voice of extremists who have the pristine courage to call ugly things by their proper names? The stance of the moderate is so often polite, respectable, soft-voiced and, worse still, tamely accommodating. Just look at history – it is the vigour and energy of the extremist who paints issues in bold colours that has been the engine of historical change, whose voice has been a clarion call to action and who will brook no delay. They may walk a hard and rough road but their spirit rides in style."[1] Interpreting Bertha's contributions as a woman, lawyer, and judge involves determining whether she spoke more in a strident voice or as a balanced incrementalist. Indeed, as this collection reveals, one of the many qualities that made Bertha such an important player in the Canadian legal landscape was her ability to alternate between these two voices.

Bertha was a woman of "firsts," although she never thought of herself like that. She was one of the earliest female graduates from a Canadian law school. After immigrating to Canada from Kirkaldy, Scotland, in 1949, Bertha spent five years as a parish minister's wife before applying to Dalhousie Law School in 1954 at the age of thirty-one. Upon submitting her application, she was told by the Dean of Dalhousie Law School that perhaps she would prefer crocheting. Undeterred, Bertha later mused, "It was hard for me to persuade him that I was a serious student; that for me a knowledge of the law was an essential part of a liberal education and that while crocheting might be a very pleasant way to spend one's leisure hours, it could not be the be-all and end-all of one's productive years."[2]

Bertha's history of firsts continued upon her graduation from law school. She was the first woman lawyer at Osler, Hoskin & Harcourt, where she practised for seventeen years. She was the first woman to make partner at the firm. In 1975 she became the first woman to sit on the Ontario Court of Appeal (where some of her male colleagues lamented the "encroachment" of a woman justice on their bench). Finally, in 1982, Bertha became the first woman to sit on the bench of the Supreme Court of Canada in the Court's 107-year history. There, she would have an incredible and direct impact for the next nine years.

In only nine years on the Supreme Court, Bertha seemed to shape a new century. On more instances than I can recall, the lights in the chamber hallways would be dimmed, and a heavy silence would have settled on the portraits of former Supreme Court justices. The building would be empty except for the spirits of those justices and a faint shaft of light creeping out from beneath Bertha's door. The majority judgment may have been written and her colleagues long departed, but Bertha would not quit until she had her concurrence or dissent penned. She had too much respect for the law and the Canadian people to give the decision anything but her most devoted efforts. I often thought that her quiet Scottish stubbornness drove her unrelenting work ethic; and it was an unrelenting work ethic indeed. In nine years, Bertha authored 179 judgments, 51 of which were formative *Charter* decisions. Between 1987 and 1990, she wrote more legal judgments than any other justice on the bench.

In each of her workplaces, Bertha brought a much needed voice, speaking for the protection and equality of women and minorities and advocating for human rights. Bertha's appointment to the Supreme Court coincided with the advent of the *Canadian Charter of Rights and Freedoms,* and her time on the bench was often defined by the strength and application of this incredible document. Her rulings in *Morgentaler,* in *Lavallee,* in *Andrews,* and in countless other cases helped shape not only Canada's legal landscape but also, indeed, our sense of who we are as Canadians. Bertha was a strong voice for the importance of a dialogue between legislature and judiciary. She saw herself as a servant of the law, of the *Charter,* and of the Canadian people. Although she was a true believer in the Canadian legal system, she nevertheless understood that it had yet to reach its full potential, and she was not prepared merely to settle for the status quo.

Bertha was not afraid to call ugly things by their proper names. She did not shy away from controversy when it was caused by standing up for social justice and equality. She recognized that the law is not a formal measuring stick to be strictly and blindly applied to each case. In short, Bertha brought judging into the twenty-first century. She believed that law is not a captive of the legal profession but rather a tool of the Canadian people. To Bertha, law was not an abstract positivist concept; nor was it removed from social context or judicial bias. By acknowledging these factors, Bertha produced judgments that were, in many cases, truly progressive and enlightened.

Bertha had an enormous influence on Canadian jurisprudence, as this collection reveals. Although she is best known for her judgments in cases such as *Operation Dismantle, Lavallee, Morgentaler,* and *Andrews,* she also had an immense effect on the evolution of Canadian law in all its aspects – from constitutional, family, and criminal law to contract, commercial, and international law. Many of Bertha's dissents and concurrent judgments were followed in later cases.

The extent of Bertha's effect on Canadian law brings me back to this collection. The chapters that follow examine many aspects of her influence on the legal system, the legal profession, and Canadian society. Although her specific judgments, publications, and committee works have been examined on their own accord, a comprehensive collection that is accessible to a wide audience is more than timely and well deserved. Bertha's presence and legacy loom in the legal world, but her effect on the legal system has also had incredible ramifications for the ordinary Canadian citizen. I am among the fortunate few who were not only privy to Bertha's incredible wisdom, intellect, and strength of character, but were also able to count her as a dearest friend, a colleague, and a mentor. This compilation examines the many roles that Bertha played: Bertha as jurist, as public figure, and as friend and role model.

Bertha was rather shy in public and often avoided the press. Yet, this shyness was never evident in her willingness to confront difficult issues and controversial topics. I do not think that Bertha failed to see the irony in that, though she personally avoided the spotlight, her words and judgments often could not hide from it. During her time on the Ontario Court of Appeal and at the Supreme Court, she never backed down, never relented, and, with a constant humility before the rule of law, settled for nothing short of justice. She was not afraid to pick up the reins of the *Canadian Charter of Rights and Freedoms* or to weigh in on complex commercial issues. Often touted as a legal pioneer, Bertha was also one who carried us into the future. This book is a tribute to her legal mind. To the late Justice Bertha Wilson: may her spirit ride in style.

Acknowledgment

I wish to acknowledge Leah Jane Kutcher, McGill University Faculty of Law, for her assistance on this project.

Notes

1 Bertha Wilson, "Gender Equality: A Challenge for the Legal Profession" (Speech delivered at the Faculty of Law, University of Ottawa, no date) [unpublished, notes on file with Kim Brooks] 5-6.

2 Rebecca Mae Salokar and Mary Volcansek, "Bertha Wilson" in *Women in Law: A Bio-Bibliographical Sourcebook* (London: Greenwood Press, 1996) 338 at 339.

Acknowledgments

As with any book, this collection would not have been possible without the hard work and support of many people. Each of the authors in the collection was wonderful to work with: responding quickly to requests, agreeing at all stages in the project to work collaboratively, writing thoughtful and reflective chapters, and delivering everything for the deadlines suggested. I am indebted to the wisdom and advice of innumerable women but might especially note Susan B. Boyd, Hester Lessard, Mary Jane Mossman, and Elizabeth Sheehy, all of whom provided advice in the early stages of the project. Many of the authors in the collection relied on the indispensable biography on Wilson's life *Judging Bertha Wilson: Law as Large as Life* authored by Ellen Anderson, and we are grateful that Anderson was able to provide us with that material with which to work. Finally, my gratitude goes to four research students who worked indefatigably through drafts of the book, Chana Edelstein, Daniel Girlando, Leah Jane Kutcher, and Palma Paciocco, to Julie Fontaine, who undertook the ugly task of bringing the whole thing together into one document, and to Randy Schmidt at UBC Press, who has worked tirelessly to bring this project to publication.

The collection would not have been possible without the support of the Social Sciences and Humanities Research Council, which, through its Aid to Research Workshops and Conferences in Canada program, supported an in-person meeting of the authors.

All royalties from this publication have been assigned to the Justice Bertha Wilson Fund established by the Women's Legal Education and Action Fund.

Introduction

Kim Brooks

> *Racine, Kamloops, Perka, Guerin, Singh, Big M Drug Mart, Operation Dismantle, Hill, Kosmopoulos, Pelech, Morgentaler, Crocker, Andrews, Vorvis, Tock, Lavallee, the Prostitution Reference, Hess/Nguyen, McKinney.*

•

These names have undoubtedly been indelibly impressed upon the consciousness of all students enrolled in law school after 1992. A good number of them are widely known among the Canadian public. The cases they represent are regularly relied upon by practising lawyers and have been the subject of heated academic commentary and debate. Justice Wilson, the first woman to be appointed to the Supreme Court of Canada, sworn in on 30 March 1982, less than three weeks before the *Canadian Charter of Rights and Freedoms* became law, wrote memorable judgments in each of these leading cases. She was, as the chapters that follow demonstrate, a prolific writer, and by the time her tenure at the Supreme Court ended in 1991, she had left an enduring mark, authoring an opinion in 179 cases.[1]

On the one hand, Bertha Wilson might seem an unlikely person to have claimed such an important role in the Canadian legal imagination. She was something of an outsider, born in Kirkcaldy, Scotland, in 1923. She immigrated to Canada in 1949.[2] She came to law later in life, enrolling at Dalhousie Law School at thirty-one years of age. She faced a number of barriers because of her gender. In many of her career choices, she was one of the first women to occupy the position: she was one of the early women law students at Dalhousie; she was the first woman to be hired by the firm Osler, Hoskin & Harcourt (in 1959), the first lawyer to head that firm's research department, and the first woman to become a partner.[3] In 1975 she was the first woman to be appointed to the Ontario Court of Appeal.

On the other hand, her personal qualities foreshadowed success. She had an enormous capacity and enthusiasm for hard work and a wide-ranging and irrepressible intellectual curiosity.[4] She was devoted to assisting in sustaining a flourishing community as reflected in her strong commitment to the legal profession, to public service,[5] and to a civil society.[6] She had a happy marriage, with a husband who both supported her career and was a partner in the work at home, without the demands of children.[7] Once on the bench, she had a high regard for those who preceded her[8] and a strong sense of the importance of the judge's role as the purveyor of incremental change.[9]

Bertha Wilson died on 28 April 2007. Her passing presented a moment for reflection on her contributions to law and legal practice and an impetus to situate her work in its current context. The chapters in this book reveal several dimensions, or themes, of Bertha Wilson's multi-faceted talents and career. First, many of them pay tribute to an aspect of her work that is sometimes overlooked: she was a marvellous legal technician. She had developed and refined her legal expertise significantly in the seventeen years that she worked at Osler. Several of the chapters draw out her ability to work with technical areas of the law in a way that reflects acuity, attention to detail, depth of understanding, and imagination. For example, she was able to translate her knowledge of fiduciary duties in family law to potential applications in commercial law,[10] and she exhibited inventiveness in building on prior common law judgments to articulate the potential for a new tort of discrimination.[11]

Second, despite, or perhaps because of, her technical facilities, Wilson was always willing to embrace controversy and challenge. Her early days in Toronto as the first woman articling student at the Osler firm presented numerous tests of her mettle.[12] Her time as the first woman on the Ontario Court of Appeal and later on the Supreme Court of Canada was no different. Her judgments in cases such as *Morgentaler,* which rendered unconstitutional Canada's criminalization of abortion, and *Lavallee,* in which the Court addressed the defence of self-defence in the context of male violence against women, brought her significant media and public notice. Other decisions garnered perhaps less media attention but have been characterized by academic commentators as controversial.[13] Any review of Wilson's judgments or other writing confirms that she did not shy away from controversy. She authored forty-one dissents, thirty-five concurrences, ten partial dissents, and thirty concurrences in plurality during her tenure on the Supreme Court.[14] Her speeches, including perhaps most notably her 1990 Barbara Betcherman Memorial Lecture "Will Women Judges Really Make a Difference?" given at Osgoode Hall Law School, also garnered a good deal of public and media attention, including a complaint to the Canadian Judicial Council on the basis that she was biased. Her articles are unabashed in taking issue with critics with whom she disagreed.[15] On the announcement of her retirement, the Montreal *Gazette* labelled her the Supreme Court's "most liberal and controversial judge."[16] After her retirement from the Supreme Court, she scarcely hid from continued controversy. She almost immediately took up the chair of the Canadian Bar Association Task Force on Gender Equality in the Legal Profession, a body charged with studying the condition of women in the legal profession, which she must have known would produce a contentious report.[17]

The controversial label, however, sits somewhat uneasily on Bertha Wilson, who, despite her remarkable list of "FW2s" (first woman to), had a complicated relationship with feminism and judicial activism. In a number of her interviews and speeches, she clearly recognized the differential treatment women receive relative to men, and in many cases she noted that such treatment amounted to discrimination.[18] In some instances, she courageously and loudly identified and condemned women's inequality, and in at least one instance, she identified herself as a "moderate feminist."[19] Yet, in the biography authored by Ellen Anderson, Justice Wilson appears as a woman who distanced herself from feminism.[20] And although her judgments and positions are clearly and carefully articulated, and although in some cases they describe the disadvantages faced by women and other equality-seeking groups, numerous scholars have critiqued her work for not going far enough to support those groups. A number of the chapters in this collection struggle with Justice Wilson's relationship to feminism, attempting to make sense of her judgments and her public positions. Regardless of whether one characterizes Justice Wilson or any of her judgments as feminist, especially in her decisions outside of criminal and constitutional law, she might be best described as an incrementalist, intent on the gradual development of the law.[21] On the face of the complete record, it would be hard to fathom Bertha Wilson as a radical who would inspire the label the "most controversial" judge.

Another aspect of Wilson's work that is emphasized in many chapters is her insistence on situating law in its wider context. In her remarks on her retirement, she reflected that "[t]he *Charter* put law into its true perspective – as large as life itself – not a narrow legalistic discipline in which inflexible rules are applied regardless of the justice or fairness of the result, but a set of values that we, as a civilized, cultured and caring people, endorse as the right of all our citizens of whatever colour or creed, male or female, rich or poor, to enjoy."[22] Although the demand for a contextual analysis seems to be a regular refrain in current judicial decision making, its pervasiveness has been attributed to the efforts of Justice Wilson at the Supreme Court. Her success in persuading the Court of the importance of a contextual analysis is not without controversy itself. She and her work have been criticized by some academic commentators who express concerns that such an analysis can easily become divorced from legal principles.[23] Nevertheless, Justice Wilson remained a constant advocate of the importance of context and supported social context training for the judiciary.[24] The authors in this collection accept the importance of context, querying instead what sort of context is relevant and questioning whether Justice Wilson went far enough in incorporating context into her own judgments.[25]

The fourth dimension of Justice Wilson's work, one related to her ability to locate law in its social, economic, and political context, is the passion she appears to have had for the protection of the equality rights of marginalized communities and "ordinary citizens," which in turn was fuelled by her capacity for "entering into the skin" of litigants.[26] These abilities, which echo through the record of her life, may have stemmed from her full and varied experience: as a student of "Enlightenment Scotland";[27] a clergyperson's wife; a receptionist in a dental office; an immigrant to Canada; a mature law student who had been discouraged from attending law school; an articling student working on prostitution cases, buggery charges, and drunk and disorderly files; a reluctantly, but eventually warmly, embraced articling student and then lawyer on Bay Street; and from her interest in reading literature. This empathy is, perhaps, what informs her strong support (whatever her identification with feminism) for women and other equality-seeking groups and for fairness and justice, broadly cast.[28] She was, for example, a strong proponent of the Court Challenges Program, a project that enabled minority language and equality challenges to be at least partially funded by the federal government,[29] and of access to justice measures generally.[30] Also, despite the demanding nature of the work and the controversy she would undoubtedly encounter, she was an enthusiastic chair of the Canadian Bar Association Task Force and a member of the Royal Commission on Aboriginal Peoples.

Finally, the degree to which the details of Justice Wilson's life inform her judgments is an underlying theme in many of the chapters in this collection. Perhaps predictably, some commentators are more focused on the implications of her personal experiences on her family and criminal law decisions, and on her views about judging more broadly, than they are on the implications of those experiences in her commercial and private law decisions.[31] Yet, even in these private law areas, connections between Bertha Wilson's life experience and her decisions receive attention.[32]

The title of this collection, *Justice Bertha Wilson: One Woman's Difference,* highlights many of the themes identified in this introduction that thread throughout the following chapters. Most obviously, it raises the question of what difference Justice Wilson made, without prejudging whether that difference might be evaluated positively or negatively in any given instance.[33] But the title also means to invoke other questions, including the one she posed for herself in her most famous speech "Will Women Judges Really Make a Difference?" This question, in turn, alludes to an issue raised in psychologist Carol Gilligan's *In a Different Voice*. Published in the year of Wilson's appointment to the Supreme Court, this book posited that women were more likely than men to engage in moral argumentation that emphasized specific contexts and relationships.[34] In addition, the title raises the often-evoked question of the possible effect of Justice Wilson's sex and gender on her judicial decision making and on her approach as lawyer and advocate. It underscores the fact that, although Wilson might have made a difference, she was only one woman, and we should not necessarily expect her to make a difference for all women. Finally, the title raises the question of whether there was something about Justice Wilson herself that made her different from other women – more likely, perhaps, to be the kind of person who would, again and again, become the "first woman to."[35]

The chapters in the collection are grouped into three parts: Foundations, Controversy, and Reflections. The first explores Justice Wilson's contributions in the areas often considered to be building blocks of the common law system, including property law, contract law, and fiduciary duties. These areas were the core of Wilson's legal practice at Osler and also the subject of her earliest articles after she graduated from law school.[36] Few commentators have explored her work in these areas.[37]

Part 1 opens with a chapter authored by Angela Fernandez and Beatrice Tice, which sets Justice Wilson's private law expertise in context by detailing her efforts to establish a research practice and department at Osler. On one level, the chapter presents a social history of law firm practice in the period from 1958 to 1975. It is rich with original research thanks to the extensive interview data gathered by the authors, who interviewed several of the lawyers who worked with Wilson during her time at the firm. The chapter reveals Wilson's meticulous and careful work habits, her facility with systems and processes, and her ability to press lightly at the boundaries and to "get along" and "fit in" without upsetting the entire workings of networks and practices that predated her arrival. These skills, along with the development of the extensive and in-depth legal knowledge of many areas of law required for the client service she provided in her practice, prepared her for the challenges she would face upon her move to the bench in 1975.

In Chapter 2, Larissa Katz focuses on Justice Wilson's property law jurisprudence. She underlines Wilson's early interest in property law and her enthusiasm for the subject (indeed, she won a scholarship, which she did not pursue, to undertake graduate work at Harvard in property law and nuisance). After a brief tour of Justice Wilson's property law contributions on the bench, the chapter turns to a rehabilitation of her decision in *Keefer,* a case addressing adverse possession, or squatters' rights, which the author argues has been misunderstood.

Building on the idea that Justice Wilson was an able technician, well versed in the difficult areas of private law, Chapter 3, by Janis Sarra, explores Justice Wilson's development of the concept of fiduciary obligation in the corporate and commercial law areas and the use of equitable remedies when those obligations are breached. Sarra's illustration of how Justice Wilson imported equitable principles into commercial law reveals Wilson's ability to abstract from legal categories that appear closed to broader underlying principles. It also underlines Justice Wilson's ability to draw connections between different areas of the law in the search for those broad and unifying principles.

Chapter 4 turns to Justice Wilson's contract law decisions, and here Moira McConnell addresses whether Wilson was primarily a skilled and careful technician, gradually developing but not altering the principles found in the common law, or an innovator bringing a unique perspective to the application of those principles. Ultimately, McConnell suggests that Justice Wilson was perhaps a bit of both. In arriving at this conclusion, she reviews a broad sample of Justice Wilson's contract law cases. The review reveals Wilson's preoccupation with reasonableness, fairness, and justice.

Wilson's willingness to recognize in the law the fullness of what it is to be human, including, for example, her recognition of the emotional side of human relationships, is one element of her judging that perhaps most distinguished her from those who preceded her on the Supreme Court. Part 1 concludes with Chapter 5, Shannon O'Byrne's illustration of how Justice Wilson provided the groundwork required to give emotions their due in the area of intangible loss in contract law. O'Byrne's analysis reviews the deep-rooted history of the devaluation of emotion in law and sets Justice Wilson's unique contributions in this area into their broader context – a context that enabled judges to strenuously resist the incursion of emotion into their reasons and remedies.

Part 2 of the collection (Controversy) examines Justice Wilson's publicly controversial contributions, largely in the area of public law. Although a number of scholars have explored her contributions in these areas, these chapters seek to take the analysis further, setting them in their wider social and economic context, and in the light of the subsequent developments in the law.

Part 2 opens with Chapter 6, by Elizabeth Adjin-Tettey, which examines the tort of discrimination. During her tenure on the Ontario Court of Appeal, Justice Wilson authored a judgment that would have enabled courts to develop a tort of discrimination. This opening was, however, quickly closed by the Supreme Court, which held that provincial human rights codes present complete systems of justice that preclude discrimination claims through the common law. Adjin-Tettey argues that a separate tort action for discrimination would rectify what has become a two-tier system of access to justice for victims of discrimination. Her piece is particularly timely since the Supreme Court revisited this issue in a 2008 decision and again concluded (contrary to Justice Wilson's holding in *Bhadauria*) that, at least at this time, there is no separate actionable tort of discrimination.

The regulation of prostitution has posed innumerable challenges for judges and legislators. In Chapter 7, Janine Benedet sets Justice Wilson's contributions to the jurisprudence on the criminal law regulating prostitution-related activities within various paradigms of prostitution. She argues that few commentators (and perhaps fewer judges) explicitly recognize the importance of the paradigm they embrace in their analysis of the criminal laws of prostitution; however, Justice Wilson at least appears to have perceived that, by and large, the paradigm chosen predetermines the legal outcome. Given that there are two cases currently before the courts that challenge Canada's prostitution-related offences, Benedet's piece is a timely and significant contribution.

In Chapter 8, Isabel Grant and Debra Parkes turn to criminal law defences, reviewing the contributions of Justice Wilson to locating law, and these defences in particular, within their social context. Wilson's developing understanding of equality in criminal law is traced through three of her most significant decisions – *Perka, Hill,* and *Lavallee*. The authors argue that courts need to build on Justice Wilson's analysis by extending a contextual inquiry beyond the facts of particular cases and into the social context of the particular criminal law defence itself, situating that defence within historical and existing inequalities.

Chapter 9 moves from criminal law to family law but remains focused on the importance of context. Gillian Calder examines the significance of the role of time and prevailing attitudes and values in *Racine*. She locates the decision within the residential school experience and the sixties scoop, and the subsequent scholarship on *Racine* and the law that builds the case. Ultimately, the author urges courts (and scholars) to be conscious of the relationship between law, culture, and time and to interrogate the linear, liberal, and individual conception of time reflected in many child welfare adjudications.

Part 2 concludes with Chapter 10, Susan Boyd's review of Justice Wilson's child custody and access decisions. Justice Wilson's family law decisions have been much critiqued by feminist scholars, and many have been considered highly controversial. Boyd locates them in their broader context by situating them within the shifting socio-legal norms relating to children, family, motherhood, and fatherhood. Perhaps not surprisingly, given her penchant for writing in dissent, in five of the seven judgments analyzed by Boyd, Justice Wilson was writing in dissent. Ultimately, Boyd explains Justice Wilson's decisions by reference to the law reform movements of the time, concluding that, though some of her decisions exposed the impact of patriarchal norms on the development of the law, others laid the groundwork for the mother blaming that has arisen in subsequent child custody decisions.

Part 3 of the collection (Reflections) includes chapters that provide an overview of Justice Wilson's contributions to the law and the legal profession.

It opens with Chapter 11, by Beverley Baines, which squarely addresses the question of whether Bertha Wilson can be called a feminist judge. In evaluating Wilson's commitment to substantive equality, Baines discusses three of her most contentious decisions – *Pelech, Morgentaler,* and *Hess; Nguyen.* Like Calder and Boyd (in Chapters 9 and 10), Baines identifies the effect of the passage of time and changing attitudes and values on our reading of these decisions. She offers a new lens through which to examine Justice Wilson's decisions – gender theory – which requires interrogating the distinctions between sex and gender. Baines concludes that, at least by the standards of her time, Justice Wilson could be called a feminist judge, although she notes that whether these three judgments line up with contemporary gender theory will require building further on the analysis she provides in the chapter.

In Chapter 12, Marie-Claire Belleau, Rebecca Johnson, and Christina Vinters provide systematic empirical evidence in approaching the question of what kind of difference Justice Wilson made. They explore the degree to which Wilson was able to manifest judicial creativity through her authorship of concurrences and dissents. Their analysis confirms her willingness to express a contrary opinion and point of view; in particular, it emphasizes her high rate of writing separate opinions and her lower rate of signing them.

In Chapter 13, a more personal account of Bertha Wilson, Lorna Turnbull addresses her importance as a role model. In innumerable accounts of Wilson, authored on her appointment to both benches, upon her retirement, and at her death, women emphasize her significance as a role model. Yet, this element of her life is hard to theorize and hence has received little sustained attention. In her chapter, Turnbull situates her own relationship with Bertha Wilson within the context of the literature on role modelling. Turnbull's analysis reveals the importance not only of the professional accomplishments of role models but also of their personal attributes.

Chapters 14 and 15 address Bertha Wilson's contributions to the Canadian Bar Association Task Force on Gender Equality in the Legal Profession and some of its ramifications for judicial education. These aspects of Wilson's work have been almost entirely ignored by commentators in the past, despite the fact that her contributions to women's advancement in the legal profession and to the process of judging and education of judges were significant. In Chapter 14, Melina Buckley, who participated with Wilson on the task force, recounts its formation and history, details its workings, and discusses the release of its report. Her analysis provides some insight into Wilson's meticulous, thorough, and thoughtful nature, as well as supports the many accounts of Wilson's industry. It also underlines the effect of these kinds of processes on the education of those involved in them.

In Chapter 15, Rosemary Cairns Way and Brettel Dawson use Bertha Wilson's public commitment to reconceptualizing the judicial role and her public stance on the importance of judicial education as the jumping-off point for a detailed social history of the evolution of social context education in Canada. The authors have each played central roles in the National Judicial Institute's social context education program and are therefore well positioned to recount this previously untold story. They conclude the chapter by referring back to Justice Wilson's own words from her Betcherman Lecture, leaving the reader on the optimistic note that women judges and women lawyers can and will continue to make a difference.

The collection ends with Chapter 16, by Mary Jane Mossman, which queries the silences in Bertha Wilson's story. To explore the way in which gender was both present and absent from the text of Wilson's life, Mossman focuses on three of her decisions – *Re Rynard, Pettkus,* and *Pelech* – and challenges a linear story of the evolution of Wilson's ideas. She urges the reader to explore Wilson's non-*Charter* decisions more carefully, something this collection begins to do, as a way of better understanding Wilson the woman. Finally, she concludes by returning to the importance of considering how Wilson's relationship with the male legal world would have influenced her feeling that she needed to prove herself repeatedly, as well as how male lawyers might have assisted her in her judicial appointments and other career successes.

This introduction opened with a list of Justice Wilson's best-known Supreme Court of Canada judgments. But those judgments represent only a small sample of her work on the Court, a smaller portion of her work as a judge, and a fragment of her work as a jurist; they give us very little insight, perhaps, about who she was as a person and as a woman. They leave us with questions about the "silences" in her record. We hope that this collection will lead its readers to speculate not only about the questions raised by Bertha Wilson's astonishing record of work but also about the questions we cannot answer from the record about who this pioneering, influential, and extraordinary woman was.

Acknowledgments
Thanks to Susan B. Boyd, Gillian Calder, and Debra Parkes for comments on an earlier version of this introduction.

Notes

1 See Chapter 12 for a review of Justice Wilson's authorial patterns while on the Supreme Court.

2 For a discussion of the characterization of the relationship between Bertha Wilson's gender and her immigrant status, see Chapter 16, 298-99, this volume.

3 For details, see Chapter 1, this volume.

4 A review of Justice Wilson's many speeches reveals an astonishing familiarity and comfort with many philosophers, legal scholars, literary scholars and authors, and political theorists, including, simply to illustrate, Aristotle, James Boswell, Robert Burns, Marc Connelly, Peter de Vries, Carol Gilligan, David Hume, Jane Jenson, Duncan Kennedy, Roscoe Pound, Peter Russell, and Henry Marshall Tory, among many others, despite her statement that she "went

to university against [her] will." See Susan Lightstone, "Bertha Wilson: A Personal View on Women and the Law" *National* (August-September 1993) 12 at 12.

5 For example, Bertha Wilson sat on the Board of Trustees of the Clarke Institute of Psychiatry, the Toronto School of Theology, and the Canadian Centre for Philanthropy, was Chair of the Rhodes Scholarship Selection Committee (Ontario), and was a member on the Board of Governors of Carleton University.

6 In a 1993 interview with Susan Lightstone, Justice Wilson stated, "I could never complain about paying taxes." See Lightstone, *supra* note 4 at 12.

7 Indeed, her partner, the Reverend John Wilson, reportedly shared in a good many of the household tasks during their marriage. His 28 June 2008 obituary in the *Ottawa Citizen* states that, since her death on 28 April 2007, "life has been kind of a shadowland, punctuated with memories of a wonderful partnership, where we shared joys and sorrows, disappointments and triumphs." John Wilson's Obituary, *Ottawa Citizen* (28 July 2008) E7.

8 See *e.g.* her comments on her 30 March 1982 Supreme Court of Canada swearing-in: "I can only pray that by being a true servant of the law, I can in some measure worthily follow in the footsteps of the distinguished predecessors who have sat on this Bench before me." Bertha Wilson, "The Honourable Madame Justice Bertha Wilson" (1982) 16 L. Soc'y Gaz. 172 at 179.

9 See *e.g.* her reportedly incendiary (and yet surprisingly tame) speech "Will Women Judges Really Make a Difference?" where she reflects that "[c]hange in the law comes slowly and incrementally; that is its nature." Bertha Wilson, "Will Women Judges Really Make a Difference?" (1990) 28 Osgoode Hall L.J. 507 at 507.

10 See Chapter 3, this volume, for a discussion of the application of Justice Wilson's *Frame v. Smith* decision in the context of commercial law.

11 See Chapter 6, this volume, for an examination of *Seneca College v. Bhadauria*.

12 For the story of the development of Bertha Wilson's research expertise at Osler, see Chapter 1, this volume.

13 See *e.g.* Chapter 2, this volume, for an analysis of Justice Wilson's decision on adverse possession.

14 For details, see Chapter 12, this volume.

15 See *e.g.* her unequivocal reply to Robert Fulford's critique of the Court's use of the *Charter* in "Law and Policy in a Court of Last Resort" in Frank E. McArdle, ed., *The Cambridge Lectures* (Montreal: Édition Yvon Blais, 1990) 219 at 220 ("It will not surprise this audience to learn that I cannot agree with Mr. Fulford").

16 See Steven Bindman, "First Woman on Supreme Court to Retire in '91: Public-Shy Wilson Inspired Controversy with Her Liberal Views" *Gazette* (21 November 1990) A1. The comment was echoed in the *Toronto Star:* see David Vienneau, "Retiring Justice Praises Charter" *Toronto Star* (5 December 1990) A11.

17 See Chapters 14 and 15, this volume.

18 See *e.g.* her interviews with Susan Lightstone and David Vienneau. Lightstone, *supra* note 4; David Vienneau, "One on One with Bertha Wilson" *Law Times* (21-27 March 1994). See also her speech on gender equality in which she asserts that gender bias "seeps like a noxious pollutant into the fibres of society in ever new and subtle forms": "Gender Equality: A Challenge for the Law Profession" (Speech delivered at the Faculty of Law, University of Ottawa, no date) at 3 [unpublished, notes on file with author]. See also her article "Women, the Family, and the Constitutional Protection of Privacy" (1992) 17 Queen's L.J. 5 at 14 ("much of women's experience of inequality, degradation, and subjugation has been perpetrated by the institution of the family and by their loved ones behind closed doors").

19 Sandra Gwyn, "Sense and Sensibility" *Saturday Night* (July 1985) 13 at 19.

20 Ellen Anderson, *Judging Bertha Wilson: Law as Large as Life* (Toronto: University of Toronto Press for the Osgoode Society for Canadian Legal History, 2001). Several reviewers of the biography focus on the degree to which it reflects a vilification of feminism. See *e.g.* Clare McGlynn, "Ellen Anderson, *Judging Bertha Wilson: Law as Large as Life* – Book Review" (2003) 11 Fem. Legal Stud. 307; Constance Backhouse, "Reviews – Ellen Anderson, *Judging Bertha Wilson: Law as Large as Life*" (2003) 51 Labour/Le Travail 295.

21 See Chapter 2, this volume.

22 See Remarks of the Honourable Mme Justice Bertha Wilson at her retirement ceremony (Tuesday, 4 December 1990) at 1-2 [unpublished, Supreme Court of Canada Library, Ottawa].
23 Robert E. Hawkins and Robert Martin, "Democracy, Judging and Bertha Wilson" (1995) 41 McGill L.J. 1.
24 For a discussion of Bertha Wilson's role in supporting social context education, see Chapter 15, this volume.
25 See *e.g.* the analysis set out in Chapters 8, 9, and 10, this volume.
26 A phrase that Justice Wilson used in her Betcherman Lecture, *supra* note 9 at 521.
27 See Alan Watson, "The Scottish Enlightenment, the Democratic Intellect and the Work of Madame Justice Wilson" (1992) 15 Dal. L.J. 23.
28 See Chapter 4, this volume, for an analysis of Justice Wilson's willingness to "enter the skin" of litigants and her penchant for reasonableness, fairness, and justice.
29 See her remarks in "Women and the Canadian Charter of Rights and Freedoms" (Keynote address to the "Tenth Biennial Conference Healing the Past, Forming the Future" of the National Association of Women and the Law, 19-21 February 1993) at 4.
30 See Hester Lessard, "Equality and Access to Justice in the Work of Bertha Wilson" (1992) 15 Dal. L.J. 35.
31 See *e.g.* Chapters 10 and 16, this volume.
32 See in particular Chapters 2 and 5, this volume.
33 See the question posed by Marie-Claire Belleau, Rebecca Johnson, and Christina Vinters in Chapter 12, this volume: "*[T]his* woman judge did indeed make a profound difference. But the inevitable rejoinder arises: What *kind* of difference?" at 229.
34 Carol Gilligan, *In a Different Voice: Psychological Theory and Women's Development* (Cambridge, MA: Harvard University Press, 1982). See in particular the discussion in Chapter 15 at 281, this volume.
35 In this vein, see the questions posted at the end of Chapter 16, this volume.
36 Bertha Wilson, "A Choice of Values" (1961) 4 Can. Bar J. 448 at 449-57; Bertha Wilson, "Equity and the Tenant for Life" (1960) 3 Can. Bar J. 117.
37 But see Maureen Maloney, "Economic Actors in the Work of Madame Justice Wilson" (1992) 15 Dal. L.J. 197.

Part 1
Foundations

1
Bertha Wilson's Practice Years (1958-75): Establishing a Research Practice and Founding a Research Department in Canada

Angela Fernandez and Beatrice Tice

Bertha Wilson created the research department at Osler, Hoskin & Harcourt, the first of its kind in Canada. The department was founded on Wilson's own interests, and the force of her personality lies behind its existence. It was also, as she herself put it, "a function of chauvinism" in the sense that she took up the practice of law at a time when many clients and other lawyers were not comfortable with the idea of a woman lawyer. Behind-the-scenes research was a way to put Wilson's talents to work while still respecting conventional attitudes toward gender in a conservative profession during the 1960s. The research department, which continued after Wilson left Osler for the Court of Appeal in 1975, proved to be a model for similar departments at other large Toronto law firms and remains a key practice area at Osler today.

This chapter explores Wilson's establishment of the department. In particular, it focuses on the research-related initiatives with which she was involved during her time at Osler, such as the law firm library and the information-retrieval systems for memoranda, opinion letters, and precedents. These are not functions that one would associate with a research department today. Knowledge-management specialization means that many of the projects in which Wilson participated would now have their own dedicated staff. However, the boundaries between roles and functions were blurry at best in Wilson's day. One of the aims of this chapter is to capture this era and its gendered dimensions. We hope to provide a snapshot of some of the on-the-ground features of law firm practice at a particular time and place: a large Toronto law firm in the 1960s and early 1970s. We also aim to provide a description of how one extraordinary woman made her way in this environment. What we are providing here is by no means a typical tale – Osler was not a commonplace law practice setting, and Bertha Wilson was an exceptional jurist and an exceptional woman.

Articling at Osler: A Legal Researcher Emerges

> Whatever your assignment, little or least,
> your great maxim is: "Make yourself indispensable."
> – Bertha Wilson, Mount St. Vincent University
> Convocation Address, 1984

In the mid-1950s very few women were practising law in Canada.[1] Wilson was confronted with this reality even before she became a law student at Dalhousie Law School, where the Dean dismissively questioned her interest in applying.[2] Wilson persisted and, having achieved top-ten standing in her class during all three years of study, received a scholarship to undertake an LL.M. at Harvard Law School. Once again, she was discouraged by the Dean, who told her that attempting to be an academic was foolhardy: "There will never be women academics teaching in law schools, not in your day."[3] Wilson did not pursue the LL.M., but her interest in an academic approach to law persisted throughout her career and manifested itself in her intense interest in research.[4] After moving with her husband, John, to Toronto, she secured an articling position with Osler in 1958 – becoming its first female associate after she was called to the bar in 1959. On 1 January 1968, she became the first female partner in the law firm's history.[5]

Osler's articling offer to Wilson did not express a tidal wave of liberal social reform at the firm. Indeed, Allan Beattie – a lawyer senior to Wilson who arrived in 1951, was made a partner in 1955, and succeeded Harold Mockridge as head of the firm – recalled "an incredibly long and solemn debate as to whether a woman could really be suited to the practice of law."[6] According to Stuart Thom, another close friend of Wilson's at Osler, these were men to whom "law was a downtown business for the man, and the lawyer[s] they hired had certain qualities and connections and patterns of behaviour. Women just didn't fit."[7] Mockridge, then head of Osler and emphatically not a social reformer, shared this view.[8] He and other skeptical members of the firm required a demonstration not only of Wilson's abilities as a lawyer but also that she could fit into the male-dominated practice environment.

The articling period was therefore a test year on many levels. Wilson herself certainly understood the importance of this probationary phase. When it was made clear to her that her position at Osler was confined to the one articling year, she replied with some spunk: "Well, I think that would be a mutually acceptable arrangement. I might not like it here either."[9] She later noted that many women entering a man's world underestimate just how important this proving stage is: "A lot of women, I think, are of the view that as soon as you get into a group, you can start trying to change things. I don't think it works. I think you have to go through this process of proving yourself first."[10] And prove herself she did. From her first assignment – "what is a bond?" – Wilson demonstrated her outstanding capacity to research, read, write, and, in Beattie's words, to *think*.[11]

Wilson remembered "getting a number of research assignments like that during the first months at the firm, and slowly realizing that she could learn the context of the research by going to the filing department and pulling the file herself."[12] Osler had a central filing system, in keeping with its philosophy that clients were firm clients and not those of individual lawyers. As Wilson's biographer Ellen Anderson put it, "The central storage meant that when presented with a research question Wilson could retrieve the file, discover the factual background to the research query, and discern the legal options open to the client and the pros and cons attaching to each."[13] Thus, Wilson took steps to enhance the quality of her work while at the same time overcoming any discomfort that her clients or immediate superiors might have felt working with her face to face. No one showed her how to access the files so as to increase the practical relevance of the advice she gave; she simply figured it out.[14]

It did not take long for the lawyers at Osler to realize they had something special in Wilson in terms of her aptitude for legal research and writing.[15] An initially skeptical Harold Mockridge grew to respect her. Justice Dennis Lane, who worked in the firm's fledgling litigation department, recalled one telling incident. Mr. Mockridge (as everyone at the firm addressed him) gave Wilson an assignment that involved the interpretation of a will for a client. He handed her the will and sent her away to construct the argument for one side. She returned with her memo. He sent her off to research the issue again from the other side, which was actually the client's side. When she returned it, he was pleased and wanted her to go to court to argue the case. However, Wilson demurred.[16]

If Mockridge was motivated to assist Wilson in her career development, she had a very different sense of what shape this was going to take. She did not want to occupy the traditional lawyer roles of the barrister who goes to court or the solicitor who sees clients to gather the relevant facts. She had an enormous appetite for books and wanted to work with them. As Lane put it, it was the law that she loved – "she left the rest of us to fiddle with the facts."[17] Anderson notes that "she preferred a minimum of client contact in her legal work, especially relishing her freedom from any of the social responsibility of rainmaking such as taking clients out to lunch ... [S]he was free [instead] to consider herself an academic lawyer."[18] Lane believes that Mockridge came to understand and respect this choice as he was interested in the business dimensions of law practice more than in the traditional barrister or solicitor functions.[19] He supported Wilson's effort to carve out a niche practice structured around what she wanted to do. And in those days, it was his support that counted in the end.

Despite any reluctance to prepare herself for traditional law practice, within a year Bertha Wilson had made herself indispensable at Osler. She recounted that, as her articling stint was nearing its end, one of the lawyers came to her with a research assignment that was expected to go on for months: "I said I think you'd better get somebody else – you do know that tomorrow is my last day. He said, 'What do you mean that tomorrow is your last day?' I said, 'I get my call to the bar tomorrow and that's when I leave.'" Horrified, the lawyer said, "'Don't go anywhere, stay here,' and off he went." He returned to tell her that everyone had taken it for granted that she was going to stay on. As Wilson put it, "I did stay on; I stayed on for seventeen years."[20]

Practice at Osler: Still Working to Make a Place of Her Own

> Next, let me deal with interpersonal relations – your responsibility to get along.
>
> – Bertha Wilson, Mount St. Vincent University Convocation Address, 1984

Wilson's own specialized practice focused on estates and trusts. However, she was not content merely to draw up wills. She therefore let it be known that she was willing to work on whatever research problem anyone doing any kind of work in the firm might have. Lane reported that, if a colleague took a problem to her, she would send back a memo that was clearly written and thoroughly researched. Lawyers could either work with her one-on-one, or they could send their request and wait to hear back.[21]

Moving among practice areas was not considered unusual in the 1950s and '60s. During this period, most lawyers, even at big firms such as Osler, were generalists. As Lane put it, you became a labour lawyer if your client had labour problems.[22] Although "the pace and scope" of a trend toward specialization such as departmentalization "varied widely from firm to firm ... by the early 1970s certain trends were clearly visible at large [Canadian] law firms."[23] Indeed, the 1971 *Income Tax Act* "appears to have been a turning point, marking the end of the all-rounder – the lawyer who was able to handle essentially any kind of case." It was "[t]he final nail in the coffin of generalization."[24]

Wilson was in her element in a generalist context. According to Lane, she earned a reputation for thorough research and soundness, putting the law together with whatever facts the client provided to create a persuasive package. She would, in essence, become an expert in whatever area of law was presented by the particular legal problem. The notion that this floating expertise could be its own kind of specialization lay at the heart of the idea for a research department. The department would consist of partners and partner-track associates who specialized in providing high-level, high-quality research on particularly complex legal problems requiring more extensive treatment than a lawyer working in an individual department would or could devote to them.

Any lawyer could send a request to the research department. It would be assigned to an associate or partner, who would perform the additional requested research. The nature of this assistance would run the gamut from help with the drafting of pleadings to the production of written memoranda on points of law where more information was desired. The research lawyer might work directly with the client, but, more often, he or she would work with the other Osler lawyers who had passed along the problem.[25]

As Wilson's reputation for sound argument and thorough research and analysis grew, her role gradually developed from that of a young lawyer assisting on matters to a seasoned expert advising her colleagues on the state of the law and its application to cases. She became, as Beattie put it, "a *lawyer's* lawyer."[26] Although it is difficult to pinpoint exactly when research became the main component of Wilson's practice, Maurice Coombs, her first junior colleague in the research department, figures that this occurred some time around 1962, approximately four years after she began articling at the firm.[27]

Lane recalls taking a problem to Wilson and watching her work. She would go to the library, select the books she wanted to use, return to her office, and line them up on her desk in the order in which she intended to treat them in the memo. Next, she would pick up the dictaphone, pause, open a book, read a passage, make a comment, and then open another book and read another passage. When transcribed, her memo would be in near-final form, typically requiring only minor edits. "Like a great athlete," Lane said, "she made it look easy." She was "a mountain of information about the law."[28]

For the most part, Wilson worked from behind the scenes through written memoranda.[29] Although she worked at arm's length, she was regarded as an approachable and collegial person. Lane recalls, for instance, that she had good relationships with the estates and trusts clients.[30] Beattie said he came to think of her as a "den mother" because she was so interested in people and had a way of talking to them about a wide range of personal and professional issues.[31] Coombs called this her "people thing," which "involved working with young lawyers, encouraging them, guiding them and looking out for their interests in the partnership," as well as "provid[ing] a sympathetic ear and wise advice to older partners struggling with the modernization of legal practice throughout the sixties and seventies."[32]

By all accounts, hiring and retaining Bertha Wilson was one of the best risks Osler ever took. However, despite the fact that her colleagues deemed her indispensable to the firm, and despite their enormous respect for, and reliance on, Wilson's judgment, she would wait nine years – three times as long as some lawyers at the time – before being made the first female partner in Osler's history.

No Gender Discrimination?

> [Y]ou have a responsibility to be patient. Promotion will appear to be painfully slow ... In fact you will begin to think that the powers that be have a vested interest in keeping you at the level you're at simply because you are so good at assisting your superiors and making them look better than they really are!
>
> – Bertha Wilson, Mount St. Vincent University Convocation Address, 1984

It was the impression of Wilson's biographer that Wilson was reluctant to acknowledge experiences of discrimination. Wilson said, "I really didn't see it that way. I didn't recognize discrimination even when I met it, probably."[33]

Wilson attributed her own delay in making partner at Osler to the unusual nature of her practice when compared with the practices of other lawyers at the firm who made partner in five years or less.[34] Former colleagues have emphasized the fact that partnerships were considered in three-year cycles; hence, depending on when a person came to the firm, missing one cycle could mean waiting for the next triennial consideration.[35] Each partner also had a veto in the decision-making process, so unanimity was required.[36] However, it is worth noting that Wilson herself wondered why she had to wait so long. When she asked, one senior colleague replied, "We never thought you would stay because you were married and you really had no reason to be working and we never saw you as a career person, looking ahead."[37] To some, the fact that she was married meant that she "did not 'really need to work' and might leave at any time."[38]

Wilson experienced many instances of sexism – both deliberate and unintended – throughout her legal career.[39] Her time at Osler was no exception. Indeed, one of the reasons she became a "lawyer's lawyer" was to avoid creating discomfort for clients who might feel uneasy working directly with a female lawyer. The research role "kept her from having direct contact with traditional male clients who might not have complete confidence in a woman lawyer."[40] Moreover, colleagues could choose to send her research requests without having face-to-face contact, and some might choose to send no requests. As laudable as the institution of the research department became, it began, as she put it, "as a function of chauvinism."[41]

Wilson was always aware of the nervousness created by those who, like her, lived between worlds – in her case, the traditional male and female spheres of work and family life of the 1950s and '60s. Her policy was to put people at ease (whatever their reason for feeling ill at ease) and to do her best to fit in "beautifully."[42] Faced with the problem of doing this at a large elite Toronto law firm, which she once described as run by "[g]entlemen of the old school," at a time when there was little reason to think that a female lawyer would be welcome there, Wilson responded with her usual practicality: she would simply work hard, demonstrate her value, and do her best, gender discrimination be damned.[43] In reference to her time sitting with Wilson on the Supreme Court of Canada from 1987 to 1991, Justice Claire L'Heureux-Dubé described this strategy as "working three times harder than everyone else."[44]

According to Anderson, Wilson "had no desire to assert herself as equal in the sense of being identical with the more prominent male lawyers."[45] Allan Beattie, for instance, emphasized that Wilson was never on the law firm management committee and would never have wanted to be.[46] Instead, Wilson was, in Anderson's words, "permitted to carve out the role she wanted, a different role. She was respected for her expertise in that role and built her own bailiwick within the firm."[47] If this role appeared to be a subordinate one – the "brains behind the big names,"[48] who operated as "a kind of resource person for everyone else"[49] – that was just fine. It was the type of work she liked to do and at which she excelled, and it was intensely appreciated by the individuals with whom she worked. Indeed, contemporaries from the time emphasize that there were few difficult files at the firm in which she was *not* involved. Picking up the phone to ask Wilson whether X or Y was sound advice that should be conveyed to a client was thought of as a sort of insurance policy, given how good she was and how much her counsel was valued around the place.[50]

Wilson's strengths and interests were a perfect match with the backroom role of a research lawyer. This complimented the role of the other lawyers at the firm who dealt directly with clients on transactions and did not have the time or inclination to take on intensive research, creating what was in many respects "a perfect marriage."[51] Indeed, some of Wilson's colleagues might have come to rely on her too much – making herself a little too indispensable for their good, and for her own. Wilson's remark in the convocation address that "assist[ing ...] your superiors and making them look better than they really are" could create "a vested interest in keeping you at the level" seems to be a reference to her own delayed promotion and a complaint about permanently inhabiting the role of helpmate.[52]

Indeed, the metaphor of marriage and the conventional role of wife as helpmate reflects in an important way Wilson's privileged middle-class background and how that helped her fit into a conservative professional milieu in law school and at Osler. The excellent liberal arts education she received in Scotland, her marriage to a minister, even her personal style and charm, including being famously shy and soft-spoken, were all aspects of her person and personality that would have reassured conventional colleagues that she was a safe and agreeable addition to the law firm despite the fact that she was a woman – and yes, she was practising law, if not in a completely traditional way.

Some of the "helpmate" projects that Wilson undertook probably came to her for gender-related reasons. For example, oversight of the law library fell to her. Indeed, some who saw her operating in her behind-the-scenes role at Osler "took her for some kind of high-grade librarian."[53] Wilson had actually acted as a law librarian from time to time when she was at Dalhousie Law School.[54] As a devout user of the library, she would have been more interested than most in its operations.

Librarianship has been a female-dominated profession throughout the twentieth century.[55] One therefore wonders whether gender played a role in the fact that library-stewardship fell to Wilson. However, it was also standard practice for there to be a library committee and for one lawyer to be responsible for the law firm library.[56] From Allan Beattie's perspective, "Bertha was the law firm library committee."[57] She was the person who took an interest in its operations and who had the clout and credibility to make bottom-line recommendations about what was most needed.

Lane, who was at times on the library committee with Wilson, recalls that her secretary handled the logistics of acquisitions.[58] Prior to the 1960s and the rise of specialized roles for law firm administration, secretaries would have done the bulk of routine work, including filing, or lawyers handled it personally.[59] Wilson operated in a pre-specialized world in which either she or her secretary probably did whatever needed to be done, big or small.

Wilson did not reject projects such as law firm library management on the grounds that a woman lawyer might quite justifiably use today – namely, that it is important to avoid getting boxed into a "pink ghetto," doing non-billable work that needs to be done and might be appreciated but that is not highly valued by the institution. It would have been hard for Wilson to think in these terms, if only because the very notion of a ghetto assumes that there are others with whom one could be ghettoized, and Wilson was the only woman lawyer at Osler for quite a few years.[60] One has the impression that she was simply trying to find a way of putting her skills to use on terms with which everyone, including herself, would be comfortable.

Even in 1960, however, carving out a comfort zone did not mean total surrender to the gender norms of the day. For instance, Wilson stood up for her need to be allowed to travel for work. Concerns were expressed about the propriety of this, given that both she and the male lawyers with whom she would be travelling were married. Yet, Wilson insisted that she be permitted to travel, and she was allowed to do so.[61] Anderson referred to her "principled boldness" on this and other issues.[62]

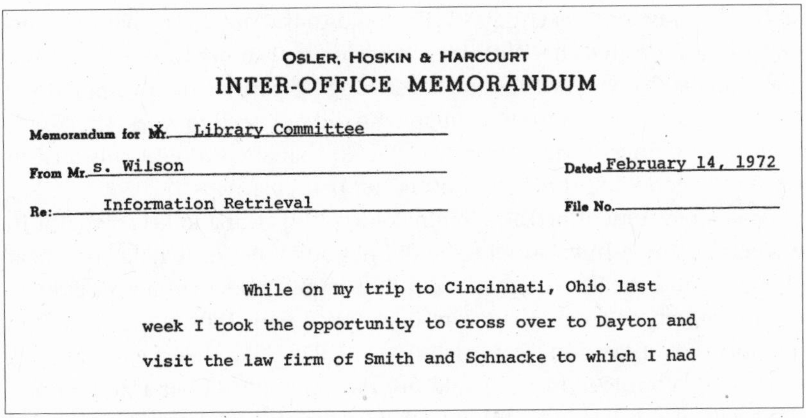

OSLER, HOSKIN & HARCOURT

INTER-OFFICE MEMORANDUM

Memorandum for Mr. X Library Committee

From Mr. s. Wilson

Dated February 14, 1972

Re: Information Retrieval

File No.

While on my trip to Cincinnati, Ohio last week I took the opportunity to cross over to Dayton and visit the law firm of Smith and Schnacke to which I had

Figure 1.1 Osler, Hoskin & Harcourt inter-office memorandum. Permission to reproduce given by Osler, Hoskin & Harcourt.

By the 1990s, the Canadian Bar Association's report on gender in the profession, of which Wilson was the chair, pointed to some of the problems that she faced while at Osler. For instance, the report noted that, in private practice, work was divided between "pink files" and "blue files," with women lawyers assigned more of the former. Pink files "involve[d] less high profile matters, less client contact and correspondence, and reduced opportunities to develop legal skills and a client base."[63] The excuse that clients would not want to work with a female lawyer was used.[64] Female lawyers felt that they were "steered into research or clerical work."[65] "Even as partners, women report[ed] that they hit a glass ceiling," with a lack of representation on powerful committees and overrepresentation on committees with less authority, such as the library committee.[66] The kinds of things that Wilson would have been willing to accept in 1960 were no longer acceptable by 1990.

Consider Figure 1.1 – the first page of a memorandum from Wilson to the library committee. Notice how she added her own "s" to "Mr." to make a "Mrs." for herself on one of the Osler standard-form memos. The date here is 1972. Wilson had been with the firm for fourteen years, and she was still required to make this alteration. Did she have her secretary add the "s" in every typed inter-office memo using this form?

Anderson noted that a theme in many of Wilson's convocation addresses was the ability to tolerate "minor injustices" in the workplace. These should be "accepted with good humour," Wilson counselled, and thought of as "so trivial as to be properly beneath notice."[67] However, what would be considered major and minor has changed substantially over time. At the present time, for instance, it is extremely difficult to imagine any woman lawyer in a law firm reacting as Wilson did to the suspicion that her married status indicated that she was not committed to her career. When the question of why she had had to wait so long for partnership prompted the suggestion that, as a married woman who did not need to work, she might leave at any time, "Wilson laughingly said that she thought this answer was 'quite good' but it did not bother her particularly."[68]

Wilson never identified as a feminist, despite a clear and keen interest in women's issues.[69] Interestingly, she did not advocate for female lawyers at Osler; nor did she act as a mentor in that respect. As Osler lawyer Barbara McGregor, whose time at the firm overlapped with Wilson's, put it, "My memory of Bertha during my articling year [1972-73] is that she was an icon – very much a role model. I would not have thought of her as a mentor – there were no such things at that time. Mentoring came later. She provided an example that it (succeeding as a lawyer in a large firm) could be done. She did not advocate for the female lawyers at Oslers – she just excelled at what she did. She broke the path."[70] Wilson may not have seen herself as a feminist or may have felt uncomfortable carrying the label. However, others at the firm associated her with the cause of women's rights. Allan Beattie recalled one lunchtime event at a restaurant during which the Osler lawyers were seated next to a table of women who, a little too loudly and rather too exuberantly, were having an office party celebration. Wilson was teased by her colleagues: "Bertha, are those the women whose rights you are fighting so hard for?"[71]

The depth and breadth of the gender stereotyping that Wilson faced might be difficult for us to appreciate now. Allan Beattie emphasized that, to a man of Mr. Mockridge's background and life experience, who had initially thought that women could not practise law, realizing what Wilson could do was the equivalent of seeing someone walk on water.[72] In McGregor's words, Wilson "broke the path," making it "less difficult for the women who followed, to carve a position for themselves."[73]

It is remarkable that the senior male lawyers at Osler were able to set aside whatever gender prejudices they had and let Wilson into their group. However, since she was so good at what she did and so valuable to the firm for that reason, one can see why they would have been motivated to do so. What is perhaps more remarkable is the way that Wilson leveraged credibility and social capital from the kind of activity one might associate with the most undesirable aspects of law practice – the "clerkish scutwork" – and made it an important and well-respected niche activity.[74] In a way, she was transforming lemons into lemonade. Wilson took her "difference" from the other, more prominent male partners, both in terms of what she liked to do and in terms of what she and others were comfortable having her do, given the times in which they were living – and founded a unique kind of law practice. In turn, this practice gave rise to a unique phenomenon: the research department. This department became a fixture at Osler and remains an important part of the firm today, which other large law firms copied.[75]

It is difficult to avoid the conclusion that the successful founding of the research department at Osler was largely due to the force of Wilson's personality: her interests, energy, credibility, and clout. However, we hesitate to say that it was solely a matter of human agency and serendipity. Timing, for instance, probably also had some role to play.

The bulk of Wilson's time at Osler has been described as a period of relative stability. In the post-war United States, until about the 1970s, "law firms [were] locked into long-term relations with major clients and handle[d] virtually all those clients' business." However, after about 1975, "corporate law practice in the United States ... entered a distinctly new phase" characterized by instability: among other things, much "legal work [went] in-house, and ... fragments of specialized work [were auctioned off] to many different outside firms," resulting in a new, highly competitive style of corporate practice.[76] Whereas America began its "boom" of large law firms during the 1950s and 1960s, Canada was slower in this respect.[77] However, the post-1975 situation in Canada seems to have been quite similar to that of the United States albeit on a smaller scale.[78]

Wilson sought institutional support for her projects in a period that predated the extremely rapid changes of the 1970s, which culminated in the intense specialization we know today. If an idea did not work out, long-term client relationships would not be endangered. However, if it met with success, there was value added in the sense of improving client service and competitiveness. At the same time, the research department's role was premised on a growing trend toward that specialization. Good economic times meant enough work to sustain divisions among lawyers, who did not all have to be cut from the same cloth, and a research practice helped bridge the gaps in knowledge and experience between those increasingly specialized lawyers.

Thus, specialized research support stood on the cusp between the old stable world and the new unstable one. It was institutionalized in a calmer time, before records management itself became professionalized, economically rationalized, and specialized. It was in this particular context that Wilson leveraged her "difference" rather than denying it. In so doing, and quite by accident in some cases, she forever changed the shape of Canadian law practice in a large firm.

Building a Research Practice: The Accidental Contributions

> Your responsibility [is] to be faithful in little things.
>
> – Bertha Wilson, Mount St. Vincent University
> Convocation Address, 1984

It is important to note that Wilson did not start out with an agenda to build a research department. According to Allan Beattie, the department grew out of her particular way of approaching the practice of law. Wilson was intensely practical in her approach to legal problems. In Beattie's words, she was "practically oriented towards the practical."[79] She took initiatives to improve the quality of her own practice wherever she saw the need, and she was willing to institute her systems on a firm-wide basis. Whether the initiative was taking on responsibility for the law library or introducing a legislation service or a synopsis service for providing client information, Wilson appeared to be tireless.[80] These projects gravitated toward her and she toward them, although it is often difficult to tell exactly how much of her time she devoted to them, and certainly her contributions to the firm went well beyond them. However, the other members of the partnership came to expect that Wilson would set these kinds of projects into motion and oversee them. At least some of these initiatives continued to be associated with the research department after her departure in 1975.

As early as 1970, Wilson was quoted in the journal of the Canadian Bar Association as saying, "What I would like to see ... is a system where, if I want a precedent I can just pick up the phone and describe what I want via certain key words and, if a document exists, it can be found and I can quickly get a copy, plus the research that may have gone into such a document."[81] In the 1972 memo, the letterhead of which is reproduced in Figure 1.1, Wilson described a visit to a law firm in Dayton, Ohio, to learn about the use of a computer for storing and retrieving "its own internal work product, *i.e.* its research memoranda, opinion letters and precedents." She noted this and compared it to "the think process" in which the Osler library committee was engaged.[82]

Lane recalls that the idea of using computers was on the library committee's agenda from about 1969 on.[83] "Of course we're all kicking around the idea of computers," Wilson remarked in 1970.[84] It is difficult to overstate just how new this technology was, although some flavour of this is captured by Wilson's description of the computer that her contact at a Cincinnati law firm was using: "[The] cathode ray tube terminal ... looks like a television set with a keyboard in front through which the lawyer can pose questions to and receive answers from the computer which appear on the television screen."[85] The first machines had no memory capacity. Coombs recalls the extreme anxiety that the new technology created for some of the Osler secretaries.[86] Wilson herself had sympathy for those, lawyers included, who had trouble making the transition to newer technologies.[87]

On her Ohio trip, Wilson received a demonstration on what the Ohio State Bar Association was doing with the computerization of Ohio statutes and case law. Encouraged by the great strides that Hugh Lawford was making with Quicklaw and Canadian law, Wilson wrote, "I am now most anxious that Osler, Hoskin & Harcourt cooperate with Professor Lawford, the Director of the computer project being conducted at Queen's University, by allowing a terminal to be installed in our office."[88] Lane recalls a trip to an American Bar Association conference in Philadelphia where Lawford's full-text retrievals "blew everyone's mind."[89] As the *Canadian Bar Journal* put it, it "[s]ounds as though Mrs. Wilson and Prof. Lawford should get together."[90] They eventually did.[91]

The Dayton law firm that Wilson visited, Smith and Schnacke, was computerizing its precedents. These consisted of thousands of forms for wills, inter vivos trusts, real estate documents, corporate financing documents, and the like.[92] However, the firm decided that handling the research memos and opinion letters with "a card index system" was "much less costly."[93] Likewise, Osler did not computerize either its precedents or the research memos and legal opinions during this period. Technologically, this was possible. Lane reported on a punch-card system he saw being used by lawyers at Aetna Life Insurance Company in Hartford, Connecticut, to store and retrieve legal memos using IBM's KWIC (Key Words in Context) system.[94] Rather, as at Smith and Schnacke, the decision was a matter of cost, compounded by the fact that Osler was told the technology would quickly become obsolete.[95]

A 1970 visit to White and Case in New York City showed Osler lawyers a perfectly acceptable non-computerized approach to precedents. Essentially, the system would be left to "run itself." Senior lawyers in each department would be responsible for identifying "starter documents" and making sure that members in their practice groups added to these documents from time to time.[96] A more hands-on approach that used the research department and the library was taken with the card system for research memos. A similar manual system was also observed at White and Case, which used "a standard library-type card catalogue by subject with a brief description of the contents of each memo appearing on each card."[97] According to Lane, "The memos themselves [were] bound in volumes by code number, roughly chronological, and the volumes [were] maintained in the library near the card catalogue."[98] The indexing was done by one individual, and the "precedent index and storage system ... [were] maintained entirely separately from the Library and from the legal research system."[99]

Wilson had a long practice of keeping research memoranda and re-using them when the opportunity presented itself. As she put it in 1970, "It's really criminal to have lawyers spending their time going over and over work that has already been done."[100] This repetition not only created the risk of inconsistency that could potentially embarrass the firm but was also a waste. Wilson "knew that she could save time and provide a more efficient service to the other lawyers in the firm by establishing an information retrieval system so that the basic research product needed only adaptation and perhaps updating for the particular client situation."[101] However, if the client paid less, the firm made less. Thus, this time-saving cut into the amount of revenue Wilson generated, created some tension for her at the firm, and ultimately led to others determining the amount of her bills.[102]

Wilson wanted to add the memos produced by other Osler lawyers to her dataset and to include a specific indication of whether a formal opinion letter had been sent out. The rendering of opinions was the area in which the potential to create embarrassing inconsistency, and to engage the firm's liability, was at its highest. This information was also easy to collect through the law firm's daybooks, or "pinks" – copies on pink paper of all correspondence that left the firm – which were deposited in binders as the letters were sent out.[103] These binders were the equivalent of daybooks, a correspondence record of the day's events.[104] Indeed, the carbon sheet separated the letter from a green copy, a yellow copy, a pink copy, and a blue copy. Coombs recalls an occasion in which one of the clerks from the mailroom presented himself to Wilson, pointing out that the wrong colour copy had been sent for the daybook. Wilson took the sheet, wrote "pink copy" at the top, and handed it back to him.[105]

In 1974, shortly before Wilson's departure for the Court of Appeal, Maurice Coombs and two articling students set to work creating a system for recording and retrieving Wilson's memos and those of other lawyers in the firm. Coombs

Identifying Number for Memorandum or Letter

{Assigned # consisting of 2 Digits [Year of Creation]/3 Digits [Number in a Physical Binder]/the letter "A" if it was an opinion letter}

Key Word 1, Key Word 2, Key Word 3, Key Word 4, Key Word 5, Key Word 6, Key Word 7, Key Word 8, Key Word 9, Key Word 10, Key Word 11, Key Word 1, etc.

Author **Matter Identifiers**

Synopsis of the matters discussed in the Memorandum or Letter

Consectetur adipiscing elit, set eiusmod tempor incidunt et labore et dolore magna aliquam. Ut enim ad minim veniam,quis nostrud exerc. Irure dolor in reprehend incididunt ut.Labore et dolore magna aliqua. Ut enim ad minim veniam, quis nostrud exercitation ullamco laboris nisi ut aliquip ex eacommodo consequat. Duis aute irure dolor in reprehenderit in voluptate velit esse molestaie cillum.Tia non ob ea soluad incommod quae egen ium improb fugiend. Of• cia deserunt mollit anim id est laborum Et harumd dereud facilis est er expedit distinct. Nam liber te conscient to factor tum poen legum odioque civiuda et tam. Nequepecun modut est neque nonor et imper ned libidig met, consectetur adipiscing elit dolor set ahmet ipsum.Lorem ipsum dolor sit amet, ligula suspendisse nulla pretium, rhoncus tempor placerat fermentum, enim integer advestibulum volutpat. Nisl rhoncus turpis est, vel elit, congue wisi enim nunc ultricies sit.

List of Cases referred to in the Memorandum or Letter

List of Statutes Referred to in the Memorandum or Letter

Figure 1.2 Mock-up index card. Permission to reproduce given by Maurice Coombs.

believed that Wilson was thinking about institutionalizing a kind of legacy to the law firm that would continue to exist after her own departure.[106]

Although the physical cards have not survived, Maurice Coombs kindly constructed the Figure 1.2 mock-up from memory. A separate card was made for each of the following pieces of information: keywords, author, matter identifier, cases, and statutes. It was therefore possible to search the system's contents using any of these categories. Such cross-indexing was not a feature of the White and Case system.[107] In 1983, when the system contained approximately seven thousand items, the proportion of research memos to opinion letters was roughly seven to three in favour of memoranda.[108] Client names were included on the original cards but were deleted when the information was sent to Quicklaw for the database.[109]

All of the cards were housed in a "rolodex contraption" with several trays stacked one over the other in a kind of pulley system. Called an "Acme Visible Stratomatic" machine, it was much like the one from Acme Visible Records reproduced in Figure 1.3. The cards were organized into plastic trays that rotated independently on parallel tracks, rather like side-by-side ferris wheels. More than one person could stand at the machine and access the plastic trays in the various wheels. Apparently, there was an issue about the noisy clacking of the plastic trays and by the fact that more than one lawyer could use the machine at the same time, creating chit-chat conditions that

Figure 1.3 Acme Visible Records, Inc. Image obtained from American Brands Inc., 1972 Annual Report, at 16.

were disruptive to those sitting in the library reading room area.[110] The machine was housed in the library and unquestionably understood to be a part of its resources.

The actual memos and opinion letters were stored in "Accogrip" binders. A person using the system would undertake a search for an item, say by keyword (*e.g.* smoke easement), would find all the cards under that keyword, and could then pull the physical documents from the binders using the assigned numbers on each card. Physical copies of the memos tended to disappear as people took them away to use them and forgot to return them. Hence, a master copy was kept to replace the gaps that would appear in the binders over time. By 1983 abstracts on the index cards were typed into a word processor, and the documents themselves were transferred onto microfiche.[111] Indeed, many of Wilson's memos are still accessible as scanned PDF documents on the current Osler system, and Osler lawyers report that they continue to pop up during routine searches on the system.[112]

Lawyers were supposed to deposit copies of their research work into the system for indexing and archiving. However, getting people to remember to give their memos to the system was difficult. Users of the system tended to be contributors to it, particularly young lawyers who were more comfortable with new technologies.[113] Research lawyers were well represented as both users and contributors. As Diane Snell, one of the indexing lawyers, put it in 1983, "[t]he research group's work is ... our motherlode."[114]

A Research Lawyer at the Supreme Court of Canada

If one were to ask oneself in the abstract "Where is the best place for an academically oriented lawyer to be in the Canadian legal system?" the last place one would choose is probably a big corporate commercial law firm in downtown Toronto. A university, yes; an appellate court such as the Ontario Court of Appeal, yes; the Supreme Court of Canada, most certainly, yes. But Osler, Hoskin & Harcourt?

Wilson did much innovative and important work in her judgments on both the Ontario Court of Appeal and the Supreme Court of Canada, as many of the essays in this collection demonstrate. The research-intensive approach that she developed during her long Osler years must have affected the way in which she approached the thinking, research, and writing of her judgments.[115] In addition to being an intensely practical person, Wilson was also (perhaps paradoxically) quite philosophical by orientation, a tendency which made many of her judgments lucid, readable, and compelling.[116] Yet in the environment that one would have expected to suit the academic and philosophical aspects of her personality best – the Supreme Court of Canada – Wilson had a difficult time. In part, the difficulty had to do with leaving Toronto after many happy years spent there.[117] It seems also to have been related to the way the Court ran at the time.

Wilson never felt comfortable with the informal consensus building around judgments, which she saw as inappropriate lobbying.[118] An individualist in outlook and operation, she thought that the consensus-oriented approach produced a "[c]alculated ambiguity."[119] She also felt excluded by informal discussions between the other justices and was in favour of implementing "set procedures or a clear protocol" to address issues: these included when judges should comment on the various positions that were emerging in the decision-making process (were they required to wait for a written draft of the majority opinion?) and how those responses were to be given (must they be in writing, and if so, would the memo be made available to everyone?).[120] Wilson's own preference for an "open process" effectuated through memo writing stemmed from her days at Osler, when she worked primarily through memos.[121]

Wilson's direct one-on-one research-intensive and memo-oriented style flourished in a large law firm setting, where meticulous solitary work was of the utmost importance, at least for the sort of practice she had. However, the memo-writing strategy that had worked so well in private practice ran into a wall at the Supreme Court. Indeed, the Court seemed to be the one place where the simple "work hard" approach did not do the trick. Perhaps this was because the Supreme Court culture included a level of give and take that Wilson had not previously been required to incorporate into her working style. A lack of support and goodwill also seemed to be an issue. With respect to the memo-writing protocol, for instance, good reasons existed for not adopting a strict formal system.[122] The fact that Wilson felt she needed one to be properly included in the collective deliberation process is quite a dramatic complaint about the collegiality of the group at that time.[123]

Wilson felt excluded by the more informal decision-making processes, many of which seemed to take place over sports-related activities. This placed a female judge "with arthritis who does not play golf or squash or tennis and does not ski or attend hockey games at something of a disadvantage."[124] The problem may also have been the specific personalities on the Court at that time. In particular, despite a reputation as "the great dissenter," Chief Justice Laskin had come to discourage dissent on the Court after 1979.[125] Laskin had not supported Wilson's candidacy, fearing in part that she would disrupt the unanimity on the Court and maintaining that there were better-qualified male candidates.[126] His attitudes could not have made for happy working conditions, at least for the two years until Brian Dickson became Chief Justice in 1984. Dickson retired in 1990, and Wilson followed suit in 1991, a full seven years early.[127]

The Canadian Bar Association report's section on judges, which Wilson oversaw and wrote, included many of the things that she personally experienced. When first appointed, many women judges "were not made to feel welcome, that in many cases they were told that they had been appointed simply because they were women and that there were male candidates 'out there' who would have been better appointees."[128] Many had left a "collegial environment" and found that "[t]hey now had to start from scratch proving themselves all over again to a fresh group of sceptics."[129] Wilson reported the comment of one defensive judge: "No woman can do my job!"[130] And she wrote that "many women judges feel a tremendous sense of alienation where they are the only one or one of a very small number on their court. They have no real sense of belonging and are unable to discuss their situation with their previous colleagues at the Bar."[131]

There is some irony in the fact that the intense academic style of Wilson's memo writing found greater support at Osler than at the high-level appellate courts where one might have thought her way of working would be most welcome.

Conclusion

It has been noted that Canadian law firms have been remarkably consistent in their "stubborn resistance to such innovations as democratic methods of firm governance, aggressive programs of client development, meritocratic hiring practices, and the adoption of new technology."[132] However, this started to change in the 1970s when the boom in capital markets led to the demise of the "old family compact," and "an aggressive, transaction-oriented meritocracy" replaced the traditional nepotism.[133] Wilson played an important role in this at Osler, as it moved away from internal autocratic rule toward more transparent and consensus-oriented law firm governance, as well as enhanced client services such as the synopsis and legislation services, and the research department itself. She herself was an example of a greater scope given to meritocracy, and, as we have seen, she advocated strongly for the adoption of new technologies.

However, positive change was accompanied by much that was negative, particularly for women in the profession, who, thanks to Wilson's example, would now be more welcome than they had been. For instance, the new, more aggressive order would see the rise of billable hours as the way to measure workplace performance, a male-model of what constitutes a dedicated associate, and a frenetic style that women with young children find difficult to keep pace with. Wilson herself had no children and an exceptionally supportive spouse.[134] Her professional coping strategy, "working three times harder than everyone else," was not one that all women could follow. Also, after the 1970s, many women would not be satisfied at being relegated to the less glamorous aspects of law practice, and they would not feel as Wilson did about operating quietly behind the scenes. Why should they be forced to make lemonade from lemons?

Wilson's Osler period is important from the point of view of legal culture in Canada, specifically on the history of the development of research procedures and protocols at Canadian law firms. It is also an important part of appreciating the legal life of Bertha Wilson and the complex role her gender played in that life. Among other things, Wilson's founding of the research department was evidence of how she broke into an exclusive, powerful, all-male institution and successfully implemented her particular way of working with the law even if it was not necessarily a template for success for all women in the profession. Her approach found support, and she institutionalized it in a way that effected lasting change on the structures of large law firms in Canada. The founding of the research department should therefore be seen as one of her most successful law reform projects.

The story of the development of the research department embodies two of the most dramatic and admirable things that we have come to associate with Wilson: creative perseverance in the face of gender discrimination and an interest in implementing lasting change in the Canadian legal system. Her initiatives succeeded in what was in many respects a hostile environment, in part because of timing, as we have seen. Wilson stood on the cusp of a new, more unstable and aggressive transaction-oriented world characterized by increased specialization, all of which was a good fit with the research function. This new more meritocratic world order could fold a Bertha Wilson comfortably into its cloak. Yet, the success of the research department was also a function of her personality: her pragmatic style, relentlessly stubborn approach to all matters, and, as she put it, her dedication to the "little things."[135]

Acknowledgments

The authors wish to thank Allan Beattie, Maurice Coombs, Dennis Lane, John Layton, Barbara McGregor, and Heather Grant for agreeing to be interviewed for this project and for providing information and (in some cases) documents relating to the issues investigated here. This chapter simply could not have been written without their participation, and we are very grateful for the enthusiasm they expressed about what we were doing. Thanks also to Mary Jane Mossman, Ellen Anderson, and Curtis Cole for their assistance, particularly at the initial stages of the research, as well as to Laura Fric, Tim Kennish, Edward Saunders, and Purdy Crawford for their input at the end stage. We would also like to acknowledge our colleagues at the University of Toronto Faculty of Law, who provided helpful feedback when we presented the piece at our faculty workshop on 25 February 2008, fellow collection contributors who participated in the conference funded by the Social Sciences and Humanities Research Council at McGill University on 18 April 2008, and the group of Osler lawyers who turned out to a lunchtime presentation kindly organized by Gail Henderson at the law firm on 26 June 2008. Matias Milet kindly liaised with Stephen Sigurdson at Osler regarding copyright permission for the Bertha Wilson memorandum reproduced in Figure 1.1. Susan Barker and Sooin Kim of the Bora Laskin Law Library at the University of Toronto, Faculty of Law, worked to get all three images into the book. Lastly, we are very grateful to collection editor Kim Brooks for her tremendous work on the project as a whole, as well as the specific suggestions and attention she gave to our chapter, from which it greatly benefited.

Notes

1 See Mary Jane Mossman, *The First Women Lawyers: A Comparative Study of Gender, Law and the Legal Professions* (Oxford: Hart, 2006) at 67-112.

2 Ellen Anderson, *Judging Bertha Wilson: Law as Large as Life* (Toronto: University of Toronto Press for the Osgoode Society for Canadian Legal History, 2001) at 38.
3 Quoted in *ibid.* at 48.
4 It has been suggested that moving to Boston to do the LL.M. was not financially feasible and that Wilson would not have wanted to leave John, who was posted in Halifax. The couple moved to Toronto after John was offered a fundraising position with the United Church there. Interview of Allan Beattie by Angela Fernandez and Beatrice Tice (3 October 2007).
5 Curtis Cole, *Osler, Hoskin & Harcourt: Portrait of a Partnership* (Toronto: McGraw-Hill Ryerson, 1995) at 143.
6 Quoted in Sandra Gwyn, "Sense and Sensibility" *Saturday Night* (July 1985) 13 at 17.
7 Quoted in Cole, *supra* note 5 at 123.
8 *Ibid.*
9 Quoted in *ibid.*
10 Quoted in Anderson, *supra* note 2 at 127.
11 Interview of Beattie, *supra* note 4.
12 Cole, *supra* note 5 at 124.
13 Anderson, *supra* note 2 at 54.
14 See Cole, *supra* note 5 at 124.
15 Interview of Beattie, *supra* note 4.
16 Interview of Dennis Lane by Angela Fernandez and Beatrice Tice (12 October 2007).
17 *Ibid.*
18 Anderson, *supra* note 2 at 64.
19 Interview of Lane, *supra* note 16.
20 Quoted in Cole, *supra* note 5 at 124-25.
21 Interview of Lane, *supra* note 16.
22 *Ibid.*
23 Carol Wilton, "Introduction: Inside the Law – Canadian Law Firms in Historical Perspective" in Carol Wilton, ed., *Essays in the History of Canadian Law: Inside the Law – Canadian Law Firms in Historical Perspective,* vol. 7 (Toronto: University of Toronto Press for the Osgoode Society for Canadian Legal History, 1996) 3 at 31.
24 *Ibid.* at 30.
25 Interview of John Layton by Angela Fernandez and Beatrice Tice (25 January 2008).
26 Quoted in Gwyn, *supra* note 6 at 17 [emphasis in original].
27 See Maurice Coombs, "Bertha Wilson: A Woman of the Law" *Briefly Speaking/En bref* (May 2007) (newsletter of the Ontario branch of the Canadian Bar Association).
28 Interview of Lane, *supra* note 16.
29 Anderson, *supra* note 2 at 192.
30 Interview of Lane, *supra* note 16.
31 Interview of Beattie, *supra* note 4.
32 Coombs, *supra* note 27.
33 Ellen Anderson, *Bertha Wilson: Postmodern Judge in a Postmodern Time,* vol. 2 (S.J.D. Thesis, University of Toronto Graduate Department in Law, 2000) at 399, n. 118 [unpublished]. The thesis is cited only where a point is not included in the published book. Please note that both the University of Toronto library copy of the thesis and that of the National Library of Canada are incomplete in that they are missing the third volume.
34 See Anderson, *supra* note 2 at 58.
35 Interview of Maurice Coombs by Angela Fernandez and Beatrice Tice (21 September 2007).
36 See Anderson, *supra* note 33, vol. 1 at 185, n. 26.
37 Quoted in *ibid.,* vol. 2 at 309, n. 132.
38 *Ibid.,* vol. 2 at 248.
39 See *e.g.* Anderson, *supra* note 2 at 94-95, 156.
40 Cole, *supra* note 5 at 125.
41 *Ibid.* Telephone conversation between Curtis Cole and Angela Fernandez (13 September 2007) (remarking that this point came from Wilson).
42 See *e.g.* Anderson, *supra* note 2 at 46.

43 Quoted in *ibid.* at 57.

44 Remarks made by Claire L'Heureux-Dubé, Women's Legal Education and Action Fund (LEAF) Equality Day Celebration, Justice Bertha Wilson Fund Launch, Cocktail Reception (17 April 2008) [L'Heureux-Dubé, Remarks]. For an empirical report of just how much work Wilson did during her time at the Supreme Court of Canada, specifically her high rate of writing when compared to the other judges, see Chapter 12 at 242, this volume. See also Robert J. Sharpe and Kent Roach, *Brian Dickson: A Judge's Journey* (Toronto: University of Toronto Press for the Osgoode Society for Canadian Legal History, 2003) at 372, for a description of Wilson's exasperation with the slow pace of work of most of her colleagues in the mid-1980s.

45 Anderson, *supra* note 2 at 64-65.

46 Interview of Beattie, *supra* note 4.

47 Anderson, *supra* note 2 at 65.

48 *Ibid.* at 58.

49 Gwyn, *supra* note 6 at 17.

50 Telephone conversation between Tim Kennish and Angela Fernandez relaying perspectives communicated to him by Edward Saunders and Purdy Crawford (11 July 2008).

51 Interview of Barbara McGregor and Heather Grant by Angela Fernandez (2 July 2008).

52 Bertha Wilson, "Remarks Made at Mount St. Vincent University Convocation upon Acceptance of an Honorary Degree" in Janet Matyskiel and Louise Lévesque, comp., *Speeches Delivered by the Honorable Bertha Wilson, 1976-1991* (Ottawa: Supreme Court of Canada, 1992) 176 at 180 [Wilson, "Remarks"].

53 Gwyn, *supra* note 6 at 17.

54 Anderson, *supra* note 2 at 39.

55 See Katherine Phenix, "The Status of Women Librarians" (1987) 9:2 Frontiers: A Journal of Women's Studies 36. See also A.R. Schiller, "Women in Librarianship" in M.J. Voight and M.H. Harris, eds., *Advances in Librarianship* (Phoenix, AZ: Oryz, 1974) 103 at 125.

56 See Joan Circa, "Variety and Routine in Law Firm Librarianship" in *Selections from Continuing Education Programme on Developing and Using Law Libraries* (N.p.: Law Society of Upper Canada, Department of Continuing Education, 1971) 155 at 159; Bette Carmichael, "Organization and Equipment in the Law Firm Library" in the same collection 135 at 141. Carmichael was the Osler librarian during Wilson's time.

57 Telephone interview between Allan Beattie and Angela Fernandez (24 September 2007).

58 Interview of Lane, *supra* note 16.

59 See George C. Cunningham and John C. Montaña, *The Lawyer's Guide to Records Management and Retention* (Chicago: American Bar Association, 2006) at 8.

60 The next woman to join the firm did so in 1966, Alicia Forgie, and she was made a partner five years later in 1971. Forgie practised real estate, an area that was relatively "friendly" to female lawyers, according to Barbara McGregor. E-mail from Barbara McGregor to the authors (6 May 2008). Heather Grant (then Frawley), who started out her practice in real estate and asked after two and half years to be switched to the corporate department, joined the firm as an associate in 1970 and became a partner in 1976. She was the first lawyer to have a baby while at Osler, triggering the development of a policy on paid maternity leave – one month for every year of work; when she had her first child, she had been at Osler for four years, so she received four months of leave. This, in her words, "set the policy for King and Bay." Interview of McGregor and Grant, *supra* note 51. The fourth female partner at the firm, Barbara McGregor, became an associate in 1974 and a partner in the real estate department in 1979. By 1981 there were sixteen women lawyers at Osler, five of whom were partners: Forgie, Grant (then Frawley), McGregor, along with Nancy Chaplick (who joined the firm in 1975 and was made a partner in 1980), and Jean Demarco (who joined Osler in 1976 and was made a partner in 1981). See Cole, *supra* note 6 at 155, 339 n. 21.

61 See Anderson, *supra* note 2 at 62.

62 See *ibid.* at 133.

63 Canadian Bar Association Task Force on Gender Equality in the Legal Profession, *Touchstones for Change: Equality, Diversity and Accountability* (Ottawa: Canadian Bar Association, 1993) at 87 [*Touchstones*].

64 *Ibid.* at 88.
65 *Ibid.* at 87.
66 *Ibid.* at 94.
67 Quoted in Anderson, *supra* note 2 at 58.
68 Anderson, *supra* note 33, vol. 2 at 309, n. 132.
69 See Anderson, *supra* note 2 at 136, 197.
70 E-mail from McGregor, *supra* note 60.
71 Interview of Beattie, *supra* note 4.
72 *Ibid.*
73 E-mail from McGregor, *supra* note 60.
74 Gwyn, *supra* note 6 at 17.
75 Other Canadian law firms with research lawyers today include Torys, Stikeman Elliott, Goodmans, Fasken Martineau, and Ogilvy Renault. This list is based on a search of law firm websites (the quality of which varies widely) and is therefore likely to be incomplete.
76 Robert W. Gordon, "A Perspective from the United States" in Carol Wilton, ed., *Beyond the Law: Lawyers and Business in Canada, 1830 to 1930,* vol. 4 (Toronto: Butterworths for the Osgoode Society for Canadian Legal History, 1990) 425 at 433-34.
77 Wilton, *supra* note 23 at 30.
78 See *ibid.* at 38; John Hagan and Fiona Kay, "Hierarchy in Practice: The Significance of Gender in Ontario Law Firms" in Wilton, *supra* note 23, 530 at 532, 541.
79 Interview of Beattie, *supra* note 4.
80 See Anderson, *supra* note 2 at 54-55, 71.
81 Quoted in L.F. Webster, "Filing: The Unsolved Problem" (February 1970) Can. Bar J. 28 at 32.
82 Memorandum from Bertha Wilson to the law firm library committee (14 February 1972) at 2. Copy provided to the authors by Dennis Lane.
83 Interview of Lane, *supra* note 16.
84 Quoted in Webster, *supra* note 81 at 30.
85 Wilson Memorandum, *supra* note 82 at 1.
86 Interview of Coombs, *supra* note 35.
87 See *e.g. Vorvis v. Insurance Corporation of British Columbia,* [1989] 1 S.C.R. 1085 at para. 32 (noting with sympathy that one of the problems the employer in the wrongful dismissal case had with plaintiff/employee/lawyer was his writing in "long-hand" as opposed to using "a dictating machine"). But see *Richardson v. Richardson,* [1987] 1 S.C.R. 857 (a spousal support case in which Wilson had little sympathy for the fact that Mrs. Richardson's clerical skills – the employment she engaged in before her marriage and intermittently throughout it – had become outdated as a result of computerization).
88 Wilson Memorandum, *supra* note 82 at 5.
89 E-mail from Dennis Lane to the authors (28 September 2007).
90 Webster, *supra* note 81 at 32.
91 Anderson, *supra* note 33, vol. 1 at 137 ("Oslers was able to arrange to store its research index (client names expunged to ensure absolute confidentiality) on QuickLaw with, of course, the further safeguard of an Oslers-only password").
92 Wilson Memorandum, *supra* note 82 at 7.
93 *Ibid.* at 6.
94 Dennis Lane, "An Approach to the Storage and Retrieval of Legal Research in a Large Law Firm" in *Selections from Continuing Education, supra* note 56, 237 at 240.
95 Interview of Lane, *supra* note 16; Diane Snell, "An Information Retrieval System – Why and How: Responses to Queries by the Canadian Association of Law Librarians Convention" (Saskatoon, SK, 1983) at 4 [unpublished]. Copies provided to the authors by Maurice Coombs and Dennis Lane.
96 Memorandum from J.T. Kennish to members of the library committee, re Proposed Commercial Precedent System (no date) at 6-7. Copy provided to the authors by Dennis Lane. Not until the 1990s did the firm became focused on its system of precedents and their computerization. Cole, *supra* note 5 at 242-43.
97 Lane, *supra* note 94 at 242.
98 *Ibid.*

99 *Ibid.* at 243.
100 Quoted in Webster, *supra* note 81 at 32.
101 Anderson, *supra* note 2 at 54.
102 See *ibid.* at 60-61. Interview of Beattie, *supra* note 4. What Wilson wanted – charging for the time required to do the work, whether that was short or long – was in keeping with current billing practices.
103 Snell, *supra* note 95 at 6.
104 E-mail from Maurice Coombs to the authors (3 October 2007).
105 Interview of Coombs, *supra* note 35.
106 *Ibid.*
107 Lane, *supra* note 94 at 242.
108 Snell, *supra* note 95 at 2.
109 *Ibid.* at 8 ("Once an in-house computer system is acquired the client's name will be re-instated and we will have the best of all possible worlds").
110 Interview of Coombs, *supra* note 35.
111 See Snell, *supra* note 95 at 7-9.
112 Comment made by Laura Fric, Osler presentation by Angela Fernandez (26 June 2008).
113 Interview of Coombs, *supra* note 35.
114 Snell, *supra* note 95 at 5.
115 See Chapter 16, this volume, for a discussion of how Wilson's academic approach played out in some of her judgments during her time at the Ontario Court of Appeal and the Supreme Court of Canada.
116 See *e.g. Perka v. The Queen,* [1984] 2 S.C.R. 232 (for a Wilson concurrence that wrestles with Kant and Hegel).
117 See Anderson, *supra* note 2 at 12.
118 See *ibid.* at 162-64.
119 *Ibid.* at 164 (Wilson thought it was "far better to have a range of judgments offering options, including a dissent and a diverging concurrence if necessary, as long as each judgment was written with crystal clarity").
120 *Ibid.* at 165.
121 See *ibid.* at 192.
122 See *ibid.* at 163-64 (arguments against a rigid procedure include not wanting to increase "the deluge of paper" and that the preservation of informal discussion is an important way to prevent positions from hardening in the decision-making process).
123 *Ibid.* See also Sandra Martin, "Bertha Wilson, 83" *Globe and Mail* (30 April 2007), online: <http://www.theglobeandmail.com> (noting that Wilson was "not fully accepted by the other members of the court").
124 Anderson, *supra* note 2 at 153. See also at 257.
125 See Philip Girard, *Bora Laskin: Bringing Law to Life* (Toronto: University of Toronto Press for the Osgoode Society for Canadian Legal History, 2005) at 433.
126 See Anderson, *supra* note 2 at 154; Girard, *ibid.* at 529; Edward Goldenberg, *The Way It Works: Inside Ottawa* (Toronto: McClelland and Stewart, 2006) at 89, quoted in Martin, *supra* note 123.
127 Anderson, *supra* note 2 at xvi. See also at 325-26 (elaborating reasons for departure, some financial and some personal, including the fact that Dickson had retired five months earlier and "[c]hange seemed, if anything, less likely with Dickson gone"). See also Martin, *supra* note 123, quoting Madame Justice Rosalie Abella of the Supreme Court of Canada, calling Wilson and Dickson "the Fred and Ginger of the Charter." L'Heureux-Dubé publicly reported that Dickson wanted Wilson to replace him as Chief Justice, but she declined for health reasons. Dickson used to say that Wilson taught him everything he knew about human rights and the *Charter.* L'Heureux-Dubé also confirmed that the decision making was very much a male club, from which she and Wilson felt excluded. For instance, they would not be invited to lunches where the male judges would be agreeing to the majority and strategizing about that. Wilson spoke up about this on one occasion during conference, which caused Dickson to turn bright red. He was not a part of that exclusion. L'Heureux-Dubé, Remarks, *supra* note 44.

128 *Touchstones, supra* note 63 at 192.
129 *Ibid.*
130 *Ibid.* at 193.
131 *Ibid.* at 194. See Anderson, *supra* note 2 at 346-51 (for a discussion of the controversy surrounding this section of the report – Chief Justice Antonio Lamer wanted to know which judges had made the complaints, but Wilson refused to disclose the information as she had elicited it personally with guarantees of confidentiality). This section of the report contains pointed criticism of the Canadian Judicial Council, which must have upset Lamer as its head. See *Touchstones, supra* note 63 at 198. See also Chapter 14 and Chapter 15 at 282-85, this volume.
132 Wilton, *supra* note 23 at 5.
133 Cole, *supra* note 5 at 207 (quoting Christopher Portner), 214 (an informal "anti-nepotism rule" was in place by the 1970s).
134 See Anderson, *supra* note 2 at 404, n. 29 (describing Wilson's childlessness as "a matter of sad happenstance rather than choice"). See also at 47, 131, 199 (in terms of domestic labour, Wilson's husband, John, did shopping and cooking, and Wilson did the house cleaning until the time of her Supreme Court appointment. John ran the household once they moved to Ottawa).
135 Wilson, "Remarks," *supra* note 52 at 179.

2
A Traditionalist's Property Jurisprudence

Larissa Katz

We remember and celebrate a judge such as Bertha Wilson by making sense of her legacy.[1] All legacies require a central story around which a person's enduring achievements are organized. The danger of a legacy, and Justice Wilson's is no exception, is that the central story has a sorting function: those contributions that tell the story are drawn into the centre, and others, real though they might be, are marginalized. Wilson's legacy is already taking shape. It lies primarily in her pioneering work in criminal[2] and constitutional law,[3] work that has fostered her reputation as a policy-oriented judge.[4] But the prominence of these areas of law in Justice Wilson's legacy is more a function of circumstance than anything else – most importantly, the timing of her appointment to the Supreme Court of Canada just as the *Canadian Charter of Rights and Freedoms* came into force.[5] Had it been up to her to choose the area of law that would dominate her life's work, she might well have opted for property law. Indeed, she came very close to pursuing an academic career devoted to researching and writing on the subject.[6]

As it turned out, Justice Wilson's interest in property law did not expire with her academic ambitions. Throughout her judicial career, she took a rigorous and scholarly approach to property law issues. Her interest in property law was not to use it as a tool for radical reform. In fact, she was a self-proclaimed conservative when it came to the subject: she thought of it as a stable area of law with little need for innovation. She made this view explicit in a 1990 lecture she gave at Osgoode Hall Law School, stating that property law's "principles and the underlying premises are so firmly entrenched and so fundamentally sound that no good would be achieved by attempting to re-invent the wheel."[7] Justice Wilson aimed throughout her judicial career to make sense of what she saw as the ancient traditions of property law handed down from feudal England to the present day.

Her view of herself as quietly following a well-trodden path might incline us to disregard her passion for the subject or to think that her property jurisprudence made no real and lasting contribution. But this would be a mistake. In fact, as I will argue in this chapter, Wilson's special regard for property law was evident in her earliest published writing and her earliest work as a judge.[8] Her contributions to this area, although perhaps outliers to the central story we tell about her, are nonetheless real and enduring.

I will begin with an overview of Justice Wilson's approach to property law generally and will argue that, in her analysis of property law issues throughout her career, she shied away from explicitly outcome-oriented reasoning. Her property jurisprudence reveals a self-conscious commitment to working out the law in terms of the values and concepts that are intrinsic to it. Next, I will focus on one aspect of her property jurisprudence in which this commitment is evident, her contribution to the law of adverse possession.

Property Fundamentals

Justice Wilson's passion for property law and the common law tradition surfaced very early in her legal career. Her first exposure to the former came at Dalhousie Law School, where she took Graham Murray's first-year property class and followed up with various property-related courses in upper years.[9] Her biographer, Ellen Anderson, describes Professor Murray's class as quite traditional, offering "a thorough grounding in the fundamental principles of property law."[10] He engendered in his students an appreciation not just of the development of the English common law on property, but of classical Roman approaches to property problems as well.[11] We see evidence of this training in the paper "A Choice of Values," which Wilson wrote in law school for a seminar with Graham Murray on municipal planning and published several years after graduating.[12] In it, she engaged in a scholarly effort to trace the ways in which, as far back as the sixteenth century, the common law resolved the classic problem of conflicting land uses. At a time when Dalhousie Law School, like most other Canadian law schools, was renouncing traditional legal history and pressing a functionalist American-style approach to the analysis of law, Justice Wilson was absorbing "ancient concepts"[13] of property law from Pollock and Maitland's *History of the English Law* and Halsbury's *Laws of England.*[14] As a student, she was sufficiently enthused about property law to plan to pursue graduate work in the area at Harvard Law School, where she had been accepted with a scholarship – a plan that the Dean of Dalhousie Law, Horace Read, persuaded her to abandon on the grounds that, as a woman, she was unlikely to secure an academic position.[15]

Justice Wilson's appreciation for the common law tradition in property law is as much in evidence in her judicial writing as in her work as a student. When she was a new judge on the Ontario Court of Appeal, fully half the decisions she wrote during her first six months concerned property law.[16] Her scholarly regard for the rich pedigree and historical context of property law is nowhere more in evidence than in her decision in *Re Rynard*.[17] Consider the opening line of this case, which captures her view, explicitly set out a decade later in her 1990 lecture at Osgoode, that property law concerns enduring, well-entrenched principles and concepts: "This appeal reminds us that the roots of some of our law are deeply embedded indeed."[18] The case concerned the application of the (medieval) rule in *Shelley's Case*, which, she notes, first appeared in the Year Books at the time of Edward II[19] and has confused and confounded lawyers and judges ever since.[20] The rule in *Shelley's Case* prevents a testator from granting a life estate to A followed by a remainder to A's heirs, where the testator meant to refer to "the whole line of inheritable issue" of A.[21] In short, the rule prevents multi-generational gifts-over, while leaving intact gifts to "heirs" in the more limited sense of specific individuals such as "next of kin living at [the testator's] death."[22]

Justice Wilson's decision in *Rynard* is striking simply because she – some have argued, perversely[23] – refused to read the rule out of existence in Ontario, notwithstanding the fact that the rule lacks a strong policy-based rationale and, indeed, on Wilson's own view, is simply a holdover from feudal times.[24] Although she found that the rule did not apply in that case, she was careful to point out that this was because the testatrix was not attempting to create a multi-generational gift and not because, as the court below had found, the rule in *Shelley's Case* was no longer part of our law. In so doing, she breathed new life into the rule in *Shelley's Case* precisely at a time when it was being abolished or limited in other jurisdictions.[25] Wilson's careful parsing of what she reverently called an "ancient rule of law"[26] is not at all out of character for someone whose first love as a student was for the history of property law.

Justice Wilson's enthusiasm for ancient solutions to enduring property problems continued when she joined the Supreme Court of Canada. Take her dissent in *Reference re Ownership of the Bed of the Strait of Georgia and Related Areas*.[27] Once again, she began her decision with a characteristic reference to the long-enduring and well-established nature of property principles: "This is one of those cases where the resolution of a very contemporary problem depends upon the application of very ancient principles of law."[28] The question posed in that case was whether British Columbia owned the land under the water between Vancouver Island and the mainland. The majority decision found quite summarily that the statutory borders of British Columbia, established by an 1866 act of British parliament, included the lands under the waters in question. Justice Wilson's dissent is a remarkable contrast. She leapt into a lengthy analysis of the property issues, carefully parsing the age-old distinction between ownership and sovereignty (and the dangers of conflating the two) and offering a rich historical overview of the common law definition of inland waters. Again, her deep respect for "ancient" principles of property law was on display in her effort to trace the history of property law concepts in order to apply them faithfully. Thus, she wrote, "In seeking to ascribe meaning to the phrase *inter fauces terrae,* it is useful to turn to its origins." Following this daunting introduction, she went on to inform us that the "earliest reference which I have been able to trace" came from the early fourteenth century.[29] She then proceeded to consider an astonishing array of cases and treatises written through the centuries that produced subtly different tests for when waters are *inter fauces terrae.*

In this decision, it is tempting to see strong evidence of Wilson's fascination with historical and doctrinal aspects of the law, if only because her elaborate discussion of the evolution of the doctrine *inter fauces terrae* was ultimately unnecessary to answer the question in the case. Indeed, she wrapped up her review of the issue by acknowledging that, because the straits had international headlands (shores on different countries), they simply were not candidates for treatment in the common law as inland waters. Certainly, her discussion of the history and meaning of this rather obscure point of law has to be one of the longest passages of *obiter dicta* penned by a judge.

Justice Wilson clearly respected and admired the centuries' worth of refinements to the common law, primarily by English judges, that have produced our modern law of property. But it would be a mistake to cast her as mechanically following English courts in her property jurisprudence, a failing common to earlier Canadian judges of which Bora Laskin and her former Dean, Horace Read, had been particularly critical.[30] For instance, in *Re Lottman Estate,*[31] Wilson declined to follow her English counterparts in restricting to personal property the requirement that trustees sell unproductive assets and invest the proceeds in order to maintain the balance between successive interest holders.[32] Citing numerous Canadian cases from the beginning of the twentieth century that applied the rule to real estate, she praised their "contemporary Canadian attitude to property." As she put it, "Real estate is not a 'sacred cow' in Canada, as it was in England when these equitable rules were developed. Sale of the family hereditaments is not fraught with trauma and disgrace."[33] She thus concluded that it was entirely appropriate to do as Canadian courts had done and to apply the rule to unproductive real estate.

Although Justice Wilson's property writing quite clearly manifests a personal interest in, and regard for, traditional principles and concepts, it would be quite wrong to dismiss her property jurisprudence as charming and quirky but ultimately of marginal significance.[34] Within the first six months of her tenure as a judge on the Ontario Court of Appeal, she had already made her mark on a foundational aspect of property law, adverse possession. Her decision in *Keefer v. Arillotta,* with which the rest of this chapter is concerned, remains an important contribution to property law, albeit one that is increasingly under attack.[35]

Salvaging a Legacy: Justice Wilson's Approach to Adverse Possession

In *Keefer,* one of her earliest property decisions, Justice Wilson steered the law of adverse possession in Ontario, and in much of Canada, in a new direction.[36] The larger context in which she decided these cases is important to understanding their significance. When she decided *Keefer,* judges elsewhere in the common law world were mainly concerned with object-level considerations about incentives in the law of adverse possession.[37] Outcomes in many adverse possession cases in England and the US reflected a general judicial reluctance to reward so-called bad-faith squatters. At the same time, the view was newly emerging in England that such policy-based restrictions on the law of adverse possession improperly distorted the law.[38] This English backlash against policy-based approaches to adverse possession has only grown stronger in subsequent years, culminating in a 2002 House of Lords decision in *J.A. Pye (Oxford) Ltd v. Graham,* which rejected the inconsistent use test on grounds that I will argue misconstrue its conceptual role and its doctrinal foundation.[39]

Justice Wilson, unlike so many of her peers, did not take a moralistic approach to adverse possession, although she is often (and I think wrongly) thought to have done so. Her decision in *Keefer* does not reflect a moral aversion to bad-faith squatters but rather proceeds from a conceptually sound analysis of the core elements of adverse possession, rooted in common law tradition and doctrine. Her approach, although controversial,[40] is defensible on conceptual and doctrinal grounds against the criticisms launched by the House of Lord's decision in *Pye* and found more recently in Canadian decisions such as *Bradford Investments (1963) v. Fama.*[41]

An Overview of *Keefer*

The *Keefer* case concerned a dispute over a strip of land belonging to the Arillottas, which lay just north of the Keefers' property. The Keefers had a right of way over the land in question to access their property to the south but had been using it far in excess of their legal rights for over ten years, well before the Arillottas had purchased it. The relationship between the Keefers and the Arillottas' predecessor, the Cloys, was non-confrontational and even amicable. The Cloys, who ran a business on their land in the summer, renting out an apartment in the back, and who spent most of the winter in Florida, tolerated and indeed facilitated the Keefers' use of the strip. There was no conflict between their uses and those the Keefers made of the property, which included parking cars on it and using the grassy area for parties from time to time in the summer and a skating rink in the winter. But when the Arillottas purchased the land from the Cloys, they did not suffer the Keefers' use of it as gladly, and the Keefers responded by claiming to have acquired possessory title to the strip. At trial, the judge found that the Keefers' possession was "open, visible and continuous for far more than the requisite number of years"[42] and also found in favour of the Keefers on what he saw as the sole remaining issue, whether the possession was exclusive. Justice Wilson heard the case on appeal. She concluded that the Keefers had not possessed the whole strip "adversely" to the true owner.

The Test of Inconsistent Use

The doctrinal innovation to emerge in *Keefer,* which Justice Wilson confirmed in *Fletcher v. Storoschuk et al.*[43] a few years later, is that, for a squatter to acquire ownership rights, she must do more than simply possess the land in the ordinary sense for the requisite number of years: she must show acts of possession that are inconsistent with the use that the true owner planned to make of the land.[44] In *Keefer,* the adverse possessors' uses of the contested strip did not interfere with the limited use that the owners wanted to make of it. The owners, in short, were not driven out of possession by the squatters' use, with the result that the squatters failed to establish that they had acquired ownership rights to the land. The test of inconsistent use places a great deal of weight on the paper-title holder's plans for the land in assessing the normative consequences of the squatter's acts of possession. Quite extensive acts of possession by a squatter are not sufficient if the owner's agenda for the property is not disturbed.[45] One implication of this focus on the owner's intended uses is that the less an owner wants to do with her land, the more effectively is she insulated from adverse possession. An owner whose plan for property is simply to hold it as an investment is unlikely to find her plans disturbed by the uses a squatter makes of it in the meantime. A squatter in such cases would thus find it very difficult to meet the requirement for inconsistent use, with the result that owners for whom real estate is an investment will have little to fear from adverse possessors.[46]

In the decades following *Keefer,* some debate focused on how the inconsistent use test bears on the elements of adverse possession. Adverse possession requires possession, the intent to possess, and dispossession of or discontinuance of possession by the true owner for the statutory period.[47] One interpretation of *Keefer* is that inconsistent use is necessary to establish that the owner has been effectively dispossessed.[48] The other interpretation is that inconsistent use is relevant merely as evidence of the squatter's mental state: acts of inconsistent use offer support for an inference of adverse intent.[49] The difference between these interpretations is significant. If inconsistent use is not strictly required to establish dispossession but is simply evidence of adverse intent, a squatter should be able to prevail against the owner even where she cannot show inconsistent use so long as other facts support a conclusion of adverse intent.[50] The *Keefer* decision, as I read it, suggests that the inconsistent use test bears both on the requisite intent and on the quality of acts necessary for dispossession. Thus, Justice Wilson wrote that the squatter must have the "intention to exclude the owner from such uses as the owner wants to make of his property" but also tells us that the "test for the acquisition of possessory title" is whether the squatter has "precluded the owner from making the use of the property that he wanted to make of it."[51] Dispossession thus depends on acts that are inconsistent with the owner's agenda for the land.

Justice Wilson's decision in *Keefer* marked a turning point in the law of adverse possession in Ontario. It cut through the ambiguity and looseness of the earlier case law and offered a clear account of the acts and intention required of an adverse possessor to succeed against the original owner. The pre-*Keefer* case law is ambiguous as to the importance and meaning of *animus possidendi* in establishing adverse possession. In *Sherren v. Pearson,* a Supreme Court of Canada decision from 1887, Chief Justice Ritchie wrote, "To enable the defendant to recover he must show an actual possession, an occupation exclusive, continuous, open or visible and notorious for twenty years. It must not be equivocal, occasional or for a special or temporary purpose."[52] No mention is made of *animus possidendi.* Henry J.'s concurring judgment in *Sherren* stated quite simply that adverse possession requires acts of possession to establish ouster: "intention has nothing to do with it."[53] And yet the traditional approach in Ontario is not quite as clear as this might suggest. Traces of an adverse intent requirement do exist in the pre-*Keefer* case law. In *Sherren,* for instance, Ritchie C.J.'s concern that there was insufficient evidence that the squatter acted "with a view to possess or to dispossess the true owner" signals that *animus possidendi* does matter after all.[54] The importance of adverse intent has surfaced even more strongly in other pre-*Keefer* cases, such as *Canada (Attorney-General) v. Krause,*[55] where the Court observed that a squatter lacked the requisite intent because he would have been willing to pay for the privilege of using the land or would have left if asked.[56] (By contrast, in a recent English case that self-consciously advocated a return to the "traditional" approach to adverse possession, the willingness of the squatter to have paid negotiated rent was found *not* to be fatal to a claim of adverse possession, the subjective intent of the squatter being irrelevant.)[57] Finally, in *Pflug and Pflug v. Collins,* the leading pre-*Keefer* case on adverse possession, the Court indicated that the squatter must prove not only actual possession and the dispossession of the true owner, but also "the intention of excluding from possession the owner or persons entitled to possession."[58] It is clear that some kind of adverse intent was required pre-*Keefer,* but it was not entirely clear what kind: an intent to possess, an intent to exclude the owner, or an intent to own.[59]

Justice Wilson's decision makes clear that the squatter must intend to drive the owner out of possession and must in fact set the agenda for the land herself. The requisite *animus* is inferred from acts of possession that are in fact inconsistent with the owner's intended use. Wilson's approach to adverse possession continues to influence the law in Canada today, although there is a growing backlash against it that, I will argue, proceeds from a misunderstanding of the purpose of the inconsistent use test and its doctrinal foundations.[60]

Although her *Keefer* decision changed the way that we view adverse possession in Canada, Justice Wilson did not, Denning-like, create an entirely novel test that diverges from the modern statutory framework for adverse possession and the common law tradition that has interpreted it.[61] Her approach in *Keefer* is drawn from an old English approach to adverse possession set out in *Leigh v. Jack,* a Court of Appeal decision from 1879.[62] In that case, Leigh had conveyed land to the defendant but had reserved from the grant a strip of property that he intended ultimately to dedicate as a public street, a plan that did not in the end materialize. For twenty years before the action was brought (twenty years being the applicable statutory period), the defendant had used the site to store materials and refuse.[63] Leigh did not occupy it, although he had repaired the fence on it during the twenty-year period prior to the action. Bramwell L.J. held that no discontinuance of possession had occurred (a small act, such as fence repair, was considered sufficient to show that an owner had not abandoned the property); nor had the defendant dispossessed the plaintiff, because there had been no inconsistent use. The defendant's use of the land for storage did not interfere with the plaintiff's plans to dedicate it in the future as a public street.

The inconsistent use test was long the accepted approach in England, Australia, and, after Justice Wilson's decision in *Keefer,* in Ontario and other Canadian jurisdictions. But it has recently been rejected in both England[64] and Australia,[65] and is increasingly questioned in Canada.[66] Wilson herself would have had the opportunity to consider and respond to some of the early criticism of *Leigh v. Jack,* which surfaced during 1977 in English cases such as *Powell v. McFarlane*[67] and *Treloar v. Nute,*[68] and in the UK Law Reform Committee's report on limitations of actions.[69] Nonetheless, in the 1981 case *Fletcher,* she affirmed the approach she had taken in *Keefer.*

In what follows, I will argue that Justice Wilson's approach in *Keefer* is not properly the target of the kinds of concerns that have been raised in England and more recently in Canada. Insofar as the inconsistent use test has fallen into disfavour, it is because it has been characterized, I think wrongly, as a judicial repeal of the modern statutory reforms to adverse possession and as a policy-motivated obstacle to adverse possession by deliberate squatters.

A Property "Heretic"?

A general criticism that might be levied against Justice Wilson's approach to adverse possession is that it distorts the law of adverse possession in order to avoid rewarding deliberate squatters for their wrongs. There would indeed be reason to criticize such a stance. I argue elsewhere that adverse possession's important role in our system of property proceeds from our concept of ownership as a position of agenda-setting authority.[70] Ownership is in certain respects analogous to sovereignty.[71] Facts on the ground matter in both cases. There comes a point when a ruler who loses effective control over her territory cannot meaningfully be said to have authority. This is so even if the revolutionaries who displaced her had no right to do so.[72] Just as the legitimacy of a claim to sovereignty is tied to some extent to the effectiveness of the authority claimed, so too is a claim of ownership. Through the law of adverse possession, we avoid vacancies in our property system by validating the adverse possessor's claims to wield agenda-setting authority in circumstances when it is clear that the paper owner no longer has effective authority. By ensuring that the form of ownership is not permanently detached from the external manifestation of ownership (*i.e.,* the *effective* authority to set the agenda), adverse possession plays an important role in a system of property. This significant role is undermined when the law of adverse possession is manipulated in order to discourage deliberate squatters.

The inconsistent use test is not vulnerable to the criticism that, as a policy tool to deter deliberate squatters, it conflicts with the more general purpose of adverse possession. On the contrary, the test plays a central role in the law of adverse possession because it determines whether or not the owner has *in fact* lost effective authority and so fails fully to occupy her position.[73] The owner's claims of agenda-setting authority may survive the physical occupation by the squatter (if her agenda does not require physical presence) but not long-term inconsistent use.

A more basic criticism of the inconsistent use test is a doctrinal one: it has been argued that the test reintroduces concepts such as non-adverse possession, which were abolished by the English reforms of the law of adverse possession in 1833.[74] Before the 1833 statutory reforms to adverse possession, certain possessors were deemed to hold "non-adversely" to the owner simply by virtue of their status and without regard to the nature of their possession.[75] This of course had the effect of insulating owners in many cases against the claims of possessors. The reappearance of the concept of non-adverse possession in the case law in effect amounts to the judicial repeal of a statutorily entrenched doctrine, a move that judges are not competent to make.[76] In 2002 the House of Lords in *Pye*[77] explicitly set out to purge the law of adverse possession of policy-based restrictions on deliberate squatters that it saw as having improperly infiltrated the modern law of adverse possession.[78] The main substantive concern of the House of Lords, as it was for the UK Law Reform Committee and Slade J. in *Powell v. McFarlane,* was the reintroduction of the concept of "non-adverse" possession.

However, this narrower criticism on doctrinal grounds is not properly directed at the inconsistent use test as it is applied in *Keefer.* Rather, it results from a conflation of the test with a rogue outgrowth of *Leigh v. Jack* introduced into the law by none other than Lord Denning. A year before Justice

Wilson wrote *Keefer,* Denning wrote a very influential decision in *Wallis's Cayton Bay Holiday Camp Ltd. v. Shell-Mex and BP Ltd.,* which ostensibly followed *Leigh v. Jack.*[79] In *Wallis's Cayton Bay,* Denning declared that deliberate squatters were to be deemed to possess non-adversely (*i.e.,* with the permission of the true owner), which prevented the statute from running against the true owner. Denning's approach proceeded from the policy view that the law ought not to assist so-called bad-faith squatters. In his words, "[I]t does not lie in the other person's mouth to assert that he used the land of his own wrong, as a trespasser."[80] This manner of correcting in law for defects in character is familiar enough from trust law: trustees, for instance, are presumed to have done what ought to have been done even when they manifestly did not, and did not intend to do so. Lord Denning's approach to squatters was novel: he imputed an implied permission to use land in circumstances that did not allow the implication of a licence for any other purpose in law and in circumstances where no licence or permission could be implied from the facts.[81] The implied licence theory is indeed deserving of criticism: it is an entirely artificial construct blatantly aimed at precluding the deliberate squatter from obtaining the assistance of the law. In so doing, it did resurrect the pre-1833 practice of deeming certain kinds of possession to be non-adverse. Parliament in the UK responded by abolishing the implied licence theory in 1980.[82]

Although, in *Pye,* Lord Brown-Wilkinson declared that "the root of the problem is caused by the concept of 'non-adverse possession,'" in the line of cases following Denning's decision in *Wallis's Cayton Bay,* he nonetheless fingered *Leigh v. Jack* and the inconsistent use test as the source of this problem. At one point, Brown-Wilkinson asserted that "Bramwell LJ's heresy [in *Leigh v. Jack*] led to the heresy in the *Wallis's Cayton Bay* line of cases ... which heresy was abolished by statute."[83] There is no doubt that Lord Denning saw himself as building on *Leigh v. Jack* in reintroducing the concept of non-adverse possession into the law. But that is not to say that the concept of non-adverse possession naturally emerges from *Leigh v. Jack.* Indeed, Justice Wilson's approach in *Keefer,* which is quite faithful to a narrow reading of *Leigh v. Jack,* employs the inconsistent use test in her definition of possession/dispossession but hardly converges with Denning's approach. Although both Denning's and Wilson's approaches are unwilling to find sufficient evidence of dispossession in mere occupation, they are importantly distinct in the tools that they offer to analyze whether sufficient possession has occurred to start the time running on the statute of limitations. The difference between Denning's and Wilson's approaches is that the former is a legal implication that operates in defiance of clear facts, whereas the inconsistent use test is entirely grounded on the facts and does not impute the grounds for ruling in favour of the owner. Although a person can, on Justice Wilson's approach, occupy the land without initiating the time for adverse possession, this is not because possession is deemed to be adverse due to the status of the adverse possessor. Rather, a person fails to possess adversely where the quality and the nature of her acts are in fact consistent with the owner's plans.

Once we properly distinguish the inconsistent use test from Denning's approach, do any grounds remain for impeaching the former? Lord Brown-Wilkinson in *Pye* suggested that the definition of dispossession in terms of actual interference with the owner's agenda added something illicit to the statutory regime. Indeed, the inconsistent use test does add substance to the idea of possession/dispossession and necessarily so. The concept of possession/dispossession is not self-defining; nor is it defined in the statutory reforms.[84] The need for further judicial definition of the terms that fit the statutory context is immediately obvious when we consider that, at the very least, possession must occur without the permission of the true owner, or else every tenant would threaten the title of the landlord. But insofar as this definition does not have the effect of reintroducing legal categories of imputed or deemed possession, it does not undermine the statutory reforms. Brown-Wilkinson's stern disapproval of any elaboration on the idea of possession/dispossession may be a response to the misleading simplicity of what counts as sufficient possession in the modern law of adverse possession. For instance, Brown-Wilkinson endorsed the view expressed in *Culley v. Doe d. Taylerson*[85] that the modern law of adverse possession required only that the squatter be in "actual possession [for the statutory period] whether adverse or not." But this statement is not in fact at odds with the approach taken in *Leigh v. Jack,* simply because it does not say much more than that we must proceed on the basis of fact, not imputation, in assessing possession. That is to say, *Culley* just confirms that the modern law of adverse possession no longer deems certain categories of persons to possess on behalf of the true owner. The approach in *Leigh v. Jack,* as Justice Wilson interpreted it, is consistent with this statement because it defines the factual circumstances that count as possession and dispossession. The simplicity of the statement in *Culley* is deceptive because it leaves unsaid what is meant by possession.

In short, nothing in the modern law of adverse possession statutorily overrides the approach that Justice Wilson took in *Keefer* such that it can fairly be called "heretical."[86] The 1833 reforms support a definition of possession that includes the test of inconsistent use, aimed as they are at the much narrower task of removing the concept of non-adverse possession.[87]

Justice Wilson shared neither Lord Denning's irreverence for established property concepts nor his willingness to mould the law of adverse possession in response to moral disapproval of "bad-faith" squatting. Her approach in *Keefer* employed the inconsistent use test to determine whether in fact the squatter had wrested agenda-setting control from the owner, on the understanding that, whereas only one person can have ultimate agenda-setting authority, ownership is left intact in circumstances where a person merely deprives another of a benefit that is ordinarily an incident of ownership.

Not only is Justice Wilson's approach to adverse possession on its face quite distinct from Denning's, it is fair to say that she deliberately distanced herself from Denning's approach. It is telling that she did not discuss or even cite his approach in *Wallis's Cayton Bay,* notwithstanding that it was decided a year before *Keefer* and several years before her decision in *Fletcher*[88] and notwithstanding her deep admiration for Lord Denning in non-property contexts.[89] Given what we know about Wilson's meticulous research practices and her general familiarity with Lord Denning's jurisprudence, I think it is fair to surmise that her omission was deliberate. Denning's tendency to produce policy-driven interpretations of property law, it has been said, "provoked the ire of traditional property lawyers."[90] When it comes to property law, Justice Wilson seems to have had much more in common with these traditionalists than with the judge, who, in her words, possessed "that pristine vigour of speaking your mind and 'damn the torpedoes.'"[91]

Post-*Keefer* Developments

I have argued that Justice Wilson's decision in *Keefer* is situated within a doctrinally sound common law approach to the ideas of ownership and adverse possession. It is post-*Keefer* case law that spins her decision as an expression of our moral distaste for so-called bad-faith squatters and thus produces the two-tier system for advertent and inadvertent squatters that we have in Ontario. In *Masidon,*[92] for instance, Justice Blair approved of Wilson's approach precisely because it made adverse possession more difficult for deliberate squatters and so avoided creating incentives for land theft.[93] The assumption that the inconsistent use test reflects a moral standard also lies behind the more lenient approach to inadvertent squatters in Ontario.[94] Justice Laskin in the *Teis* case explicitly construed the test as a tool to restrict and punish land thieves "by strengthening the hand of the true owner in the face of an adverse possession claim by a knowing trespasser."[95] In Laskin J.'s view, it would defeat this policy to apply the test to claims by persons who honestly, though mistakenly, use land that is not their own.[96] Insofar as Justice Wilson introduced the inconsistent use test to punish or restrict knowing squatters, an exemption for good-faith squatters arguably follows:[97] Inadvertent squatters would find it more difficult than advertent squatters to meet the requirements of the test.[98] A good-faith squatter cannot have had the intent to oust the true owner where she thought she herself was the true owner. Further, in cases of mutual mistake, it would be impossible for the inadvertent squatter to have acted in a way inconsistent with the owner's plans, because the true owner would not have known to make any plans for the land.[99]

This two-tier system makes sense insofar as the inconsistent use test is aimed at deterring deliberate squatters. But no explicit appeal to the immorality of deliberate squatting appears in *Keefer;* nor does the inconsistent use test depend for its coherence on such questionable moral assumptions. As I argued earlier and elsewhere, there is a conceptual explanation for why inconsistent use is an important part of the law of adverse possession. The conceptual implications of inconsistent use hold true whether a deliberate or an inadvertent squatter takes over the function of agenda setter.

Justice Wilson's work on property law generally, and adverse possession in particular, complicates our view of the judge and her legacy. At least in her property jurisprudence, she was not a "Canadian Denning." She cleaved to doctrine, to the "ancient law" of property, sometimes with a reverence that surprises a reader who knows her for her innovative *Charter* jurisprudence. What she has left us through her property writing is a richer understanding of basic concepts in property law and of the common law tradition in which these concepts are at play.

Acknowledgments
I am grateful to Kim Brooks, Mary Jane Mossman, Shannon O'Byrne, Malcolm Thorburn, Bruce Ziff, and two anonymous reviewers for their helpful comments and to Heather Webb for research assistance.

Notes

1 See *e.g.* Moira L. McConnell, special editor, "The Democratic Intellect: Papers Presented at a Symposium to Honour the Contribution of Madame Justice Bertha Wilson, Dalhousie Law School, October 5, 1991" (1992) 15 Dal. L.J. i at iii; Brian Dickson, "Madame Justice Wilson: Trailblazer for Justice (1992) 15 Dal. L.J. 3; Ellen Anderson, *Judging Bertha Wilson: Law as Large as Life* (Toronto: University of Toronto Press for the Osgoode Society for Canadian Legal History, 2001).

2 See *R. v. Perka,* [1984] 2 S.C.R. 232 (dissenting); *R. v. Tutton,* [1989] 1 S.C.R. 1392 (dissenting); *R. v. Daviault,* [1994] 3 S.C.R. 63; *R. v. Lavallee,* [1990] 1 S.C.R. 852.

3 See Brian Dickson, "Madame Justice Wilson: Trailblazer for Justice" (1992) 15 Dal. L.J. 1. See also *Singh v. Minister of Employment and Immigration,* [1985] 1 S.C.R. 177; *R. v. Big M Drug Mart Ltd.,* [1985] 1 S.C.R. 295; *Reference Re Section 94(2) of the Motor Vehicle Act,* [1985] 2 S.C.R. 486; *Clarkson v. The Queen,* [1986] 1 S.C.R. 383; *R. v. Edwards Books and Art Ltd.,* [1986] 2 S.C.R. 713; *R. v. Morgentaler,* [1988] 1 S.C.R. 30; *R. v. Wigglesworth,* [1987] 2 S.C.R. 541; *Andrews v. Law Society of British Columbia,* [1989] 1 S.C.R. 143; *Irwin Toy Ltd. v. Quebec (A.G.),* [1989] 1 S.C.R. 927.

4 See Anderson, *supra* note 1 at 225 (noting Wilson J.'s reputation as Canada's Lord Denning, an English Court of Appeal judge famous for his unorthodox outcome-oriented decisions). By "policy oriented," I mean what James Harris calls "the utility model of rationality." This is a mode of legal reasoning in which a court "opts between different rulings by assessing the consequences in terms of moral, social or economic considerations 'extrinsic' to legal materials." See J.W. Harris, "Legal Doctrine and Interests in Land" in John Eekelaar and John Bell, eds., *Oxford Essays in Jurisprudence* (Oxford: Clarendon Press, 1987) 167 at 175.

5 Dickson, *supra* note 3 at 14. *Canadian Charter of Rights and Freedoms,* Part 1 of the *Constitution Act, 1982,* being Schedule B to the *Canada Act 1982* (U.K.), 1982, c. 11.

6 See *infra* note 15 and accompanying text.

7 Bertha Wilson, "Will Women Judges Really Make a Difference?" (1990) 28 Osgoode Hall L.J. 507 at 515.

8 See Bertha Wilson, "A Choice of Values" (1961) 4 Can. Bar J. 448.
9 Anderson, *supra* note 1 at 40, 99.
10 *Ibid.* at 40, 47.
11 *Ibid.* at 40.
12 Wilson, *supra* note 8 at 449-57.
13 *Ibid.* at 450.
14 See Philip Girard, "Who's Afraid of Canadian Legal History?" (2007) 57 U.T.L.J. 727 at 735-36, 747-49.
15 Anderson, *supra* note 1 at 48.
16 All six concerned private law: *Coulson v. Secure Holdings Ltd.,* [1976] O.J. No. 1459 (C.A.); *Dominion Chain Co. Ltd. v. Eastern Construction Co. Ltd.* (1976), 12 O.R. (2d) 201 (C.A.); *Gilbert Steel Ltd. v. University Construction Ltd.* (1976), 12 O.R. (2d) 19 (C.A.); *Bouskill v. Campea et al.* (1976), 12 O.R. (2d) 265 (C.A.); *Brown v. Bouwkamp* (1976), 12 O.R. (2d) 33 (C.A.); *Keefer v. Arillotta* (1977), 13 O.R. (2d) 680 (C.A.) [*Keefer*].
17 *Re Rynard* (1980), 31 O.R. (2d) 257 (C.A.) [*Rynard*]. In Chapter 16, this volume, Mary Jane Mossman makes a convincing case that *Rynard* can also be read as an attempt to promote the agency of women by honouring the testatrix's wishes. For other cases that signal Justice Wilson's delight in the internal logic of the law and its historical roots, see *e.g. Smibert v. Shore Estate,* [1978] O.J. No. 1278 at para. 34, where she discusses, unprompted by counsel, the applicability of the equitable doctrine of notional conversion found in *Lawes v. Bennett* (1785), 1 Cox Ch. 167.
18 *Rynard, supra* note 17 at para. 1.
19 *Ibid.* at para. 5. See also *Van Grutten v. Foxwell,* [1897] A.C. 658 (H.L.). The rule takes its name from a much earlier case, *Shelley's Case* (1581), 76 E.R. 206 (K.B.).
20 M.M. Litman and Bruce Ziff, "*Shelley's* Rule in a Modern Context: Clearing the 'Heir'" (1984) 34 U.T.L.J. 170 at 196.
21 *Rynard, supra* note 17 at para. 18. On this threshold issue of construction, see also Litman and Ziff, *supra* note 20 at 174.
22 *Rynard, supra* note 17 at para. 18.
23 Wilson considered and rejected the position of the trial judge: that s. 31 of the *Wills Act,* R.S.O. 1927, c. 149, abolished the rule in *Shelley.*
24 Indeed, the rule has long been abolished in England (see the *Law of Property Act 1925* [U.K.], 15 Geo. V., c. 20) and limited elsewhere. See Bruce H. Ziff, *Principles of Property Law,* 4th ed. (Toronto: Thomson Carswell, 2006).
25 At least, she ensured that, formally, the rule in *Shelley* remains the law in Ontario. There are virtually no other cases in Ontario or indeed in Canada in which the rule has been at issue, with the possible exception of *Taylor Estate v. Taylor,* [1986] O.J. No. 1472 (S.C.).
26 *Rynard, supra* note 17 at para. 6.
27 *Reference re Ownership of the Bed of the Strait of Georgia and Related Areas,* [1984] 1 S.C.R. 388.
28 *Ibid.* at 427.
29 *Ibid.* at 427 and 441. A literal translation of *inter fauces terrae* is "between the jaws of land," meaning inland waters.
30 Girard, *supra* note 14 at 738.
31 *Re Lottman Estate* (1978), 2 E.T.R. 1 [*Lottman*] (reversed by *Lottman et al. v. Stanford et al.,* [1980] 1 S.C.R. 1065).
32 *Ibid.* at para. 13, citing the English case *Re Woodhouse,* [1941] Ch. 332.
33 *Lottman, supra* note 31 at para. 14.
34 See Litman and Ziff, *supra* note 20 at 192 (criticizing *Rynard* as needlessly perpetuating the rule in *Shelley's Case*).
35 *Keefer, supra* note 16.
36 Wilson confirmed her approach in *Keefer* in *Fletcher v. Storoschuk et al.* [1982] 35 O.R. (2d) 722 (C.A.) [*Fletcher*]. In *Fletcher,* the true owner intended to create a buffer zone between his neighbour's lot and the land on which he himself grazed cattle. Wilson J. found that the use the defendant made of this strip of land, including various measures to keep the weeds down, was not inconsistent with its use as a buffer.

37 In England, Lord Denning provided a doctrinal basis for this approach, the implied licence theory, which I discuss later in this chapter. In the US, judges were less systematic in their efforts to exclude bad-faith squatters, content to decide against them even in the absence of a doctrinal basis for doing so. See R.H. Helmholz, "Adverse Possession and Subjective Intent" (1983) 61 Wash. U.L.Q. 331; Thomas W. Merrill, "Property Rules, Liability Rules, and Adverse Possession" (1984) 79 Nw. U.L. Rev. 1122.

38 See Slade J.'s decision in *Powell v. McFarlane* (1977), 38 P. & C.R. 452 (Ch.D.) [*Powell*]; UK, Law Reform Committee, "Final Report on Limitation of Actions," Cmnd. 6923 (1977) ["Final Report"].

39 *J.A. Pye (Oxford) Ltd v. Graham,* [2003] 1 A.C. 419 (H.L.) [*Pye*].

40 In Newfoundland, the approach in *Keefer* has been followed in *Fitzpatrick's Body Shop Ltd. v. Kirby* (1992), 315 A.P.R. 42 (T.D.), 1992 CarswellNfld 218 (Nfld. S.C. (T.D.)); *Bussey v. Maher,* [2006] N.J. No. 136 (Nfld. S.C.) (citing *Fitzpatrick's*). *Masidon Investments Ltd. v. Ham* (1984), 45 O.R. (2d) 563 (C.A.) [*Masidon*], which itself follows *Keefer,* has been cited with approval in *Re McEachern,* [1996] P.E.I.J. No. 127 (S.C. (T.D.)); *R. v. Roch,* [1994] Y.J. No. 151 (S.C.); *Landry v. Landry,* [1991] N.B.J. No. 622 (C.A.).

41 *Bradford Investments (1963) v. Fama,* [2005] O.J. No. 3258 (Sup. Ct. Jus.) [*Bradford*].

42 *Keefer,* supra note 16 at para. 38.

43 *Fletcher, supra* note 36.

44 Wilson's decision was foreshadowed by the trial decision in *St. Clair Beach Estates Ltd. v. MacDonald et al.* (1974), 5 O.R. (2d) 482 (Div. Ct.).

45 *Fletcher, supra* note 36 at para. 8 (finding defendants' acts of possession insufficient to oust the true owner when considered relative to the true owner's plans for the land).

46 See *e.g. Masidon, supra* note 40.

47 *Pflug and Pflug v. Collins,* [1952] O.R. 519, [1952] 3 D.L.R 681 (S.C.) [*Pflug*].

48 *Masidon, supra* note 40.

49 This is how Laskin J. understood Justice Wilson's decision. See *Teis v. Ancaster (Town),* [1997] O.J. No. 3512 (C.A.) [*Teis*].

50 See *Bradford, supra* note 41. *Bradford* was a case of unilateral mistake. The Court held that the squatter could prevail even in the absence of inconsistent use because there was *other* evidence of adverse intent. *Ibid.* at paras. 42-44, 80. But see *Tecbuild Ltd. v. Chamberlain* (1969), 20 P. & C.R. 633 at 643 [*Tecbuild*] ("In general intent has to be inferred from the acts themselves"). See also *Powell, supra* note 38 at 476, n. 31 (noting that declarations of intent, even contemporaneously made, are of little evidential value, because they are self-serving). See also Larissa Katz, "Exclusion and Exclusivity in Property Law" (2008) 58 U.T.L.J. 275.

51 *Keefer, supra* note 16 at 193. See also *Fletcher, supra* note 36 at paras. 8, 11, where Wilson J. suggests that, without inconsistent use, the squatter cannot establish either an intent to exclude the owner from possession or the discontinuance for the statutory period of possession by the owner.

52 *Sherren v. Pearson,* [1887] S.C.J. No. 23, (1887), 14 S.C.R. 581 at para. 3 [*Sherren*]. See also *Mechanic and Mechanic v. Karnov,* [1943] 2 D.L.R. 201 (Ont. C.A.); *Laing and Laing v. Moran and Moran,* [1952] 2 D.L.R. 468 (Ont. C.A.); *Pflug, supra* note 47; *Rains v. Buxton* (1880), 14 Ch. D. 537.

53 *Sherren, supra* note 52 at 593.

54 *Ibid.,* at para. 4.

55 *Canada (Attorney-General) v. Krause,* [1955] O.J. No. 270 (S.C.).

56 See also *Bell and Maedel v. Bell and Bell* (1957), 9 D.L.R. (2d) 767 (Ont. H.C.), where the claim failed because there was no admissible evidence that the possession was adverse.

57 *London Borough of Southwark v. Williams and another,* [1971] 2 All E.R. 175 (C.A.).

58 *Pflug, supra* note 47 at 527.

59 See *George Wimpey & Co., Ltd. v. Sohn,* [1966] 1 All E.R. 23 (C.A.) at paras. 42-44, 80 (accepting the evidence the defendants offered about their intent); *Powell, supra* note 38 at 475, n. 23 (citing Sachs L.J. in *Tecbuild, supra* note 50 at 642-43).

60 For cases applying the inconsistent use test, see *Mueller v. Lee,* [2007] O.J. No. 2543 (Sup. Ct. J.) *(obiter)* [*Mueller*]; *Laurier Homes (27) Ltd. v. Brett* (2005), 42 R.P.R. (4th) 86, 2005

CarswellOnt 702; *Masidon, supra* note 40. For cases criticizing the inconsistent use test, see *Beaudoin et al. v. Aubin et al.* (1981), 33 O.R. (2d) 604 at para. 18; *Fazio v. Pasquariello,* [1999] O.J. No. 703 (C.J. (Gen. Div.)); *Raso v. Lonergan,* [1996] O.J. No. 2898 (C.J. (Gen. Div.)); *Gorman v. Gorman* (1998), 110 O.A.C. 87, 1998 CarswellOnt 1366 (Ont. C.A.); *1636539 Ontario Ltd. v. W. Bradfield Ltd.,* [2007] O.J. No. 973, 2007 CarswellOnt 1562 (Ont. Sup. Ct.). *Cf. Bradford, supra* note 41, which approvingly considered the criticisms in *Pye, supra* note 39, but was precedent-bound to follow *Keefer; Gibbins v. Gibbins* (1977), 18 O.R. (2d) 45, 1977 CarswellOnt 134 (H.C.J.).

61 In fact, Wilson, who seems to have admired Denning's work in other contexts, chose not to follow his own take on the question. In a controversial case decided two years before *Keefer,* Denning determined that any use of an owner's land to which she did not object was by her implied permission and hence not adverse. See *Wallis's Cayton Bay Holiday Camp Ltd. v. Shell-Mex and BP Ltd.,* [1974] 3 W.L.R. 387, 3 All E.R. 575 [*Wallis's Cayton Bay*].

62 *Leigh v. Jack* (1879), 5 Ex. D. 264.

63 The defendant also enclosed part and then all of the planned street, though for a total of fifteen years, not the required twenty (the action was brought eleven years after he did so).

64 *Pye, supra* note 39.

65 See Adrian J. Bradbrook, Susan V. MacCallum, and Anthony P. Moore, *Australian Real Property Law,* 4th ed. (Pyrmont, NSW: Lawbook, 2007) at 688-94.

66 See *e.g. Teis, supra* note 49; *Bradford, supra* note 41.

67 *Powell, supra* note 38.

68 *Treloar v. Nute,* [1977] 1 All E.R. 230 (C.A.).

69 "Final Report," *supra* note 38 at 44-46.

70 See Katz, "Exclusion and Exclusivity," *supra* note 50. Other reasons commonly offered for the importance of adverse possession include removing stale claims, punishing dormant owners, and protecting third parties who mistake the possessor for the owner of the land. Although each of these reasons is partially valid, taken either alone or together, they do not explain why adverse possession is an important element of property law. For a discussion of the shortcomings of these rationales, see Lee Ann Fennell, "Efficient Trespass: The Case for 'Bad Faith' Adverse Possession" (2006) 100 Nw. U.L. Rev. 1037.

71 Katz, *supra* note 70 at 293-95.

72 The discussion that follows is from Larissa Katz, "The Moral Paradox of Adverse Possession Resolved: Sovereignty and Revolution in Property Law," 2009 SSRN, online: <http://papers.ssrn.com/sol3/papers.cfm?abstract_id=1444986> (developing the analogy between revolution and adverse possession).

73 Katz, *supra* note 70 at 292.

74 *Real Property Limitation Act, 1833* (U.K.), c. 27, repealing *An Act for Limitation of Actions, and for avoiding of Suits in Law,* 1623 (U.K.) 21 Jac. I, c. 16.

75 See *e.g.* John M. Lightwood, *A Treatise on Possession of Land* (London: Stevens and Sons, 1894) at 161-67 (describing pre-1833 rules and presumptions of non-adverse possession).

76 See *e.g.* "Final Report," *supra* note 38 (criticizing certain policy-based restrictions on adverse possession by deliberate squatters as "judicial repeal of the statute").

77 *Pye, supra* note 39.

78 See also *Bradford, supra* note 41 at para. 80. In his *A History of English Law,* 2d ed., vol. 7 (London: Methuen, 1966) at 80, Sir William Holdsworth described the effect of the 1833 *Act* as follows: "[The statute] takes away from every owner ... his title to the property ... whether the possession of that other has or has not been adverse."

79 *Wallis's Cayton Bay, supra* note 61. See also *Gray v. Wykeham-Martin* (17 January 1977), Transcript No. 10A of 1977 (C.A.).

80 *Wallis's Cayton Bay, supra* note 61 at 392.

81 See *Powell, supra* note 38 at 469.

82 See the *Limitation Act, 1980* (U.K.) 1980, c. 58, s. 8(4).

83 *Pye, supra* note 39 at para. 45.

84 Indeed, Brown-Wilkinson offers a definition of possession sufficient to start the statute running as physical control and intent to possess: *Pye, ibid.* at para. 32, citing Slade J. in *Powell, supra* note 38.

85 *Culley v. Doe d. Taylerson* (1840), 11 Ad. & El. 1008 at 1015.

86 It has also been argued that this definition of possession is simply contrary to the "ordinary" meaning of the word. See *Bradford, supra* note 41 at para. 82 (inconsistency relates solely to the future intentions of the owner rather than to any existing connection with the property).

87 See *Masidon, supra* note 40 at para. 17: "Before 1833, some acts of possession were deemed to be acts on behalf of the owner and hence not 'adverse.' As a consequence of the reforming statutes of the 1830s, adverse possession is established where the claimant's use of the land is inconsistent with the owner's 'enjoyment of the soil for the purposes for which he intended to use it'" [citation omitted].

88 Denning's decision in *Wallis's Cayton Bay* made its way into Ontario case law in *Masidon,* where it was considered by the lower court: *Masidon Investments Ltd. et. al. v. Ham,* [1982] O.J. No. 3541, 39 O.R. (2d) 534 (H.C.J.).

89 On Wilson's admiration for Denning in other contexts, see Anderson, *supra* note 1 at 324 and 351.

90 J.W. Harris, *Property and Justice* (Oxford: Oxford University Press, 1996) at 89, quoting D.J. Hayton, "Equity and Trusts" in J.L. Jowell and J.P.W.B. McAuslan, eds., *Lord Denning: The Judge and the Law* (London: Sweet and Maxwell, 1984) 79.

91 Quoted in Anderson, *supra* note 1 at 324.

92 *Masidon, supra* note 40.

93 *Ibid.* at para. 33, citing Burton J.A. in *Harris v. Mudie* (1882), 7 O.A.R. 414 at 421. See Brian Bucknall, "Two Roads Diverged: Recent Decisions on Possessory Title" (1984) 22 Osgoode Hall L.J. 375 at 382 (inconsistent use test creates moral standard). There is also an older precedent for the view that deliberate adverse possession amounts to land theft. See *Campeau v. May,* [1911] O.J. No. 644, 19 O.W.R. 751 at para. 12.

94 See *Teis, supra* note 49 at para. 27 ("the law has always been less generous when a knowing trespasser seeks its aid to dispossess the rightful owner"); *Kreadar Enterprises Ltd. v. Duny Machine Ltd.* (1994), 42 R.P.R. (2d) 274 at para. 19 (Ont. Gen. Div.); *Lepore v. Girolami Estate,* [1994] O.J. No. 528 (Gen. Div.); *Giouroukos v. Cadillac Fairview Corp. Ltd. et al.,* [1982] O.J. No. 3323 at 187-88 (H.C.J.). See also Katz, "Moral Paradox," *supra* note 72.

95 *Teis, supra* note 49 at para. 28. See also *Mueller, supra* note 60 at paras. 21-22; *Wood v. Gateway of Uxbridge Properties Inc.,* [1990] 75 O.R. (2d) 769 (Gen. Div.) [*Wood*]. See also *Fazio v. Pasquariello,* [1999] O.J. No. 703; *Key v. Latsky,* [2006] O.J. No. 71; *Murray Township Farms Ltd. v. Quinte West (City),* [2006] O.J. No. 2956; *BCM International (Canada) Inc. v. Joannette,* [2006] O.J. No. 756 (even though the claimant did not succeed).

96 *Teis, supra* note 49.

97 For an analysis of unilateral mistake, see *Bradford, supra* note 41.

98 As Laskin J. pointed out in *Teis, supra* note 49 at para. 27, "Thus applied, the test would reward the deliberate squatter and punish the innocent trespasser."

99 *Ibid.; Wood, supra* note 95.

3

Power, Discretion, and Vulnerability: Justice Wilson and Fiduciary Duty in the Corporate/Commercial Context

Janis Sarra

> Change in the law comes slowly and incrementally; that is its nature. It responds to changes in society; it seldom initiates them. And while I was prepared – and, indeed, as a woman judge, anxious – to respond to these changes, I wondered to what extent I would be constrained in my attempts to do so by the nature of the judicial office itself.
>
> – Bertha Wilson, "Will Women Judges Really Make a Difference?" 1990

The Translation of Concepts between Areas of the Law

The Honourable Bertha Wilson recognized at the outset of her judicial tenure that the law develops incrementally and that although the courts will respond to changing social norms, their response will be measured and balanced. As the first woman appointed to an appellate court in Canada and the first woman appointed to the Supreme Court of Canada, she was able to view this dynamic first-hand and, in turn, to play an important role in advancing particular aspects of the law. She is most widely recognized for her judgments in respect of equality and diversity. However, her time on the bench marked another significant role: her contribution to the development of corporate and commercial law in Canada. Her seventeen years' experience at the law firm Osler, Hoskin & Harcourt writing corporate and commercial memos and opinions stood her in good stead in this respect. An important aspect of this contribution has perhaps been unrecognized, specifically, using principles and concepts established for one legal framework to discern and grant a remedy in an entirely different context. In this respect, Justice Wilson offers a lesson to legal scholars, practitioners, and adjudicators regarding their collective capacity to think about the law and the development of its overarching principles in a comprehensive and integrated manner.

Although Wilson never described herself as a feminist, she did acknowledge that certain areas of the law were more susceptible to analysis viewed through a woman's experience, whereas others were less so. Writing in 1990, she observed,

> Taking from my own experience as a judge of fourteen years' standing, working closely with my male colleagues on the bench, there are probably whole areas of the law on which there is no unique feminine perspective. This is not to say that the development of the law in these areas has not been influenced by the fact that lawyers and judges have all been men. Rather, the principles and the underlying premises are so firmly entrenched and so fundamentally sound that no good would be achieved by attempting to re-invent the wheel, even if the revised version did have a few more spokes in it. I have in mind areas such as the law of contract, the law of real property, and the law applicable to corporations.[1]

The passage illustrates Wilson's acknowledgment that judging is grounded in the experience and norms of the judges, including gender as a lens through which evidence is assessed and cases are determined. Equally, however, the quote illustrates that she found a number of commercial law principles fundamentally sound and that she was not persuaded of a need for a change when viewed from the perspective of gender. Yet, where Justice Wilson concluded that commercial law was in need of adjustment, she did not hesitate to express her opinions, either writing for the court, which she did many times, or in a dissenting judgment.

This chapter deals with two aspects of her contribution: specifically, development of the concept of fiduciary obligation in the corporate and commercial context and the need for an equitable remedy where such obligations are breached; and her recognition of the court's signalling role in development of corporate commercial law through the exercise of its leave powers.

"Fiduciary" comes from the Latin *fiducia,* meaning "trust."[2] "Fiduciary" as a term is derived from Roman law, meaning a person holding the character of, or analogous to, a trustee, including the requirement of utmost good faith and candour. Such a person has duties created by his or her undertaking to act primarily for another's benefit in matters connected with the undertaking.[3] The imposition of a fiduciary obligation by the court draws on equity to find a remedy where an abuse of that trust has occurred.[4] Since commercial transactions do not necessarily involve notions of trust, the application of equitable principles or remedies is a challenging issue.

Justice Wilson's reasoning in respect of fiduciary obligation can be summed up in two sentences. First, parties to a commercial relationship will not, in the usual course, owe fiduciary obligations to one another, but occasions may arise in which the recognition of such a duty is appropriate and necessary. Second, three general characteristics are common to situations in which a fiduciary obligation has been recognized: the fiduciary has scope for the exercise of some discretion or power; the fiduciary can unilaterally exercise that power or discretion so as to affect the beneficiary's legal or practical interests; and the beneficiary is peculiarly vulnerable to, or at the mercy of, the fiduciary holding the discretion or power.[5] Justice Wilson's approach was novel as it recognized that, beyond the historically defined categories of fiduciary relationships, other circumstances may also give rise to fiduciary obligations without creating broad new categories. Her approach also acknowledged the importance of drawing out broad principles in respect of power and vulnerability and applying them to areas of law that one might not intuitively have considered.

Developing an Analysis of Fiduciary Obligation beyond Recognized Categories

> [R]esort to equity is entirely appropriate so that no just cause shall go without a remedy.
>
> – Bertha Wilson, *Frame v. Smith,* 1987

The now widely adopted approach to determining whether a fiduciary obligation exists in a corporate commercial context drew initially on a judgment not in the field of business law but, rather, on the reasoning in a dissent authored by Justice Wilson in a family law case, *Frame v. Smith.*[6] In that case, the Supreme Court addressed the conduct of a custodial parent toward a non-custodial parent. The issue arose in the context of an application to strike out the plaintiff's statement of claim as disclosing no reasonable cause of action. Wilson, in a dissenting judgment, held that although the custodial parent's actions did not give rise to a cause of action based on the torts of conspiracy, intentional infliction of mental suffering or unlawful interference, or a right at common law of access to children, they would give rise to a cause of action for breach of fiduciary duty.[7]

Prior to *Frame v. Smith,* the courts had approached the issue of whether a particular relationship was subject to a fiduciary obligation by determining whether or not it fit into one of the categories of relationships in which a fiduciary obligation was held to be present, such as directors of corporations, trustees, and agents.[8] In her dissenting judgment in *Frame v. Smith,* Wilson noted the reluctance in the common law to affirm the existence of, and give content to, a general fiduciary principle that could be applied in appropriate circumstances, suggesting that perhaps the biggest obstacle to the development of such a principle was the fact that the content of the fiduciary duty varied with the type of relationship to which it was applied.[9] She observed that "the failure to identify and apply a general fiduciary principle has resulted in the courts relying almost exclusively on the established list of categories of fiduciary relationships and being reluctant to grant admittance to new relationships despite their oft-repeated declaration that the category of fiduciary relationships is never closed."[10]

Justice Wilson's dissent proposed a different way of analyzing fiduciary obligation. She found that common features were discernible in the contexts in which fiduciary duties had been held to exist and that these features provided a "rough and ready guide" to whether or not the imposition of a fiduciary obligation in a new situation would be appropriate and consistent. She wrote that relationships in which a fiduciary obligation had been imposed seemed to possess three general characteristics: the fiduciary had scope for the exercise of some discretion or power; the fiduciary could unilaterally exercise that power or discretion so as to affect the beneficiary's legal or practical interests; and the beneficiary was peculiarly vulnerable to, or at the mercy of, the fiduciary holding the discretion or power because the beneficiary was unable to prevent the injurious exercise of that power and because of the inadequacy of remedies to redress the wrongful exercise. Wilson observed,

> With respect to the second characteristic it is, of course, the fact that the power or discretion may be used to affect the beneficiary in a damaging way that makes the imposition of a fiduciary duty necessary. Indeed, fiduciary duties are frequently imposed on those who are capable of affecting not only the legal interests of the beneficiary but also the beneficiary's vital non-legal or "practical" interests. For example, it is generally conceded that a director is in a fiduciary relationship to the corporation. But the corporation's interest which is protected by the fiduciary duty is not confined to an interest in the property of the corporation but extends to non-legal, practical interests in the financial well-being of the corporation and perhaps to even more intangible practical interests such as the corporation's public image and reputation.[11]

Justice Wilson focused on the power relationship in particular circumstances and its ability to harm rather than on fixed broad categories of relationship, opening up the potential for finding a fiduciary obligation in commercial situations. Her view was that equity was the appropriate tool to tailor a cause of action, providing not only a remedy in the circumstances, but creating an incentive for others similarly situated.[12] She also recognized that the imposition of fiduciary duties could protect both legal and non-legal or "practical interests" in appropriate cases. To deny relief because of the nature of the interest involved, and to afford protection to material interests but not to human and personal interests, would be arbitrary; hence, other "non-economic interests should also be capable of protection [in] equity through the imposition of a fiduciary duty."[13] The protection of non-legal and practical interests suggests that Wilson understood relationships as complex, layered, and dynamic, and that the interests affected were equally complex and nuanced where harm was caused by the inequitable exercise of power. In this respect, her judgments are a strong example of contextual reasoning.

Wilson deployed an interesting technique of judicial reasoning that appears in some of her other judgments, conducting the principled analysis by using examples far removed from the subject at hand and then applying the principles to the case before her. In *Frame v. Smith,* she utilized examples from the corporate context to make her points about potential fiduciary obligation in the family law context. The use of differing contexts illustrates how she was able to draw linkages between disparate areas of the law in order to identify broad principles that should be applied. This technique aligns with her views in respect of the role of the Supreme Court of Canada generally. In an article she wrote during her second year on the Supreme Court, she observed that the Court's role was overseeing the development of the law, consciously creating a framework for the law, and setting its boundaries.[14]

Arguably, also, the use of this interpretative technique allowed her to advance new indicia or principles in a non-threatening way, before applying them to particular circumstances that might be highly emotive, such as in the family law context.[15] This technique created an analysis that was subsequently adopted by courts in the context of commercial litigation, with the result that Wilson's dissenting *Frame v. Smith* analysis of fiduciary obligation became the most often quoted family law judgment in the commercial law context, as discussed later in this chapter.

The significance of this interpretive approach is illustrated by the number of judgments in which Wilson's reasoning has been endorsed. As she recognized, the development of the law is incremental, whether through the democratic legislative process or the development of the common law. The courts face a tension regarding the extent to which they should signal their views on matters that are not directly before them but that touch on public policy issues of significance to society. Wilson's recognition of this tension is evident in her views of the Supreme Court's leave process, as examined below. Her broad principled contextual approach, together with her willingness to reason across diverse legal categories, presents an interesting judicial tool to raise broad principles and paves the ground for their further development in the appropriate case.

Another significant aspect of Wilson's judgment in *Frame v. Smith* was her observations in respect of whether statutory language ousts the common law or prevents recognition of a fiduciary obligation in equity. She noted that strong statutory language is required to remove the jurisdiction of the court to grant equitable relief for an equitable wrong such as breach of fiduciary duty, again using the corporate context to point out that extensive statutory intervention had not succeeded in ousting the equitable jurisdiction of the court to grant relief for breach of fiduciary duty.[16] Historically, courts of equity have even been willing to grant equitable relief supplementing statutory relief for a statutory wrong.[17]

Justice Wilson's observation that clear and compelling statutory language is required to oust equity's broad jurisdiction to give equitable relief in appropriate circumstances is significant. In the commercial law context, as in other areas of the law, courts frequently struggle to find the appropriate remedy that makes commercial sense and is fair and predictable. Occasionally, the degree of statutory codification has made courts reluctant to consider equitable remedies. Wilson's analysis is helpful in understanding that equity interacts with statutory language and that the court's ability to grant equitable relief for harms from a breach of fiduciary responsibilities is not negated absent statutory language expressly ousting its authority.

Elsewhere, Justice Georgina Jackson of the Saskatchewan Court of Appeal and I have suggested that the courts should first engage in statutory interpretation to determine the limits of authority, adopting a broad, liberal, and purposive interpretation that may reveal the authority.[18] Statutory interpretation may reveal a discretion and determine the extent of the discretion, or it may reveal a gap.[19] The application of equitable principles may fill the gap; if it does, the court retains discretion as to whether it will invoke the authority. Justice Wilson's reasoning illustrates these distinctions. Her analysis in respect of fiduciary obligation distinguishes between the authority of the courts under statutory language and their equitable jurisdiction where the statute has not expressly ousted that jurisdiction. In this respect, her description of the contours of these sources of authority has been helpful to courts in subsequent cases.[20]

Application of Justice Wilson's Reasoning in the Commercial Law Context

Justice Wilson's reasoning in respect of fiduciary obligation was endorsed by the Supreme Court of Canada for the first time in a commercial context in *Lac Minerals Ltd. v. International Corona Resources Ltd.*,[21] where both the majority and the minority judgments relied on her analysis of fiduciary obligation in *Frame v. Smith*. The case involved a junior mining company, International Corona Resources, which had discovered a valuable property through its extensive exploration program. Corona showed Lac Minerals, a senior mining company, confidential geological findings during negotiations for financing and development of a joint venture. The matter of confidentiality was not raised. Lac Minerals subsequently acquired the property itself but never informed Corona of its intention to do so.[22] The trial judge held Lac Minerals liable under breaches of confidence and fiduciary duty for its actions, finding that the appropriate remedy was to give the property to Corona.[23] The Ontario Court of Appeal affirmed the findings of the trial judge with respect to breach of fiduciary duty and confirmed the remedy of a constructive trust as an appropriate remedy.[24]

On appeal to the Supreme Court of Canada, the Court dealt with the issue of whether a fiduciary relationship existed between Corona and Lac Minerals and whether it was breached by Lac Minerals' acquisition of the property. Justice La Forest relied on Justice Wilson's reasoning in *Frame v. Smith* to find that a fiduciary obligation existed and that it had been breached in the circumstances of the case. He held that Lac Minerals had breached a duty of confidence owed to Corona.[25] La Forest held that the receipt of confidential information in circumstances of confidence established a duty not to use that information for any purpose other than that for which it was conveyed and that Lac Minerals acted to Corona's detriment when it employed the confidential information to acquire the property.[26]

La Forest further held that the relationship of trust and confidence that developed between Corona and Lac Minerals was a factor worthy of significant weight in determining if a fiduciary obligation existed between the parties and that the existence of such a bond played an important role in determining whether one party could reasonably expect the other to act or refrain from acting against its interests.[27] Fiduciary law is concerned with the duty of loyalty. La Forest further held that although breach of confidence has a jurisdictional base at law and accordingly can draw on remedies available in both law and equity, fiduciary obligations arise only in equity and can draw only on equitable remedies.[28]

Justice La Forest held that a fiduciary relationship did not normally arise between arm's-length commercial parties; however, the facts here supported the imposition of a fiduciary obligation based on trust and confidence, industry practice, and vulnerability.[29] Applying Wilson's analysis, he held that both parties would reasonably expect that a legal obligation would be imposed on Lac Minerals not to act in a manner contrary to Corona's interest with respect to the property.[30] He further held that industry practice, though not conclusive, should be given significant weight in determining what Corona could reasonably expect of Lac Minerals; here, it was the importance of the industry practice of not acting on disclosure of confidential information. He held that vulnerability or its absence was not conclusive of the question of fiduciary obligation; rather, "the issue should be whether, having regard to all the facts and circumstances, one party stands in relation to another such that it could reasonably be expected that that other would act or refrain from acting in a way contrary to the interests of that other."[31]

Justice La Forest further held that the Court should not deny the existence of a fiduciary obligation simply because the parties could have regulated their affairs by means of a confidentiality agreement.[32] Such agreements should not be presumed where it was not established that entering into them was a common, usual, or expected course of action, particularly when the law of fiduciary obligations could operate to protect the reasonable expectations of the parties, and there was no reason to clutter normal business practice by requiring a contract.[33] La Forest expressly rejected the argument that finding a breach of fiduciary obligation here would create uncertainty in commercial law or result in determination of the rules of commercial conduct on the basis of *ad hoc* moral judgments rather than on the basis of established principles of commercial law, finding that certainty in commercial law is an important value, but not the only value.[34]

In discussing the remedy to be imposed in the circumstances, La Forest drew on Justice Wilson's reasoning in another judgment, *Hunter Engineering Co. v. Syncrude Canada Ltd.,* in determining that a constructive trust was the appropriate remedy in the circumstances.[35] Specifically, Wilson had held that no special relationship between the parties was necessary for a finding of constructive trust, as to do so would be to impede the growth and impair the flexibility crucial to the development of equitable principles. Constructive trust was refused in *Hunter Engineering Co.* because the claim for unjust enrichment was not made out, not because of the nature of the relationship.[36] Justice La Forest held that the imposition of a constructive trust could both recognize and create a right of property.[37]

Of the five members of the Supreme Court who heard the appeal in *Lac Minerals,* only Justices La Forest and Wilson recognized that a fiduciary duty to Corona had arisen, although Justice Lamer joined to make a majority on the remedy awarded, whereas the other two judges would have awarded damages only for breach of confidence. Hence, the majority endorsed Wilson's express extension of the equitable doctrine of constructive trust to the commercial law context. La Forest, writing for the majority, held that a constructive trust was the only appropriate remedy, given the uniqueness of the property, the fact that Corona would have acquired it but for Lac Minerals' breach of duty, and the virtual impossibility of accurately valuing the property.[38]

Justice Sopinka, dissenting in *Lac Minerals* in respect of the finding of a fiduciary relationship, concurred in the finding of breach of confidence but disagreed on the remedy. However, in doing so, he expressly endorsed

Wilson's analysis in *Frame v. Smith* as the indicia of fiduciary obligations and agreed that such duties could arise in the commercial context.[39]

Acknowledging the criteria developed by Wilson, Sopinka then wrote that, in his view, the lower courts had erred in finding that a fiduciary obligation existed between Corona and Lac Minerals as they did not give sufficient weight to the essential ingredient of dependency or vulnerability and too much weight to other factors such as the supply of confidential information and the practice in the mining industry.[40] Sopinka held that the vital ingredient of vulnerability was missing in the case and that where confidential information was misused, there was a remedy that fell short of classifying the relationship as fiduciary. Again, he quoted from Wilson's *Frame v. Smith* analysis of vulnerability to find that there was no inability to seek a remedy for the conduct.[41] Hence, in the combined majority and minority judgments, the Supreme Court endorsed Wilson's notion that fiduciary obligation was available as an equitable remedy in the corporate commercial context, although the Court split on whether it was appropriate in the circumstances.

In a concurring judgment in *Lac Minerals,* Justice Wilson observed,

> It is my view that, while no ongoing fiduciary relationship arose between the parties by virtue only of their arm's length negotiations towards a mutually beneficial commercial contract for the development of the mine, a fiduciary duty arose in Lac Minerals Ltd. ("Lac") when International Corona Resources Ltd. ("Corona") made available to Lac its confidential information concerning the Williams property, thereby placing itself in a position of vulnerability to Lac's misuse of that information. At that point Lac came under a duty not to use that information for its own exclusive benefit. Lac breached that fiduciary duty by acquiring the Williams property for itself.
>
> It is, in other words, my view of the law that there are certain relationships which are almost per se fiduciary such as trustee and beneficiary, guardian and ward, principal and agent, and that where such relationships subsist they give rise to fiduciary duties. On the other hand, there are relationships which are not in their essence fiduciary, such as the relationship brought into being by the parties in the present case by virtue of their arm's length negotiations towards a joint venture agreement, but this does not preclude a fiduciary duty from arising out of specific conduct engaged in by them or either of them within the confines of the relationship. This, in my view, is what happened here when Corona disclosed to Lac confidential information concerning the Williams property. Lac became at that point subject to a fiduciary duty with respect to that information not to use it for its own use or benefit.[42]

Hence, Justice Wilson again distinguished between relationships that are fiduciary in nature and those that are not in essence fiduciary, such as that brought into being by the parties in their arm's-length negotiations toward a joint venture agreement; but she found that this latter type of relationship did not preclude a fiduciary duty from arising out of specific conduct engaged in within its confines.[43] She held that where this conduct gave rise to alternative causes of action, one at common law and the other at equity, the Court should consider what would provide the more appropriate remedy to the innocent party.[44] Here, she found that both causes of action involved concepts of good conscience and vulnerability.[45] Since the result of Lac Minerals' breach of fiduciary duty was its unjust enrichment through the acquisition of the property at the expense of Corona, she held that Corona would be fully compensated only by the imposition of a constructive trust on Lac Minerals in favour of Corona with respect to the property.[46] She held that the imposition of a constructive trust also ensured that the wrongdoer did not benefit from its wrongdoing, an important consideration in equity that may not be achieved by a damage award.[47] The constructive trust was aimed at correcting the harm that arose from Lac Minerals' course of conduct. It was significant in that Corona had not previously owned the property, and thus constructive trust was used as an equitable tool to place Corona where it would have been but for the breach of fiduciary obligation.

The Supreme Court's recognition that fiduciary obligations could arise in the commercial context and that the Court was not confined solely to certain categories of relationships marked a significant shift in the jurisprudence. It was one of the relatively rare occasions in which the Court signalled that it would interfere in private relationships to ensure equity and to advance a broader public policy of not allowing a wrongdoer to benefit from the inappropriate exercise of power imbalances. The Supreme Court's endorsement of Justice Wilson's analysis of when fiduciary obligations may arise was accompanied by language to the effect that certainty in commercial relations was an important objective. Wilson herself noted in numerous judgments that certainty was an important value in commercial law and important to businesses in the conduct of their economic activities.[48] In this respect, she believed that judges should not lightly import additional responsibilities in the corporate commercial context, although she was not hesitant to do so in the appropriate case.

Fiduciary Obligation Post–*Lac Minerals*

Justice Wilson's *Frame v. Smith* analysis of the circumstances in which a court may recognize fiduciary obligations has been cited in more than four hundred judgments in Canada. More than one hundred of these are in the corporate and commercial context.[49] As she predicted, her approach was not one of opening up a broad category of fiduciary relationships that would create commercial uncertainty. Quite the contrary – an examination of the subsequent case law reveals that the courts adopt the criteria and, in applying it, typically do not find that a fiduciary relationship or obligation has arisen, given the hallmark criteria articulated by Justice Wilson. Hence, fiduciary duty as an equitable remedy remains a sparingly used but powerful one in appropriate circumstances. The availability of the remedy arguably creates incentives for commercial parties, tempering their conduct in the commercial context.

For example, in a recent case alleging damages for breach of contract, breach of fiduciary duty, and breach of confidence, the New Brunswick Court of Appeal used Wilson's reasoning to dismiss a claim of fiduciary relationship between contracting parties.[50] The Court held that the employee or controlling mind of the corporation did not owe a fiduciary obligation to a party with whom the corporation had contracted, even where the employee signed the contract on behalf of the corporation. On the facts, Imperial Oil terminated its sales agency agreement with the respondent H.H.L. Fuels. The agreement was a standard form contract used by Imperial with parties whose services were required to exclusively sell and deliver Imperial products to assigned customers in a defined market area. The agreement was initially for a term of one year, and thereafter the contract automatically renewed for successive periods of one year unless terminated either for cause or on notice.[51] Imperial terminated for cause, specifying in the termination letter that H.H.L. had defaulted in its financial and custodianship responsibilities to Imperial and its promise not to "divulge or communicate to any person, firm or corporation any information which [it] may receive or obtain in respect of Imperial's business or affairs."[52]

The Court of Appeal held that the contract was an arm's-length commercial contract between two corporate entities, each experienced in their sphere of activity of selling and delivering the products defined in the agreement.[53] The Court held that the rupture of the contractual relationship did not itself create a fiduciary duty, applying Justice Wilson's broad principles in *Frame v. Smith* as to when a fiduciary duty may be found.[54] The Court quoted Wilson's analysis of vulnerability as one factor that may give rise to a fiduciary obligation, specifically, that "vulnerability arises from the inability of the beneficiary (despite his or her best efforts) to prevent the injurious exercise of the power or discretion combined with the grave inadequacy or absence of other legal or practical remedies to redress the wrongful exercise of the discretion or power."[55] Here, there were experienced businesspeople of similar bargaining strength, and there were no facts such that a fiduciary relationship should be recognized.[56]

The Supreme Court of Canada further considered fiduciary obligation in *Hodgkinson v. Simms,* holding that where the ingredients giving rise to a fiduciary duty are present, its existence will not be denied simply because of the commercial context.[57] The case involved material non-disclosure in which the appellant allegedly breached his fiduciary duty to the respondent in the performance of a contract for investment advice and other tax-related financial services. Justice La Forest, for the majority, opted for a broad approach to the application of fiduciary concepts in a commercial setting, stating that the existence of a contract in itself does not preclude the existence of fiduciary obligations, and even where a contract does exist, "the facts surrounding the relationship will give rise to a fiduciary inference where the legal incidents surrounding the relationship might not lead to such a conclusion."[58] The majority, however, cautioned that commercial interactions between parties at arm's length normally derive their social utility from the pursuit of self-interest, and the courts are rightly circumspect when asked to enforce a fiduciary duty that vindicates the very antithesis of self-interest.[59] The Court held that, in assessing the existence of fiduciary obligations, it should take a contextual approach.[60] The existence of a contract and its terms were factors to consider in assessing the nature of the relationship between the parties. The majority adopted Wilson's analysis in *Frame v. Smith,* concluding that the desire to protect and reinforce the integrity of enterprises is prevalent throughout fiduciary law, because the law has recognized that not all relationships are characterized by a dynamic of mutual autonomy and that the marketplace cannot always set the rules.[61]

The Court held that fiduciary obligations can exist where, though not innate to a given relationship, they arise as a matter of fact out of the specific circumstances. The question to ask is whether, given all of the surrounding circumstances, one party could reasonably have expected that the other party would act in the former's best interests with respect to the subject matter at issue. The Court held that discretion, influence, vulnerability, and trust are non-exhaustive examples of evidentiary factors to be considered in making this determination. Parties, in all other respects independent, will rarely be justified in surrendering their self-interest so as to invoke the fiduciary principle.[62] The Court held that policy considerations support fiduciary relationships in the case of financial advisors, and by enforcing a duty of honesty and good faith, courts are able to regulate an activity that is of great value to commerce and society generally. Concepts such as trust, independence from outside interests, and disregard for self-interest are all hallmarks of the fiduciary principle.[63]

In *Cadbury Schweppes Inc. v. FBI Foods Ltd.,* the Supreme Court of Canada considered another commercial law case involving a breach of confidence in respect of a manufacturer that used confidential information obtained under a licensing agreement to manufacture a competing product. Justice Binnie, delivering the judgment of the Court, relied on Wilson's reasoning in *Frame v. Smith* to acknowledge that fiduciary duties can arise in a commercial relationship, even though fiduciary relationships do not generally apply to business entities dealing at arm's length.[64] The Court held that equity, as a court of conscience, directs itself to the behaviour of those who come into possession of confidential information and that equity will pursue such information into the hands of third parties who receive it with the knowledge it was communicated in breach of confidence. Under these circumstances, the Court will award a remedy. The Court, on allowing the appeal on the basis of a breach of confidence, cited Wilson's reasoning to find that strong evidence should be required before a breach of confidential information situation is metamorphosed into one of fiduciary relationship.[65] The Court held that the overriding deterrence objective applicable to situations of particular vulnerability to the exercise of a discretionary power did not operate in these circumstances.[66] Although the law will supplement the contractual relationship by importing a duty not to misuse confidential information, the Court held that there was nothing special in this case to elevate the breached duty to one of a fiduciary character.[67]

Although Justice Wilson's indicia of fiduciary obligation have been extensively relied on, the actual imposition of fiduciary obligation in the commercial context continues to be relatively rare. This infrequent recognition of a duty is in keeping with the notion that commercially sophisticated parties should be allowed to conduct their activities and make their bargains in their self-interest, if they comply with all the legal requirements imposed on them through statute and under the common law. What her analysis of fiduciary obligation contributed to the development of corporate and commercial law is that it rendered such relationships subject to examination by the courts on equitable grounds, subjecting private relationships to scrutiny for public policy reasons in appropriate circumstances.

Delineating the Contours of Commercial Law through the Supreme Court's Leave Power

Justice Wilson's contribution to the development of fiduciary obligation in the corporate/commercial context attests to the strength of drawing on broad principles and of translating concepts between differing areas of the law to advance law's evolution. She recognized both the substantive and procedural contours of this project, as illustrated by her analysis of the Supreme Court's role in development of the law through control of its docket. In 1975 the Court introduced the leave to appeal provisions to allow it to manage its caseload.[68] Prior to that time, commercial parties could appeal decisions to the Supreme Court of Canada as of right, provided they had the resources to do so and sought greater clarity or commercial certainty. Amendments to the *Supreme Court Act,* which imposed a leave requirement in civil litigation, meant that the Court was required to develop criteria for granting leave to appeal.[69] This new authority was a subject of great interest to Justice Wilson, who wrote a paper in 1983 on how a mechanism to control the Court caseload had the substantive effect of limiting the types of cases that would be heard based on how the "national importance" test was interpreted.[70]

Wilson appreciated the significance of the change, challenging the legal bar and the judiciary to understand how it had shifted the role of the Court to that of a supervisory tribunal with oversight over the development of the law. The leave power has considerably more substantive significance in its developmental role than would be conveyed by a screening tool or a docket management tool.[71] Wilson observed that, once one goes beyond constitutional and other issues that are by their nature of public importance, the Court required a stronger framework for determining how commercial cases were to be analyzed in terms of public importance.[72]

She noted that the Court tends to open up a principle or its application to further scrutinize it or to provide it with a protective shield, consciously creating a framework for the law. If the guiding principle of granting leave is the importance of a case, she queried how the Court would determine importance in a commercial context, indicating that she recognized the tensions inherent in the Supreme Court's policy role. At the same time, she embraced the notion that this role was to be played in the domain of commercial and other activity as well as in the more immediately apparent public law issues.

In the same article, Justice Wilson also raised the question of the extent to which the Court, in dealing with matters of public importance, became a policy maker in addition to being an adjudicator, by using its findings and *obiter dicta* to identify policy directions in the law, closing off some avenues and opening up others, which she viewed as fundamental.[73] These observations align with her development of fiduciary law and her method of translating concepts and principles across differing areas of the law. Through control of its docket, the Supreme Court signals to potential parties its view of areas of law that require its attention and those that are currently sufficiently developed that predictability in commercial dealings may be more important than revisiting existing principles. In the area of fiduciary obligation, the Court's decision to hear and determine cases such as *Lac Minerals* and *Hodgkinson v. Simms* conveyed its view that further development of the contours of the duty was required in order to advance fairness and predictability.[74]

Conclusion

Justice Wilson left us a number of interpretive challenges to contend with in the future. She outlined a principled approach to fiduciary obligation in the corporate and commercial context, and though more than a hundred judgments have relied on that analysis, they have been slow to further develop the contours of those principles. Second, it is not readily apparent that the legal community has embraced Wilson's call to more fully understand the substantive law and policy powers granted to the Supreme Court of Canada in its leave decision function, particularly in the commercial context, in terms of advancing fiduciary and other aspects of the law. Third, she posited the question, still unanswered, as to whether a gender-specific view of commercial law exists, or whether the current principles serve women equally well once they achieve equality in bargaining power.

Notwithstanding these challenges, the Honourable Bertha Wilson has left us with a strong legacy in the commercial area. The attention she drew to the necessity of a long-term view of the Court's role and its decisions in advancing commercial law is an important *aide memoire* to those of us who seek to analyze the law from a feminist viewpoint. Her contextual and purposive analysis is a helpful reminder that such tools can move the law forward. Her technique of developing broad principles in one context that are naturally applicable to corporate and commercial contexts offers insight for feminist adjudicators working in these areas of the law. In this respect, her dissents frequently set the stage for majority judgments in subsequent cases. Legal scholars and practitioners can draw a helpful lesson in this respect regarding the power and potential of translating concepts between areas of the law and the importance of thinking creatively and holistically about the law when confronted with a novel challenge and the need for equity's assistance. Finally, the depth of Justice Wilson's understanding of the normative role of the courts, and the particular challenges for that role, serves to inspire us to think more deeply about the nature of judicial decision making and its function in society, in all its facets, including the corporate and commercial spheres.

Acknowledgment
My thanks to Tara Kyluik, UBC Law II, for her research assistance.

Notes

1 Bertha Wilson, "Will Women Judges Really Make a Difference?" (1990) 28 Osgoode Hall L.J. 507 at 515.
2 *Girardet v. Crease & Co.* (1987), 11 B.C.L.R. (2d) 361 at 362 (Southin J.).
3 *Black's Law Dictionary,* 8th ed., *s.v. "fiducia"* and "fiduciary."
4 A rich literature exists on fiduciary obligation generally, which I do not address in this brief essay. For reference see Peter Birks, *An Introduction to the Law of Restitution* (Oxford: Clarendon Press, 1985); P.D. Finn, *Fiduciary Obligations* (Sydney: Law Book Company, 1977); John McCamus, "The Role of Proprietary Relief in the Modern Law of Restitution" in Frank E. McArdle, ed., *The Cambridge Lectures 1987* (Montreal: Les Éditions Yvon Blais, 1989) at 124; D.W.M. Waters, *Law of Trusts in Canada* (Toronto: Carswell, 1984).
5 Wilson first undertook this analysis in a family law case, in a dissenting judgment in *Frame v. Smith,* [1987] 2 S.C.R. 99 at para. 60 [*Frame*].
6 *Ibid.* at para. 77.

7 *Ibid.* Interestingly, breach of fiduciary duty was not originally advanced by counsel, but since the issue before the Court was whether the statement of claim should be struck out as disclosing no reasonable cause of action, the Court was of the view that it should be addressed. Thus, counsel were invited to file written submissions, which the Court then considered. *Ibid.* at para. 56.

8 *Ibid.* at para. 57.

9 *Ibid.* at para. 58.

10 *Ibid.*

11 *Ibid.* at paras. 60-63.

12 Wilson held, "Accordingly, it would be my view that the cause of action for breach of fiduciary duty should be extended to this narrow but extremely important area of family law where the non-custodial parent is completely at the mercy of the custodial parent by virtue of that parent's position of power and authority over the children. If this is a situation which for very good reason the common law is ill-equipped to handle, resort to equity is entirely appropriate so that no just cause shall go without a remedy." *Ibid.* at para. 77.

13 *Ibid.* at para. 68.

14 Bertha Wilson, "Leave to Appeal to the Supreme Court of Canada" (1983) 4 Advocates' Q. 1 at 5.

15 Although it is beyond the scope of this discussion, her position recognizing the potential cause of action of a non-custodial father arguably might have generated considerable concern from the feminist community in respect of how this recognition further exacerbated the imbalance in power relationships between men and women, although her judgment did attempt to draw attention to the risks inherent in the recognition of such obligations. *Frame, supra* note 5 at paras. 65-68.

16 *Ibid.* at para. 75.

17 *Ibid.*

18 Georgina Jackson and Janis Sarra, "Selecting the Judicial Tool to Get the Job Done: An Examination of Statutory Interpretation, Discretionary Power and Inherent Jurisdiction in Insolvency Matters" in Janis P. Sarra, ed., *Annual Review of Insolvency Law, 2007* (Toronto: Carswell, 2008) at 41-96. We suggest that it is important that courts first interpret the statute before them and exercise their authority pursuant to the statute, before reaching for other tools in the judicial toolbox, including the exercise of equitable jurisdiction.

19 *Ibid.* The common law may permit the gap to be filled. If it does, the judge still has discretion as to whether he or she invokes the authority revealed by the discovery of jurisdiction.

20 See *e.g. Cadbury Schweppes Inc. v. FBI Foods Ltd.*, [1999] 1 S.C.R. 142 [*Cadbury Schweppes*]; *Lac Minerals Ltd. v. International Corona Resources Ltd.*, [1989] 2 S.C.R. 574 [*Lac Minerals* (SCC)].

21 *Lac Minerals* (SCC), *supra* note 20.

22 Lac Minerals advised Corona to pursue the property aggressively. Negotiations between Lac Minerals and Corona failed.

23 *International Corona Resources Ltd. v. Lac Minerals Ltd.* (1986), 53 O.R. (2d) 737 at paras. 186, 199-200 (H.C.J.). The trial judge relied on the category of partnership and fiduciary obligation, finding that, though the joint venture had not been concluded, it was being negotiated, the judgment predating the Supreme Court judgment in *Frame v. Smith*. Holland J. held, "I conclude that in these circumstances Lac and Corona owed fiduciary duties each to the other to act fairly and not to act to the detriment of the other and that Lac was in breach of that duty by acquiring the Williams property." *Ibid.* at paras. 183, 185.

24 *International Corona Resources Ltd. v. Lac Minerals Ltd.* (1987), 62 O.R. (2d) 1 (C.A.). The Court of Appeal held that the trial judge correctly concluded that the law of fiduciary relationships can apply to parties involved in arm's length negotiation of a joint venture or partnership. *Ibid.* at 9-10.

25 *Lac Minerals* (SCC), *supra* note 20 at para. 130 (finding three elements of the test had been established: the information conveyed was confidential; it was communicated in confidence; and it was misused by the party to whom it was communicated).

26 *Ibid.* at para. 135. La Forest held that, although confidentiality had not been raised, a mutual understanding existed that valuable private information was communicated by Corona to

Lac Minerals under circumstances giving rise to an obligation of confidence. *Ibid.* at para. 130.

27 *Ibid.* at para. 160.

28 *Ibid.* at para. 169. Quoting Justice Wilson, he held that vulnerability is not a necessary ingredient in every fiduciary relationship, agreeing with her proposition that, if new classes of relationship are recognized as giving rise to fiduciary obligations, the vulnerability of the class of beneficiaries of the obligation is a relevant consideration.

29 *Ibid.*

30 *Ibid.*

31 *Ibid.* at para. 171.

32 *Ibid.* at para. 174. He observed that Lac Minerals knew the information to be confidential, that it was being received in circumstances of confidence, and that a claim for breach of confidence would clearly be available were the information misused; thus, neither party would enter into a confidentiality agreement simply to confirm what both parties knew.

33 *Ibid.*

34 *Ibid.* at paras. 117-78.

35 *Hunter Engineering Co. v. Syncrude Canada Ltd.*, [1989] 1 S.C.R. 426 at 519.

36 *Lac Minerals* (SCC), *supra* note 20 at para. 193.

37 *Ibid.* at paras. 193-94.

38 *Ibid.* at para. 198.

39 *Ibid.* at paras. 32-33. McIntyre J. and Lamer J. agreed with Sopinka J. in respect of not finding a fiduciary obligation, using Wilson J.'s reasoning on the tests, but Lamer J. agreed with the majority on the appropriate remedy in the circumstances. *Ibid.* at paras. 111-14.

40 *Ibid.* at paras. 38, 45.

41 *Ibid.* at paras. 50, 51.

42 *Ibid.* at paras. 116-17.

43 *Ibid.* at para. 117.

44 *Ibid.* at para. 119.

45 *Ibid.* at para. 120.

46 *Ibid.* at para. 119.

47 *Ibid.*

48 See *e.g. Dominion Chain Co. Ltd. v. Eastern Construction Co. Ltd.* (1976), 12 O.R. (2d) 201.

49 See *e.g. 155569 Canada Limited v. 248524 Alberta Ltd.*, 2000 ABCA 41, 255 A.R. 1, which held at para. 90, "Factors indicative of fiduciary obligations include: exercise of some discretion or power by the fiduciary; unilateral exercise of power to affect the beneficiary's legal or practical interest; and vulnerability of the beneficiary to the fiduciary holding the discretion or power: Wilson J. (in dissent) in *Frame v. Smith* (1987), 42 D.L.R. (4th) 81 at 98-99, adopted by Sopinka J. (for the majority) in *Lac Minerals, supra* at 62-63."

50 *Imperial Oil v. H.H.L. Fuels Ltd.*, 2006 NBCA 1, 294 N.B.R. (2d) 371.

51 *Ibid.* at para. 1. Notice was prior to an anniversary date.

52 *Ibid.* at paras. 2, 17.

53 *Ibid.* at paras. 45, 46.

54 *Ibid.* at paras. 46, 47.

55 *Ibid.* at para. 48, quoting *Frame, supra* note 5 at para. 63.

56 *Ibid.* at para. 8.

57 *Hodgkinson v. Simms*, [1994] 3 S.C.R. 377.

58 *Ibid.* at para. 28.

59 *Ibid.* at para. 38.

60 *Ibid.* at para. 32.

61 *Ibid.* at para. 48.

62 *Ibid.* The law does not object to one party taking advantage of another *per se*, so long as the particular form of advantage is not otherwise objectionable.

63 *Ibid.* at para. 58.

64 *Cadbury Schweppes, supra* note 20.

65 *Ibid.* at para. 30.

66 *Ibid.* at para. 32.

67 *Ibid.* at para. 32.
68 *An Act to Amend the Supreme Court Act and to Make Related Amendments to the Federal Court Act,* S.C. 1974-75-76, c. 18, s. 5.
69 *Supreme Court Act,* R.S. 1985, c. S-26.
70 Wilson, *supra* note 14 at 1.
71 *Ibid.* at 2-4.
72 *Ibid.* at 4.
73 *Ibid.* at 7.
74 In her biography of Bertha Wilson, Ellen Anderson described Wilson's views in respect of granting leave in private law disputes as the Court's indication that it was prepared to implement change where necessary. She also suggested that Wilson understood that people tend to pattern their business transactions in reliance on the predictability of the law, which can be more pertinent than a perception of whether the law is just. Ellen Anderson, *Judging Bertha Wilson: Law as Large as Life* (Toronto: University of Toronto Press for the Osgoode Society for Canadian Legal History, 2001) at 241.

4

A Few More Spokes to the Wheel: Reasonableness, Fairness, and Justice in Justice Bertha Wilson's Approach to Contract Law

Moira L. McConnell

Entering the Skin

In her now (in)famous speech about the potential impact of female judges on the development of Canadian law, Justice Wilson observed that, in some areas of law, including contracts, "the principles and the underlying premises are so firmly entrenched and so fundamentally sound that no good would be achieved by attempting to re-invent the wheel, even if the revised version did have a few more spokes in it."[1] Justice Wilson's observation, informed by fourteen years' experience on the bench and many years of practice in commercial and corporate law, suggests, despite her numerous and often solitary dissents from her male colleagues in contracts cases, that she believed she was simply applying well-established rules rather than developing new approaches.[2]

Yet, in that same speech, she also commented that there was "merit" in Carol Gilligan's research on the differences between women's and men's approaches to moral problems and on the development of women's particular ethical sense.[3] Quoting favourably from an article[4] on feminist theory and judging that argued for the need to first "connect" with litigants' stories before the separation that necessarily characterizes judging, she described the visceral nature of this experience: "Obviously, this is not an easy role for the judge – *to enter into the skin of the litigant and make his or her experience part of your experience* and only when you have done that, to judge. But we have to do it; or at least make an earnest attempt to do it."[5] Not surprisingly, the few academic comments that exist on Wilson's contract and commercial law decisions have largely responded to, and countered, her rejection of a female view on economic actors and on these specific areas of the law.[6]

This chapter aspires to add a few more "spokes" to the debate about Justice Wilson's contributions to contract law: Was she, as she seems to suggest, a skilled and careful technician, gradually developing but not altering the principles found in the common law of contracts? Or was she an innovator who brought a unique perspective to the application of these principles? Through a careful review of her judgments, this chapter ultimately finds that she was, perhaps, both. Indeed, any attempt to classify Wilson's contributions as fitting within one camp invariably obfuscates the underlying themes of her judicial contribution. For example, her contract decisions reveal, *inter alia,* a respect for the primacy of private ordering and autonomy, combined with a marked reluctance to enter the quagmire of assessing power discrepancies in negotiations between parties.[7] Although not "results driven," they reflect a deep concern for the consequences of her determinations and a preference for what she often described as the "virtue" of certainty and predictability: intervention by the courts is reserved for contexts wherein the enforcement of a contractual arrangement would be unreasonable[8] or unfair, or where an injustice would *result from the court's action* in condoning the situation. In Justice Wilson's decisions, the court becomes an actor in the legal drama, and each judge is held morally responsible for the decision and its outcomes. Notions of what is fair often seem to be visceral, reflecting a communal or common sense experience of right and wrong and a just outcome rather than a more abstract philosophical exposition.

In short, Justice Wilson's approach to contract law was guided by concerns about reasonableness, fairness, and justice between the parties concerned. This chapter argues that her determinations of what these concerns would actually entail in each case are explained, at least in part, by her willingness to "enter into the skin" of the parties and engage directly with their stories.[9] To some extent, this approach is captured by Ellen Anderson's statement in her biography of Bertha Wilson that "[c]ontingency and contextuality run as deep principle in Wilson."[10] This chapter suggests that Wilson's determinations were also guided by her values, ideas, and internalized rules of what constitutes "good" or appropriate conduct between parties.

As a preliminary matter, it might be noted that defining what constitutes a contract case is more difficult than would first appear. On a narrow classification, Justice Wilson authored contract law decisions in more than twenty cases. However, if a broader view is taken, contract law analysis underpins many of her decisions in the areas of employment, labour, insurance, corporate, and family law, and even in some criminal law cases. This discussion focuses on a broad spectrum of judgments that rely on contract principles and seeks to delineate the underlying themes and values that these judgments reflect.

The judgments are explored under the rubric of three adages: "chickens come home to roost";[11] "having their cake and eating it too";[12] and "the proof of the pudding is in the eating."[13] These common sense or folk wisdom axioms are used because, either explicitly or implicitly, they capture the experiential aesthetic and approach that informed Justice Wilson's determination of what is reasonable, fair, or just in each particular case.[14]

Chickens Come Home to Roost

This adage captures the idea that a person's misbehaviour will ultimately come back to haunt him or her. Justice Wilson's decisions on the issue of misrepresentation inducing a contract, and on the availability of punitive damages in contractual situations, suggest that she was unwilling to ignore "misbehaviour": rather, she felt that it should be exposed and sanctioned. This section considers several decisions in connection with issues such as misrepresentation and other behaviours in a contractual setting. In each decision, Wilson held the misbehaving party to the consequences of its wrongful behaviour. These decisions also illustrate how her notion of what constitutes misbehaviour, though nuanced and context sensitive, also reflects a particular, almost retributive, sense of what is a "just" outcome; where such misbehaviour occurs, chickens do, indeed, come home to roost.

Two years after her appointment to the Ontario Court of Appeal, Justice Wilson wrote the majority decision in *Fine's Flowers Ltd. et al. v. General Accident Assurance Co. of Canada*.[15] She tells us that the plaintiff, Mr. Fine, "believed in insurance"[16] and had always insured his business with the defendant company (and its predecessors). At issue was the liability of the defendant company for a loss that was not covered under the plaintiff's policy. The plaintiff sued the insurance agent in contract (for breach of contract to obtain the appropriate coverage) and in tort (for negligence in obtaining the coverage). The trial judge found for the plaintiff in both contract and tort.[17]

Justice Wilson's majority decision says remarkably little about theory or case law. She was prepared to agree with the trial judge, without comment, that a contract existed between the plaintiff and the defendant whereby the latter undertook to obtain "full coverage" for the plaintiff's business. Her decision did not address the question of why she concluded that a contract existed; nor did she rely on case law to reach her conclusion that a contractual liability existed.[18] Rather, she seems to have simply accepted the trial judge's conclusion that the relationship was contractual.

With respect to the question of whether a breach had occurred, Justice Wilson appeared less comfortable, as the defendant led evidence to suggest that the kind of coverage the plaintiff wanted was not actually available. However, she concluded that this evidence "[fell] far short of establishing that coverage for the loss in question could not be obtained."[19] Of particular interest is her presentation of the dilemma as a script or conversation with the reader in which the ethical problems and the defendant's story were weighed: "Is it open to an agent to say: 'I do not think I should be held liable for doing nothing because even if I had done what I should have done on one possible interpretation of my instructions my principal would still not have been covered for the loss he suffered'?"[20] Justice Wilson concluded that this response was not open to the defendant, who did not claim to have misconstrued the instructions; rather, he argued that he was not required to insure the particular equipment at all. In Justice Wilson's view, the defendant did not comply with the instructions of his principal.

It is clear that Justice Wilson struggled with reaching a fair result between the two parties. She was influenced by the trial judge's preference for Mr. Fine's evidence over that of the defendant and by his finding that "Mr. Fine [was] an honest and credible witness."[21] She noted that the findings of fact and credibility were crucial to the outcome of the appeal, as was the trial judge's finding of a close and continuing relationship between the two parties and of the plaintiff's reliance on the defendant. It is evident that her determination of the fair result stemmed, ultimately, from her view that the defendant was bound by the terms of the contract (or the representation), or, as she came to describe it in subsequent cases, by the relationship of reliance that the defendant had put in place.

In 1981, in *Carman Construction Ltd. v. Canadian Pacific Railway Co.*, Justice Wilson rendered the brief decision at the Ontario Court of Appeal.[22] The case involved a tendering situation, an exemption clause, and a negligent misrepresentation by an employee of the defendant. Justice Wilson upheld the exemption clause and the trial judge's "reluctant" dismissal of the plaintiff's claim.[23] She did not found her judgment on the negligent misrepresentation case law, but rather on a view of what would have been unfair or "wrongful" behaviour toward the defendant.[24] The judgment serves to emphasize her fact-based storytelling approach – a kind of internal script about what seemed to be fair and unfair behaviour. Justice Wilson's decision presents a situation in which it is perhaps the plaintiff who is being unfair in seeking damages, since the plaintiff knowingly took a risk in seeking information from the defendant's employee:

> The plaintiff was aware of these provisions [in the contract] before it approached the defendant's employees seeking information as to the quantity of rock to be removed. *It knew that this precise matter was dealt with in clear and unambiguous terms in the contract on which it was tendering.* Indeed, the provisions were clearly meant for the sole purpose of ensuring that, if prospective bidders got any information on this subject from the defendant's employees, they would be relying on it at their own risk. Likewise, the defendant knew that if its employees gave out any information or made an estimate in response to requests from prospective bidders, the risk of the information's being wrong was not on it but on the bidders who used it. This was the context in which they conducted their business.[25]

In Justice Wilson's view, having taken the risk, the plaintiff must live with the consequences.

Although it seems a stretch to conclude that either of these early decisions served to clarify or even address the law on misrepresentation in Canada, Justice Wilson did deal with this issue in delivering the Supreme Court of Canada's decision in *V.K. Mason Construction v. Bank of Nova Scotia*.[26] Her judgment shows a marked departure from her readiness to accept the existence of a contract in *Fine's Flowers*. In *V.K. Mason,* the defendant (the Bank of Nova Scotia) made a representation to the plaintiff in relation to the financial situation of one of its clients. The trial judge found in favour of the plaintiff on the basis of contract and, alternatively, negligent misrepresentation. Justice Wilson agreed with the trial judge's findings of fact, but her views on the contractual aspect of the case differed. By way of "put[ting] the case in perspective," she wrote,

> This is not a simple situation in which a bank makes a representation about the creditworthiness of one of its clients to a third party. This is a case in which the Bank made a representation to a third party for the specific purpose of inducing the third party to enter into a contract with one of the Bank's own clients, thereby enabling that client to enter into a substantial loan transaction with the Bank ... It is quite clear that [the Bank's manager] wished to check the letter with the Bank's solicitor precisely because he realized that the Bank was inducing [the plaintiff] to enter into a contract and he wanted to avoid the prospect of the Bank's incurring a liability.[27]

Although she considered the possibility that this situation could be characterized as a unilateral contract, Justice Wilson concluded that it lacked sufficient certainty to give rise to a contract.[28] Here, unlike her decision in *Fine's Flowers,* she preferred an approach based on tort law. Concluding that no contractual relationship existed between the parties, she wrote,

> Negligent misrepresentation is, in my view, the appropriate basis of liability in this case. The disadvantage in implying a contract in a commercial context like this is that much of the value of commercial contracts lies in their ability to produce certainty. Parties are enabled to regulate their relationship by means of words rather than by means of their understanding of what each other's actions are intended to imply. I think this is one reason why the common law imposes an objective rather than a subjective test for the creation of an agreement. The objective test is important because it prevents parties from avoiding obligations which a reasonable person would assume they had undertaken, simply on the ground that there is no document embodying the precise nature of the obligation. On the other hand, *if too*

broad a view is taken of what a reasonable person assumes will give rise to an agreement or obligation, the certainty which is one of the principal virtues of contract may be undermined.[29]

On Justice Wilson's analysis, a key value of contracts is that they promote the "virtue" of certainty by enabling parties to regulate their relationships, subject to a "reasonable person" test. Of course, to then impose a special relationship entailing tort liability instead of a contract could be seen as creating even greater uncertainty. In the end, however, Justice Wilson's principal concern in the case was addressing what seems to have been unethical business behaviour on the part of the bank manager.[30]

Justice Wilson's interest in establishing consequences for unethical or unfair behaviour came to the fore at the Supreme Court of Canada in *Vorvis v. Insurance Corp. of British Columbia.*[31] This employment contract case considered the nature of damages available for a wrongful dismissal. Along with the cases that followed it, *Vorvis* has been the subject of extensive academic commentary about the majority's approach to awarding aggravated and punitive damages for breach of the contract and with respect to the utility of imposing a duty of good faith in contracts.[32] However, my interest lies with Justice Wilson's decision, a partial dissent supported by Justice L'Heureux-Dubé. Unlike the majority, Justice Wilson saw no difficulty, in principle, with using ordinary concepts of forseeability to award damages for mental distress in breach of contract cases. However, she would not have awarded these damages in this case. She would award punitive damages where the conduct was, in her view, "deserving of punishment."[33]

Despite the fact that, in other cases, Justice Wilson displayed a discomfort with assessing power disparities in negotiations,[34] her decision in *Vorvis* strongly supported this approach. She recognized and condemned bullying behaviour in the context of what she characterized as an "unjust dismissal." Indeed, she felt strongly that harsh or vindictive conduct should be punished, a view she reiterated several times in the judgment. For example, she remarked that "punitive damages should be available in order to deter the strong from deliberately and callously disregarding the legal rights of the weak whenever it is in their economic interests to do so,"[35] adding that "the correct approach is to assess the conduct in the context of all the circumstances and determine whether it is *deserving of punishment because of its shockingly harsh, vindictive, reprehensible or malicious nature.*"[36] She also referred to "the duty of civilized behaviour"[37] and to "the court's awareness and condemnation of flagrant wrongdoing."[38] Clearly, despite her earlier reluctance to ground decisions on an imbalance of power in relationships, Justice Wilson was willing to identify unethical behaviour and to make the condemnation of that behaviour a focus of her decision.

The three decisions examined in this section reveal Justice Wilson's consistent interest in the facts of the case and in the ethical decisions and behaviours of the individuals involved. Despite a recitation of the reasonable person test, her judgments suggest a marked interest in the story of the parties' subjective motives and of what each party must have known or thought. As Alan Watson notes in his examination of one of Justice Wilson's cases, what emerges is, *inter alia,* "an empathy with humans involved in the case. She has a strong understanding of the human condition."[39] This understanding is characterized by her appreciating (and judging) of a full range of behaviours and motivations, both good and bad. Justice Wilson's application of this understanding is characterized, in part, by her sense that parties should be forced to accept the consequences of their misbehaviours. In this sense, all of the cases considered under the adage that chickens come home to roost reflect this particular interest in ensuring that misbehaving parties are forced to confront their past behaviour and live with the consequences.

Having Their Cake and Eating It Too

This adage encapsulates the theme of greed: in particular, the idea that there is something inherently immoral about wanting to have the benefits of, for example, a contract or promise – and not its attendant burdens. This moral tenet is explicit in a number of Justice Wilson's decisions, including, most significantly, that in *Hunter Engineering Co. v. Syncrude Canada Ltd.*[40]

Before *Hunter v. Syncrude* is examined, three of her earlier decisions are reviewed since they set the stage for this focal decision. In *Hamelin v. Hore,* a 1976 case decided by the Ontario Court of Appeal, Justice Wilson referred to the idea of "unfairness" in relation to a party seeking to take the benefits of a contract without the burdens.[41] *Hamelin* involved a narrow issue: namely, whether or not a condition relating to a severance in an agreement for purchase and sale had been complied with. If it had been, a contract had come into existence; if it had not, the transaction had ended. In her view (supported by Justice Brooke's, concurring, with Justice McKinnon dissenting), the severance did not occur, and the contract did not come into existence. Wilson characterized the required event as a true condition precedent and held that it had not been satisfied. Of interest to the present analysis is her comment concerning "unfairness" on the part of the vendor. As she stated, "This [was] not a case of a contracting party trying to take advantage of his own delinquency."[42]

A similar approach is reflected in her 1979 Ontario Court of Appeal judgment in *Chomedy Aluminum Co. v. Belcourt Construction (Ottawa).*[43] *Chomedy* involved the difficult issue of the effect of a fundamental breach on the plaintiff's waiver of its lien rights. Justice Wilson cast the issue in terms of fairness and reasonableness:

> Many exclusionary clauses ... which in isolation seem unfair and unreasonable are not so when viewed in their contractual setting and may, indeed, constitute part of the quid pro quo for benefits received through hard negotiation. It seems to me, therefore, that what we are to ask ourselves is not whether the exclusionary clause is fair and reasonable in its contractual setting (this is, indeed, to be assumed in a contract between sophisticated parties) but *whether it is fair and reasonable that it survive the disintegration of its contractual setting.* If it is, then presumably that is what the parties must be taken to have intended. But if it is not, then such an intention is not [to] be attributed to the parties.[44]

She faced a dilemma: should she allow one party to breach the contract but at the same time to benefit from the Court's enforcement of a clause that operated in its favour? She resolved the dilemma (which she had constructed) by concluding, in essence, that it would not be fair or reasonable for the Court to enforce the clause.[45]

In 1987, writing for the majority of the Supreme Court on a different area of law, Justice Wilson revisited her concerns about the ability of individuals to benefit from their bad conduct. *Kosmopoulos v. Constitution Insurance Co.*[46] considered the identity between a sole proprietor and a corporation established to carry out his business within the context of insurable interests.[47] She found in the plaintiff's favour and refused to lift the corporate veil, thereby overruling prior case law relating to insurable interests. Her reasons reflected her concern with the defendant's desire to have the benefit of the law without accepting the burden, or, as she put it, "to 'blow hot and cold' at the same time":[48]

> There is a persuasive argument that "those who have chosen the benefits of incorporation must bear the corresponding burdens, so that if the veil is to be lifted at all that should only be done in the interests of third parties who would otherwise suffer as a result of that choice" ... Mr. Kosmopoulos was advised by a competent solicitor to incorporate his business in order to protect his personal assets ... Having chosen to receive the benefits of incorporation, he should not be allowed to escape its burdens.[49]

This insistence that a party should not have its cake and eat it too permeates Justice Wilson's decision in *Hunter v. Syncrude*,[50] a case that remains the subject of a significant amount of academic commentary on the Supreme Court's approach to fundamental breach.[51] At issue in *Hunter* was the effect of one party's behaviour, which allegedly amounted to a fundamental breach, on limited liability clauses. The facts of the case are complicated. Indeed, many authors appear to disagree about the case's outcome on the question of fundamental breach. In his recent review of the case, Richard Devlin points out that the Supreme Court's decision is generally understood to be an even split between the approach put forward by Chief Justice Dickson and an alternative approach suggested by Justice Wilson.[52]

In her decision, Justice Wilson considered the ambiguities in the law of fundamental breach and considered several possible approaches to the issue. Under one approach, the concept of fundamental breach was discarded and exclusion or limitation of liability clauses were given their true construction, regardless of the *nature* of the breach. Another approach imported a "reasonableness" requirement into the analysis, which allowed a court to refuse to enforce a clause where that enforcement would create unfairness or unreasonableness. Justice Wilson also considered, and discarded, the approach proposed by Chief Justice Dickson, whereby the doctrine of fundamental breach was replaced by a concern for unconscionability, including inequality of bargaining power.[53] In her view, this third approach would involve assessing the fairness and reasonableness *per se* of the provision (at the time it was negotiated), and courts are not well placed to *post facto* assess the bargain between the parties as understood at the time the contract was negotiated.[54] As she put it, "A contractual provision [*i.e.,* an exclusion clause] that seems unfair to a third party may have been the product of hard bargaining between the parties and, in my view, deserves to be enforced by the courts in accordance with its terms. It is, however, in my view an entirely different matter for the courts to determine after a particular breach has occurred whether an exclusion clause should be enforced or not."[55] Having rejected these alternatives, Justice Wilson focused on the choice that a court would have to make to arrive at a fair and reasonable result: "[S]hould a party be able to commit a fundamental breach secure in the knowledge that no liability can attend it? Or should there be room for the courts to say: *this party is now trying to have his cake and eat it too. He is seeking to escape almost entirely the burdens of the transaction but enlist the support of the courts to enforce its benefits.*"[56] This theme – trying to have one's cake and eat it too – is the nub of the ethical problem that Wilson sought to resolve. She was prepared to tackle the issue of whether the behaviour in question offended some common sense of fair play, thereby upsetting the bargain struck in the agreement. She commented on her understanding of the role of the courts in this context. In her opinion, the essential question for the court was as follows: "[I]n the circumstances that have happened should the court lend its aid to A to hold B to this clause?"[57] Interestingly, although Justice Wilson was attentive to the nature and extent of the breach as a contextual factor in the Court's assessment of what was fair and reasonable, she was principally concerned with the conduct of the parties. She also provided some guidance regarding what, in her view, would be unfair or unreasonable:

> Turning to the case at bar, it seems to me that, even if the breach of contract was a fundamental one, there would be nothing unfair or unreasonable (and even less so unconscionable, if this is a stricter test) in giving effect to the exclusion clause. The contract was made between two companies in the commercial market place who are of roughly equal bargaining power. Both are familiar and experienced with this type of contract ... There is no evidence to suggest that Allis-Chalmers who seeks to rely on the exclusion clause was guilty of any sharp or unfair dealing ... *This is not a case in which the vendor or supplier was seeking to repudiate almost entirely the burdens of the transaction and invoking the assistance of the courts to enforce its benefits.* There is no abuse of freedom of contract here.[58]

Thus, she focused on the behaviour of the parties; and in assessing that behaviour, she considered a host of factors, including the question of whether a party sought to have it both ways. Her comments reveal that the ethical status of the conduct of the party seeking the court's assistance (was the plaintiff guilty of sharp or unfair dealing, or was it seeking to escape the burdens and take the benefits?) was an aspect of what, in her reasoning, constituted "appropriate circumstances."

One factor that does *not* feature prominently in Justice Wilson's analysis of what constitutes appropriate circumstances is the balance of power. Indeed, it seems that the main difference between her judgment and that of Chief Justice Dickson is her reluctance to analyze power *per se*. Outside of the most obvious consumer situations, how is one to assess inequalities of bargaining power? Justice Wilson's discomfort with making assumptions about power imbalances[59] may well stem from her concerns about *whose* idea of power is involved: a concern that she explored in other contracts decisions, as discussed in the next section. In Justice Wilson's view, the issue seemed to be less about the court's role in righting discrepancies of power and more about its disapprobation of unethical or unfair behaviour.

The cases discussed in connection with the adage "having one's cake and eating it too" demonstrate that, in assessing what counts as unethical or unfair behaviour, Justice Wilson was concerned with the court's role in delineating "tolerable conduct."[60] In her view, seeking to have it both ways was intolerable.

The Proof of a Pudding Is in the Eating

This chapter has already alluded to Bertha Wilson's concern for outcomes and to her discomfort with entering the messy arena of power analysis. The decisions considered so far also reveal her belief in individual autonomy, freedom of contract, and the "virtue of certainty," restrained, in some circumstances, by the intervention of the court. This section more directly considers Justice Wilson's interrelated concerns about power, certainty, and her outcome-orientation approach. It does so by examining her reasoning in three cases under the rubric "the proof of the pudding is in the eating." This proverb refers to evidence that reveals the true value of something and is often used to convey the idea that the end result is what matters.

Pelech v. Pelech[61] has been given a thorough analysis from a gender perspective.[62] *Pelech* involved the issues of gender and inequality in connection with the enforcement of separation agreements. According to Justice Wilson, who wrote the majority decision, the issues facing the Supreme Court related to the judicial supervision of separation agreements and to whether a court should refuse to enforce such agreements, thereby intervening in the bargains freely struck by the parties on the advice of counsel, where those agreements were seen to reflect inequities.[63]

In *Pelech,* Justice Wilson presented the issue in a manner that is structurally similar to her approach in the fundamental breach cases. She identified two main alternative approaches in the existing cases. These were roughly cast as freedom of contract and individual responsibility versus a more "paternalistic" approach that would "minimize the importance of freedom of contract and impose on the parties a judicial standard of reasonableness notwithstanding their agreement to the contrary."[64] In searching for a middle ground between these two approaches, Justice Wilson reviewed the benefits and disadvantages of each:

> The need to compensate for systemic gender-based inequality ... forms a counterpoint to the need for finality ... The Alberta Court of Appeal in *Jull* describes the tension in terms of the competing values of fairness and freedom ...
>
> I believe that [a] case by case approach and the continuing surveillance by the courts over the consensual arrangements of former spouses ... will ultimately reinforce the very bias [that those who advocate this approach seek] to counteract. In addition, I believe that every encouragement should be given to ex-spouses to settle their financial affairs in a final way so that they can put their mistakes behind them and get on with their lives ...
>
> I do, however, agree with ... [the] emphasis on the importance of finality in the financial affairs of former spouses and that considerable deference should be paid to the right and the responsibility of individuals to make their own decisions.
>
> It seems to me that where the parties have negotiated their own agreement, freely and on the advice of independent legal counsel, as to how their financial affairs should be settled on the breakdown of their marriage, and the agreement is not unconscionable in the substantive law sense, it should be respected. People should be encouraged to take responsibility for their

own lives and their own decisions. This should be the overriding policy consideration.[65]

Ultimately, she endorsed a compromise between the various considerations and focused on the existence of a causal link between the needs of the claiming party and the circumstances of the marriage: "[W]here an applicant seeking maintenance or an increase in the existing level of maintenance establishes that he or she has suffered a radical change in circumstances flowing from an economic pattern of dependency engendered by the marriage, the court may exercise its relieving power. Otherwise, the obligation to support the former spouse should be, as in the case of any other citizen, the communal responsibility of the state."[66]

Once again, Justice Wilson was essentially concerned with the parties' conduct. As in *Hunter v. Syncrude,* she demonstrated her preference for enforcing parties' arrangements, as well as her inclination to avoid considering the relative power between the parties. Also, much as in *Hunter,* Justice Wilson expressed the view that courts should intervene where there seemed to be some element of unfairness, subsequent to the making of the agreement, that was causally linked to a benefit conferred on one of the parties. On this approach, the Court did not focus on assessing whether the formation of the initial agreement was fair, but rather on the later situation in relation to that agreement. Her judgment in *Pelech* also illustrated her concern about a "longer-term" outcome of her decision. She was concerned about the potential that a power analysis would ultimately result in negative consequences for women by re-creating and entrenching the very bias it sought to address.

As mentioned earlier, and as reflected in *Pelech,* a recurrent theme in Justice Wilson's decisions is her conviction that one objective of judicial decision making within contract law is certainty and consistency, which enable people to plan their affairs. The 1987 case *Keneric Tractor Sales v. Langille* provides another illustration of this preoccupation.[67] *Keneric* dealt with a technical question regarding the appropriate method of calculating damages in connection with leases of chattels. Justice Wilson wrote the majority decision for the Supreme Court, which reflected her interest in consistency. For example, she wrote that *"if the law in this area is to be coherent and principled it would make good sense* to abolish artificial legal distinctions between leases of land and leases of chattels. However, *the pursuit of consistency* today mandates a different result in this case."[68]

Justice Wilson's view that one of the functions of the courts is to provide consistency and, where necessary, to squarely face up to changing the rules, has also been pointed out by Ellen Anderson in her biography of Bertha Wilson: "[It was not] so much Wilson's multiplicity of perspectives but her longer perspective which could give rise to conflicts with colleagues ... If something appeared unfair, unjust or outmoded and needed change she tended to look beyond the limitations of the particular situation ... [W]hat appeared to be a conflict between idealistic and pragmatic vanished when viewed from her longer term perspective."[69] This concern was clearly illustrated in *Keneric*. It is also a focus in Justice Wilson's judgment in *Reference re ss. 193 and 195.1(1)(c) of the Criminal Code*.[70] This was not a contract law case. It rather considered the constitutionality of changes proposed to the *Criminal Code* that would prohibit communication for the purposes of prostitution and the keeping of a bawdy house. The majority decision, delivered by Chief Justice Dickson, found that, although the provisions infringed on rights under the *Canadian Charter of Rights and Freedoms*, they were a reasonable limit under s. 1. Justice Wilson's dissenting judgment, supported by Justice L'Heureux-Dubé, took the view that the provisions violated *Charter* rights and were not saved under s. 1. The gender split represented by the Court's decision is itself of interest, as is the question of why the two women judges did not support legislation aimed at what is often seen as the exploitation of women.[71]

The decision is examined in this chapter in connection with contract law because Justice Wilson's decision provides insight into aspects of her approach to contract law cases. Interestingly, she adopted an economic and contracts-based approach. Once again, her emphasis was on the primacy of private ordering and autonomy: "The provision prohibits persons from engaging in expression that has an economic purpose. But economic choices are, in my view, for the citizen to make (provided that they are legally open to him or her) and, whether the citizen is negotiating for the purchase of a Van Gogh or a sexual encounter, s. 2(b) of the Charter protects that person's freedom to communicate with his or her vendor."[72] More fundamentally, her judgment illustrates her aforementioned pragmatism in focusing on the consequences of the Court's decisions. She was preoccupied with the long-term implications of her decision in the case. Her decision also reveals almost a disdain for what she regarded as an unfair and hypocritical approach to the issue:

> While it is an undeniable fact that many people find the idea of exchanging sex for money offensive and immoral, it is also a fact that many types of conduct which are subject to widespread disapproval and allegations of immorality have not been criminalized ... Whatever the reasons may be, the persistent resistance to outright criminalization of the act of prostitution cannot be treated as inconsequential ...
>
> [T]he legality of prostitution must be recognized in any s. 7 analysis and must be respected regardless of one's personal views on the subject. As long as the act of selling sex is lawful it seems to me that this Court cannot impute

> to it the collective disapprobation reserved for criminal offences. We cannot treat as a crime that which the legislature has deliberately refrained from making a crime.[73]

Essentially, she concluded that this legislation was hypocritical and that upholding its constitutionality would have a negative impact in the long term. It is notable that she opened her remarks at the 1987 Schumiatcher Lecture with a whimsical reflection on the passing of these *Criminal Code* amendments relating to prostitution:

> I had recalled, somewhat perversely an anecdote in Lord Wavell's Anthology of Poetry "Other Men's Flowers." He and a friend were walking ... when a lady of the night accosted them. His friend paused, pointed to the stars and the moon, and addressed the lady in the magnificent words of Sir Henry Wotton.
>
> You meaner beauties of the night,
> That poorly satisfy our eyes
> More by your number than your light,
> You common people of the skies;
> What are you, when the Moon shall rise?[74]

She said no more on the topic. Justice Wilson's deliberate musing on the legislation in this speech is instructive. It captures her broad understanding and acceptance of the human condition. In pointing to the romanticization[75] of the behaviour now cast as "public nuisance," she also reveals a streak, if not of perversity, then certainly of irony. It reflects her concerns about the overall impact and potential consequences for individuals of the legal decisions that she was called on to make.

Conclusion

This chapter has sought to capture both the breadth and depth of Justice Wilson's contributions to contract law, which have been underappreciated, in part because of the more obvious interest in the *Charter*/human rights cases. Nevertheless, her ethos has been influential and has emerged as the way to address many issues of business ethics and practice. Many of Justice Wilson's decisions are still engaging scholars more than a decade later and will continue to do so.

I have argued that some basic, what we might call "homespun," approaches to assessing fairness, reasonableness, and justice inform and are embedded in her judgments. These approaches are presented in Justice Wilson's judgments as if they are self-evident truths. For that reason, her decisions are often appealing at the visceral level. At the same time, she evinces an interest in the parties' story, and her decisions give some voice to that story.

Finally, perhaps the most "long run" of Justice Wilson's many ethical commitments and approaches is her uneasiness with power categorizations and with the portrayal of women as categorically disempowered and dependent. Perhaps this disquiet is a reflection of the fact that she had managed to make her own way and may therefore have been less sympathetic to the struggles of others. But perhaps she was also suspicious of the double edge, the potential trap that this portrayal of women might present. Ultimately, such an approach may have proven to be a disservice to the goal of women's equality.

At the very least, however we understand and construe Bertha Wilson's views on the potential of women judges, and however she herself would have described her approach to contract law, we can conclude that, in adding these "few spokes" – as she might have characterized her contribution – she significantly affected the wheel's shape and its course.

Acknowledgments

The research assistance of William Hayes, LL.B. (2009), Dalhousie University, and of Palma Paciocco and Daniel Girlando at McGill University, Faculty of Law, is gratefully acknowledged. So too is the support and editorial advice provided by Professor Kimberley Brooks, editor of this book.

Notes

1 Bertha Wilson, "Will Women Judges Really Make a Difference?" (1990) 28 Osgoode Hall L.J. 507 at 515.
2 See Chapter 12, this volume.
3 Wilson, *supra* note 1 at 520.
4 P.A. Cain, "Good and Bad Bias: A Comment on Feminist Theory and Judging" (1988) 61 S. Cal. L. Rev. 1945 at 1954, cited by Wilson, *supra* note 1 at 521, n. 44.
5 Wilson, *ibid.* at 521 [emphasis added].
6 This characterization is at least applicable to comments by feminist scholars. See *e.g.* Maureen Maloney, "Economic Actors in the Work of Madame Justice Wilson" (1992) 15 Dal L.J. 197. In her biography, Ellen Anderson comments on the symposium to honour Bertha Wilson on her retirement: "It is striking how little attention was accorded the civil cases which comprised so much of Wilson's judicial career ... [O]nly Maureen Maloney had much to say about the substantial contribution Wilson made to the development of business law doctrines." Ellen Anderson, *Judging Bertha Wilson: Law as Large as Life* (Toronto: University of Toronto Press for the Osgoode Society for Canadian Legal History, 2001) at 269.
7 At least in some areas: but see Chapter 3, this volume.
8 See *e.g.* M.H. Ogilvie, "'Reasonable' Exemption Clauses in the Supreme Court of Canada and the House of Lords," Case Comment (1991) 25 U.B.C. L. Rev. 199; M.H. Ogilvie, "Fundamental Breach Excluded but Not Extinguished: Hunter Engineering v. Syncrude Canada" (1990) 17 Can. Bus. L.J. 175.
9 For discussion of the potential role of stories and narrative, see Carol M. Rose, "Property as Storytelling: Perspective from Game Theory, Narrative Theory and Feminist Theory" (1990) 2 Yale J.L. & Human. 37 at 55. A good example of this kind of projection and storytelling is found in Justice Wilson's dissenting (in part) decision in *Boise Cascade Canada Ltd. v. R.* (1982), 34 O.R. (2d) 18, where she recounts, from the perspective of one of the contracting parties, what it might have understood their arrangement was in 1905 (as an argument for the business efficacy test for implied terms). See also her dissent in *Tom Jones & Sons Ltd. v. Thunder Bay (City)*, [1978] O.J. No. 1503 at para. 28 (Lexis). This is also extended to reviewing

a trial judge's decision and what he or she must have meant: see *Thermo King Corp. v. Provincial Bank of Canada et al.* (1982), 34 O.R. (2d) 369.

10 Anderson, *supra* note 6 at 134.

11 This maxim is inspired from the well-known fact that chickens return to their nesting places to rest and sleep. Credo Reference, online: <http://www.xreferplus.com> *s.v.* "chickens come home to roost," citing Christine Ammer, *The American Heritage Dictionary of Idioms* (Boston: Houghton Mifflin, 1997).

12 To do or get two things that are seen as incompatible or impossible to have at the same time. The adage is usually stated as criticism. Credo Reference, online: <http://www.xreferplus.com> *s.v.* "you can't have your cake and eat it too," citing E.D. Hirsch, Joseph F. Kett, and James Trefil, eds., *The New Dictionary of Cultural Literacy,* 3d ed. (Boston: Houghton Mifflin, 2002). I have used the term "adage," but I note that Dale Gibson, in "On Having Cake and Eating It: A Review of Jeremy Webber's *Reimagining Canada,*" Book Review of *Reimagining Canada* by Jeremy Webber (1995) 41 McGill L.J. 312, describes it as a rule.

13 The true value of something is best proved or tested by actual use. It is often employed to convey the idea that the end result is what counts. Credo Reference, online: <http://www.xreferplus.com> *s.v.* "the proof of the pudding is in the eating," citing E.D. Hirsch, Joseph F. Kett, and James Trefil, eds., *The New Dictionary of Cultural Literacy,* 3d ed. (Boston: Houghton Mifflin, 2002). The saying dates back to at least 1615 when Miguel de Cervantes published *Don Quixote.*

14 I have not attempted to track this as a peculiarly Scottish approach but note a similar reliance in the famous contract law case of *McCutcheon v. David MacBrayne Ltd.,* [1964] 1 W.L.R. 125 at 137 (H.L. Scot.), where Lord Devlin remarked that "[i]t is just as legitimate, but also just as vain, for the respondents to say that it was only a slip on their part, that it is unfair and unreasonable of the appellant to take advantage of it and that he knew perfectly well that they never carried goods except on conditions. The law must give the same answer: they must abide by the contract they made. *What is sauce for the goose is sauce for the gander*" [emphasis added].

15 *Fine's Flowers Ltd. et al. v. General Accident Assurance Co. of Canada* (1977), 17 O.R. (2d) 529 [*Fine's Flowers*].

16 *Ibid.* at para. 32.

17 *Fine's Flowers Ltd. et al. v. General Accident Assurance Co. of Canada* (1974), 5 O.R. (2d) 137 (the tort case was argued in the alternative with the contract claim as the primary basis. The trial judge agreed with both bases, relying, *inter alia,* on *Hedley Byrne & Co. v. Heller & Partners Ltd.,* [1964] A.C. 465).

18 *Fine's Flowers, supra* note 15. In a minority decision, the Chief Justice of Ontario, Justice Estey, reached the same conclusion on the defendant's liability but on the basis of negligence. He was unable to conclude that there was a contract at all between the plaintiff and the insurance agent because of a lack of certainty with respect to the meaning of "full coverage" (essentially there was no *consensus ad idem*). Interestingly, when on the Supreme Court of Canada, Justice Wilson had the opportunity to refer to *Fine's Flowers* in *Fletcher v. Manitoba Public Insurance Co.,* [1990] 3 S.C.R. 191, a negligence case, and in so doing she relied on Justice Estey's decision. *Fine's Flowers* was also raised in connection with the issue of fiduciary obligations and relationships that might involve such obligations: *Hodgkinson v. Simms,* [1994] 3 S.C.R. 377.

19 *Fine's Flowers, supra* note 15 at para. 41.

20 *Ibid.* at para. 55.

21 *Ibid.* at para. 39.

22 *Carman Construction Ltd. v. Canadian Pacific Railway Co.* (1981), 124 D.L.R. (3d) 680 [*Carman Construction*].

23 *Carman Construction Ltd. v. Canadian Pacific Railway Co.* (1980), 109 D.L.R. (3d) 288 at 304. The trial judge stated he was bound by a prior decision of the Ontario Court of Appeal *Ronald Elwyn Lister v. Dunlop Canada* (1978), 85 D.L.R. (3d) 321.

24 *Carman Construction, supra* note 22. There was a more extensive dissent by Justice Brooke arguing that this was an unjust result and finding that the exemption clauses did not apply

to the issue in question and that there was a breach of a collateral warranty and a negligent misrepresentation.

25 *Ibid.* at para. 1 [emphasis added].

26 *V.K. Mason Construction v. Bank of Nova Scotia,* [1985] 1 S.C.R. 271.

27 *Ibid.* at para. 17.

28 *Ibid.* at para. 21.

29 *Ibid.* at para. 22 [emphasis added].

30 *Ibid.* at para. 23 ("It seems to me that a negligent misrepresentation analysis properly focuses attention on the *gravamen of the cause of action in this case, namely the fact that the Bank's representation to Mason was false*" [emphasis added]).

31 *Vorvis v. Insurance Corp. of British Columbia,* [1989] 1 S.C.R. 1085 [*Vorvis*]. In terms of assessing Justice Wilson's contribution to the development of the law on this point, it is of interest to note that the Supreme Court of Canada quoted her view regarding the availability of punitive damages in a contractual situation that, arguably, did not constitute an actionable wrong. See *Whiten v. Pilot Insurance Co.,* 2002 SCC 18 at para. 78. See also G.E. Kruk, "The Supreme Court of Canada in *Whiten* v. *Pilot Insurance:* Judicial Rationality or Supreme Outrage?" (2002) 35 C.C.L.I. (3d) 112 at 119 (the author goes so far as to argue that the Court in *Whiten* essentially agreed with the minority in *Vorvis*).

32 See *e.g.* John Swan, "Now, Can You See Why You Must Start a Contracts Course with 'Remedies'? Extended Damages and *Vorvis v. Insurance Corporation of British Columbia,*" Case Comment (1990) 16 Can. Bus. L.J. 213; Judy Fudge, "The Limits of Good Faith in the Contract of Employment: From *Addis* to *Vorvis* to *Wallace* and Back Again" (2007) 32 Queens L.J. 529; Nicholas Rafferty, "Developments in Contract and Tort Law: The 1988-89 Term" (1990) 1 Sup. Ct. L. Rev. (2d) 269; David Stack, "The Two Standards of Good Faith in Canadian Contract Law" (1999) 62 Sask. L. Rev. 201; Bruce Feldthusen, "Notes of Cases" (1990) 69 Can. Bar. Rev. 169.

33 *Vorvis, supra* note 31 at para. 27. See also Chapter 5, this volume.

34 But see Chapter 3, this volume.

35 *Vorvis, supra* note 31 at para. 55, referring to the approach taken by Linden J. in *Brown v. Waterloo Regional Board of Commission of Police* (1982), 37 O.R. (2d) 277; and Galligan J. in *Nantel v. Parisien* (1981), 18 C.C.L.T. 79 at 292-93.

36 *Vorvis, supra* note 31 at para. 59 [emphasis added].

37 *Ibid.* at para. 60.

38 *Ibid.* at para. 62.

39 Alan Watson, "The Scottish Enlightenment, the Democratic Intellect and the Work of Madame Justice Wilson" (1992) 15 Dal. L.J. 23 at 31.

40 *Hunter Engineering Co. v. Syncrude Canada Ltd.,* [1989] 1 S.C.R. 426 [*Hunter*].

41 *Hamelin v. Hore* (1976) 16 O.R. (2d) 170.

42 *Ibid.* at para. 43.

43 *Chomedy Aluminum Co. v. Belcourt Construction (Ottawa)* (1979), 97 D.L.R. (3d) 170. The judgment was affirmed on appeal to the Supreme Court of Canada: [1980] 2 S.C.R. 718.

44 *Ibid.* at para. 22 [emphasis added].

45 *Ibid.* at para. 28.

46 *Kosmopoulos v. Constitution Insurance Co.,* [1987] 1 S.C.R. 2 [*Kosmopoulos*].

47 Watson, *supra* note 39, commented at length on this case and noted Wilson's sympathy for the "underdog."

48 *Kosmopoulos, supra* note 46 at para. 13.

49 *Ibid.*

50 *Hunter, supra* note 40.

51 Richard F. Devlin, "Return of the Undead: Fundamental Breach Disinterred" (2007) 86 Can. Bar. Rev. 1 at 13, provides a good overview of the range of "Canonical Reponses."

52 *Ibid.* See also Maloney, *supra* note 6 at 199. John D. McCamus also described the case in this way; however, his comments relate specifically to the arguments on unjust enrichment/restitution. John D. McCamus, "Restitution and the Supreme Court: The Continuing Progress of the Unjust Enrichment Principle" (1991) 2 Sup. Ct. L. Rev. (2d) 505. See also Ogilvie,

supra note 8; Anderson, *supra* note 6 at 247, describes it as a strong and detailed partial dissent.

53 *Hunter, supra* note 40 at para. 59: "I am much inclined to lay the doctrine of fundamental breach to rest, and ... to deal explicitly with unconscionability. In my view, there is much to be gained by addressing directly the protection of the weak from over-reaching by the strong, rather than relying on the artificial legal doctrine of 'fundamental breach.' There is little value in cloaking the inquiry behind a construct that takes on its own idiosyncratic traits, sometimes at odds with concerns of fairness. This is precisely what has happened with the doctrine of fundamental breach ... I wish to add that, in my view, directly considering the issues of contract construction and unconscionability will often lead to the same result as would have been reached using the doctrine of fundamental breach, but with the advantage of clearly addressing the real issues at stake."

54 *Ibid.* at para. 161: "I would reject this approach because the courts, in my view, are quite unsuited to assess the fairness or reasonableness of contractual provisions as the parties negotiated them. Too many elements are involved in such an assessment, some of them quite subjective."

55 *Ibid.* at paras. 151-52.

56 *Ibid.* at para. 152 [emphasis added].

57 *Ibid.* at para. 164.

58 *Ibid.* at para. 161 [emphasis added].

59 But see Chapter 3, this volume, for a differing analysis in connection with fiduciary obligations.

60 *Hunter, supra* note 40 at para. 159.

61 *Pelech v. Pelech,* [1987] 1 S.C.R. 801 [*Pelech*].

62 Brenda Cossman, "A Matter of Difference: Domestic Contracts and Gender Equality" (1990) 28 Osgoode Hall L.J. 303. See also the very interesting analysis provided by Mary Jane Mossman, Chapter 16 at 306-10, this volume.

63 *Pelech, supra* note 61 at para. 1.

64 *Ibid.* at para. 46.

65 *Ibid.* at para. 81.

66 *Ibid.* at para. 83.

67 *Keneric Tractor Sales v. Langille,* [1987] 2 S.C.R. 440.

68 *Ibid.* at para. 18 [emphasis added].

69 Anderson, *supra* note 6 at 133.

70 *Reference re ss. 193 and 195.1(1)(c) of the Criminal Code (Man.),* [1990] 1 S.C.R. 1123 [*Ref re Criminal Code*].

71 M.L. McConnell, "Protecting Public Places: Prostitution, Pollution and Prohibiting a 'Perfectly Legal' Profession" (1991) 2 N.J.C.L. 197. *Criminal Code,* R.S.C. 1985, c. C-46; *Canadian Charter of Rights and Freedoms,* Part 1 of the *Constitution Act, 1982,* being schedule B to the *Canada Act 1982* (U.K.), 1982, c. 11.

72 *Ref re Criminal Code, supra* note 70 at para. 71.

73 *Ibid.* at paras. 192-93 [emphasis added].

74 Bertha Wilson, "The Scottish Enlightenment: The Third Schumiatcher Lecture in 'the Law as Literature'" (1986-87) 51 Sask. L. Rev. 251 at 252.

75 It may also reflect the ideas put forward by Shannon O'Byrne, Chapter 5, this volume, with respect to recognition of the place of emotion.

5

Giving Emotions Their Due: Justice Bertha Wilson's Response to Intangible Loss in Contract

Shannon Kathleen O'Byrne

The Role of Emotion in Contract Law

Until the 2006 Supreme Court of Canada decision in *Fidler v. Sun Life Assurance Co. of Canada,* the law generally derided, decried, and admonished the presence of emotion in the contractual realm.[1] As the House of Lords observed in 2001, "Contract-breaking is to be treated as an incident of commercial life which players in the game are expected to meet with mental fortitude."[2] In a similar vein, an American court commented, "Life in the competitive world has at least equal capacity to bestow ruin as benefit, and it is presumed that those who enter this world do so willingly, accepting the risk of encountering the former as part of the cost of achieving the latter. Absent clear evidence to the contrary we will not presume that the parties to a contract such as the one before us meant to ensure each other's emotional tranquility."[3] For these and related reasons, the general rule in common law Canada has been – at least until *Fidler* in 2006 – that compensation for mental distress in a breach of contract action could be recovered only in exceptional cases and according to a specialized set of rules. In short, the law regarded emotional response in the face of breach as largely unworthy of legal recognition.

The purpose of this chapter is to illustrate how Justice Wilson led the process of giving emotions their due, thereby launching the modern approach to recovery for mental distress damages. To set the stage for the scope of her conceptual breakthrough in the legal arena, the second section of this chapter explores how intransigently Western thought has regarded emotions, including how closely and negatively they have been associated with women. The third section provides a brief explanation of the pre-*Fidler* law, to show how an impoverished and blinkered understanding of emotion precipitated an erroneous approach to the recovery of intangible loss. Section four assesses how Justice Wilson set the stage for recognizing emotion in a legal context. She refused to see emotion as dangerous to the law, concluding that parties should be entitled to enforce their bargain or recover damages suffered as a reasonably foreseeable consequence of breach. Section five shows how Justice Wilson's perspective inspires and infuses the joint reasons offered by Chief Justice McLachlin and Justice Abella in *Fidler.* Section six offers some brief concluding remarks.

The Law's Abhorrence of Emotion: A Potted History

It is well known to feminist analysis that men and women have been defined as differing in masculocentric and dichotomous ways. Most significant for the purposes of this discussion is that Western thought has historically regarded reason as superior and masculine, emotion as inferior and feminine.[4] The history of women and emotion is complex in that women are not consistently associated with any one *kind* of emotion. However, as this section of the chapter will demonstrate, the emotion always chosen for such association is of the uncontrolled and uncontrollable variety – whether it be fierce anger, blinding rage, or wild hysteria.

The foundation for this understanding of women and emotion began at least as early as the sixth century BC, with the creation of the Pythagorean table of opposites. As Genevieve Lloyd points out, this table expressly connected femaleness with the unbounded (the vague and indeterminate), as contrasted with maleness and its association with the bounded (the "precise and clearly determined").[5] As Lloyd explains in more depth,

> The Pythagoreans saw the world as a mixture of principles associated with determinate form, seen as good, and others associated with formlessness – the unlimited, irregular or disorderly – which were seen as bad or inferior. There were ten such contrasts in the table: limit/unlimited, odd/even, one/many, right/left, male/female, rest/motion, straight/curved, light/dark, good/bad, square/oblong. Thus 'male' and 'female,' like the other contrasted terms, did not here function as straightforwardly descriptive classifications. 'Male,' like the other terms on its side of the table, was constructed as superior to its opposite; and the basis for this superiority was in its association with the primary Pythagorean contrast between form and formlessness.[6]

Lloyd expertly traces how this Pythagorean world view profoundly influenced the philosophical thought of Plato,[7] Aristotle,[8] and beyond.[9] In this way, "reason, masculinity, truth, and intellect" began to establish a longstanding association in superior opposition to "sense, femininity, error, and emotion."[10]

Significant aspects of the symbolic dichotomization of reason as male and emotion as female can be traced to a portrayal of women's anger in the Latin Vulgate Bible, which was commissioned by Pope Damasus in AD 382.[11] As noted by Sarah Westphal, female anger described in the Book of Ecclesiasticus[12] is not even distantly heroic.[13] On the contrary, it is wild and malignant. According to Ecclesiasticus:

> There is no head worse than the head of a serpent:
> And there is no anger above the anger of a woman.
> It will be more agreeable to abide with a lion and a dragon, than to dwell with a wicked woman.
> The wickedness of a woman changeth her face: and she darkeneth her countenance as a bear: and showeth it like sack-cloth.[14]

This representation of women's anger was carried forward into the Middle Ages, and following the lead of Roman law,[15] it was conceptually integrated into legal codes in order to justify rules that excluded women from the legal process.[16] Though Westphal acknowledges that medieval law codes do not provide a comprehensive account of how women actually functioned in the legal context of the day, they nonetheless manifest a social ideal[17] and therefore help to illustrate the gendering process of law.

Offering an instance of how women's anger as described in Ecclesiasticus was reflected in medieval secular law,[18] Westphal traces the history of Calefurnia, a fictitious female character who almost certainly appeared as early as 1235 in a German legal text – the *Sachsenspiegel*.[19] The *Sachsenspiegel* constituted a record of long-standing legal knowledge, as well as of practices observed in parts of Europe.[20] What follows is Westphal's account of Calefurnia's story, which she based on Maria Dobozy's English translation of the illustrated Wolfenbüttel manuscript of the *Sachsenspiegel* (dated approximately 1300):

> Calefurnia [in foreground] is pictured in both word and image arguing a case before the emperor [also in foreground] in the highest court in the land. Presumably she is arguing on her own behalf in a personal matter and not as a pleader or advocate on behalf of another person, since there is not a second figure in the image. The substance of her case is never revealed. The text anecdote of Calefurnia begins with the general principle of law that arises from her actions: "No woman may be a pleader, nor may she bring a suit without a guardian. Calefurnia forfeited this [right] for all [women] when she misbehaved before the emperor in a fit of rage ... because her demands could not proceed without a spokesman. Of course, any man may be a pleader and a witness, and bring suit and defend himself except in the district in which he is outlawed or if he is in royal outlawry."[21]

Ironically, infuriatingly, and in strategic defiance of logic (which somehow creates no rift in the close association of reason with men), the Emperor uses

Figure 5.1 Fol. 10v of the manuscript "Heidelberger Sachsenspiegel" (CPG 164), reproduced with permission.

Calefurnia's anger at his decree that she could not plead her own case as justification for an exclusion that could only have goaded such a response to begin with. In short, the crime did not provoke the punishment: the punishment provoked the crime.

But not only is Calefurnia the "Eve"[22] of women's diminished legal capacity (in that the punishment for her individual actions is visited on all womankind) – she can also be regarded as a feminist prototype for non-violent direct action. As Westphal explains, and as can be seen in Figure 5.1, an unexplained hairy brush-like object is located next to Calefurnia's derrière. This may represent the fact that, in one version of the story, Calefurnia "mooned" the Emperor in response to being denied standing by him.[23] Alluding to the brush-like object, Professors Charles Nelson and Madeline Caviness, commentators from Tufts University, observe that the illustrator has "done his best to represent this event with decorum."[24]

Following the tradition of ancient Greece,[25] the Renaissance continued the negative association of emotion with women through its focus on the Great Chain of Being. This concept – regarded by Arthur Lovejoy as "one of the half-dozen most potent and persistent presuppositions in Western thought"[26] – has been described by E.M. Tillyard as serving "[t]o express the unimaginable plenitude of God's creation, its unfaltering order, and its ultimate unity. The chain stretched from the foot of God's throne to the meanest of inanimate objects. Every speck of creation was a link in the chain, and every link except those at the two extremities was simultaneously bigger and smaller than another: there could be no gap. The precise magnitude of the chain raised metaphysical difficulties; but the safest opinion made it short of infinity though of a finitude quite outside man's imagination."[27]

And predictably, the Great Chain of Being privileged a masculocentric universe that Val Plumwood has described in the following terms: "Reason, the 'manly' element in the soul, was opposed to the inferior and corrupting 'female' elements, which included the supposedly 'soft' areas of the emotions and the senses. So rationalism inscribes in culture a series of dualistic oppositions between reason, abstraction, spirit and mind on the one hand, and materiality, the body, the emotions, and the senses on the other."[28]

Like the Renaissance, the eighteenth-century neo-classical age that followed (also known as the Age of Reason and the Enlightenment) was much influenced by the Great Chain of Being and its dichotomous, hierarchical understanding of the world.[29] Curiously, this perspective co-existed with other influences of the time, including a fervent interest in science and "patient empirical inquiry."[30] Of course, male writers of conduct books did not regard women as fit for reason-based education; instead, they relegated women to learning "home economics and sewing."[31] In response to the characterization of woman as "innately emotional, intuitive, illogical, capable of moral sentiment but no rational understanding,"[32] Mary Wollstonecraft famously remarked in her own 1792 treatise, "My own sex, I hope, will excuse me, if I treat them like rational creatures, instead of ... viewing them as if they were in a state of perpetual childhood, unable to stand alone."[33] She also disparaged the "prevailing opinion" that women were created "rather to feel than reason, and that all the power they obtain, must be obtained by their charms and weakness."[34]

This is not to suggest that emotion of all kinds was eschewed by the Enlightenment, for this was also the age of sensibility and sentimentalism, and with it came the tendency to aggrandize emotion.[35] According to Janet Todd, for instance, sensibility "came to denote the faculty of feeling, the capacity for extremely refined emotion and a quickness to display compassion for suffering."[36] This was a cultural movement tied to demonstrations of "pathos and unqualified virtue."[37] For example, in his 1759 *A Theory of Moral Sentiments,*[38] the philosopher Adam Smith saw emotion as essential to a "decent ethical life."[39]

Related to Enlightenment sensibility was the ongoing work of nerve doctors,[40] who regarded upper-class males as being especially susceptible to hypochondria (and other similar nervous disorders) as the condition was caused by a luxurious diet.[41] But notwithstanding the inclination of prosperous men to suffer from hypochondria, diseases of the nerves were largely gendered as female. According to G.J. Barker-Benfield, "[N]ot only were women's nerves interpreted as more delicate and more susceptible than men's, but women's ability to operate their nerves by acts of will ... was seriously questioned."[42] The association between madness and nerves was noted, for example, as early as 1757 in the writings of William Battie[43] and over time (*i.e.*, in the late eighteenth century and beyond) came to be associated with hysteria.[44]

By the 1770s, Enlightenment sentimentality began to be criticized, and the notion's popularity was on the wane.[45] Sentimentality was now seen as indulging in "affected feeling" out of proportion with the "stimulus" that prompted it.[46] As summarized by Todd, sensibility was regarded by the poet Coleridge, for example, as "female, unstrenuous, anti-social and self-indulgent, a physical manipulation and a sensation of the body. The sensation was felt by men and women alike, but was especially associated with the selfish, effeminate side of the personality which, in men, needed proper and manly curbs."[47] Even more relevant for the purposes of this chapter, Todd relates Coleridge's conclusion that "[r]eason, law and duty clarify, but sensibility, amoral and passive, exists in 'the twilight between vice and virtue.'"[48]

Modern contract law emerged largely during the nineteenth century, developing in the overlapping Romantic and Victorian eras that followed the Enlightenment. An important nineteenth-century treatise writer appeared to embrace the Victorian regard for all things scientific and reason-driven,[49] as the following quotation from *Anson's Law of Contract* (1879) demonstrates: "The law of contract so far as its general principles are concerned has been happily free from legislative interference; it is the product of the vigorous common sense of English Judges; and there can hardly be a healthier mental exercise than to watch the mode in which a judicial mind of a high order applies legal principles to complicated groups of facts."[50] As A.W.B. Simpson observes, "[T]there are hints here of the idea that the principles [of contract law] were essentially rational and in some sense given."[51] A similar perspective emerged at Harvard Law School through the work of its first dean, who was appointed in 1870. During his tenure, Dean Christopher Columbus Langell instituted a new system of legal education – the case method – which also manifested a belief in law as a science.[52]

It is well known that the nineteenth-century coverture laws governed married women and extracted from them all vestiges of legal personhood.[53] The imposition of legal incapacities stemmed from women's presumed inherent inferiority and inability to reason fully. Indeed, the guardianship theory – one of two historic theories that supported coverture – saw women as juvenile, fragile, and unable to care for themselves.[54] As Carole Pateman demonstrates, the marriage contract thereby subordinates women and works to exclude them from full membership in society.[55] To put it another way, as she does, the legal and political subject is male.[56]

Considered emotionally unstable and susceptible to insanity, nineteenth-century women were openly regarded as inherently unfit to engage in the scientific method so valued by the Victorians.[57] Jane Ussher notes,

> The rise of the Victorian madwoman marked a turning point in both the history of women's madness and in its institutional misogyny. Madness was certainly not a new concept in itself. Eminent scholars had speculated on the origins of insanity or melancholia from the time of the ancient Greeks. The institutionalization of the application of science and rationality to the problem of the insane, a particular hallmark of the Victorian epoch, was not new either. Yet the Victorian era marked an important change in the discursive regimes which confined and controlled women, because it was in this period that the close association between femininity and pathology became firmly established within the scientific, literary and popular discourse: madness became synonymous with womanhood.[58]

Although both men and women were diagnosed with neurasthenia (or hysteria) during this time, the vast majority of sufferers were women.[59] According to the French physician Dr. August Fabre (writing in 1883), "As a general rule, all women are hysterical and ... every woman carries with her the seeds of hysteria. Hysteria, before being an illness, is a temperament, and what constitutes the temperament of a woman is rudimentary hysteria."[60] The nervous Victorian-era woman between puberty and age thirty was regarded as particularly prone to hysteria.[61] Studies cited by Ussher indicate that it was often the "strong and outspoken women" who were diagnosed with hysteria and that these diagnoses were a form of social control over such women.[62] Laura Briggs summarizes the scholarship of those writing from a women and gender perspective: "[H]ysteria is at once a diagnostic gesture of dismissal of women as competent participants in public life, a social role uncomfortably inhabited by suffering women, and a warning about the dangerous consequences for women of engaging in 'unfeminine' behavior."[63]

One of the best-known proponents of the "rest cure" for hysterical women was S. Weir Mitchell, an American neurologist. His commonly held view was that women's inherent inferiority to men and the related irritability of their nervous systems made them more prone to suffer from nervous disorders.[64] Though, theoretically, both the Victorian male and female hysteric were to undergo the rest cure, most patients described in the literature were "nervous females."[65] According to Mitchell's regime, once the patient began to respond to bed rest, the cure turned to "moral reeducation" whereby the woman was instructed regarding how to "keep feelings under control."[66] In Mitchell's words, the goal was to "make clear to her how she is to regain and preserve domination over her emotions."[67] In all these ways, the ancient conjunction of emotion, madness, and womankind continued to mark history.

Feminist analysis suggests that hysteria is actually an expression of a woman's anger at her oppression[68] and a "semiotic language which speaks to patriarchy in ways which can't be expressed."[69] As Marta Caminero-Santangelo states, "The theory that madness is related in some way to the violence of particular types of social order has received much attention from feminists ... Critics such as Hélène Cixous and Carroll Smith-Rosenberg, for example, have suggested that the nineteenth-century hysteric was in fact enacting a protest against the traditional feminine role."[70] On this basis, there is a strong symbolic link between the enraged medieval Calefurnia and her hysterical Victorian counterpart. Both manifest a woman's socially induced anger, which is then turned against her to justify women's compromised legal status (in Calefurnia's case) or her mandatory confinement (in the case of the Victorian "hysteric").[71]

Contract Law's Rejection of Emotion

The negative characterization of emotion embedded in the Pythagorean table of opposites, the Great Chain of Being, the biography of Calefurnia, and the histories of all the women diagnosed with hysteria in Victorian England had far-reaching consequences. Indeed, over the course of history, male and female became imbued with "literary dimensions"[72] and "symbolic content"[73] as driven by gender. This gendering phenomenon has been observed in the philosophical text[74] and in a variety of other disciplines including the sciences, which are all characterized as male.[75] It is also the case for the jurisprudential or legal text[76] and more specifically for contract law.[77]

The law, including contract law, classically regarded emotion as antagonistic to its domain. Law is ordered, stalwart, objective, steady, and just. Emotion is erratic, subjective, arbitrary, irrational, anarchical, destructive, endarkening, anti-reason, anti-male, and anti-law. Emotion is anti-law because it is inexorably associated with the feminine, the destabilizing, and the unstable. Emotion thereby symbolizes legal failure embodied by women and emerging from their association with the "inferior" side of every germane ancient dichotomy permeating history. The social context within which the principles of modern contract law became established over the course of the nineteenth century was clear: prevailing belief gendered madness, instability, and emotion as female, whereas coherence, order, and reason were regarded as male. Given this context, the common law was unable to develop a manner of addressing recovery for mental distress in a breach of contract action. Modern contract law refused to develop generalized principles to enforce the non-pecuniary content of a contract, even when doing so would be consistent with enforcing the plaintiff's expectation interest. Instead, modern contract law linked arms with the Pythagoreans and their successors by adopting the dichotomies of antiquity. As the next section shows, the common law established an elaborate and exclusionary system for recovery of mental distress damages.

Recovery for Mental Distress in a Breach of Contract: Pre-*Fidler* Common Law

As I have discussed in more detail elsewhere,[78] Canadian common law prior to *Fidler* held that, as a general proposition, there could be no recovery for intangible loss in a breach of contract.[79] In the stylized and robust universe of the reasonable businessman, hurt, disappointment, or distress should not be experienced by the innocent party, and even if they were, such a response could not be regarded as a risk to be borne by the party in default.

The traditional rule denying recovery illustrates how contract law routinely favours what it regards as reason over emotion. This genders the law because it privileges the "male" perspective while defining and simultaneously diminishing the ascribed "female" one. Such an approach impoverishes and introduces error into contract law by forcing it to deny what is plainly evident – that contracts often *do* contain implied terms regarding emotion and, furthermore, that distress in the face of breach can be an *entirely* foreseeable consequence. As will be discussed below, the principle of reasonable foreseeability emphasized by Justice Wilson is the means through which contract law can acknowledge the legitimacy of recovery for intangible loss.

Those writing from a law and emotions perspective have offered illuminating commentary on the role of emotion in the law from a variety of theoretical outlooks.[80] In fact, Terry Maroney counts no fewer than six analytical approaches within the law and emotions movement.[81] According to Kathryn Abrams, the conversation regarding law and the emotions has evolved beyond the early questions about whether emotion can co-exist with reason in the legal arena – it resoundingly can – and has moved on to more sophisticated inquiries regarding, for example, the ways in which emotion and reason are interconnected.[82] Abrams also cites Susan Bandes' outstanding collection *The Passions of Law* as evidence of this evolution.[83] In Bandes' words, the book focuses on such matters as "which emotions deserve the most weight in legal decision making, and which emotions belong in which legal contexts," *not* the extent to which emotions belong there in the first place.[84]

Although Abrams correctly states that targeting the dichotomous relationship between reason and emotion can be both archaic and counterproductive by raising old discredited arguments,[85] this does not mean, nor does she suggest, that the symbolism residing in the reason/emotion dichotomy has itself disappeared from legal doctrine. In contract law, the symbolic dimensions of male and female generate powerful narratives that negatively impact real people's lives. Because of what emotion *signifies* within that narrative context, contract law historically chose the path of "excess abstraction,"[86] even driving itself at times to the point of theoretical incoherence. That is, though contract law was mandated to compensate for expectation interests, it nonetheless compromised the enforceability of a promise regarding intangibles because of its female timbre.

As the next section of this chapter illustrates, Justice Wilson refused to participate in the gendering of reason and emotion. Instead, she demonstrated a willingness to give emotions their due, thus providing the necessary catalyst for the Supreme Court's analysis in *Fidler.*

Vorvis v. Insurance Corp. of British Columbia: Justice Wilson's Breakthrough Decision

In *Vorvis,* the plaintiff sued for wrongful dismissal and sought damages for mental distress caused by his supervisor's abusive, berating conduct in the time leading up to his dismissal.[87] The majority denied recovery for mental distress (which it collapsed into the term "aggravated damages") because, as a general proposition, only damages arising from a failure to give notice should be awarded.[88] The Court went on to say, however, that aggravated damages could be recoverable "particularly where the acts complained of were independently actionable."[89] In this case, the supervisor's objectionable conduct was insufficient to constitute an independent actionable wrong.[90] In addition, there could be no recovery for aggravated damages, because the supervisor's offensive conduct did not arise out of the dismissal itself – that is, the conduct was not associated with the *manner* of breach, but preceded it.[91] Although the Court was correct to assert that damages for disappointment caused by the termination of a contract were not recoverable (given that either side to an indeterminate contract of employment can end it on notice), it missed the mark in other crucial aspects.

In short, the majority decision is a bit of a mess. Aggravated damages and general damages for mental distress are both called aggravated damages, which is confusing since aggravated damages go to the *manner* of breach, whereas general damages for mental distress relate to the *fact* of breach.[92] Sometimes the Court seemed to regard aggravated damages as involving two distinct areas (fact of breach and manner of breach), but, for the most part, it seemed disinterested in systematically distinguishing between them. The confusion in nomenclature is complicated by logical inconsistencies. For example, why should intangible damages be restricted to the *manner* of breach absent exceptional circumstances, and why must the plaintiff prove an independent actionable wrong to secure aggravated damages? Such unjustified preconditions to recovery betray a fear of intangible claims and an inability to properly analyze when it comes to compensating emotions. Though the majority in *Vorvis* admittedly nodded in the direction of foreseeability,[93] it declined to develop the idea and did not reject the traditional exclusionary approach to recovery for mental distress.

Dissenting in part, Justice Wilson (Justice L'Heureux-Dubé concurring) forged the modern perspective. She disagreed with the majority's view, contending that an independent actionable wrong should not be a precondition to recovery for mental distress. According to her, "Rather than relying on a characterization of the conduct as an independent wrong, I think that the proper approach is to apply the basic principles of contract law relating to remoteness of damage."[94] Wilson rejected the view that mental distress is recoverable only when the "very object of the contract" is to provide peace of mind, since this prerequisite would "categorically exclude the availability of damages for mental distress in the employment contract."[95] Rather, her approach was to apply *Hadley v. Baxendale* and enquire whether mental distress in the face of breach was a reasonably foreseeable consequence.[96] She also rejected the majority view that conduct preceding dismissal could not be considered.[97] However, somewhat surprisingly, she still would have denied recovery on the basis that the plaintiff's distress *was not* reasonably foreseeable: the plaintiff had not been employed by the defendant for very long, a replacement position would have been easy to find,[98] and no promise of promotion or other special elements of trust existed.[99] Such preconditions, even when given by way of example, seem to place too much responsibility on Vorvis (the plaintiff) for not avoiding the abusive situation. Justice Wilson's conclusion is jarring, given that, each Monday morning, Vorvis' supervisor subjected him to "productivity meetings" that, in the trial judge's words, "became an inquisition," causing Vorvis to be "tense, agitated and distressed, finally resorting to medical attention and a tranquillizer."[100] It would seem reasonably foreseeable – regardless of the alternative employment options that the plaintiff could or should have pursued – that abusive conduct by the employer would cause Vorvis mental distress.

In a countermand to this aspect of her decision, Justice Wilson did create the modern legal structure for mental distress claims, and this in a time when the common law was particularly hostile to emotion. Furthermore, she went on to reject the majority's approach to punitive damages and, on this basis, was one of only two judges on the panel who would have offered Vorvis any compensation at all for his ill-treatment. Wilson saw no reason to require the plaintiff to establish an independent actionable wrong before punitive damages could be awarded:[101] "[T]he facts of this case disclose reprehensible conduct on the part of the respondent towards a sensitive, dedicated and conscientious employee. The appellant was harassed and humiliated and, so the learned trial judge found, ultimately dismissed for no cause after a sustained period of such treatment."[102] As will be developed in more depth below, the *Fidler* decision was founded on both Justice Wilson's overall perspective that the defendant's conduct could justify damages and her reliance on the elementary contract law principle of foreseeability. Like the Court in *Fidler,* she refused to invoke the special categories approach, which required that the contract be of a certain type before recovery was permissible:

> [T]he established principles of contract law set out in Hadley v. Baxendale provide the proper test for the recovery of damages for mental suffering. The principles are well-settled and their broad application would appear preferable to decision-making based on a priori and inflexible categories of damages. The issue in assessing damages is not whether the plaintiff got what he bargained for, i.e., pleasure or peace of mind (although this is obviously relevant to whether there has been a breach), but whether he should be compensated for damage the defendant should reasonably have anticipated that he would suffer as a consequence of the breach.[103]

Locating the Roots of *Fidler* in the *Vorvis* Dissent

In *Fidler,* Sun Life, the plaintiff's disability insurer, terminated the plaintiff's benefits for no valid reason.[104] Over the next few years, Sun Life continued to ignore medical evidence that Fidler was not yet able to work.[105] By the time the matter went to trial, the only issues were Fidler's entitlement to aggravated and punitive damages for Sun Life's breach of the disability insurance contract.

Early in their unanimous decision, Chief Justice McLachlin and Justice Abella acknowledged the suspicion with which the law historically regarded claims for intangible loss: "Until now, damages for mental distress have not been welcome in the family of remedies spawned by ... [*Hadley*'s foreseeability] principle. The issue in this appeal is whether that remedial ostracization continues to be warranted."[106] Like Justice Wilson in *Vorvis,* the Supreme Court in *Fidler* went on to conclude that nothing in *Hadley* required mental distress damages to be treated differently from claims for pecuniary loss.[107]

In a brief but well-reasoned analysis, the Supreme Court noted its own historical requirement that compensation for mental distress "be grounded in independently actionable conduct"[108] and went on to reverse that rule.[109] Though the Court cited the majority in *Vorvis* (*Vorvis* acknowledged that, in certain special cases, mental distress is a contemplated consequence of breach),[110] its decision exactly resonated with Justice Wilson's dissenting view in *Vorvis* that an independent actionable wrong should *not* be a precondition to recovery.[111]

Instead of regarding the recovery of mental distress as being premised on a set of specialized rules, the Court in *Fidler* determined that its role was simply to ask "what did the contract promise?"[112] If the object of the contract "was to secure a psychological benefit which brings mental distress upon breach within the reasonable contemplation of the parties," mental distress was recoverable, provided it was of a degree "sufficient to warranty compensation."[113] In this way, the Court, like Justice Wilson in *Vorvis,* approached the question of mental distress damages from a more general standpoint instead of relying on the old exception-driven approach. This assessment was confirmed by the *Fidler* Court: "We conclude that the 'peace of mind' class of cases should not be viewed as an exception to the general rule of the non-availability of damages for mental distress in contract law, but rather as an application of the reasonable contemplation or foreseeability principle that applies generally to determine the availability of damages for breach of contract."[114] In short, the Supreme Court recognized that "*[Hadley v. Baxendale]* is the single and controlling test for compensatory damages in cases of breach of contract"[115] just as Justice Wilson opined that *Hadley* provided the applicable principles for determining when mental distress damages should be recoverable.[116]

As well as following the *type* of analysis espoused by Justice Wilson, the Supreme Court adopted a similar *attitude* to those experiencing emotional upset in the face of breach. Like Wilson, who bemoaned the supervisor's harsh treatment of Vorvis, the Court in *Fidler* openly acknowledged that contracts could be infused with emotions, noting, "[i]f benefits [under a disability policy] are unfairly denied, it may not be possible to meet ordinary living expenses. This financial pressure, on top of the loss of work and the existence of a disability, is likely to heighten an insured's anxiety and stress ... People enter into disability insurance contracts to protect themselves from this very financial and emotional stress and insecurity. An unwarranted delay in receiving this protection can be extremely stressful."[117] The parallels between Justice Wilson's dissent in *Vorvis* and the unanimous decision in *Fidler* are unmistakable. Justice Wilson and the Supreme Court in *Fidler* refused to regard mental distress recovery as meriting special handling: both Courts refused to regard emotion as a legal outcast, and both relied on the ordinary tools of contract law to weigh claims for intangible loss. Though emotion may have been gendered and derided since antiquity, these female judges would have none of it.

Conclusion

To contextualize the contribution made by Justice Wilson to modern law's approach regarding claims for intangible loss, this chapter emphasized the historic gendering of emotion and the association of women with the inferior side of long-standing dichotomies. The ancient despising of emotion severely compromised the ability of contract law to fashion a coherent response to loss of expectation and consequential loss when that loss related to the emotions. Accordingly, contract law fell into early contradiction by elevating pecuniary interests and diminishing non-pecuniary ones. In so doing, it compromised its foundational principles – including freedom of contract and the plaintiff's entitlement to her expectation interest – because the alternative was regarded as much worse.

Contract law's aversion to emotion not only produced theoretical inconsistency, it also created tremendously regrettable results – including the *Vorvis* outcome, which left unsanctioned (by the majority) a sustained pattern of badgering, demeaning, and harassing behaviour. Fortunately, Justice Wilson generated a perspective that ultimately ended the ostracization of intangible loss claims in the contractual arena by emphatically rejecting the caricatures of antiquity and giving emotions their due.

Acknowledgments

I would like to thank the following people for their helpful commentary on an earlier draft of this chapter: Dean David Percy, Faculty of Law, University of Alberta; Professor Heather Zwicker of the Department of English and Film Studies, University of Alberta; Professor Lise Gotell of the Women's Studies Program, Faculty of Arts, University of Alberta; Professor Elizabeth Adjin-Tettey of the Faculty of Law, University of Victoria; Professor Kim Brooks of the Faculty of Law at McGill University; and James McGinnis of the Edmonton law firm Parlee McLaws. I could not have written this chapter without their inspiration and insights. I would also like to thank for their outstanding research assistance third-year law student Stephanie Aldersey; Ph.D. candidate (English) Susan C. McNeill-Bindon; M.A. candidate (Political Science) Gabrielle Mason; and LL.M. candidate Yemi Alawode. Errors and omissions remain my own. I gratefully acknowledge research funding assistance from the Faculty of Law, University of Alberta, as well as from the Small Faculties Grant Program (Endowment Fund for the Future, Support for the Advancement of Scholarship).

Notes

1 *Fidler v. Sun Life Assurance Co. of Canada,* [2006] 2 S.C.R. 3 [*Fidler*].

2 *Johnson v. Gore Wood,* [2001] 2 W.L.R. 72 at 108 (H.L.).

3 *Hatfield v. Max Rouse & Sons Northwest,* 606 P. (2d) 944 at 952 (Idaho 1980).

4 Genevieve Lloyd, "Maleness, Metaphor, and the 'Crisis' of Reason" in Louise Antony and Charlotte Witt, eds., *A Mind of One's Own: Feminist Essays on Reason and Objectivity,* 2d ed. (Boulder: Westview Press, 2002) 73 at 82. See more generally Genevieve Lloyd, *The Man of Reason: "Male" and "Female" in Western Philosophy,* 2d ed. (Minneapolis: University of Minnesota Press, 1993); Moira Gatens, *Feminism and Philosophy: Perspectives on Difference and Equality* (Bloomington: Indiana University Press, 1991) at 94-95. Note that many other theorists have observed and commented on the phenomenon of reason being male and emotion being female. See *e.g.* Alison Jaggar, "Love and Knowledge: Emotion in Feminist Epistemology" in Ann Garry and Marilyn Pearsall, eds., *Women, Knowledge, and Reality: Explorations in Feminist Philosophy,* 2d ed. (New York: Routledge, 1996) 166 at 166, noting that, "[n]ot only has reason been contrasted with emotion, but it has also been associated with the mental, the cultural, the Universal, the public and male, whereas emotion has been associated with the irrational, the physical, the natural, the particular, the private, and of course, the female." See also Carole Pateman, *The Sexual Contract* (Stanford: Stanford University Press, 1988), arguing that Western thought is harmfully permeated with dichotomies in hierarchy. She explains that many of these dichotomies are manifest in the male/female dichotomy, *e.g.* reason/emotion, masculine/feminine.

5 Lloyd, *The Man of Reason, supra* note 4 at 3.

6 *Ibid.*

7 *Ibid.* at 4-8.

8 *Ibid.* at 8-9.

9 Lloyd also explores the work of Augustine, Aquinas, Descartes, Hume, Rousseau, Kant, and Hegel.

10 Gatens, *supra* note 4 at 94-95, summarizing the work of Lloyd, *supra* note 4.

11 See Princeton University, "Cataloguing Biblical Materials: Summary Descriptions of Versions of the Bible," online: Princeton University Library's Cataloging Documentation <http://library.princeton.edu/departments/tsd/katmandu/bible/versions.html>.

12 Sarah Westphal, "Calefurnia's Rage: Emotions and Gender in Late Medieval Law and Literature" in Lisa Perfetti, ed., *The Representation of Women's Emotions in Medieval and Early Modern Culture* (Gainesville: University Press of Florida, 2005) 164 at 175.

13 *Ibid.* at 176.

14 Ecclesiasticus 25:22-24, quoted in Westphal, *ibid.* at 175-76.

15 Westphal, *ibid.* at 173.

16 *Ibid.* at 165.

17 *Ibid.* at 166.

18 *Ibid.* at 176.

19 *Ibid.* at 166.

20 *Ibid.*

21 *Ibid.* at 167. As Westphal demonstrates at 173-74, this rule restricting women to partial legal capacity is based on Roman law compiled between AD 530 and 533 and justified on the Calefurnia story or, as it was known in Rome, the Carfania story. According to the Justinian scholars quoted by Westphal at 174, "The origin of this restriction [on women's legal capacity] was derived from the case of a certain Carfania, an extremely shameless woman, whose effrontery and annoyance of the magistrate gave rise to this Edict." *Ibid.* at 167 [footnote omitted].

22 *Ibid.*

23 *Ibid.* at 170.

24 *Ibid.*, quoting Charles G. Nelson and Madeline H. Caviness, "Women's Bodies, Women's Property," online: Tufts University Archives and Special Collections <http://dca.tufts.edu/features/law/Group1/index.html>.

25 Page duBois, *Centaurs and Amazons: Women and the Pre-history of the Great Chain of Being* (Ann Arbor: University of Michigan Press, 1982) at 152 (explaining how the hierarchical implications of the dualistic structures informing the Great Chain of Being originated in the mind/body, male/female, human/foreigner dichotomies of Plato and Aristotle).

26 Arthur O. Lovejoy, *The Great Chain of Being: A Study of the History of an Idea* (Cambridge: Harvard University Press, 1961) at vii.

27 E.M.W. Tillyard, *The Elizabethan World Picture* (London: Chatto and Windus, 1948) at 23.

28 Val Plumwood, *Environmental Culture: The Ecological Crisis of Reason* (Florence: Routledge, 2002) at 20.

29 Lovejoy, *supra* note 26 at 183.

30 *Ibid.*

31 Anne Mellor, "Introduction" in Mary Wollstonecraft, *"A Vindication of the Rights of Woman,"* and *"The Wrongs of Woman, or Maria,"* Anne Mellor and Noelle Chao, eds. (New York: Pearson Longman, 2007) 3 at 5. Popular conduct books included the Marquis of Halifax, George Savile, *The Lady's New Years' Gift, or Advice to a Daughter* (London: Randal Taylor, 1688); John Gregory, *A Father's Legacy to His Daughters* (London: G. Robertson, 1774).

32 Mellor, *supra* note 31 at 5.

33 Wollstonecraft, *Vindication, supra* note 31 at 25.

34 *Ibid.* at 84.

35 G.J. Barker-Benfield, *The Culture of Sensibility: Sex and Society in Eighteenth-Century Britain* (Chicago: University of Chicago Press, 1992) at xix.

36 Janet Todd, *Sensibility: An Introduction* (London: Methuen, 1986) at 7.

37 *Ibid.* at 8.

38 Adam Smith, *A Theory of Moral Sentiments,* A.L. McFie and D.D. Raphael, eds. (Indianapolis: Liberty Press, 1982), first published in 1759.

39 Charles L. Griswold, *Adam Smith and the Virtues of Enlightenment* (Cambridge: Cambridge University Press, 1999) at 14.

40 George S. Rousseau, *Nervous Acts: Essays on Literature, Culture and Sensibility* (Houndmills: Palgrave Macmillan, 2004) at 27.

41 George Cheyne, *The English Malady: A Treatise of Nervous Diseases of All Kinds, as Spleen, Vapours, Lowness of Spirits, Hypochondriacal, and Hysterical Distempers* (London and Dublin: George Risk, George Ewing and William Smith, 1733) at 33-34 (E-Source through University of Alberta library).
42 Barker-Benfield, *supra* note 35 at xvii-xviii.
43 Cited in Rousseau, *supra* note 40 at 33 and 75, n. 135.
44 *Ibid.* at 36.
45 Todd, *supra* note 36 at 8.
46 *Ibid.*
47 *Ibid.* at 140.
48 *Ibid.* at 141.
49 As John van Wyhe notes in *The Victorian Web: Literature, History and Culture in the Age of Victoria,* online: Victorian Science, an Introduction <http://www.victorianweb.org/science/intro.html>, it was during this era that sciences gained their "great cultural authority."
50 A.W.B. Simpson, *Legal Theory and Legal History: Essays on the Common Law* (London: Hambledon Press, 1987) at 325, quoting from the preface of the first edition of *Anson's Law of Contract.*
51 Simpson, *supra* note 50 at 325.
52 *Ibid.* at 3-5.
53 For an excellent account of the nineteenth-century law of coverture, see Margaret Valentine Turano, "Jane Austen, Charlotte Brontë, and Marital Property Law" (1998) 21 Harv. Women's L.J. 179.
54 *Ibid.* at 190. (The other theory that supported coverture was the unity theory. As Turano, *ibid.* at 188, notes, this model focused on the domination of the husband and the submission of the wife.)
55 Pateman, *supra* note 4 at 154-58.
56 For instance, as Pateman, *ibid.* at 156, discusses, a woman's legal and civil status disappears upon her marriage and is subsumed into that of her husband. At 184, Pateman reveals how the liberal idea of the "individual" is itself a patriarchal category. She states, at 187, that, "[w]hen contract and the individual hold full sway under the flag of civil freedom, women are left with no alternative but to (try to) become replicas of men."
57 In reference to Donna Haraway's analysis of this matter, George P. Landow notes, "Donna Haraway explains the central importance of a particular kind of witness with specifically non-female modesty as one of the founding virtues of what we call modernity. This is the virtue that guarantees that the modest witness is the legitimate and authorized ventriloquist for the object world, adding nothing from his mere opinions, from his biasing embodiment. And so he is endowed with the remarkable power to establish the facts." See George P. Landow, "Haraway on Modest Witness and the Scientific Method" in *The Victorian Web: Literature, History, and Culture in the Age of Victoria,* online: <http://www.victorianweb.org/science/boyle.html>.
58 Jane M. Ussher, *Women's Madness: Misogyny or Mental Illness?* (New York: Harvester Wheatsheaf, 1991) at 64, quoted in Michele Cammers Goodwin, "The Black Woman in the Attic: Law, Metaphor and Madness in Jane Eyre" (1999) 30 Rutgers L.J. 597 at 638.
59 Laura Briggs, "The Race of Hysteria: 'Overcivilization' and the 'Savage' Woman in the Late 19th-Century Obstetrics and Gynecology" (2000) 52 American Quarterly 246 at 247.
60 Quoted in Elaine Showalter, "Hysteria, Feminism, and Gender" in S. Gilman, H. King, R. Porter, G.S. Rousseau, and E. Showalter, eds., *Hysteria beyond Freud* (Berkeley: University of California Press, 1993) 286 at 287.
61 See Ussher, *supra* note 58 at 74 (for Burrow's pronouncement to this effect in 1828 as well as her analysis of the supposed role of the wandering womb in the etiology of madness).
62 *Ibid.* at 76, referencing E. Showalter, *The Female Malady* (London: Virago, 1987); B. Ehrenreich and D. English, *For Her Own Good: 150 Years of the Experts' Advice to Women* (New York: Anchor Doubleday, 1978).
63 Briggs, *supra* note 59 at 246.
64 Ellen L. Bassuk, "The Rest Cure: Repetition or Resolution of Victorian Women's Conflicts?" (1985) 6 Poetics Today 245 at 251.

65 *Ibid.* at 247.
66 *Ibid.* at 249.
67 *Ibid.* at 249, quoting S. Weir Mitchell, *Doctor and Patient* (Philadelphia: J.B. Lippencott and Co., 1888) at 8.
68 Ussher, *supra* note 58 at 75.
69 *Ibid.*, quoting E. Showalter, "Double Flowers: Hysteria, Feminism and Gender" (Paper presented at the "Wellcome Symposium on the History of Medicine: History of Hysteria," London, 6 April 1990).
70 Marta Caminero-Santangelo, *The Madwoman Can't Speak: Or Why Insanity Is Not Subversive* (Ithaca: Cornell University Press, 1998) at 3.
71 For a very brief application of aspects of Cixous' work to Calefurnia, see Westphal, *supra* note 12 at 170. Note also that the Emperor's dismissal of Calefurnia (due to her rage) parallels that of Victorians such as Eliza Lynn Linton, who dismissed as "wild" those women who sought political and social equality. Eliza Lynn Linton, "The Wild Women: As Politicians" at 161 and "The Wild Women: As Social Insurgents" at 170 in Susan Hamilton, ed., *Criminals, Idiots, Women, and Minors: Victorian Writing by Women on Women* (Peterborough: Broadview Press, 1995) at 188, 198. For example, Linton writes at 188, "All women are not always lovely, and the wild women never are. As political firebrands and moral insurgents they are specially distasteful, warring as they do against the best traditions, the holiest functions, and the sweetest qualities of their sex."
72 Lloyd, "Maleness, Metaphor," *supra* note 4 at 75.
73 *Ibid.*
74 Lloyd, *The Man of Reason, supra* note 4 at xviii. (Lloyd discusses how "[t]he maleness of the Man of Reason ... is no superficial linguistic bias. It lies deep in our philosophical tradition." Lloyd has occasionally been criticized for giving certain philosophers a skewed reading in order to support her thesis.) See *e.g.* Penelope Deutscher, *Yielding Gender: Feminism, Deconstruction and the History of Philosophy* (London: Routledge, 1997) at 2 and following.
75 See *e.g.* Vandana Shiva, "Science, Nature, and Gender" in Garry and Pearsall, *supra* note 4, 264 at 264, and Evelyn Keller, *Reflections on Gender and Science* (New Haven: Yale University Press, 1985).
76 Katherine O'Donovan, *Sexual Divisions in Law* (London: Weidenfeld and Nicholson, 1985) at 3 notes: "'Public' may be used to denote state activity, the values of the market-place, the male domain or that sphere of activity which is regulated by law. 'Private' may denote civil society, the values of family, intimacy, the personal life, home, women's domain or behaviour unregulated by law."
77 See *e.g.* Bela Bonita Chatterjee, "Different Space, Same Place? Feminist Perspectives on Contracts in Cyberspace" in Linda Mulcahy and Sally Wheeler, eds., *Feminist Perspectives on Contract Law* (London: GlassHouse Press, 2005) 109 at 119, where Chatterjee explains how contracts have helped to create and structure gender relationships. See 113, n. 24, for her discussion of how concentration on the market "reinforces the connection of contracts and contract law with the public sphere, the sphere of masculine power and interest."
78 Shannon Kathleen O'Byrne, "Damages for Mental Distress and Other Intangible Loss in a Breach of Contract Action" (2005) 28 Dal. L.J. 311; Ronnie Cohen and Shannon O'Byrne, "Cry Me a River: Recovery of Mental Distress Damages in a Breach of Contract Action – A North American Perspective" (2005) 42 Am. Bus. L.J. 97. Both these articles are cited with approval in *Fidler, supra* note 1.
79 *Fidler, ibid.* Note that Quebec civil law has historically refused to make a qualitative distinction between tangible and intangible loss. See Pierre Gabriel Jobin and Nathalie Vézina, *Les obligations* (Cowansville, QC: Editions Yvon Blais, 2005).
80 See *e.g.* Susan A. Bandes, ed., *The Passions of Law* (New York: New York University Press, 2000) at 1. Bandes notes that emotion "pervades the law" and offers a collection of essays that demonstrate the range of emotions present.
81 Terry A. Maroney, "Law and Emotion: A Proposed Taxonomy of an Emerging Field" (2006) 30 Law and Human Behavior 119 at 123.

82 Kathryn Abrams, "The Progress of Passion" (2002) 100 Mich. L. Rev. 1602 at 1602 and 1620. See also Kathryn Abrams, "Legal Feminism and the Emotions: Three Moments in an Evolving Relationship" (2005) 28 Harv. J. L. and Gender 325.
83 Bandes, *supra* note 80.
84 Abrams, "Progress of Passion," *supra* note 82 at 1602, quoting Bandes, *supra* note 80 at 7.
85 Abrams, "Progress of Passion," *ibid.* at 1602, 1620.
86 I borrow this term from Robert Hillman, *The Richness of Contract Law: An Analysis and Critique of Contemporary Theories of Contract Law* (Dordrecht: Springer, 1997) at 156-57.
87 *Vorvis v. Insurance Corp. of British Columbia,* [1989] 1 S.C.R. 1085 at para. 33 [*Vorvis*].
88 *Ibid.* at para. 21.
89 *Ibid.* at para. 22.
90 *Ibid.* at para. 29.
91 *Ibid.* at para. 23.
92 The Supreme Court of Canada in *Fidler* has since regularized this area.
93 *Vorvis, supra* note 87.
94 *Ibid.* at para. 44.
95 *Ibid.* at para. 45.
96 *Ibid.* at para. 46; *Hadley v. Baxendale,* [1843-60] All E.R. 461 at 465.
97 *Ibid.* at para. 44.
98 *Ibid.* at para. 49.
99 *Ibid.*
100 *Ibid.* at para. 33, quoting the trial judge.
101 *Ibid.* at para. 59.
102 *Ibid.* at para. 61.
103 *Ibid.* at para. 46.
104 *Fidler, supra* note 1 at para. 8.
105 *Ibid.* at para. 17.
106 *Ibid.* at para. 28.
107 *Ibid.* at para. 30.
108 *Ibid.* at para. 37.
109 *Ibid.* at para. 44.
110 *Ibid.* at para. 42.
111 *Vorvis, supra* note 87 at para. 44.
112 *Fidler, supra* note 1 at para. 44.
113 *Ibid.* at para. 47.
114 *Ibid.* at para. 49.
115 *Ibid.* at para. 55.
116 *Ibid.* at para. 46.
117 *Ibid.* at paras. 57-58.

Part 2
Controversy

6

Picking Up Where Justice Wilson Left Off: The Tort of Discrimination Revisited

Elizabeth Adjin-Tettey

> If one were to identify a single case which stands out as the best known contribution [Justice] Wilson made at the Court of Appeal, it might be Bhadauria v. Seneca College in which she ... recognized a new tort of discrimination. [The decision was characterized as] 'a creative and progressive application of the best public policy principles in the development of the common law.'
>
> – Ellen Anderson, *Judging Bertha Wilson: Law as Large as Life*

Remedying Discrimination

An employee is diagnosed with a disabling condition that impairs her ability to work. The employer doubts the legitimacy of the disability and engages in intimidating and harassing conduct that culminates in the employee's termination and total working disablement. The employee alleges that she was treated differently than those with physical illnesses and that the employer's conduct amounted to discrimination and harassment contrary to her right not to be discriminated against on the basis of her disability. She sues the employer for wrongful dismissal and discrimination on the basis of her disability. The employer challenges the court's jurisdiction, arguing that, since the claim includes allegations of discrimination, the appropriate forum is the human rights system.

As a specialized system mandated to address human rights violations, does the human rights tribunal have the jurisdiction and expertise to redress the breach of contract claim? Should the employee be entitled to have all aspects of the claim addressed by a court? Addressing all aspects of the claim in one forum would reveal the interconnected nature of her experiences. How should the jurisdictional quandary be resolved?

Jurisdictional problems also arise in other contexts, such as where discrimination occurs outside of the jurisdiction of human rights systems or other administrative bodies empowered to interpret and apply human rights legislation, and this conduct does not constitute a traditional common law cause of action. Even if the claim falls within the jurisdiction of human rights tribunals, should a complainant be able to opt for a judicial remedy, for example, because that would be the most appropriate one?

These dilemmas would have been avoided had the tort of discrimination recognized by Justice Wilson in *Board of Governors of Seneca College of Applied Arts and Technology v. Bhadauria* survived.[1] A tort of discrimination would have allowed courts to address issues of discrimination when the discriminatory conduct gives rise to other common law causes of action or when it falls outside the jurisdiction of the human rights system. In these cases of overlapping jurisdiction, the plaintiff would be provided with a choice of forum. Justice Wilson's decision was, however, reversed by the Supreme Court, which held there was no common law tort of discrimination or common law action for violation of human rights legislation.[2]

In *Honda Canada Inc. v. Keays,* the Supreme Court, for the first time since *Bhadauria,* had the opportunity to reconsider a common law tort of discrimination.[3] However, the Court decided that doing so was unnecessary because there was no evidence of discrimination to support a human rights claim. As a consequence, victims of discrimination are limited to seeking remedies in the human rights system, unless the impugned conduct also constitutes a common law cause of action.

The outcome in *Keays* could have been different. Much has changed since *Bhadauria* was decided in 1981. First, the privative clause in the *Ontario Human Rights Code (OHRC)* that allegedly accorded the human rights tribunal exclusive jurisdiction over human rights violations has since been repealed. Administrative bodies can interpret and apply provisions of human rights legislation.[4] Allegations of discrimination may be considered and remedied in common law actions.[5] Second, the introduction of the *Canadian Charter of Rights and Freedoms,* which guarantees fundamental human rights, especially freedom from discrimination, buttresses the need to provide effective avenues for remedying discrimination.[6] Finally, inconsistent judicial responses to claims of discrimination following *Bhadauria* confirm the necessity of explicitly recognizing a common law tort of discrimination. These incremental developments have effectively overtaken *Bhadauria,* yet the general rule rejecting the tort of discrimination remains. The response to an unjust rule is not to create more exceptions but to examine its validity – an approach that Justice Wilson took in many cases, including *Bhadauria.*[7]

Overview of *Bhadauria* and Its Implications for Victims of Discrimination

In *Bhadauria,* the plaintiff, a woman of East Indian origin, sought damages from Seneca College for harms suffered arising from the college's refusal to employ her, allegedly because of her ethnicity. She claimed that depriving her of the opportunity to earn a living as a teacher caused her "mental distress, frustration and loss of dignity and self-esteem."[8] Her claim was dismissed as disclosing no cause of action because violation of the *OHRC* did not give rise to a civil action.

Justice Wilson reversed the trial decision, noting that the appeal raised two distinct issues: the alleged breach of a common law duty and a statutory duty not to discriminate. She held that the appellant had a common law right not to be discriminated against, a violation of which gives rise to a cause of action. It was therefore unnecessary for her to consider whether there was a common law remedy for breach of the statute. Justice Wilson acknowledged that she was recognizing a new tort and justified this as consistent with the evolutionary nature of the common law and Ontario's public policy of protecting human rights as expressed in the *OHRC*.[9]

Justice Wilson emphasized that, although the *OHRC* and the tort of discrimination have a common goal – protection of the fundamental human right to be free from discrimination – the common law right and remedy for its violation should be independent of, and distinct from, rights and obligations under the *OHRC*. Specifically, she noted that Ontario's public policy against discrimination predated the enactment of the *OHRC;* although the *OHRC* recognizes the right against discrimination, it did not create that right. Further, she found no express legislative intent in the *OHRC* to exclude a common law remedy for discrimination, *inter alia,* because establishing a board of inquiry to hear complaints about *Code* violations is discretionary. Since freedom from discrimination is a fundamental right that exists independent of the *OHRC,* the remedy for its vindication must be guaranteed and not subject to ministerial discretion and competing political interests. The two systems are complementary: victims of discrimination can choose to pursue their claim under the *OHRC* or through the civil courts.

Justice Wilson's decision reflects her commitment to substantive equality, her appreciation of the vulnerability of marginalized groups in a pluralist society, and her attention to context. She seemed conscious of the particular ways in which discrimination is manifested in contemporary society and its deleterious effects on victims, their community, and society generally. For example, Richard Delgado, a leading critical race scholar, notes that racism excludes racialized people from participating equally in society, impedes self-fulfillment, and entrenches a class system in which these individuals are second-class citizens.[10]

Bhadauria reflects Justice Wilson's judicial philosophy of empathy and contextualization as seen by her willingness to "enter into the skin of the litigant" so as to identify with her experiences as a precondition to fair and reasonable adjudication,[11] and to counter hegemonic epistemologies as a way of promoting equality and justice for litigants.[12] In this way, she humanized the actors involved in the case rather than viewing them as abstract legal subjects.

A tort of discrimination recognizes the pervasiveness of discrimination and its effects on marginalized groups. Redress is not denied simply because the discriminatory conduct does not affect the victim's access to employment, accommodation, service, or state benefits, or because the impugned conduct does not constitute a traditional common law cause of action such as assault, battery, or mental distress. Discrimination *per se* is actionable as it violates a fundamental human right and is an affront to human dignity. A common law action for discrimination allows courts to exercise holistic jurisdiction over cases involving discrimination without having to defer to the human rights system for the discrimination aspect of the plaintiff's claim. Given the reality that experiences of discrimination often intersect with other causes of action, effectively dealing with all aspects of the plaintiff's complaint in a single forum is preferable.

The tort of discrimination as an alternative to a human rights claim was short-lived. In the respondent's appeal to the Supreme Court, Chief Justice Laskin, speaking for a unanimous Court, held that there was no tort of discrimination and hence no common law remedy. Consequently, breach of the *OHRC* provisions did not give rise to a civil cause of action but could be remedied only within the human rights system. Laskin commended Justice Wilson's position as "bold" and "an attempt to advance the common law"[13] but noted that, regrettably, this option had been foreclosed by the legislature. He inferred that, by creating a comprehensive regime for addressing discrimination, the legislature intended the *OHRC* to supplant the common law. Although courts are part of the *OHRC*'s enforcement mechanism, their role is purely supervisory.[14] A common law tort of discrimination would have undermined Laskin's view that issues of discrimination were best addressed through an administrative system with expertise, institutional capacity, and sensitivity to such matters.[15] Was Justice Laskin justified in excluding all common law actions based on discrimination? Not all instances of discrimination fall within the scope of human rights legislation. Victims of these forms of discrimination deserve to have an avenue for redress.

In *Keays,* the Supreme Court reiterated the remedial purpose of the *Code,* noting additionally that a tort of discrimination could result in indeterminate liability and punishment for discriminatory conduct contrary to the purpose of the *Code.*[16] Justice LeBel, dissenting, cast doubt on the appropriateness of precluding civil actions for all forms of discrimination. He noted that Justice Laskin's statements in *Bhadauria,* which foreclosed civil actions for discrimination, were *obiter* and should not stall the development of tort law:[17] "The development of tort law ought not to be frozen forever on the basis of this *obiter dictum*. The legal landscape has changed. The strong prohibitions of human rights codes and of the *Charter* have informed many aspects of the development of the common law."[18]

Limitations of the Human Rights System in Redressing Discrimination

Foreclosing civil actions for discrimination was based on an optimistic view of the human rights system as a publicly funded, non-adversarial, and specialized system to provide timely, effective, accessible, and inexpensive resolution of complaints of discrimination.[19] It was also intended to avoid a two-tier system of access to justice. However, this optimistic vision for the evolution of remedies for discrimination has not come to fruition.[20] Administrative bodies empowered to interpret and apply human rights legislation do not provide remedies for all instances of discrimination. Those who allege discrimination and a common law cause of action may have to seek redress in two forums – the human rights and common law systems – as neither may have the jurisdiction to adjudicate on all the issues raised. Furthermore, there are a number of procedural and practical reasons why complainants would prefer a common law action to a remedy through the human rights system.[21] For example, individuals who experience discrimination may be deterred from filing human rights complaints because of the discretion involved in dismissing complaints with or without a hearing.[22] They may also be deterred by the short time limits for initiating human rights complaints compared with those for common law actions,[23] or claimants who miss the limitation period may be without a remedy absent a common law cause of action.[24] Moreover, the conciliatory nature of the human rights system, with its focus on settlement rather than determining the strength of the complaint, may be inappropriate for some complainants. It often results in parties feeling coerced to settle,[25] undermining the anti-discrimination focus of human rights regimes and the expected therapeutic benefits of the process, possibly exacerbating complainants' vulnerability.[26]

Human rights systems have broader functions than do courts, including public education, facilitating conciliation, and making non-monetary orders.[27] For some complainants, they may provide the ideal solution, as in the example where an employee wants reinstatement. The public dimension of remedies under human rights regimes is commendable from a utilitarian perspective and will probably yield long-term benefits for marginalized groups. However, these may not necessarily align with complainants' needs in particular cases.

Further, remedies in the human rights system are limited. Harms arising from discrimination are often intangible – emotional and psychological, and an affront to dignity. These may be more appropriately remedied by aggravated and punitive damages. However, these types of damages may be unavailable or capped in the human rights system.[28]

Lastly, the finality of tribunal decisions (whether to accept or dismiss a complaint in whole or in part) may leave victims with few and/or ineffective options in the event of an unsatisfactory decision.[29] Complainants can seek judicial review,[30] but the scope of intervention may be limited based on the reasonableness standard,[31] and it affords no right of appeal. The resulting denial of access to justice for alleged discrimination may cause resentment in victims and reinforce the perception of lack of state interest in responding to their victimization. For such persons, commitments to equality and the public policy against discrimination become rhetorical. The denial also violates victims' sense of justice, undermines their well-being, and could threaten social harmony.[32]

Limitations of Traditional Tort Actions in Redressing Discrimination

The current state of tort law is also inadequate to remedy discrimination. It provides remedies for violation of bodily integrity (battery) and threats of offensive physical contact (assault) but none for psychological harms *per se*. Meanwhile, the consequences of discrimination tend to be emotional and psychological and to leave intangible scars.[33] Persistent discriminatory conduct may not threaten the victim's physical and bodily integrity in obvious ways. Hence, assault and battery offer limited assistance to victims of discrimination.

One possible tort action that could be used to remedy discrimination is intentional infliction of mental distress. However, the requirements of this tort significantly limit its utility in responding to discrimination. The defendant's conduct must be "extreme and outrageous," going beyond "mere insults." The plaintiff must prove that the defendant intended to inflict harm on her or him, and a physical manifestation of the psychological injury must exist. Although discrimination often has detrimental effects on victims, they do not always manifest themselves as physical or psychological illness.[34] Medical testimony may not be required to substantiate claims of intentional infliction of mental distress.[35] However, plaintiffs are still required to adduce evidence of the tangible effects of the defendant's conduct on them. Unless we adopt a more expansive view of harm based simply on the outrageousness and undesirability of certain conduct, it is unlikely that a remedy will be available without such evidence.

The benefits of a tort of discrimination alongside other human rights causes of action include giving victims a choice of forum and avoiding paternalism by recognizing that victims are capable of making decisions regarding the appropriate forum. As well, victims can seek remedies for discrimination *per se*, without having to subsume that experience under another cause of action, if one exists. This can be empowering and is important for victims of discrimination.[36] The opportunity for integrated hearings would allow courts to acknowledge the interconnection between the various causes of action and would also be more time- and cost-efficient.

Judicial Responses to Claims of Discrimination: Judicial and/or Jurisdictional Lottery

Judicial responses to *Bhadauria* have been mixed, ranging from express denial of claims involving discrimination, to the assertion of jurisdiction only over aspects of the claim not based on discrimination, to disregarding *Bhadauria* as foreclosing a civil action. These conflicting responses and their disparate impact on victims of discrimination reflect a sense of unease about precluding civil actions for discrimination and the need for a tort of discrimination.

Deference to *Bhadauria:* Dismissing Claims Alleging Discrimination and Other Causes of Action

Some courts decline jurisdiction over claims alleging discrimination, even if they also raise common law causes of action.[37] This position was recently affirmed in *Taylor v. Bank of Nova Scotia,* where it was held that *Bhadauria* precludes discrimination from giving rise to a civil cause of action.[38] In *Keays,* the plaintiff argued that his wrongful dismissal due to his disability, which was found to constitute discrimination and harassment in breach of the *OHRC,* should be recognized as an independent cause of action. At the trial court in *Keays,* following *Taylor,* Justice McIsaac dismissed the plaintiff's claim with marked reluctance.[39]

The strictest adherence to *Bhadauria* can be seen in cases involving sexual harassment. In *Janzen v. Platy Enterprises,* the Supreme Court held that sexual harassment was a prohibited form of discrimination for which broad remedies may be sought under human rights legislation.[40] The effect of *Janzen,* when combined with *Bhadauria,* has been to preclude civil actions for sexual harassment. In dismissing the plaintiff's action for sexual harassment by her employer in *Chaychuk v. Best Cleaners & Contractors,*[41] the Court held that the Supreme Court had effectively ruled that sexual harassment and sexual discrimination were the same, and thus any common law action the plaintiff might have had for sexual harassment was excluded by the *Canadian Human Rights Act (CHRA).*[42] Similarly, in *Nicholas v. Mullin,* following *Bhadauria,* the Court dismissed the plaintiffs' claim for assault, battery, intentional infliction of mental distress, negligence, and breach of fiduciary duty.[43] The Court noted that, although the conduct could constitute the alleged torts, it had no jurisdiction because the claims were couched in terms of sexual assault and should have been brought under the *Human Rights Act.*

Dismissing discrimination claims based on *Bhadauria,* often in the employment context, effectively forces claimants to seek redress in the human rights system or other administrative tribunals such as labour arbitration where the parties are governed by a collective agreement even if the complainant would have preferred a common law remedy. A blanket application of *Bhadauria* may deprive complainants of a civil remedy irrespective of a remedy within an administrative system. This is an extraordinary position and is inconsistent with equality before and under the law. As Justice LeBel, dissenting, noted in *Keays,* it is doubtful and undesirable that *Bhadauria* be given such a wide interpretation.[44]

Distinguishing *Bhadauria*

Sometimes, courts try to minimize the impact of *Bhadauria* by distinguishing its application in the case at bar. For example, in *Perera v. Canada,*[45] the Court distinguished *Bhadauria* because, unlike the *OHRC* under which *Bhadauria* was decided, the *CHRA* did not contain a privative clause giving the human rights tribunal exclusive jurisdiction over discrimination.[46] Thus, *Bhadauria* could not be relied on to foreclose civil actions based on discrimination under the *CHRA*.[47]

Manitoban courts have also distinguished *Bhadauria,* based on differences in wording in the Manitoba and Ontario *Codes*. In *Lajoie v. Kelly,* without referring to *Bhadauria,* Justice Smith said that a reading of the Manitoba *Code* and case law showed that, in Manitoba, victims of discrimination were not limited to complaints in the human rights system and that they were entitled to initiate civil actions for discrimination.[48] Similarly, in *Billinkoff v. Winnipeg School Division No. 1,* the Court of Appeal held that it had jurisdiction to hear the plaintiff's complaints of religious discrimination.[49] The Court noted that complainants had a right of appeal to the Court under the *OHRC* in existence when *Bhadauria* was decided. This influenced Justice Laskin's decision that the human rights tribunal had exclusive jurisdiction over discrimination. The Manitoba *Code* provided for judicial review instead and contemplated an initial consideration of certain preliminary matters by the court. The Court also cited a practical reason to support its decision – namely, that it allowed for consideration of both *Charter* and human rights issues at one hearing.[50]

Although distinguishing *Bhadauria* based on the differences in wording allows complainants to proceed with civil actions, its legitimacy has been doubted.[51] In *Allen v. C.F.P.L. Broadcasting,* Justice Leitch stated that *Bhadauria* was still applicable notwithstanding repeal of the privative clause and enactment of the *Charter.*[52]

De-Emphasizing Discriminatory Aspects of Plaintiffs' Claims

Bhadauria precludes discrimination as a basis of a common law claim. Conduct constituting a recognized common law cause of action, such as the tort of intentional infliction of mental suffering, may also involve elements of discrimination. Therefore, a claim can be framed based on a recognized common law cause of action. Arguably, *Bhadauria* did not oust courts' jurisdiction over these claims.[53] Discrimination is not considered the basis of the common law action but will be considered a relevant factor in assessing the defendant's conduct.[54] The integrated approach is often used in cases of wrongful dismissal, where plaintiffs' claims for breach of contract also allege discriminatory treatment by the employer.[55] In *Kaiser v. Dural,* Justice Hamilton commented on the efficiency of the integrated approach, which allows all aspects of the plaintiff's claim to be considered together.[56]

There is, however, the danger that plaintiffs may feel compelled to downplay the discrimination aspect of their claims in order to survive the jurisdictional hurdle, when in fact discrimination may be central.[57] It may not always be possible to adopt an integrated approach to adjudicate on the discrimination claim together with the common law cause of action.[58] In such cases, some courts simply limit exercise of their jurisdiction to the latter actions,[59] leaving the plaintiff to seek vindication of the discrimination claims in the human rights system. This is a decontextualized approach that presupposes watertight human experiences. It ignores the reality that discrimination may be intertwined with other causes of action and that it deserves holistic remedies reflecting the multi-faceted and complex nature of a plaintiff's victimization. Some may never obtain any remedy for the discrimination, because they may not pursue a complaint in the human rights system, or their claim could be dismissed because the issue was implicitly or explicitly addressed in the civil action, or the court could determine that the discrimination claim was not validated.[60]

Overlapping Jurisdiction

When the plaintiff invokes a common law cause of action and discrimination on a prohibited ground, most courts assert jurisdiction on the ground that courts and human rights tribunals have concurrent jurisdiction over such claims. For example, in *Alpaerts v. Obront,* the Court heard the plaintiff's allegations of sexual harassment against her employer, reasoning that the facts of her case were distinguishable from *Bhadauria* because they also disclosed a cause of action for constructive dismissal.[61] Similarly, in *Lehman v. Davis,* the plaintiff filed a human rights complaint alleging workplace sexual harassment and instituted a civil action for constructive dismissal four months later.[62] In allowing her claim to proceed, the Court distinguished *Bhadauria,* holding that the action was not founded on a breach of the *Human Rights Code.* It noted that courts generally have very broad jurisdiction and cautioned that they should not lightly decline to exercise such jurisdiction absent clear legislative direction.[63] The Court also emphasized that the remedial purpose of human rights legislation supported concurrent jurisdiction of courts and human rights tribunals to adjudicate human rights complaints.[64] Human rights commissions are also not averse to recognizing overlapping jurisdiction with other statutory agencies when the complainant has not yet filed a claim with the other agency.[65]

Concurrent jurisdiction has been justified on the ground that the human rights system was not intended to be the sole forum for redressing discrimination and that civil courts remain an alternative forum, as, for instance, where there is unreasonable delay in obtaining a remedy in the human rights system or the possibility of prejudice to the plaintiff.[66] However, courts avoid duplicative proceedings with possible inconsistent outcomes, prejudice to the defendant, or abuse of process.[67] Court proceedings may be stayed when a human rights complaint is already under way.[68] Some courts have refused to stay proceedings where the basis of the civil action can also ground a human rights complaint.[69] Plaintiffs may be required to inform defendants when they file human rights complaints, and courts may stay proceedings in such an event.[70]

Discrimination as a Basis for Awarding Punitive Damages

Prior to the Supreme Court decision in *Keays,* some courts held that, although discrimination *per se* cannot ground an award of compensatory damages, it may justify aggravated and/or punitive damages.[71] In such cases, the *Code* violation was considered ancillary to the plaintiff's main action, although it could satisfy the separate actionable wrong requirement for punitive damages for breach of contract.[72] Although not directly foreclosing the possibility of punitive damages for discriminatory conduct where the plaintiff had a common law cause of action, the Supreme Court based its approach on *Bhadauria* to hold in *Keays* that breach of human rights legislation did not constitute an actionable wrong to ground punitive damages for breach of contract.[73] An award of punitive damages must be independently justified. Following *Keays,* it may be difficult to obtain punitive damages for wrongful dismissal.

Further, reliance on punitive damages is an indirect and ineffective way of remedying discrimination. Punitive damages are not compensatory and hence have no correlation with the plaintiff's harm from discrimination; the focus of the award is on the defendant's misconduct.[74] Also, punitive damages are available only in exceptional cases where the defendant's conduct is perceived to be harsh, malicious, reprehensible, or egregious.[75] Availability of punitive damages depends on the common law action open to a plaintiff. Punitive damages may be readily available in tort actions, especially intentional torts, but not in breach of contract cases where an independent actionable wrong is required.[76] Furthermore, the availability and quantum of punitive damages are constrained by the rationality test; punitive damages may be awarded only where the combined effect of compensatory damages, including aggravated damages, does not sufficiently punish the defendant and where additional deterrence is necessary in the circumstances.[77]

A further flaw in the punitive damages approach is that it is vulnerable to attack on appeal; there is a greater scope of appellate review for punitive damages compared to compensatory damages.[78] In *Keays,* the award of punitive damages appeared difficult to rationalize on the face of the case and was no doubt in recognition of the discrimination allegedly experienced by the plaintiff.[79] The amount was reduced on appeal and ultimately set aside by the Supreme Court, which held that Honda's (Keays's employer) conduct was not discriminatory and did not constitute an actionable wrong to justify the award.[80] It would therefore be preferable to remedy discrimination by compensatory damages and without requiring the conduct to be harsh, reprehensible, and independently actionable.

Alternative Avenues for Redressing Discrimination: Another Jurisdictional Lottery?

Inconsistency in the degree of access to courts following *Bhadauria* is amplified by the uneven recognition of concurrent regimes for redressing discrimination across Canadian jurisdictions. A civil alternative to human rights claims will provide victims of discrimination access to courts regardless of the jurisdiction where the incident occurs.

Currently, alternative avenues for redressing discrimination exist in Newfoundland, Quebec, and British Columbia. Under the Quebec *Charter of Human Rights and Freedoms,* victims of discrimination may pursue a civil action instead of a human rights claim.[81] Similarly, victims in Newfoundland and Labrador can initiate civil action for *Code* violations.[82] Under the British Columbia *Civil Rights Protection Act (CRPA),*[83] persons (individuals or member[s] of a class) subjected to a "prohibited act" can pursue a statutory tort actionable without proof of damage.[84] A "prohibited act" is defined as "conduct ... promoting (a) hatred or contempt of a person or class of persons, or (b) the superiority or inferiority of a person or class of persons in comparison with another or others, on the basis of colour, race, religion, ethnic origin or place of origin."[85] Successful claimants may obtain compensatory and/or punitive damages or injunction.[86] Furthermore, the statutory remedy is not limited to discrimination in any particular context, as is the case under human rights regimes.

Such alternative avenues for redressing discrimination are absent in other Canadian jurisdictions. In addition, the existing alternative avenues are not without their limitations. For instance, under the *CRPA,* the grounds of a prohibited act do not include sex, sexual orientation, and analogous grounds. A tort of discrimination could fill the lacunae, without requiring jurisdictions to adopt new legislation or amend existing legislation.

Mapping Out a Tort of Discrimination

Justice Wilson's recognition of a tort of discrimination in *Bhadauria* simply meant that the appellant could proceed with her claim. Given the Supreme Court's rejection of the tort of discrimination, there was no opportunity to develop the objectives and elements of that action. As well, because the Supreme Court found it unnecessary to reconsider *Bhadauria* in *Keays,* it did not address what the tort of discrimination might entail. What should it entail, and what are some potential difficulties in proving discrimination?

The tort of discrimination should take a broader view of civil wrongs that is not limited to tangible harms, but focuses on the wrongful conduct of discrimination and the resulting affront to human dignity and security. It should therefore be aimed at vindicating fundamental rights, human dignity, and self-worth of victims and at promoting social harmony and egalitarianism in a pluralist society. It should be grounded in a rights-based theory of tort liability consistent with equality jurisprudence. It should protect personal liberty, human dignity, and the right of all individuals to fully participate in society free from discrimination.[87] Given that harms from discrimination tend to be emotional and psychological, affecting a person's sense of self-worth and his or her familial and social relations, the tort should be actionable without proof of tangible harm, consistent with the Canadian law on trespass to the person.[88]

This vision of the tort of discrimination is consistent with substantive equality and also in line with corrective justice, despite the latter's narrow focus on repairing direct losses caused by another's wrongdoing.[89] Corrective justice demands that wrongful loss that diminishes the overall well-being of victims requires rectification.[90] The tort of discrimination could therefore be a mechanism for reinforcing the public policy against discrimination, as embodied in *Charter* values. If the tort is to be effective in protecting the interests of marginalized people, it should focus not on the defendant's state of mind, but on how his or her interference has adversely affected the victim. Absence of discriminatory intent should not be a defence.

A potential objection to recognizing a tort of discrimination is the difficulty in establishing a causal link between the defendant's conduct and the victim's harm, as well as the extent of the latter's injuries. The cumulative effect of discrimination may generate injuries that seem disproportionate to the perpetrator's conduct.[91] However, this should not affect the perpetrator's liability. His or her wrongful conduct need not be the *sole* or even a sufficient cause of the plaintiff's injury. It will suffice that the defendant's conduct is a necessary factor that, when combined with other elements, produces the harm in question.[92] This is the basis of the thin-skull doctrine, whereby a defendant is liable for the plaintiff's injury even if it is unexpectedly severe due to the latter's pre-existing vulnerability and regardless of the defendant's moral blameworthiness.[93] There is an even stronger reason to adopt such an approach in cases of discrimination where the defendant has engaged in undesirable conduct.

In addition, given the pervasiveness of discrimination and its cumulative effect on victims, it ought to be reasonably foreseeable to people who engage in discriminatory behaviour that their victims may have been previously exposed to discrimination and may be particularly susceptible to harm. Delgado argues persuasively that this approach to recognizing the necessary causal link between a defendant's wrongful conduct and the resulting harm to the victim accords with justice and avoids the revictimization of vulnerable people.[94] This also aligns with the notion of outcome responsibility, which shifts the focus away from the defendant's actions to the resulting injuries.[95] As well, such an approach to causation is consistent with the principle that a wrongdoer's liability for harms directly resulting from her conduct is not limited to the reasonably foreseeable or intended consequences.[96]

The Way Forward

Evolution in the approaches to discrimination following *Bhadauria* has resulted in a potpourri of responses. No clear and consistent jurisprudence has emerged for remedying discrimination. Whether an alleged victim of discrimination will obtain a common law remedy may depend on the jurisdiction in which the incident occurs and the court that hears the complaint. It is unsatisfactory to leave to chance protection of an interest crucial to the dignity of individuals and their meaningful participation in society. The problem may be resolved with an amendment to human rights legislation or the adoption of legislation that gives victims direct access to a civil remedy for discrimination alongside the human rights system. However, this depends on the political will of legislators, and there is no guarantee that any such amendment or legislation will ensure an independent tort of discrimination.[97] The uneven access to alternative avenues for redress is likely to continue.

Expectations of the human rights system as a forum for timely, effective, and accessible remedies for discrimination have not been realized. Limiting victims of discrimination to seek a remedy only in the human rights system unless they can manipulate their pleadings to gain access to court, with the possibility of diminishing the importance of the discrimination claim, is unsatisfactory. A tort of discrimination can minimize these flaws in remedying discrimination. Discrimination is a complex social problem, and it is reasonable to have alternative avenues for redress.[98] The tort of discrimination is not intended to be a panacea for systemic discrimination but simply to add to the ways of responding to this social phenomenon. Concerns about litigation costs and differential access to courts are not unique to the human rights context and do not justify limiting redress for discrimination to administrative bodies. The force of *Bhadauria* has been weakened significantly by legislative and judicial recognition of alternative avenues for redressing discrimination and compensation for *Code* violations in civil actions. Although the Supreme Court did not find it necessary to revisit *Bhadauria* in *Keays,* one may hope that it will seize the opportunity to reconsider *Bhadauria* when presented with the "right" facts.

Notes

1 *Board of Governors of Seneca College of Applied Arts and Technology v. Bhadauria* (1979), 105 D.L.R. (3d) 707 (Ont. C.A.) [*Bhadauria* (C.A.)]. The *Bhadauria* decision may have been the ultimate factor that sealed Justice Wilson's appointment to the Supreme Court of Canada. See Ellen Anderson, *Judging Bertha Wilson: Law as Large as Life* (Toronto: University of Toronto Press for the Osgoode Society for Canadian Legal History, 2001) at 125.

2 *Seneca College of Applied Arts and Technology v. Bhadauria,* [1981] 2 S.C.R. 181 [*Bhadauria*].

3 *Honda Canada Inc. v. Keays,* 2008 SCC 39 at paras. 67, 91 [*Keays*]. The Legal Education and Action Fund (LEAF) intervened in the appeal of *Keays* before the Supreme Court. I was a member of the LEAF subcommittee for this intervention.

4 See *Tranchemontagne v. Ontario (Director, Disability Support Program),* [2006] 1 S.C.R. 513 [*Tranchemontagne*]; *Ontario Human Rights Code,* R.S.O. 1990, c. H-19, s. 34(1)(a) [*OHRC*].

5 Ontario courts are now empowered to remedy *Code* violations where conduct giving rise to a civil claim also constitutes a breach of the *Code. OHRC, supra* note 4, s. 46.1.

6 *Canadian Charter of Rights and Freedoms,* Part I of the *Constitution Act, 1982,* being Schedule B to the *Canada Act 1982* (U.K.), 1982, c. 11.

7 See Alan Watson, "The Scottish Enlightenment, the Democratic Intellect and the Work of Madame Justice Wilson" (1992) 15 Dal. L.J. 23 at 27-28. See also *Becker v. Pettkus* (1978), 87 D.L.R. (3d) 101 (Ont. C.A.) (constructive trust in favour of common law spouses); *Kosmopoulos v. Constitution Insurance Co.,* [1987] 1 S.C.R. 2 at para. 14 (factual expectation test for insurable interest); *R. v. Lavallee,* [1990] 1 S.C.R. 852 (battered woman syndrome); *Vorvis v. Insurance Corporation of British Columbia,* [1989] 1 S.C.R. 1085 (dissenting) (non-pecuniary damages for breach of contract, a view adopted by the Supreme Court of Canada in *Fidler v. Sun Life Assurance of Canada,* [2006] 2 S.C.R. 3 [*Fidler*]); Chapters 4 and 5, this volume.

8 *Bhadauria* (C.A.), *supra* note 1 at 708. Bhadauria had filed twenty-two complaints with the human rights commission regarding previous applications for teaching positions. None of her complaints reached a board of inquiry stage. Her claims were investigated and dismissed for "lack of substance." See Philip Girard, *Bora Laskin: Bringing Law to Life* (Toronto: University of Toronto Press for the Osgoode Society for Canadian Legal History, 2005) at 496; Anderson, *supra* note 1 at 122.

9 *Bhadauria* (C.A.), *supra* note 1 at 714.

10 Richard Delgado, "Words That Wound: A Tort Action for Racial Insults, Epithets and Name-Calling" (1982) 17 Harv. C.R.-C.L.L. Rev. 133 at 140-42, 175-76.

11 Bertha Wilson, "Will Women Judges Really Make a Difference?" (1990) 28 Osgoode Hall L.J. 507 at 520-21.

12 See Hester Lessard, "Equality and Access to Justice in the Work of Bertha Wilson" (1992) 15 Dal. L.J. 35 at 60-63; Chapter 8, this volume.

13 *Bhadauria, supra* note 2 at 203.

14 *Ibid.* at 203.

15 Girard, *supra* note 8 at 482, 497; Allen M. Linden and Bruce Feldthusen, *Canadian Tort Law,* 8th ed. (Markham, ON: LexisNexis, 2006) at 63.

16 *Keays, supra* note 3 at paras. 63, 65.

17 LeBel noted that Laskin should simply have held that the interest at stake was not protected at common law and should not have excluded all civil actions for discrimination. *Ibid.* at paras. 91-92.

18 *Ibid.* at para. 92.
19 Girard, *supra* note 8 at 493-94, 497. See also *Keays, supra* note 3 at para. 66.
20 See Linden and Feldthusen, *supra* note 15 at 63-64; Girard, *supra* note 8 at 496-97; *Tranchemontagne, supra* note 4 at para. 49.
21 See Tamar Witelson, "Retort: Revisiting *Bhadauria* and the Supreme Court's Rejection of a Tort of Discrimination" (1999) 10:2 N.J.C.L. 149 at 160-67; Girard, *supra* note 8 at 496.
22 See BC *Human Rights Code,* s. 27(1).
23 Generally, tort actions must be brought within two years from the time the plaintiff "discovered" his or her right of action: *Limitation Act,* R.S.B.C. 1996, c. 266, ss. 3(2), 6(3), 6(4), 6(5); *Limitations Act,* S.O. 2002, c. 24, Sch. B, ss. 4, 5; *Central Trust Co. v. Rafuse,* [1986] 2 S.C.R. 147. In contrast, human rights complaints must be initiated within six months in many jurisdictions (*e.g.* BC *Human Rights Code,* s. 22), or one year from the time the alleged conduct occurred (*e.g. Canadian Human Rights Act,* R.S.C. 1985, c. H-6, s. 41(1)(e); *Human Rights Code,* R.S.N.L. 1990, c. H-14, s. 20(2)). There is discretion to hear complaints not brought within the specified period where it is in the public interest to do so, where no person will be substantially prejudiced by the delay, and where the delay was in good faith. See BC *Human Rights Code,* s. 22; *OHRC, supra* note 4, s. 34(1)(d).
24 See *Sulz v. Canada (Attorney General)* (2006), 54 B.C.L.R. (4th) 328 (S.C.), aff'd (2006), 60 B.C.L.R. (4th) 43 (C.A.) [*Sulz*]. The plaintiff's action was time-barred under the *Human Rights Act,* and she could have had no redress had the Court not allowed her claim to proceed on the basis of overlapping jurisdictions between the human rights system and common law courts. See also *Lajoie v. Kelly* (1997), 116 M.R. (2d) 221 (Q.B.) [*Lajoie*].
25 For example, complainants may be required to attempt to resolve the problem with the alleged perpetrators or at least to determine the position of the other party before making an application to the tribunal. See *BC Human Rights Tribunal Rules of Practice and Procedure,* Rule 24 (January 2008), online: <http://www.bchrcoalition.org/files/BCHRTsub0304.pdf>.
26 See M. Kaye Joachim, "Reform of the Ontario Human Rights Commission" (2000) 13 Can. J. Admin. L. & Prac. 51 at 67, 69-70.
27 Responses to complaints may include encouraging parties to settle, ordering reinstatement of the complainant, limited monetary compensation, and mandatory employment equity programs. See *Canadian Human Rights Act,* R.S.C. 1985, c. H-6, s. 53(2); BC *Human Rights Code,* s. 37(2); *OHRC, supra* note 4, s. 41; *Human Rights Code,* C.C.S.M., c. H175, s. 43(2).
28 See *Schmidt v. Elko Properties Ltd.* (2005), 45 C.C.E.L. (3d) 297 at para. 18 (Ont. S.C.J.), leave to appeal refused (2005), 50 C.C.E.L. (3d) 252 (Ont. S.C.J.). Under the *Canadian Human Rights Act,* ss. 53(2)(e) and 53(3), successful complainants may be awarded non-pecuniary damages for pain and suffering up to $20,000 and special compensation not exceeding $20,000 where the perpetrator wilfully or recklessly engaged in discriminatory conduct (equivalent of aggravated and/or punitive damages).
29 See *BC Human Rights Tribunal Rules of Practice and Procedure, supra* note 25, Rule 14(9); *OHRC,* s. 45.8. Human rights complaints that have been dismissed as disclosing no cause of action have sometimes been successful in civil courts where courts entertain the claim on the basis of concurrent jurisdiction: *Boothman v. Canada,* [1993] 3 F.C. 381 (T.D.); Witelson, *supra* note 21 at 179.
30 *BC Human Rights Tribunal Rules of Practice and Procedure, supra* note 25, Rule 39.
31 *Dunsmuir v. New Brunswick,* [2008] 1 S.C.R. 190.
32 See Lucie Léger, "The Culture of the Common Law in the 21st Century: Tort Law's Response to the Needs of a Pluralist Society" in Ken Cooper-Stephenson and Elaine Gibson, eds., *Tort Theory* (North York, ON: Captus University Publications, 1993) 162 at 166.
33 See R.A. Lenhardt, "Understanding the Mark: Race, Stigma, and Equality in Context" (2004) 79 N.Y.U. L. Rev. 803; Delgado, *supra* note 10 at 143-47; Léger, *supra* note 32 at 170.
34 See Delgado, *supra* note 10 at 136-43.
35 *Nolan v. Toronto (Metropolitan) Police Force,* [1996] O.J. No. 1764 (Gen. Div.); *Rahemtullah v. Vanfed Credit Union* (1984), 51 B.C.L.R. 200 (S.C.).
36 *Aziz v. Adamson,* [1979] O.J. No. 278 at para. 9 (C.A.).

37 See *Allen v. C.F.P.L. Broadcasting* (1995), 24 C.C.L.T. (2d) 297 at para. 23 (Ont. Gen. Div.) [*Allen*]. See also *Chapman v. 3M Canada Inc.* (1995), 24 C.C.L.T. (2d) 304 (Ont. Gen. Div.), aff'd (1997), 37 C.C.L.T. (2d) 319 (Ont. C.A.) [*Chapman*]; *Nicholas v. Mullin* (1998), 199 N.B.R. (2d) 219 [*Nicholas*].

38 *Taylor v. Bank of Nova Scotia,* [2005] O.J. No. 838 (C.A.) [*Taylor*].

39 *Keays v. Honda Canada Inc.* (2005), 40 C.C.E.L. (3d) 258 at para. 50 (Ont. S.C.J.), aff'd, *Keays, supra* note 3.

40 *Janzen v. Platy Enterprises,* [1989] 1 S.C.R. 1252.

41 *Chaychuk v. Best Cleaners & Contractors* (1995), 11 C.C.E.L. (2d) 226 (B.C.S.C.).

42 *Ibid.* at paras. 233, 242. See also *Chapman, supra* note 37 at para. 47, where the plaintiff's claim for discrimination and harassment on the basis of sex was dismissed as disclosing no civil cause of action. *Canadian Human Rights Act, supra* note 27.

43 *Nicholas, supra* note 37.

44 *Keays, supra* note 3 at paras. 91-92 (Justice LeBel, dissenting).

45 *Perera v. Canada* (1997), 97 C.L.L.C. 230-016, [1997] F.C.J. No. 199 (T.D.), aff'd in part, [1998] 3 F.C. 381 (C.A.).

46 *Ibid.* at para. 14.

47 See also *Sulz, supra* note 24 at para. 78; *Kaiser v. Dural* (2003), 219 N.S.R. (2d) 91 at para. 27 (C.A.) [*Kaiser*]; *White v. Bay-Shep Restaurant & Tavern* (1995), 16 C.C.E.L. (2d) 57 at para. 5 (Ont. Gen. Div.) [*White*].

48 *Lajoie, supra* note 24 at para. 39.

49 *Billinkoff v. Winnipeg School Division No. 1,* [1999] 7 W.W.R. 489 at paras. 48-54 (Man. C.A.).

50 *Ibid.* at paras. 47, 50-51. See also *Sparrow v. Manufacturers Life Insurance Co.,* 2004 MBQB 281 at paras. 16-19 (where the Court notes that the *Code* does not preclude civil actions for violations of its provisions).

51 See David Mullan, "Tribunals and Courts – The Contemporary Terrain: Lessons from Human Rights Regimes" (1999) 24 Queen's L.J. 643 at 648.

52 *Allen, supra* note 37 at para. 23; see also *Chapman, supra* note 37 at para. 42.

53 See *Kaiser, supra* note 47; Amnon Reichman, "Professional Status and the Freedom to Contract: Toward a Common Law Duty of Non-discrimination" (2001) 14 Can. J.L. & Jur. 79 at 84.

54 See *e.g. Taylor, supra* note 38 at para. 2.

55 See *L'Attiboudeaire v. Royal Bank of Canada* (1996), 131 D.L.R. (4th) 445 at para. 8 (Ont. C.A.) [*L'Attiboudeaire*]. See also *Gnanasegaram v. Allianz Insurance Co.* (2005), 74 D.L.R. (4th) 340 at para. 10 (Ont. C.A.).

56 *Kaiser, supra* note 47 at para. 28.

57 See *Petrovics v. Canada* (1999), 210 N.B.R. (2d) 109 (plaintiff amended her statement of claim to delete references to sexual harassment).

58 See *Kaiser, supra* note 47 at para. 28.

59 See *Ayangma v. Prince Edward Island Eastern School Board* (2000), 187 D.L.R. (4th) 304 (P.E.S.C.A.D.).

60 See *OHRC, supra* note 4, s. 45.1.

61 *Alpaerts v. Obront* (1993), 46 C.C.E.L. 218 at para. 5 (Ont. Gen. Div.) [*Alpaerts*].

62 *Lehman v. Davis* (1993), 16 O.R. (3d) 338 (Ont. Gen. Div.) [*Lehman*].

63 *Ibid.* at para. 43.

64 *Ibid.* at paras. 41, 43. See also *Thomas v. Woolworth* (1996), 22 C.C.E.L. (2d) 96 (Ont. Gen. Div.).

65 See *Ford Motor Co. of Canada v. Ontario (Human Rights Commission)* (2001), 209 D.L.R. (4th) 465 (Ont. C.A.); *Snow v. Honda of Canada Manufacturing,* 2007 HRTO 45, 2007 CarswellOnt 8707 (Ont. Hum. Rt. Trib.).

66 See *Lehman, supra* note 62 at para. 42; *McKinley v. BC Tel* (1996), 23 B.C.L.R. (3d) 366 at para. 67 (S.C.), additional reasons (1997), 25 B.C.L.R. (3d) 255 (S.C.), aff'd (1997), 31 C.C.E.L. (2d) 214 (C.A.) [*McKinley*]; *White, supra* note 47.

67 In *Farris v. Staubach Ontario Inc.* (2004), 32 C.C.E.L. (3d) 265, [2004] O.J. No. 1227 (Ont. S.C.J.), Justice Lederman held that it was not a precondition for the judicial proceeding

that the plaintiff suspend the human rights complaint; although the evidence in the two proceedings would probably be similar, the two systems had differing remedial purposes and could be pursued in tandem provided the defendant would not be prejudiced.

68 *Bhasin v. Home Depot (Canada) Inc.* (2007), 58 C.C.E.L. (3d) 265 (Ont. S.C.J.).

69 See *e.g. McKinley, supra* note 66.

70 *Alpaerts, supra* note 61; see also *Lehman, supra* note 62.

71 See *McKinley, supra* 66 at para. 54; *L'Attiboudeaire, supra* note 55 at para. 8; *Greenwood v. Ballard Power Systems,* 2004 BCSC 266; *Collinson v. William E. Coutts Co.,* [1995] B.C.J. No. 2766 (S.C.).

72 *McKinley, supra* note 66 at paras. 68-74. *McKinley v. BC Tel* (2001), 200 D.L.R. (4th) 385 at paras. 88-89 (S.C.C.).

73 *Keays, supra* note 3 at para. 64.

74 *Whiten v. Pilot Insurance Co.,* [2002] 1 S.C.R. 595 at para. 73 [*Whiten*]; *Keays, supra* note 3 at para. 69.

75 *Whiten, supra* note 74 at para. 36; *Hill v. Church of Scientology of Toronto,* [1995] 2 S.C.R. 1130 at para. 196 [*Hill*]; *Keays, supra* note 3 at para. 68.

76 See Jamie Cassels and Elizabeth Adjin-Tettey, *Remedies: The Law of Damages,* 2d ed. (Toronto: Irwin Law, 2008) at 282. See also *Vorvis v. Insurance Corporation of British Columbia,* [1989] 1 S.C.R. 1085; *Whiten, supra* note 74; *Fidler, supra* note 7 at paras. 62-63.

77 See *Whiten, supra* note 74 at paras. 67, 71, 74, 101; *Hill, supra* note 75; *Keays, supra* note 3 at para. 69; Cassels and Adjin-Tettey, *supra* note 76 at 281-82.

78 *Hill, supra* note 75 at para. 195; *Whiten, supra* note 74 at para. 96.

79 The trial judge found Honda's purported manner of accommodating Keays – requiring him to submit doctors' notes for his absences for chronic fatigue syndrome – was discriminatory because employees with "mainstream" illnesses had no such requirement.

80 *Keays, supra* note 3 at para. 69. Justice LeBel, dissenting (Justice Fish, concurring), doubted this finding, noting that Honda's alleged manner of accommodation was insensitive to the nature of Keays' disability and arguably discriminatory. *Ibid.* at paras. 93-96.

81 Quebec *Charter of Human Rights and Freedoms,* R.S.Q. 1977, c. C-12. See Part I, c. 1-1, ss. 10-20.1.

82 *Human Rights Code,* R.S.N.L. 1990, c. H-14, s. 34.

83 *Civil Rights Protection Act,* R.S.B.C. 1996, c. 49 [*CRPA*]. For a discussion of the *CRPA,* see *Maughan v. University of British Columbia,* 2008 BCSC 14; Benjamin L. Berger, "Using Statutory Measures to Redress Discrimination" (2001) 24 Advocates' Q. 449 at 462-66.

84 *CRPA, supra* note 83, s. 2.

85 *Ibid.,* s. 1.

86 *Ibid.,* s. 3.

87 See Richard W. Wright, "Right, Justice and Tort Law" in David G. Owen, ed., *Philosophical Foundations of Tort Law* (Oxford: Clarendon Press, 1995) 159 at 163-65.

88 See Linden and Feldthusen, *supra* note 15 at 44; Ruth Sullivan, "Trespass to the Person in Canada: A Defence of the Traditional Approach" (1987) 19 Ottawa L. Rev. 533 at 546.

89 See Jules L. Coleman, "The Practice of Corrective Justice" in Owen, *supra* note 87, 53 at 57; Wright, *supra* note 87 at 181.

90 Coleman, *supra* note 89 at 66.

91 See Delgado, *supra* note 10 at 168.

92 See Tony Honoré, "The Morality of Tort Law – Questions and Answers" in Owen, *supra* note 87, 73 at 80 (noting that corrective justice requires only that the defendant's conduct be a necessary and not a sufficient cause of the plaintiff's harm). *Athey v. Leonati,* [1996] 3 S.C.R. 458 at paras. 16-17 [*Athey*]. See also *Minet v. Kossler,* [2007] Y.J. No. 30 (S.C.) [*Minet*].

93 *Athey, supra* note 92 at para. 34.

94 See Delgado, *supra* note 10 at 169-70.

95 See Stephen Perry, "Responsibility for Outcomes, Risk and the Law of Torts" in Gerald Postema, ed., *Philosophy and the Law of Torts* (Cambridge: Cambridge University Press, 2001) 72.

96 See *Bettel v. Yim* (1978), 20 O.R. (2d) 617 (Co. Ct.), cited with approval by the Supreme Court of Canada in *Non-Marine Underwriters, Lloyds of London v. Scalera,* [2000] 1 S.C.R. 551 at para. 99; *Minet, supra* note 92 at paras. 35, 48; Linden and Feldthusen, *supra* note 15.

97 For example, although recent amendments to the *OHRC* permit courts to remedy violations of the *Code* in the course of civil actions, *Code* violations *per se* do not give rise to a common law action. *OHRC, supra* note 4, s. 46.1.

98 In *R. v. Keegstra,* [1990] 3 S.C.R. 697 at para. 129, Chief Justice Dickson acknowledged the desirability of alternative measures for addressing hate propaganda and its impact on its victims.

7
Paradigms of Prostitution: Revisiting the *Prostitution Reference*

Janine Benedet

> When a prostitute propositions a customer, or vice versa, we are not dealing with the free expression of ideas ... I think that Milton and Mill would have been astounded to hear that their disquisitions were being invoked to protect the business of whores and pimps. I confess my own astonishment.
>
> – Huband J.A., in the Manitoba Court of Appeal, the *Prostitution Reference*

> The provision prohibits persons from engaging in expression that has an economic purpose. But economic choices are, in my view, for the citizen to make (provided that they are legally open to him or her) and, whether the citizen is negotiating for the purchase of a Van Gogh or a sexual encounter, s. 2(b) of the Charter protects that person's freedom to communicate with his or her vendor.
>
> – Wilson J., dissenting, in the Supreme Court of Canada, the *Prostitution Reference*

> Prostitution: what is it? It is the use of a woman's body for sex by a man, he pays money, he does what he wants. The minute you move away from what it really is, you move away from prostitution into the world of ideas. You will feel better; you will have a better time; it is more fun; there is plenty to discuss, but you will be discussing ideas, not prostitution. Prostitution is not an idea ... It is more like gang rape than it is like anything else.
>
> – Andrea Dworkin, "Prostitution and Male Supremacy"

Canada's prostitution laws are once again the subject of constitutional challenge. In Ontario, the criminal laws prohibiting communicating in a public place for the purposes of prostitution, pimping (procuring), and indoor prostitution (bawdy houses) are being challenged as violating the liberty and security of the person contrary to s. 7 of the *Canadian Charter of Rights and Freedoms.*[1] In British Columbia, the same provisions are being challenged as violations of the s. 7 right to security of the person and the right to sex equality in s. 15(1) of the *Charter.*[2] The applicants in these challenges have not been charged with any criminal offences. Instead, civil libertarian or "social justice" lawyers are leading the challenges, with groups of women who identify as "sex workers" added as applicants to their motions for declaratory relief.[3]

It is an opportune time to revisit the first *Charter* challenge to Canada's prostitution laws, *Reference re ss. 193 and 195.1(1)(c) of the Criminal Code (Man.),* commonly referred to as the *Prostitution Reference,* decided by the Supreme Court of Canada in 1990.[4] That challenge was based on the s. 7 protection of the right to liberty, as well as the rights to expression and association in ss. 2(b) and 2(d) of the *Charter.* The Supreme Court unanimously found an infringement of freedom of expression contrary to s. 2(b), but a majority of the Court held that the law was a reasonable limit on expression under s. 1 of the *Charter.* Justice Wilson, with Justice L'Heureux-Dubé concurring, would have held that both ss. 2(b) and 2(d) were violated and that the infringements could not be saved under s. 1.

In this chapter, I contend that it is impossible to evaluate the strength of the legal claims concerning the constitutional validity of the criminal laws of prostitution without recognizing directly, and choosing among, the multiple paradigms of prostitution that frame these arguments. I use the term "paradigm" to signify a way of understanding prostitution in its social context. Most of the time, scholars and judges adopt one or more of these paradigms without much scrutiny, in ways that often predetermine the legal result. I consider whether this occurred in the *Prostitution Reference* and whether the same risk is evident in the current challenges. The issue is not merely what paradigm of prostitution is most accurate – an important evidentiary question – but also whether the outcome of the challenge is affected if the paradigm animating the legislation (Parliament's paradigm) is not the "right" one.

What follows is a brief summary of the diverse paradigms of prostitution that appear in public and legal discourses. These paradigms are presented in rough chronological order, although it should be evident from the discussion that all of them persist and reappear in differing ways today. I then turn my attention to the various reasons for judgment in the *Prostitution Reference* itself, to identify the multiple paradigms of prostitution that influenced the justices' reasons in that case. In so doing, I argue that only Justice Wilson explicitly recognized the existence of these paradigms and their importance to the legal outcome. Rather than identify her own paradigm, she evaluated the legislation from the vantage point of Parliament's choice. In holding the legislature to its choice, she found the legislation constitutionally deficient. Her reasons suggest that she was troubled by the hypocrisy of the criminal law of prostitution but fell into the trap of assuming that prostitution must be normalized in order to show respect for prostituted women. In my view, the same false correlation underlies the current challenges.

Paradigms of Prostitution

Prostitution as Immorality (for Women)

Historically, the public discourse of prostitution was framed in terms of sexual immorality. Prostitution was linked to the sin of fornication, the spread of disease, and the destruction of the family. These consequences were visited on the prostituted woman herself by making prostitution a "status offence" in which a conviction for vagrancy could follow if, when found in a public place, a woman failed to "give a good account of herself" and was thus judged to be a "common prostitute."[5]

The immorality paradigm was attached predominantly to the woman rather than to the men who bought and sold her. For example, evidence of past acts of prostitution was considered to diminish the credibility of a woman who testified as a witness because evidence of immorality was proof of a tendency to dishonesty.[6] No such rule ever applied to proof that a male witness had bought or sold women in prostitution.

This view of prostitution is still reflected in the organizational structure of prostitution law policing. Many Canadian police forces continue to employ the term "vice" or "morality" squad to describe this work.[7] The use of these labels tells us something about how law enforcement views the practice of prostitution. Moving child pornography and juvenile prostitution investigations from the "morals squad" to "child exploitation" or "sex crime" units is an example of how a shift in nomenclature reflects a shift in public attitude. This shift does not yet appear to be widespread in the case of adult prostitution, perhaps because the fact that prostitution is not criminalized directly legitimizes or normalizes it to some degree.

Although the morality paradigm is much less publicly prominent today than in the past, some courts continue to view the prostitution transaction asymmetrically. In one 1990s case, the trial judge refused to issue the mandatory publication ban on the identity of a sexual assault complainant because she was "a 'liar' and a 'prostitute'" who didn't deserve protection.[8] In 2007 a Manitoba court acquitted a man who had been charged with "engaging in prostitution" after he had offered an undercover police officer money for oral sex. The Court reasoned that, as the buyer, he was not engaging in prostitution; only the prostitute herself could do that.[9]

Currently, the morality paradigm is perhaps most significant as a tactic used by advocates of decriminalization and legalization to rally prostituted women in support of their cause. These groups tell prostitutes that they are despised or looked upon as immoral by middle-class society and that legalization in the form of red-light districts or licensed brothels will both promote respect for them and encourage police to take seriously the violence committed against them.[10]

Prostitution as Sexual Freedom (for Men)

In the 1970s, a paradigm of prostitution as sexual freedom emerged to dispute the immorality characterization. Civil libertarians and left-wing activists argued that the state should not concern itself with the private sexual behaviour of its citizens and that prostitution was a consensual act that was of benefit to both parties.[11] These arguments were framed in the language of choice, freedom, and privacy. The primacy and inevitability of male sexual "needs," and the expectation that they should be met by women, were implicitly accepted. A few advocates for "sexual liberation" actually argued that prostitution would disappear once true sexual freedom had been achieved because women would then willingly fulfill male sexual needs for free.[12] The prostitution-as-freedom discourse persists today in the attempts to show that some, most, or all women in prostitution want to perform that role and that they enjoy being sexually available to all men on demand.[13] The pornography industry promotes this view of women generally and of prostituted women in particular.[14] The industry also goes to great lengths to distinguish between pornography and prostitution, even though both involve payment for sexual acts, and many women in prostitution are used to make pornography.[15]

The prostitution-as-freedom paradigm relies heavily on the age of consent, treating prostitution with those below that line as subject to strong public condemnation and prostitution with women above the line assumed to be consensual.[16] Men are also afforded a mistake of age defence, just in case they enjoy straying close to the line.[17]

The freedom paradigm is less visible in current debates concerning prostitution, perhaps because it bears so little correlation with the tangible reality of prostituted women's lives. Recently, its advocates have wrapped their views in the guise of feminism, using language about supporting women's choices and transferring the focus from male entitlement to female autonomy. They have also shifted to speaking in the language of "harm reduction" and the inevitability of prostitution, as discussed later in this chapter. Reliance on the freedom paradigm in any of its guises typically leads to calls for complete decriminalization of prostitution, perhaps with some regulation to minimize the risk that women will transmit diseases to men.[18]

Prostitution as Public Nuisance

Modern Canadian legislative responses to prostitution have been influenced by the prostitution-as-sexual-freedom or choice paradigm inasmuch as they do not directly proscribe prostitution. Instead, both the judicial interpretation of the solicitation offence passed in 1972 and the communicating offence that replaced it in 1985 focused on the nuisance aspects of prostitution. The 1972 solicitation law made it an offence to "solicit any person in a public place for the purpose of prostitution."[19] In *R. v. Hutt,* the Supreme Court of Canada held that, if a prostitute were to be convicted, the solicitation had to be "pressing or persistent."[20] The consensus among law enforcement officials was that this definition made the provision extremely difficult to enforce.[21]

Provincial and municipal governments then tried a number of measures to move prostitutes out of neighbourhoods where residents were concerned about noise, litter, and a general decline in their enjoyment of their properties, and into areas that were either non-residential or too low income/high turnover to generate much complaint.[22] These initiatives were struck a serious blow when the Supreme Court ruled that control of prostitution was properly the subject of the criminal law and therefore in the exclusive jurisdiction of the federal Parliament.[23] In so doing, the Court invalidated a municipal bylaw that made it an offence to be on the street for the purpose of prostitution. In his unanimous judgment, Chief Justice Laskin rejected the attempt of the municipal government to assert legislative authority over prostitution as a matter of public nuisance, noting that it was a matter of morality and therefore in pith and substance a matter for the criminal law.[24]

Parliament, however, chose to base its next version of the criminal law of prostitution not on morality but, rather, on public nuisance. The solicitation law was replaced in 1985 with the communicating law in what is now s. 213 of the *Criminal Code.* It proscribes behaviour that impedes the free flow of pedestrian or vehicular traffic, as well as any public communication for the purpose of buying or selling sexual services. The definition of "public place," which is very broad, extends to cars that are on public property or open to public view.[25] The communicating law is quite clearly directed at visible prostitution, particularly that which occurs on the street. Although the provision does not prohibit all prostitution, it has the effect of prohibiting all street prostitution, which invariably requires some public communication between the parties. The bawdy house laws, which prohibit keeping or being found in any premises retained for the purpose of prostitution, remained largely unchanged and prohibit most indoor prostitution as well.[26]

Focusing on the nuisance aspects of prostitution is attractive to legislators because this justification tends to enjoy at least some support across a variety of other paradigms that address the act of prostitution itself. Even people who disagree vehemently on whether prostitution is necessary, useful, inevitable, or exploitative will usually agree that the legal system has some role to play in assisting citizens who are being propositioned in their front yards by johns and whose local playgrounds are polluted with needles and condoms. However, the issues of how best to reduce those nuisances and whether the law should target prostituted persons themselves remain subjects of debate. Critics of nuisance-based approaches argue that they privilege middle-class property owners and do nothing to address the abuse in prostitution itself, being content instead with keeping it out of sight.[27]

On its own, the nuisance paradigm is inadequate to explain what framework ought to guide legal and public policy responses to prostitution. It is not enough to focus on public nuisance associated with prostitution without deciding if prostitution itself is harmful. Nuisance alone is not a paradigm but needs to be attached to a narrative of prostitution itself.

Prostitution as Sex Inequality

A more substantive paradigm understands prostitution as an expression of male dominance or sex inequality. There is little doubt that the prostitution industry is deeply gendered: most buyers and pimps are male; most prostitutes are girls and women. This is not a coincidence. The paradigm of prostitution as sex inequality or male dominance does not reject the claim that the practice of prostitution can produce public nuisance; it simply does not view this as a predominant or independent harm. Being kept awake all night by the screams of the abused woman who lives next door is certainly a nuisance, but this is hardly the "harm" of battering that demands the primary focus of state intervention. In the same way, being propositioned by a trick as you walk home from work is demeaning and likely also frightening, but it pales in comparison to how demeaning and frightening it is to be in prostitution.

Understanding prostitution as a reflection of a socially constructed hierarchy that eroticizes male dominance over women is also not inconsistent with a critique of a morals-based approach. If prostitution is a form of violence against women, or if it reflects women's position of social and sexual inequality, its morality in a personal or religious sense is not a significant concern. The supposed immorality of prostitution has always been one-sided, or at least fleeting, where male buyers are concerned.

The sexual violence that is prostitution becomes evident when the practice of prostitution is placed in social context. How girls and women (and some boys) end up in prostitution is crucial to understanding the position of those in it. Many women who enter prostitution do so at a young age: in one study, a majority of prostituted women in Vancouver indicated that they entered as girls or adolescents.[28] Factors that push girls into prostitution include incest or other forms of sexual abuse, poverty (local and global) and neglect, homelessness, addiction, the glamorization of prostitution in the popular media, and, for Aboriginal women, the legacy of colonialism and the persistence of racism.[29] Rates of post-traumatic stress disorder among prostituted women are high; more than half of prostituted women surveyed met the clinical diagnosis for that condition.[30] This should not be surprising, since verbal abuse, beatings, and other violent acts are commonplace in prostitution. Most prostituted women report having been raped; a majority also report being forced to make pornography or to perform acts presented in it.[31] In the 1980s, the Fraser Committee on Prostitution and Pornography estimated that the mortality rate of prostituted women was forty times the national average.[32] Murders of prostituted women in Vancouver and Edmonton, and the disappearance of hundreds of Aboriginal women, some of whom were prostituted, are only beginning to attract public attention.[33]

When asked, 90-95 percent of women in prostitution say that they want out of prostitution immediately but see no viable way of doing so.[34] Few have much formal education or other credentials; many have criminal records and are disabled by addictions, mental illness, and infections such as hepatitis and HIV.[35] They lack conventional work histories, and their job prospects are not high. If they started in prostitution as youth, they may have few life skills or contacts outside of street life.[36] Welfare rates in Canada are deliberately kept below subsistence levels, and specialized counselling and addiction services for women are lacking.[37] If a prostituted woman has appeared in pornography, it may circulate endlessly on the Internet with no recourse to end its distribution, further complicating her exit.

The men who buy women have, by definition, some disposable income. For the most part, they expect sexual access to women on demand in a transaction in which money substitutes for force. Large numbers of men buy women and girls (and sometimes other men and boys) for sex; some are judges, police officers, Crown attorneys, surgeons, and other prominent citizens.[38] Most are married or in long-term relationships.[39]

Prostitution as Work

Compelling evidence reveals that prostitution itself is a practice of sex discrimination that violates women's physical and sexual integrity. When men buy access to women's bodies, they take advantage of women's social and economic inequality to coerce sexual contact with them. In this context, the focus on supporting the "choice" of women to remain in prostitution seems misplaced, to say the least. Yet the choice argument is the red herring that is typically trotted out to distract us from the stark brutality of prostitution. Supporters of legalization are quick to point out cases of women choosing prostitution as a way of supporting themselves instead of working in a bank or a restaurant. They assert that the experiences of these women ought to guide the analysis of legislative change. They argue that prostitution should be considered work and prostituted women, "sex trade workers."

The rhetoric of prostitution as career choice tells us nothing about whether prostitution can or should be the subject of legal restriction or prohibition. The fact that a person "chooses" to engage in an activity for remuneration tells us nothing about whether the activity ought to be prohibited. Trafficking in drugs, brokering the sale of human organs, and selling fake lottery tickets are examples of choices to earn income, but they are not constitutionally immunized from legislative prohibition as a result.

The law and the s. 7 *Charter* right to liberty are not about protecting the right to make choices in the abstract. The impact of the choice is obviously relevant. The Supreme Court of Canada has rejected the idea that choosing to perform an act that harms no one but the actor is immunized from criminal sanction by the *Charter*.[40] If a minority of women in prostitution do in fact participate in the industry free from these significant constraints, their restriction in aid of the majority who do not is not really problematic for them. Presumably, these women could choose another "career" that is more attractive on a simple cost-benefit analysis. Far more often, the contextual factors that make this the best "choice" for some women mean that their real options are limited.

In any event, the vast majority of prostituted women do not consider prostitution to be their career. They prostitute episodically when money runs out, when they need a hit of drugs, or when their pimps tell them to. Prostitution is not a career choice but a survival strategy. This is equally true for women who are prostituted indoors, even in jurisdictions where prostitution is legal.[41] Many women move between escort services, massage parlours, strip clubs, pornography, street solicitation, and referrals by word of mouth.[42]

The irony of treating prostitution as work is that the act of prostitution meets the definition of sexual harassment in employment, a form of sex discrimination prohibited by human rights laws. Sexual harassment in employment includes conditioning the receipt of income on the performance of sexual acts. In other words, when a woman is required to engage in sexual activity as a condition of employment, this is recognized as sex discrimination that limits or prevents women's economic equality. Consent is not a defence: people cannot agree to contract out of human rights legislation.[43]

Reports pushing for the legalization of prostitution as work, and the consequent amendment of employment-related statutes to include prostituted women, either usually ignore this point or argue that human rights codes should not apply to this situation.[44] But the refusal to recognize that prostitution is sexual harassment leads to the result that, when women are paid for typing and a blow job, they are being discriminated against, but when they are paid solely for the blow job, they are not. Rather than dignifying women's choices, this result actually divides prostituted women from the rest of us, who are entitled to earn income without being expected to fulfill the sexual demands of any man who holds economic power over us.[45]

Prostitution as Inevitable (Harm Reduction for Men)

Those arguing for the legalization of prostitution and its recognition as work encounter a problem when confronted with the brutality endemic in prostitution. The obvious question is why the men who buy or pimp women should be immune from criminal sanction. To answer this, proponents of legalization minimize that brutality, claiming it applies only to a subset of women and that it can be managed under the right conditions. At the same time, they assert that total decriminalization is necessary to help women whose safety would otherwise be at greater risk. They suggest that, when pimping and buying women are prohibited, women are forced to turn tricks in dangerous, isolated locations. Since prostitution is inevitable, the argument goes, we ought to accept it and try to reduce any associated harms.[46] General laws on assault, extortion, and public disorder can be used to deal with excessive behaviour.

This "harm reduction" argument is superficially more attractive than one based on choice of work, but on closer inspection, it proves unconvincing. First, it tends to focus on the desirability of moving street prostitutes to legal, supervised brothels. The argument is that street prostitution is unsafe (and so must be completely decriminalized) and that brothels are safe, or at least would be if they were legalized too. But legalizing street prostitution will increase demand for prostitutes on the street, not decrease it.[47] The legalization of prostitution supports its normalization and increases demand for both its legal and illegal forms.[48] If the demand is there, women who need money will meet it. If women working on the street were willing or able to move indoors, and were influenced by the state of the law, they would be doing so now, since they are much less likely to be arrested indoors than on the street.

Second, this argument illogically assumes that, if all prostitutes were confined to supervised brothels, the men who beat, rape, and kill them would either be thwarted in their efforts or lose interest in doing so. There is evidence of violence in legalized brothels, although the amount is difficult to measure since operators have an incentive not to report it. Even those men who are not intent on additional violence take a prostitute to isolated locations because they do not want to be publicly observed in the act of using her.

It is a dangerous fallacy that men who rape and kill prostituted women will stop, or be prevented from doing so, if their purchase of women for sex is fully legalized. They will still find women in bars, on street corners, or in rooming houses who are willing to come with them to secluded locations in the bush, in trailers, or on pig farms. The women may be sent there by their pimps or taken to places where they can be filmed. As in Robert Pickton's case, a female companion may be used to help lure women.[49] The simple fact is that women in prostitution often go where the men who pay tell them to go. Making it completely legal for men to arrange these meetings does not make women safer; it actually gives police one less tool they could use against such men before the violence actually occurs.

If prostitution is a fully legal and regulated activity, treating it differently than any other business becomes difficult to justify. Promoting prostitution tourism to Canada will become a legal business. "Employers" of prostitutes should be able to take advantage of immigration programs designed to recruit foreign "workers," as occurred until recently with employment visas for "exotic dancers."[50] The government will have no need to fund exit programs to encourage women to leave a legal and regulated profession.

"Harm reduction" is a term borrowed from strategies to assist injection drug users, such as needle-exchange programs and supervised injection sites.[51] In the drug context, advocates of harm reduction strategies claim that they are more effective than a strictly prohibitionist approach. Some advocates of harm reduction programs support them as a way of increasing the likelihood that users will enter treatment programs to get them off drugs entirely, whereas others see the programs as ends in themselves and do not privilege treatment or abstinence as an outcome.[52] Proponents of more traditional approaches to addiction recovery may view them solely as prolonging the harms of addiction.[53] Others suggest that harm reduction lacks a broader understanding of inequality and oppression, leading to its co-option by neo-liberals as an inexpensive way of keeping the disadvantaged under control.[54]

These debates are significant to prostitution because the "harm reduction" label is often raised in that context without much thought as to the various ways in which it can be used, or who benefits and who is harmed by capitulating to the inevitability of prostitution in this way. There are many programs that could reduce the harms of prostitution, either by reducing the number of women who enter prostitution or by supporting the exit of women currently being prostituted. Raising welfare rates would help at both ends. Decriminalizing the women in prostitution, so that they are less likely to be saddled with criminal records, is another. The only harm specifically reduced by the legalization of pimps and johns is the harm to men from the risk of criminal conviction.

Harm reduction arguments in which legalization and condom distribution are the beginning and end of the strategy are, in my view, actually grounded in the choice paradigm. If proponents of legalization in the name of harm reduction were truly committed to the idea that nothing short of total decriminalization will reduce violence against women in prostitution, they would be calling for the total decriminalization of child prostitution as well. Surely underage girls, like those preyed on by Judge Ramsay, are most in need of this supposed benefit.[55] Yet proponents of harm reduction are quick to clarify that they do not wish to challenge the current laws prohibiting engaging in prostitution with a person under eighteen, even though those laws are asymmetrical and punish only the buyer, not the girl he is buying. They justify this distinction on the grounds that girls do not have the capacity to consent to sexual activity, but adult women in prostitution do. Supporters of the prostitution industry need to maintain the illegality of child prostitution to justify their reliance on the choice of adult women to prostitute. The line is, of course, artificial for the customer as well as for the prostitution industry; legalized prostitution expands the demand for prostitutes and encourages the entry of more girls into prostitution.

Harm reduction, as presently understood, offers the same false promise of neutrality as the nuisance paradigm: that we can all get on board no matter how we understand prostitution itself. Implicit in harm reduction arguments is the claim that humane people can and should support decriminalization even if they do not support prostitution. But harm reduction advocates very clearly have a point of view about prostitution, which is that increasing the demand for prostituted women through legalization is not harm enhancing. Harm reduction proponents return to the language of sexual freedom and choice when faced with other strategies that might actually reduce the supply or demand. Harm reduction also has similarities with the nuisance paradigm, since both share the goal of keeping women out of public view.

The *Prostitution Reference*

In December 1988, the *Prostitution Reference* was heard in the Supreme Court along with two companion cases: *R. v. Stagnitta,* in which a female accused was charged after offering sex for money to an undercover policeman, and *R. v. Skinner,* in which a male accused was arrested for soliciting oral sex from an undercover policewoman.[56] The Court sat with a coram of seven justices, but Justice McIntyre had retired before the decisions were released some eighteen months later in May 1990.

In the *Prostitution Reference,* the Court dismissed the appeal by a margin of four to two. Writing for the plurality, Chief Justice Dickson, with Justices La Forest and Sopinka concurring, held that the communicating offence in s. 195.1(1)(c) of the *Criminal Code,* but not the bawdy house offence in s. 193, violated s. 2(b) of the *Charter* but that the infringement was a reasonable limit under s. 1. They rejected the s. 7 vagueness claim and the claim that the principles of fundamental justice were violated by criminalizing street solicitation while prostitution itself was legal.

Justice Lamer, concurring, came to similar conclusions as the plurality, but added that s. 7 of the *Charter* did not extend to the right to exercise a chosen profession. He also preferred a more expansive understanding of the government's objective in the s. 1 analysis, noting that there was evidence about the sexual exploitation of women intrinsic in prostitution.

Justice Wilson, with Justice L'Heureux-Dubé concurring, dissented. She would have found that the s. 2(b) infringement was not justified under s. 1.

The legislation failed the minimal impairment test because no possibility of nuisance to others need be shown for conviction and because it was over-broad.

In the companion case of *R. v. Skinner,* the majority held that s. 195.1(1)(c) did not infringe the right to freedom of association under s. 2(d); the mere fact that a provision limited the possibility of commercial activity was insufficient. Once again, Justices Wilson and L'Heureux-Dubé dissented. They would have held that s. 2(d) was violated because it prohibited parties from associating in order to pursue a lawful common objective, the sale of sex for money. They again found the violation not justified under s. 1, pointing to the breadth of the statutory definition of "public place."

A close reading of the *Prostitution Reference* shows that the contradictory paradigms of prostitution discussed above are reflected in the arguments of the parties and the judges' reasons. The parties characterized the purpose of the legislation, and indeed the act of prostitution, in differing ways that replicated these varying paradigms of prostitution. The s. 7 argument of those challenging the legislation was very clearly tied to the model of prostitution as work or commerce and, to a lesser degree, as sexual freedom. The s. 7 challenge was based on the claim that the sale of sex for money is not directly a criminal act. It was argued that stigmatizing a legal activity with criminalization deprived individuals of their liberty and offended the principles of fundamental justice. In addition, the s. 7 claim asserted that prostitution was work and that s. 7 protected the right to practise one's chosen profession. The ss. 2(b) and 2(d) claims were very much tied to these same principles and grounded in the notion that prostitution is a lawful commercial transaction.

The government's s. 1 arguments, by contrast, attempted to justify the legislation by different paradigms. Its primary focus was on nuisance – the public nuisance of traffic, noise, litter, and crowding but also the larger "social nuisance" of being unwillingly exposed to the display of prostitution in one's own neighbourhood. Thus, the harms identified encompassed somewhat of a moral justification, one based on the offensiveness of prostitution in plain view. The intervenor Attorney General for Ontario appears to have been the only party to identify harms to women from prostitution itself, pointing out that most prostitutes were women and that they were subjected to violence and control from pimps and buyers.

How the three sets of reasons in the *Prostitution Reference* reflect these multiple paradigms reveals the conflicting ways in which the judges understood prostitution. The short plurality reasons, written by Justice Dickson, accepted Justice Wilson's conclusion that the communicating provision infringed the freedom of expression protected by s. 2(b). Justice Dickson's s. 1 analysis also appeared to accept that prostitution is an instrument of sex inequality for women but rejects the argument that addressing this inequality is part of the purpose of the *Code* provision. Instead, like Wilson J., he viewed the provision as being about eradicating nuisance: "In prohibiting sales of sexual services in public, the legislation does not attempt, at least in any direct manner, to address the exploitation, degradation and subordination of women that are part of the contemporary reality of prostitution. Rather, in my view, the legislation is aimed at taking solicitation for the purposes of prostitution off the streets and out of public view."[57] Yet, the plurality also assumed that prostitution was a form of trade or commerce and used that fact to diminish the value of expression designed to facilitate that trade: "Here the activity to which the impugned legislation is directed is expression with an economic purpose. It can hardly be said that communications regarding an economic transaction of sex for money lie at, or even near, the core of the guarantee of freedom of expression."[58]

Justice Dickson did not see the asserted "legality" of prostitution itself as relevant to Parliament's constitutional ability to criminalize street solicitation, an issue that would arise only if the Court were "faced with the direct question of Parliament's competence to criminalize prostitution."[59] This is somewhat paradoxical, of course, because the Court had already stated that the control or regulation of prostitution lay, for the purpose of the division of powers, within the federal criminal law power.[60] If that power were to be enjoined by the operation of the *Charter,* prostitution would be entirely immune from direct legislative intervention.

Justice Lamer, concurring, wrote lengthier reasons in which he rejected the s. 7 challenge on the ground that the section did not protect the right to work or to practise a profession. He asserted that prostitution was not illegal in Canada, a fact that needed to be kept in mind. He continued, "[W]e find ourselves in the anomalous, some would say bizarre, situation where almost everything related to prostitution has been regulated by the criminal law except the transaction itself. The appellants' [liberty and security of the person] argument then, more precisely stated, is that in criminalizing so many activities surrounding the act itself, Parliament has made prostitution *de facto* illegal if not *de jure* illegal."[61] Here, then, he considered the paradigm of prostitution as lawful commercial activity and appeared to find it compelling but not determinative.

Justice Lamer rejected the more expansive definition of "liberty" favoured by Justice Wilson in cases such as *R. v. Jones* and *R. v. Morgentaler,* which recognized the liberty to work or to make important personal choices, preferring instead a definition that focused on deprivations of liberty tied to the operation of the legal system.[62] Of course, Justice Lamer could have reached the same conclusion by challenging the assumptions that prostitution is "work" and that it furthers any liberty other than male liberty to sexually access women on demand. The work paradigm carried over into the s. 2(b) analysis, where he characterized communication for the purposes of prostitution as commercial expression, a contract for services in which the act for which the communication takes place was lawful.

Yet Justice Lamer's paradigm shifted when he turned to the s. 1 analysis and the government's objective. He argued that the scope of regulation implied that Parliament's goal was not merely to eradicate nuisance but also to eradicate the practice of prostitution itself. With apparent approval, he quoted from a brief prepared by the Ontario Advisory Council on the Status of Women, which described prostitution as "a form of violence against women and young persons ... a blatant form of exploitation and abuse of power. Prostitution is related to the traditional dominance of men over women."[63] Justice Lamer described prostitution "at its most basic level [as] a form of slavery. It is degrading to the prostitute and is commonly accompanied by physical violence and brutality."[64]

This shift in understanding is important because it justifies a more expansive scope to the criminal law. Despite this promising start, however, Justice Lamer reverted to the moral justification for limiting prostitution in his minimal impairment analysis, noting that the issue of how best to deal with it was contentious and "morally-laden."[65] Ultimately, he upheld the s. 2(b) violation under s. 1.

In her dissenting reasons, Justice Wilson also invoked multiple paradigms of prostitution, but she was the only judge who seemed to recognize explicitly these varying views of prostitution in society:

> While it is an undeniable fact that many people find the idea of exchanging sex for money offensive and immoral, it is also a fact that many types of conduct which are subject to widespread disapproval and allegations of immorality have not been criminalized. Indeed, one can think of a number of reasons why selling sex has not been made a criminal offence. First, as Lamer J. notes in his s. 1 analysis ... more often than not the real "victim" of prostitution is the prostitute himself or herself. Sending prostitutes to prison for their conduct may therefore have been viewed by legislators as an unsuitable response to the phenomenon. Or the legislators may have realized that they could not send the female prostitute to prison while letting the male customer go and been reluctant for that reason to make prostitution a criminal offence. Another explanation may be a reluctance on the part of legislators to criminalize a transaction which normally occurs in private between consenting adults. Yet another possibility is that the legislature simply recognized that prostitution is the oldest trade in the world and is clearly meeting a social need. Whatever the reasons may be, the persistent resistance to outright criminalization of the act of prostitution cannot be treated as inconsequential.[66]

In this passage, Justice Wilson recognized prostitution as immorality ("many people find [it] ... offensive and immoral"), as exploitation and inequality ("the real 'victim' of prostitution is the prostitute"), as a gendered institution that reflects male privilege ("could not send the female prostitute to prison while letting the male customer go"), as personal liberty ("in private between consenting adults"), and as work ("the oldest trade in the world"). She stated that she was not endorsing any particular theory, apparently content to rely on the government's asserted objective for the communication law of curbing social nuisance.

In one sense, she can be commended for holding the government to its choice and asserting that its case stood and fell on the paradigm it had used. On the other hand, it is disingenuous to suppose that Justice Wilson's own reasons were value-neutral. She repeatedly labelled prostitution as a commercial bargain or transaction, suggesting tacit acceptance of the "prostitution as work" paradigm. But more fundamentally, she clearly believed that an absence of criminalization signified a lack of collective censure.

Much more than the other two opinions, hers appears to be influenced by the supposed "legal" status of prostitution. The link between legalization and normalization is clear in her reasons. She argued that, just as the act of criminalization expresses society's collective disapproval of certain acts, "it is equally true that where the legislature has *not* criminalized a certain activity it is because the legislator has determined that this uniquely coercive and punitive method of expressing society's collective disapprobation is not warranted."[67] In finding that the violation of freedom of expression could not pass the proportionality analysis in s. 1, she went further, describing the legislation as affecting "persons engaged in a lawful activity which is not shown to be harming anybody."[68]

Yet, this analysis of prostitution as lawful and harmless sits in awkward juxtaposition to her conclusion that prostitution is a "degrading way for women to earn a living."[69] It may be that, in her focus on legalization, Justice Wilson (and Justice L'Heureux-Dubé, who concurred with her) was concerned that prostituted women not be further victimized by criminal punishment. I suspect that her reasons were a response to what she perceived as the hypocrisy of the current law, which claims to be concerned about public nuisance but actually seeks to ban all street prostitution through punishing predominantly women. In so doing, she fell into the trap of thinking that the only way to affirm the dignity of prostituted women was to normalize prostitution itself. She never considered (and it appears that she was not asked to consider) whether the asymmetry in who is responsible for the harms of prostitution might mean that the law is unconstitutional only to the extent it is applied to prostituted women themselves.

The irony in Justice Wilson's approach to the communicating offence is that Parliament probably would have been in a much better position for the purposes of *Charter* review if it had simply prohibited street prostitution directly. Regardless of its motivation for enacting the law, finding a *Charter* violation under the sections at issue in the *Prostitution Reference* would be difficult. Section 2(b) would not be engaged, since the act of prostitution itself is not intended to convey a meaning and would probably not meet the definition of "expression."

Although the scope of s. 2(d) has been expanded in recent years, a purposive approach to the section would probably not extend constitutional protection to the act of two people engaging in fellatio in an underground parking garage, for payment or otherwise. The argument that there is a s. 7 liberty interest in engaging in prostitution was similarly not appealing to any members of the Court. The deprivation of liberty that comes from criminalizing such conduct, once again, would not appear to violate any recognized principle of fundamental justice.[70] Thus, it would not be necessary to consider s. 1 or even to articulate the government's purpose. Instead, by focusing on the least harmful component of prostitution, the public discussion of price, the government found itself in the position of having to justify an infringement on fundamental rights under s. 1.

New Constitutional Challenges

Paradigms of prostitution matter because they are the lens through which law reform and judicial review take place. These differing views are sometimes glossed over as unimportant, most recently by proponents of "harm reduction," on the ground that we all agree that the important thing is to protect women in prostitution from violence, or that women in prostitution should be decriminalized. But the differences cannot be elided, and sometimes the points of common ground are more apparent than real. Those who assert that prostitution is a career choice may agree with those who argue that it is a form of sexual exploitation that prostituted women should not be punished by a criminal conviction, but their underlying paradigms are fundamentally different, and they produce quite distinct results when applied to buyers and pimps.

The recent constitutional challenges raise two grounds that were not considered in the 1990 *Prostitution Reference:* the s. 7 right to security of the person and the s. 15(1) right to sex equality. The security of the person argument is based on the claim that indirectly criminalizing buyers and pimps, as well as prostituted women themselves, increases the vulnerability of such women to violence. Although a full consideration of this claim is beyond the scope of this chapter, it seems clear that legalizing men's buying and selling of women will not diminish their tendency to act violently toward prostitutes. Nor is it likely to make them want to engage in acts of prostitution in highly visible places. Those men who seek to brutalize and kill prostituted women will simply pay them to come to secluded areas, much like Robert Pickton and Judge David Ramsay did.[71] Moreover, such an argument assumes that prostitution is not, in and of itself, coercive.

If the courts do accept this argument, however, they must consider whether any deprivation of personal security offends the principles of fundamental justice. For this to be true, the applicants must point to a legal principle that is a basic tenet of our legal system and that is capable of definition with some precision.[72] Presumably, the principle must go to the substantive fact of criminalization itself. It is hard to imagine what sort of principle could apply here, since similar arguments were rejected in *Rodriguez* and *Malmo-Levine,* but there is little doubt that the analysis will be influenced by the paradigm according to which prostitution is understood.

If prostitution is understood as a legal activity that concerns acts in private between consenting adults, or as women's work, to criminalize all public communications concerning it in a way that is thought to increase women's vulnerability may violate some form of principle that respects individual privacy, or even the right to equality, if equality is understood as a principle of fundamental justice. The Supreme Court's recent decision that sexual acts in commercial sex clubs are not harmful may signal a growing tolerance for indoor prostitution, especially if it can be depicted as a consensual business transaction between adults.[72] If the paradigm adopted is public nuisance, the provision is vulnerable to an overbreadth argument similar to Justice Wilson's minimal impairment analysis in the *Prostitution Reference.* But if prostitution is to be understood as part of the continuum of male violence against women, to strike down in full a law that criminalizes men's sexual exploitation of women is illogical.

This brings us to the s. 15(1) argument where, once again, the analysis depends on which paradigm of prostitution one applies. The current laws on prostitution do violate s. 15(1) inasmuch as they punish women through criminal conviction for their own sexual exploitation by men. Complainants in rape cases have long argued that rape is the only offence that puts the victim/witness on trial rather than the accused. But prostitution offences actually go further and criminalize the victimized woman herself. The paradigm of prostitution as a practice of sex inequality by definition should support a s. 15(1) claim.

A s. 15(1) claim cannot justify the further step of decriminalizing the buyers and pimps unless this is somehow necessary for their equality relative to women, or for the equality of the women themselves. The former argument can succeed only if a court accepts the paradigm of prostitution as an expression of male sexual freedom. The latter can succeed only if a court accepts the asserted evidentiary foundation for the s. 7 claim and operates according to a paradigm of prostitution as chosen work.

This is more than a mere question of evidence: the paradigm chosen will be fundamentally important in structuring the analysis of the rights claim.

A judgment regarding the inherent violence and inequality of prostitution is required before a consideration of the effects of decriminalizing it is possible. Decriminalization of buyers and pimps in the name of harm reduction locates the harm of prostitution outside the act of prostitution itself. Decriminalization of buyers and pimps also concedes the inevitability of prostitution, since it does nothing to keep women and youth from entering prostitution and even less to assist them in exiting it. More fundamentally, harm reduction erases the fact that prostitution is gendered. A paradigm of prostitution that names it as sex inequality, on the other hand, would not choose decriminalizing those directly responsible for those harms as a logical step to ending prostitution and would never conclude that the *Charter* demands it.

The paradigm adopted is also important, as the *Prostitution Reference* demonstrates, to the s. 1 analysis. If prostitution as nuisance is selected, justifying any s. 7 or 15 violations under s. 1 will be difficult. A threat to women's safety cannot be justified in the name of curbing the social nuisance of street prostitution, especially if the claim that prostitution is a legal activity is given weight in the rights analysis itself.

The question then arises as to whether the government is stuck with the objective that it identified in passing the law, or if it can identify other objectives that might support its continued use. Justice Wilson clearly did not approve of the idea that Parliament could use one objective to get a law passed and another to defend its constitutionality. She demanded consistency in the courts of law and of public opinion. But this consistency ought to extend to the courts' analysis as well, which is why the refusal of all the Supreme Court judges in the *Prostitution Reference* to acknowledge their own prostitution paradigms and how they influenced their reasons for judgment is problematic.

If prostitution is truly degrading to those who are prostituted, and if most prostitutes are women, we can believe either that women want to be degraded more often than do men or that sexism is at work in creating the prostitution industry. I hope that the judges deciding the current constitutional challenges are given the evidence that confronts the physical and psychological brutality of prostitution and the way in which that brutality is fused with societal sex inequality. With that paradigm in place, we can judge whether the current laws relieve, ignore, or further that inequality. This may permit the laws to be struck down only to the extent that they apply to those who are prostituted. If not, it will at least permit new laws to be passed that are grounded in reality.

The danger, however, is that the judges in the current challenges will mistakenly assume that their genuine concern for the dire situation of prostituted women should be addressed through normalizing prostitution so as to promote respect for prostitutes. In fact, this merely fuses these women with what is being done to them – prostitution becomes their identity. Respect for these women means taking seriously the fact that they are human beings who deserve better than prostitution. If, as Justice Wilson's words at the beginning of this chapter suggest, the total legalization or decriminalization of the men who use women in prostitution contributes to the elision of negotiation for back-alley sexual acts to those for the purchase of a painting, it ought to be resisted at all costs.

Acknowledgments

This chapter benefited from conversations with Lee Lakeman, Erin Graham, and other members of the Abolition Coalition. I am grateful for their insights.

Notes

1 *Bedford et al. v. Canada (Attorney-General)* (23 April 2007), Superior Court of Justice, Toronto Court File No. 07-CV-329807PD1; *Canadian Charter of Rights and Freedoms,* s. 7, Part I of the *Constitution Act, 1982,* being Schedule B to the *Canada Act 1982* (U.K.), 1982, c. 11.

2 *Downtown Eastside Sex Workers United against Violence Society v. Attorney General (Canada),* "Statement of Claim" (3 August 2007) Vancouver Registry No. S075285 (B.C. Sup. Ct.). As of April 2009, the future of this litigation is uncertain as the applicants are appealing their denial of standing: *Downtown Eastside Sex Workers United against Violence Society v. Attorney General (Canada),* 2008 BCSC 1726 (CanLII).

3 The lawyer for the Ontario applicants is law professor Alan Young, who has a long history of representing civil libertarian causes; he represented Terri Bedford when she was convicted of bawdy house charges. See *R. v. Bedford,* (2000) 131 O.A.C. 101, 33 C.R. (5th) 143. The Pivot Legal Society, which is pursuing the Vancouver litigation, describes itself as an independent law firm that advances the interests of marginalized persons: for its homepage, see online: <http://www.pivotlegal.org>. Pivot has close ties to the British Columbia Civil Liberties Association.

4 *Reference re ss. 193 and 195.1(1)(c) of the Criminal Code (Man.),* [1990] 1 S.C.R. 1123 [*Prostitution Reference*].

5 *Criminal Code,* R.S.C. 1970, c. C-34, s. 175(1)(c). The provision was repealed in 1972, an act referred to by some commentators as "legalizing" prostitution.

6 *R. v. Moulton* (1979), 19 A.R. 286, 51 C.C.C.(2d) 154 (Alta. C.A.).

7 *R. v. Skinner,* [1990] 1 S.C.R. 1235. For example, the Vancouver Police Department's "Vice Unit" polices prostitution. Its website refers specifically to the "moral" nature of prostitution-related offences. See "Vice Unit" (15 December 2008), online: Vancouver Police Department Investigation Division <http://www.city.vancouver.bc.ca/police/investigation/sis/vice.htm>.

8 Cristin Schmitz, "Can't Lift Publication Bans without Consent: SCC" *Lawyers' Weekly* 15:33 (12 January 1996). The decision was reversed by the Supreme Court of Canada on a s. 40 application on the ground that trial judges lack the discretion to rescind the ban. *R. v. Adams,* [1995] 4 S.C.R. 707.

9 *R. v. Baumgarthuber,* 2007 MBQB 286, 222 Man. R. (2d) 229, [2008] 3 W.W.R. 709 (Q.L.).

10 I am grateful to Lee Lakeman for this observation. Vancouver's "Living in Community" consultation process is an example of this approach. See *e.g.* the discussion of stigmatization in "Action Plan: Final Action Plan" at 23 (June 2007), online: Living in Community <http://www.livingincommunity.ca> ["Living in Community"]. See also Christine Stark, "Girls to Boyz: Sex Radical Women Promoting Pornography and Prostitution" in Christine Stark and Rebecca Whisnant, eds., *Not for Sale: Feminists Resisting Prostitution and Pornography* (Melbourne: Spinfiex, 2004) 278 at 281

11 See *e.g.* the position of John Lowman, criminologist, succinctly summarized in his commentary "Reconvening the Federal Committee on Prostitution Law Reform" (20 July 2004) 171:2 Canadian Medical Association Journal 147.

12 See *e.g.* the comments of "J," prostituted during the 1970s in New York City, in Kate Millett, *The Prostitution Papers* (New York: Ballantyne, 1976) at 58: "I think as long as you're going to have compulsive families and compulsive marriage I think you're going to have prostitution ... Monogamy and prostitution go together."
13 The romanticized presentation of women in prostitution as in control and erotically engaged with their tricks is popular in films and television, from *The Happy Hooker* (1975) to *Pretty Woman* (1990) – promoted with the tagline "Who Knew It Was So Much Fun to Be a Hooker?" – to the new Australian Broadcasting Series *Power Prostitutes,* which follows the legalization of brothels in Australia.
14 Chyng F. Sun, "The Fallacies of Fantasies" in David E. Guinn, ed., *Pornography: Driving the Demand in International Sex Trafficking* (Los Angeles: Captive Daughters Media, 2007) 233 at 234-39, 243-45; Ken Franzblau, "Slavefarm, Sex Tours and the Pimp John T.: Using Pornography to Advance Trafficking, Sex Tourism and Prostitution" in Guinn, *ibid.,* 261 at 261.
15 Ann Russo, "Feminists Confront Pornography's Subordinating Practices: Politics and Strategies for Change" in Gail Dines, Robert Jenson, and Ann Russo, eds., *Pornography: The Production and Consumption of Inequality* (New York: Routledge, 1998) 9 at 10-13, 16-29.
16 For a critique of this distinction, see Sheila Jeffreys, "Challenging the Child/Adult Distinction in Theory and Practice on Prostitution" (2000) 2 Int. Fem. J. of Politics 359. Alternatively, the argument is made that concerns about juvenile prostitution result from a moral panic that overstates the extent and the harm: Deborah Rose Brock, *Making Work, Making Trouble: Prostitution as a Social Problem* (Toronto: University of Toronto Press, 1998).
17 *Criminal Code,* R.S.C. 1985, c. C-46, s. 150.1(5).
18 In Nevada's legalized brothels, the women are forced to undergo sexually transmitted disease (STD) testing and are fired if they test positive. Male customers are not obligated to disclose whether they are infected with any STD, including HIV. Melissa Farley, *Prostitution and Trafficking in Nevada: Making the Connections* (San Francisco: Prostitution Research and Education, 2007).
19 *Criminal Code,* R.S.C. 1970, c. C-34, s. 195.1(1)(c), S.C. 1972, c. 13, s. 15.
20 *R. v. Hutt,* [1978] 2 S.C.R. 476 at 482.
21 *Report of the Subcommittee on Solicitation Laws, the Challenge of Change: A Study of Canada's Criminal Prostitution Laws* (Ottawa: Public Works and Government Services Canada, 2006) c. 4.
22 In Vancouver, the Attorney General was successful in getting an injunction prohibiting street solicitation in the residential West End of downtown. This moved prostitutes out of the West End to the industrial/commercial area on the edge of what is now Yaletown and then into the low-income neighbourhoods of Hastings and Main, Strathcona, and Mount Pleasant. *British Columbia (A.G.) v. Couillard* (1984), 42 C.R. (3d) 273 (S.C.).
23 *R. v. Westendorp,* [1983] 1 S.C.R. 43 [*Westendorp*].
24 *Ibid.*
25 *Criminal Code, supra* note 17 at s. 213(2).
26 *Ibid.* The *Criminal Code* defines "common bawdy house" in s. 197(1) and prohibits being a landlord, keeper, inmate, or "found-in" at a common bawdy house in s. 210.
27 See Lowman, *supra* note 11.
28 Vednita Carter and Evelina Giobbe, "Duet: Prostitution, Racism and Feminist Discourse" (1999) 10 Hastings Women's L.J. 37 at 43-45.
29 *Ibid.*
30 Melissa Farley, ed., *Prostitution, Trafficking and Traumatic Stress* (Binghamton: Haworth Maltreatment and Trauma Press, 2003).
31 Melissa Farley, Jacqueline Lynne, and Ann Cotton, "Prostitution in Vancouver: Violence and the Colonization of First Nations Women" (2005) 42 Transcultural Psychiatry 242.
32 Special Committee on Pornography and Prostitution (Fraser Committee), *Pornography and Prostitution in Canada* (Ottawa: Department of Supply and Services, 1985).
33 Amnesty International, *Stolen Sisters: Discrimination and Violence against Indigenous Women in Canada* (October 2004), online: <www.amnesty.ca/campaigns/resources/amr.2000304.pdf>; Native Women's Association of Canada, *Sisters in Spirit Initiative* (June 2007), online: <http://www.nwac-hq.org/en/NationalAboriginalWomensSummit.htm>.

34 Melissa Farley, "Bad for the Body, Bad for the Heart: Prostitution Harms Women Even If Legalized or Decriminalized" (2004) 10 Violence Against Women 1187; Farley, Lynne, and Cotton, *supra* note 31; Lisa A. Kramer, "Emotional Experiences of Performing Prostitution" in Farley, *supra* note 30 at 187.
35 Melissa Farley, Ann Cotton, and Jacqueline Lynne, "Prostitution and Trafficking in Nine Countries: An Update on Violence and Post-traumatic Stress Disorder" (2003) 2 J. Trauma Practice 33 at 56, 58.
36 "Living in Community," *supra* note 10, takes this view and uses it to emphasize how unlikely it is that persons in prostitution can ever rejoin "regular" society.
37 Lee Lakeman, Alice Lee, and Suzanne Jay, "Resisting the Promotion of Prostitution in Canada: A View from the Vancouver Rape Relief and Women's Shelter" in Stark and Whisnant, *supra* note 10 at 210.
38 Wilbert Keon, heart surgeon and senator, was arrested in Ottawa for soliciting an undercover police officer for prostitution. He was later inducted into the Canadian Medical Hall of Fame. In 2006 BC Provincial Court Judge David Ramsay was sentenced to seven years' imprisonment for his sexual assaults and beatings of teenage Aboriginal girls whom he picked up on the streets of Prince George; he died in jail. Thunder Bay, Ontario, Crown attorney Agnew Johnston was convicted in 1996 for paying teenage girls for sex. One of the girls was a complainant in a sexual assault case he was prosecuting.
39 Scot Wortley and Benedikt Fischer, *An Evaluation of the Toronto John School Diversion Program: Report Prepared for the National Crime Prevention Council and the Department of Justice* (Toronto: Centre of Criminology, University of Toronto, 2001).
40 *R. v. Malmo-Levine; R. v. Caine,* [2003] 3 S.C.R. 571 [*Malmo-Levine*].
41 Mary Sullivan, *What Happens When Prostitution Becomes Work? An Update on the Legalisation of Prostitution in Australia* (Amherst: Coalition against Trafficking in Women, 2005), online: Coalition against Trafficking in Women, <http://www.catwinternational.org/index.php>.
42 Jody Raphael and Deborah L. Shapiro, "Violence in Indoor and Outdoor Prostitution Venues" (2004) 10 Violence Against Women 126.
43 See *e.g.* the definition of sexual harassment in Ontario's *Human Rights Code,* R.S.O. 1990, c. H.19, s. 7(2).
44 Pivot Legal Society, *Beyond Decriminalization: Sex Work, Human Rights and a New Framework for Law Reform* (Vancouver: Pivot Legal Society, 2006), online: Pivot Legal Society, <http://www.pivotlegal.org/Publications/reports.htm>.
45 Margaret A. Baldwin, "Strategies of Connection: Prostitution and Feminist Politics" (1993) 1 Mich. J. Gender & L. 65.
46 Gunilla Ekberg, "The Swedish Law That Prohibits the Purchase of Sexual Services: Best Practices for Prevention of Prostitution and Trafficking in Human Beings" (2004) 10 Violence Against Women 1187.
47 Nevada, which has legalized brothels, also has an active illegal street prostitution industry.
48 Janice G. Raymond, "Prostitution on Demand: Legalizing the Buyers as Sexual Consumers" (2004) 10 Violence Against Women 1156.
49 *R. v. Pickton,* British Columbia Supreme Court, New Westminster Registry, Docket No. X065319-62.
50 Audrey Macklin, "Dancing across Borders: 'Exotic Dancers,' Trafficking, and Canadian Immigration Policy" (2003) 37 International Migration Review 464.
51 G. Allan Marlatt, ed., *Harm Reduction: Pragmatic Strategies for Managing High-Risk Behavior* (New York: Guilford Press, 1998).
52 These have been referred to as the UK (Merseyside) Model and the Dutch Model, respectively. See *ibid.*
53 For a description of the use reduction versus harm reduction debate, see Tom Waller and Daphne Rumball, *Treating Drinkers and Drug Users in the Community* (Oxford, MA: Blackwell Science/Addiction Press, 2004) at 15. A more nuanced critique of harm reduction from a feminist perspective is found in Erin Graham, *Rounding 'Em Up on the East Side of the Wild West: Four Pillars, or One Big Corral?* (M.A. Thesis, University of British Columbia, 2007) at 39-69 [unpublished, on file with the author].

54 For critiques of harm reduction from this perspective, see A. Hathaway, "Shortcomings of Harm Reduction: Toward a Morally Invested Drug Reform Strategy" (2001) 12 Int'l J. of Drug Policy 125. G. Roe, "Harm Reduction as Paradigm: Is Better Than Bad Good Enough?" (2005) 15 Critical Public Health 243.
55 *R. v. Ramsay,* [2004] 22 C.R. (6th) 76 (B.C.S.C.).
56 *R. v. Skinner,* [1990] 1 S.C.R. 1226.
57 *Prostitution Reference, supra* note 4 at 1135, Dickson, C.J.
58 *Ibid.* at 1136.
59 *Ibid.* at 1142.
60 *Westendorp, supra* note 23.
61 *Prostitution Reference, supra* note 4 at 1162.
62 *R. v. Jones,* [1986] 2 S.C.R. 284; *R. v. Morgentaler,* [1988] 1 S.C.R. 30.
63 *Prostitution Reference, supra* note 4 at 1193, Lamer J. quoting from the Ontario Advisory Council on the Status of Women, "Pornography and Prostitution" (1984).
64 *Ibid.* at 1194, Lamer J.
65 *Ibid.* at 1199, Lamer J.
66 *Ibid.* at 1216-17, Wilson J.
67 *Ibid.* at 1216.
68 *Ibid.* at 1215.
69 *Ibid.* at 1210.
70 *Malmo-Levine, supra* note 40; *Rodriguez v. B.C. (A.G.),* [1993] 3 S.C.R. 519 [*Rodriguez*].
71 *R. v. Pickton, supra* note 49.
72 *Rodriguez, supra* note 70
73 *See R. v. Labaye,* [2005] 3 S.C.R. 728, in which the Supreme Court held that a club in which patrons paid a fee to engage in public group sex was not harmful and therefore not "indecent" within the meaning of the *Criminal Code.* To sustain a conviction under the bawdy house law, by contrast, it is not necessary to prove that the acts are indecent or harmful, because the *Criminal Code* prohibits the keeping of any place for the purposes of prostitution. But *Labaye* does indicate that the court requires more than commercialization to prove harm and that it will accept claims of "consent" at face value.

8

Contextualizing Criminal Defences: Exploring the Contribution of Justice Bertha Wilson

Isabel Grant and Debra Parkes

In her influential 1990 speech "Will Women Judges Really Make a Difference?"[1] Justice Bertha Wilson urged judges to make an earnest attempt to "enter into the skin of the litigant and make his or her experience part of your experience and only when you have done that, to judge."[2] Much has been written about the ways in which Justice Wilson made a difference in Canadian law, the legal profession, and the judiciary. In this piece, we examine her work in the area of criminal law defences, asking what her suggestion that judges "enter into the skin" of accused persons might mean for this area of the law. Specifically, we focus on three cases where she examines the conceptual basis of various defences that include an objective reasonableness test; we suggest that these decisions are significant because of the way in which equality informs her attention to the context of the accused's actions and the context of the particular defence at issue.

It can be argued that, in all areas including criminal law, judging involves choosing to consider some contextual or explanatory factors over others; therefore, the question becomes *what sort of* context is relevant rather than *whether* context is relevant.[3] Judges regularly state that they are taking a contextual approach to adjudication in a variety of areas from constitutional law[4] to administrative law[5] to tax law,[6] but it is often unclear what exactly is meant by "context" in a given area. Examination of some of Justice Wilson's opinions on the nature of criminal defences reveals that her contextual approach was informed by her developing conception of equality.

For Justice Wilson, acknowledging the role of context did not necessarily involve applying defences differently to different defendants. She expressly denounced an approach that would *personalize* defences to account for individual characteristics of accused persons, arguing that such personalization undermined equality.[7] We examine whether the distinction between contextualization and personalization is supportable and consider some of the implications and complications inherent in assessing the actions of accused persons *in context.*

In the years since Justice Wilson's retirement, the Supreme Court has more firmly entrenched the doctrine of "moral involuntariness" (sometimes called "normative involuntariness"), which was first developed in *R. v. Perka*[8] as the conceptual basis for several criminal defences.[9] We suggest that this concept, combined with a trend toward personalizing objective tests for these defences, has led, in some cases, to a masking of the normative judgments at stake in criminal law[10] and a departure from the kind of contextual, equality-promoting analysis that Justice Wilson championed in cases such as *R. v. Lavallee.*[11]

In the following section, we survey the opinions penned by Justice Wilson in three important criminal defence cases: *R. v. Perka, R. v. Hill,* and *R. v. Lavallee.* These cases reveal the development in her understanding of equality in criminal law from a formal individualistic understanding of equality in *Perka* through to a nuanced substantive approach to equality in *Lavallee.* Next, we discuss two different ways that context figures in those opinions, first, to understand the accused's actions, and second, to locate the defence itself in its social and historical context to reveal biases and inequalities reflected therein. We then move to examine the Supreme Court's more recent approach to defences, highlighting the ways in which Justice Wilson's equality-informed contextual approach has been both present and absent in some of the Court's recent decisions.

The Role of Context in Defences: Normative Involuntariness and *R. v. Perka*

One of the earliest expressions of Justice Wilson's view on defences can be seen in *Perka,*[12] a case dealing with the defence of necessity. In *Perka,* the accused were smuggling cannabis from Colombia to Alaska. The ship in which they were travelling developed mechanical problems off the coast of Vancouver Island requiring them to land for their own safety. The crew had been ordered to offload the cannabis so that the ship would not capsize. The accused were charged with importing cannabis into Canada for the purposes of trafficking. The primary defence was necessity, a common law defence. Justice Dickson wrote the majority judgment in which he conceptualized necessity as an excuse. Justice Wilson wrote separate concurring reasons questioning the exclusive focus on an excuse analysis and leaving open the option of conceptualizing necessity as a justification. An excuse-based defence is one that recognizes the wrongfulness of the accused's actions but holds that those actions should not be punished, because of some characteristic or circumstance specific to the accused. By contrast, conceptualizing a defence as a justification indicates that, in the circumstances, the conduct was not wrongful. To put it another way, justifications look at the blameworthiness of the act, whereas excuses focus on the circumstances of the actor.[13] Self-defence has been characterized as a justification, whereas duress generally has been considered an excuse.[14] The majority judgment in *Perka* introduced the concept of normative involuntariness, derived from the work of American scholar George Fletcher, as the foundation of the defence.[15] Although the conduct in question is not literally involuntary, the accused is seen as having had no real choice in the circumstances but to break the law. Exculpation is based on a concession to human frailty where the accused could not have been expected to act otherwise in an emergency situation.

Justice Wilson's judgment in *Perka* demonstrates her early views on the way that equality informs and shapes defences. She disagreed with the majority view that the necessity defence was based on a concession to human frailty. Rather, she would have left open the option of basing necessity on a theory of justification[16] whereby an actor's behaviour would be justified if he or she had two conflicting legal duties and chose the one that caused the least harm. In Justice Wilson's view, compassion for the actor must be considered in sentencing but not at the stage of assessing liability, because to do so would undermine principles of equality.[17] Culpability must be based on a normative assessment of the act, not on compassion for the actor. Relying on the famous *R. v. Dudley and Stephens* necessity case,[18] she posited equality as an underlying principle of criminal liability and exculpation: "The underlying principle here is the universality of rights, that all individuals whose actions are subjected to legal evaluation must be considered equal in standing. Indeed, it may be said that this concept of equal assessment of every actor, regardless of his particular motives or the particular pressures operating upon his will, is so fundamental to the criminal law as rarely to receive explicit articulation."[19] In questioning the concession to human frailty analysis, she rejected compassion as the basis for defences: "Where ... a defence by way of excuse is premised on compassion for the accused or on a perceived failure to achieve a desired instrumental end of punishment, the judicial response must be to fashion an appropriate sentence but to reject the defence as such. The only conceptual premise on which necessity as an excuse could rest is the inherent impossibility of a court's responding in any way to an act which, although wrongful, was the one act which any rational person would commit."[20] Justice Wilson's concerns about using human frailty as the basis for defences are clear in *Perka,* but her analysis of equality is undeveloped and, at times, resembles a formal equality approach, focusing on sameness and identical treatment for accused persons.[21] As demonstrated in *Lavallee,* discussed later in this chapter, Justice Wilson later utilized a substantive equality analysis, which goes beyond sameness and difference to acknowledge and address existing inequalities including, for example, the law's failure to respond adequately to the situation of women who have experienced violence and abuse.[22] Arguably, though the facts in *Perka* did not raise substantive equality concerns in the same way as did *Lavallee,* there may be room in future cases to consider what a substantive equality approach might mean for the defence of necessity, particularly in light of concerns that the defence has failed to address class-based inequality.[23]

A Limited Recognition of Context: *R. v. Hill*

Justice Wilson returned to the role of equality in conceptualizing and applying defences in her dissenting opinion in *Hill,*[24] where the issue was the scope of the "ordinary person" or "objective" component of the provocation defence. Provocation, if successful, reduces what would otherwise have been murder to manslaughter on the basis that the accused, provoked by an act or insult of the victim, lost self-control and acted in a sudden, violent manner. The trier of fact must find that an ordinary person would also have lost self-control in the face of the insult. Historically, the characteristics and circumstances of the accused were not attributed to the ordinary person. In *Bedder v. DPP,* for example, the English Court of Appeal held that insults regarding a man's impotence had to be assessed from the standard of an ordinary person who was not impotent.[25] In *R. v. Parnerkar,* the accused's race was not considered relevant to the ordinary person test, even though the provocative insult was a racial one.[26] It could be argued that this very narrow approach to objective tests is falsely premised on a formal equality analysis with the implication that, to achieve equality, the law must treat everyone in the same way: devoid of any unique characteristics and regardless of their circumstances.

Gradually, courts began to look at the circumstances in which the accused found him- or herself in order to understand whether an ordinary person would lose self-control under a particular provocation. Thus, in *R. v. Daniels,* the Northwest Territories Court of Appeal recognized that a history of infidelity and violence was relevant to the final-straw provocative insult when the accused was taunted by her husband's lover.[27] In *Hill,* the Supreme Court accepted the relevance of surrounding circumstances from *Daniels,* going one step further to acknowledge that personal characteristics of the accused may also be considered in applying the objective test, with Justice Wilson's minority opinion being most explicit about the role of this contextual evidence in the jury's task.

Hill involved a fifteen-year-old boy who was accused of killing an older man, allegedly in response to a sexual advance. The victim was the accused's volunteer "Big Brother," and the two had apparently been drinking on the night in question. The issue was whether the jury should be told that the objective inquiry should be undertaken from the position of an ordinary person of the same age and gender as the accused. The majority judgment of Chief Justice Dickson held that gender and age could be considered by a trier of the fact but that the trial judge did not necessarily have to instruct the jury as such. In his view, jury members could use their common sense to determine which factors were relevant to the analysis. Hill's appeal from conviction was thus denied. Justice Wilson wrote one of three dissenting judgments. She held that both age and gender were relevant to the ordinary person analysis. Again, starting with the principles of equality and individual responsibility, she outlined the purpose of the objective test, keeping in mind that the provocation defence was based on a loss of self-control: "The objective standard, therefore, may be said to exist in order to ensure that in the evaluation of the provocation defence there is no fluctuating standard of self-control against which accuseds are measured. The governing principles are those of equality and individual responsibility, so that all persons are held to the same standard notwithstanding their distinctive personality traits and varying capacities to achieve the standard."[28] Given this introduction, one might have expected that Justice Wilson would take a narrow approach to the defence, rejecting the relevance of the accused's characteristics in the name of equality. To the contrary, she based her analysis on a consideration of context that, unlike a personalized objective test, does not depart from the basic premise of equality under the law. In her view, one must understand the context of the provocative insult, not to demonstrate compassion toward the accused, but rather because it sheds light on the nature of the insult and ultimately informs the normative assessment of the reasonableness of the accused's response.[29]

Justice Wilson distinguished between two different ways of using context to satisfy the objective test. First, evidence about the circumstances and characteristics of the accused can put the insult in context. For example, in light of the reality of racism in contemporary society, a racial taunt is likely to provoke an accused of the race in question.[30] Considering the race and gender of the accused does not undermine principles of equality if those factors shed light on the nature of the provocative insult in question. Thus, human frailties may be relevant to the provocation analysis, not because of sympathy or compassion for the accused, or as a recognition of weakness, but rather because they shed light on the ordinariness of the accused's response.

The second use of such evidence would be to argue that the standard of self-control we expect from people with certain characteristics or from certain social groups is lowered. Justice Wilson argued that allowing such characteristics to alter the standard of self-control expected of the accused would almost always undermine the overarching principle of equality. She made an exception, however, for young persons. Acknowledging a lower standard of self-control for young people is consistent with equality and society's recognition that young people are "in the developmental stages *en route* to full functioning capacity as adults."[31]

A Richer Understanding of Context: *R. v. Lavallee*

Lavallee presents the quintessential example of Justice Wilson taking context into account where the law had previously refused to do so.[32] In *Lavallee,* the Court examined a self-defence claim by a woman who had been in a relationship involving repeated abuse. Self-defence, as codified in ss. 34 and 35 of the *Criminal Code,* justifies the use of force, including deadly force, where an individual has been threatened with grievous bodily harm or death.[33] For deadly force to be justified, the accused must reasonably have perceived she was at risk of grievous bodily harm or death and that she could have preserved herself only by using deadly force.

The accused, Angelique Lyn Lavallee, had been repeatedly abused by her partner, the deceased, Kevin Rust. After an argument in an upstairs bedroom, Rust apparently handed Lavallee a gun and indicated that either she must kill him or he would kill her. He also told her she would "get hers later." As Rust was leaving the room, she shot him in the back of the head, killing him.

The difficulty with her self-defence claim was that, because Rust was leaving the room and was unarmed, it could not be argued that Lavallee was under an immediate or imminent threat of grievous bodily harm or death. Accordingly, she did not need to shoot him to preserve herself – she could simply have left the home.

Justice Wilson's analysis focused on the evidence necessary to assist the jury to understand both why the accused felt her life was threatened and why she was unable to escape the violence. In *Lavallee,* Justice Wilson took the analysis further than she did in *Hill,* looking beyond the factual context of the case in question to critique the social context of self-defence by demonstrating the gendered nature of its development.

She noted that the historical and ongoing acceptance of violence against women has meant that it remains underreported and that the experiences of the women involved remain misunderstood. In her view, the jury must be equipped to understand the accused's conduct in its social context so that it could accurately assess the reasonableness of her actions. This context was particularly important because of the gendered way in which self-defence law had evolved and because of the (often false) assumptions made about women in abusive relationships. The jury in a self-defence case is asked to decide what a reasonable person would do if faced with these circumstances. In an oft-quoted passage, Justice Wilson observed the disadvantage imposed on women by the traditional doctrine of self-defence: "If it strains credulity to imagine what the 'ordinary man' would do in the position of a battered spouse, it is probably because men do not typically find themselves in that situation. Some women do, however. The definition of what is reasonable must be adapted to circumstances which are, by and large, foreign to the world inhabited by the hypothetical 'reasonable man.'"[34]

The link between contextualization and equality is also clear in Justice Wilson's judgment in *Lavallee*. In order to give effect to women's equality, it is necessary to recognize that their circumstances and experiences, as well as their perceptions, may differ from those of men because of the ongoing reality of sex inequality and violence in intimate relationships. Justice Wilson quoted from an American decision in *State v. Wanrow*[35] to establish the connection between the development of self-defence law and sex inequality: "The respondent was entitled to have the jury consider her actions in the light of her own perceptions of the situation, including those perceptions which were the product of this nation's 'long and unfortunate history of sex discrimination.' Until such time as the effects of that history are eradicated, care must be taken to assure that our self-defense instructions afford women the right to have their conduct judged in light of the individual physical handicaps which are the product of sex discrimination."[36] This is not to suggest that all women who experience abuse respond in the same way or that all those who kill their abusive spouses are entitled to an acquittal. Justice Wilson acknowledged that women who have been battered may well kill their partners other than in self-defence. The focus is not on who the woman is, but on what she did and the reasonableness of her actions when viewed in that broad social context.[37] With respect to Lavallee herself, Justice Wilson concluded that there was sufficient evidence to demonstrate that the accused was acutely aware of when violence was likely to follow and that she was reasonable in believing that she could not extricate herself from it. Thus, the jury's decision to acquit was upheld.

We recognize that *Lavallee* can (and has) been interpreted as, in essence, utilizing contextual evidence in a manner consistent with a "concession to human frailties" approach to self-defence. In particular, expert evidence of "battered woman syndrome" (which is based on the assumption that "learned helplessness" results from persistent abuse) may be interpreted as focusing the inquiry on what standard of behaviour can be expected of a "helpless" battered woman. It is this interpretation that has been criticized as creating a new stereotype of the battered woman and for seeming to lower the standard expected of her, rather than focusing on the reasonableness of her actions in a context that may not be easily understood.[38] We argue that *Lavallee* should, instead, be seen as utilizing social context evidence to understand the reality faced by women who experience persistent abuse, an understanding that is necessary to applying a standard of reasonableness to their use of violence against an abusive partner. Part of that reality is the recognition that women are most in danger of lethal violence when they try to extricate themselves from a violent relationship[39] and that they may reasonably believe the police will not protect them.[40] In addition, women who have experienced persistent abuse may have a heightened awareness of impending violence and its severity.

We see a significant distinction between a contextual inquiry focused on discerning the reasonableness of an accused person's actions and a more personalized inquiry focused on the particular frailties of an accused, leading to a potentially lower standard of behaviour expected of a person with those experiences or characteristics.[41] *Lavallee* recognizes that the prevailing inequality in heterosexual relationships may shed light on the reasonableness of a woman's actions in ways jurors might not otherwise understand.

In light of allegations that Justice Wilson was a "judicial activist,"[42] it is significant to note that she grounded her analysis firmly in legal doctrine.[43] In *Lavallee,* for example, she did not depart from the statutory framework of self-defence but rather incorporated an equality-sensitive examination of social context into that framework. It is the s. 34(2) criteria that form the foundation of the self-defence claim.

Two Roles for Context: Contextualizing the Accused's Actions and the Defence Itself

Justice Wilson's view of the individual is essentially a liberal one that emphasizes "individual responsibility"[44] and autonomy.[45] However, the contextual approach she championed pays close attention to the relationships between individuals and their environment and community.[46] We argue that Justice Wilson's consideration of context in criminal defences focuses on two key inquiries, both of which are infused with conceptions of equality.

First, context helps decision makers understand the actions of accused persons in their circumstances, particularly where those circumstances may be outside the trier of fact's everyday understanding. As discussed earlier, this differs from "personalizing" a defence, which would essentially lower the standard expected of the accused. Rather, this approach sheds light on the reasonableness of the accused's actions.

Juries construct stories out of the evidence provided to them, cobbled together with their own life experiences. Justice Wilson's opinions in both *Hill* and *Lavallee* are about helping the jury to assemble the story that will most accurately and fairly evaluate the actions of the accused.[47] This is not to take pity on the accused but rather to help the jury, particularly where the context may differ from its own, to construct a narrative that actually incorporates the experience of the accused.[48]

Second, Justice Wilson extended the contextual inquiry to examine the social context of the defence itself, allowing the decision maker to assess the values promoted by the defence and the requisite normative judgments to be made about the accused's conduct. This sort of contextual inquiry, rooted in a commitment to gender equality in *Lavallee,* expanded the application of self-defence to take into account the experiences of women in abusive relationships and might be employed in a similar way to render duress[49] and necessity[50] more inclusive and consistent with gender equality. Such an approach could, however, result in circumscribing other defences, such as provocation, that may perpetuate inequality.

This second use of context looks at the defence itself, its history and development, the values associated with its application, and how it relates to the case at issue. Recognizing context is never a value-neutral exercise. Justice Wilson's opinion in *Lavallee* was grounded in this recognition, meaning that an evaluation of the normative foundation and paradigmatic narrative of the defence itself was vital to her contextual inquiry. Essentially, Justice Wilson asked in *Lavallee,* "what would self-defence look like if it were inclusive of women's experiences of gendered violence?" The social context evidence of women in abusive relationships was directed at answering this question, as well as at assessing the reasonableness of Lavallee's actions within this newly contextualized framework.

Justice Wilson's analysis in *Lavallee* was more attuned to social context than was her judgment in *Hill.* The defence of provocation cries out for an analysis that locates it within its historical context. Provocation is rooted in a long history of excusing male violence against women[51] and, more recently, excusing homophobic violence against gay men.[52] The inquiry of whether an "ordinary person" would lose self-control in the face of a particular insult carries the potential to excuse male violence against women or against gay men, particularly if gender inequality and homophobia are sufficiently "ordinary" in Canadian society.[53] In *Hill,* gender was effectively used as a proxy for sexual orientation, with the underlying assumption being that a same-sex sexual advance is more likely than a heterosexual advance to deprive the ordinary (presumptively heterosexual) man of self-control to the point of lethal violence.[54]

The above analysis of the three judgments of Justice Wilson demonstrates that her understanding and use of context evolved through her early decision in *Perka,* culminating in *Lavallee* where she explicitly used context in the second way referred to here, to develop the doctrine of self-defence to promote gender equality. Noting the extent to which the norm of equality informed these opinions demonstrates that a contextual methodology can avoid the critics' charge of being an unprincipled purely result-oriented inquiry into a range of background facts.

Defences in the Supreme Court of Canada after Justice Wilson

Since Justice Wilson's retirement, the Supreme Court has developed its jurisprudence of criminal defences in two significant ways. First, the Court has entrenched the personalized objective test for all "affirmative defences" such as duress, necessity, self-defence, and provocation.[55] Second, the Court has adopted moral voluntariness as a principle of fundamental justice under s. 7 of the *Charter,* meaning that morally involuntary conduct cannot be criminally punished.[56] Both of these doctrinal developments came in cases involving duress, a defence that was not the subject of a Wilson opinion at the Supreme Court, but that is closely related to necessity and self-defence and can be informed by her analysis relating to these other defences. We consider each of these developments in turn and use the Court's approach to personalizing the objective test for provocation in *R. v. Thibert* to demonstrate the difference between personalization and a full contextual inquiry, as well as the potential dangers of an open so-called contextual inquiry.[57]

Personalizing the Objective Test: *R. v. Hibbert* and *R. v. Latimer*

Throughout the mid- to late-1990s, the Supreme Court adopted an approach to adjudicating criminal defences that incorporated the personal characteristics and experiences of the accused into the objective test. *R. v. Hibbert*[58] was a landmark decision because it settled that "a personalized objective test" was appropriate for defences, although the Court had earlier rejected such an approach for objective tests in the definition of offences such as those involving criminal negligence.[59] The Supreme Court held in *Hibbert* that, in applying the objective elements of duress, the accused's "perceptions of the surrounding facts can be highly relevant to the determination of whether [his or her] conduct was reasonable under the circumstances, and thus whether his or her conduct is properly excusable."[60]

Lawrence Hibbert was charged with the attempted murder of his friend Fitzroy Cohen, on the basis that he was a party to the offence. Hibbert called the victim down to the lobby of his apartment building, allegedly under threats from a co-accused who ultimately shot Cohen. The jury convicted Hibbert of the included offence of aggravated assault. The Supreme Court ordered a new trial for Hibbert, in part because the trial judge erred in not instructing the jury that the existence of a "safe avenue of escape" from the threats was to be determined on a personalized objective basis, to include consideration of the accused's ability to perceive an alternative course of action.

In his analysis for the Court, Chief Justice Lamer stated that each of the three defences of duress, necessity, and self-defence employs a personalized objective test that "takes into account the ... human frailties of the accused."[61] At various points throughout the decision, he lumped the three defences together under the rubric of excuse-based defences,[62] even though self-defence is conventionally characterized as a justification.[63] He also relied on the concept of normative involuntariness as the theoretical basis for at least the defences of necessity and duress.[64] He explained that it was important to take the particular frailties of an accused into account, stating that "a person does not 'choose' inaction when he or she is *incapable* in the first place of acting, or of knowing when to act."[65] The focus was on the degree to which the accused could be expected to make a rational judgment, given his or her experiences or characteristics, an approach that may amount to lowering the standard of behaviour expected of some accused persons. In this way, personalizing an objective test is different from the contextualization we see in *Lavallee.*

Most recently, the Supreme Court has personalized elements of the objective test for the defence of necessity. In *R. v. Latimer,* the only Supreme Court decision to consider that defence since *Perka,* the Court held unanimously that there was no air of reality to Robert Latimer's claim that he was acting out of necessity when he killed his daughter, Tracy, who had a severe form of cerebral palsy.[66] In analyzing the necessity claim, the Court held that the first two elements of the defence – namely, whether the accused was in a situation of imminent peril and whether there was no reasonable legal alternative to breaking the law – were assessed by using a personalized objective test. The Court confirmed that the proportionality element (*i.e.,* weighing the harm caused by the accused's conduct against the harm avoided) was not personalized. It remained a true objective assessment "since evaluating the gravity of the act is a matter of community standards infused with constitutional considerations (such as, in this case, the section 15(1) equality rights of the disabled)."[67] Nevertheless, for the first two elements, the Court relied on *Hibbert* for the proposition that "it is appropriate, in evaluating the accused's conduct, to take into account personal characteristics that legitimately affect what may be expected of that person."[68]

Given Justice Wilson's rejection of an exclusive excuse-based analysis for necessity, together with her concern about personalizing objective tests to effectively lower the standard expected of the accused rather than to assess the reasonableness of his or her actions, we suggest that she may have had reservations about the conceptual approach taken to necessity in *Latimer,* while agreeing with the proportionality analysis and the result. If one looks beyond *Latimer,* it is clear that necessity is closely circumscribed in Anglo-Canadian law. It has been limited to situations of "imminent peril" that the courts have confined to unusual emergencies, rather than persistent social emergencies such as homelessness.[69] Personalizing the objective test to account for individual human frailties, particularly when necessity is conceptualized as excusing normatively involuntary behaviour, does not address the broader context and critiques of the defence.

The Perils of Context Unlimited: *R. v. Thibert*

The Court's decision in *Thibert,* involving the provocation defence, demonstrates some potential dangers of an open so-called contextual inquiry where the objective test is personalized to effectively lower the standard of conduct expected of the accused, without attending to social inequalities underlying the defence.[70] In a narrow three-to-two decision, the Court developed an analysis of provocation resting on a recognition of human frailty. Thibert, the accused, was charged with murdering his estranged wife's lover. Carrying a sawed-off shotgun in his car, he went to meet his wife at her workplace to plead with her to return to the marriage. He admitted that he had planned to use the gun to kill the deceased but claimed that he changed his mind before arriving at his wife's workplace. He met her outside the workplace, and the victim soon joined them. Thibert confronted the pair with the loaded gun. In the alleged provocative act, the deceased stood behind the accused's wife, moving her body back and forth like a shield and saying, "[C]ome on big fellow, shoot me. You want to shoot me? Go ahead and shoot me."[71]

In holding that there was an air of reality to the defence of provocation, Justice Cory began by linking the objective test to the recognition of human frailties: "I think the objective element should be taken as an attempt to weigh in the balance those very human frailties which sometimes lead people to act irrationally and impulsively against the need to protect society by discouraging acts of homicidal violence."[72] Conceptually, an understanding of human frailties may justify the subjective branch of the provocation defence (*i.e.,* the requirement that the accused was, in fact, provoked), but such an approach has never been used as the basis for determining whether an ordinary person would have been so provoked. To the contrary, in *Hill,* for example, Chief Justice Dickson stated that the objective test was intended to set a minimum standard of behaviour for all persons: "It is society's concern that reasonable and non-violent behaviour be encouraged that prompts the law to endorse the objective standard. The criminal law is concerned, among other things with fixing standards for human behaviour. We seek to encourage conduct that complies with certain societal standards of reasonableness and responsibility."[73]

The majority in *Thibert* took what we can only describe as a generous approach to the ordinary person component of the provocation defence. Relying on *Hill* and *Daniels,* the majority considered the following evidence as "context": that Thibert's wife had planned to leave him on a previous occasion, but he had convinced her to return; that Thibert was distraught and had not slept for thirty-four hours; that he wanted very badly to speak to his wife in private; and that the deceased held Ms. Thibert "by her shoulders in a proprietary and possessive manner and moved her back and forth in front of him while he taunted the accused to shoot him."[74] This, in the view of the majority, was sufficient to put the defence to the jury. It was suggested that, under such circumstances, an ordinary married man faced with the breakup of his marriage might well have lost his self-control in the face of such provocation.[75]

In a stinging dissent, Justice Major found no evidence to support putting the defence to the jury. The uncontradicted evidence was that Thibert confronted the deceased with a loaded weapon and remained in control of that weapon throughout the encounter. It was inappropriate for the law to tell victims how they were expected to respond when faced with such a threat. The accused had no right to demand a private meeting with his wife: "At law, no one has either an emotional or proprietary right or interest in a spouse that would justify the loss of self-control that the appellant exhibited."[76]

How can our understanding of Justice Wilson's approach to context help to explain what went wrong in *Thibert*? Both the majority and the dissent attempted to contextualize the objective test. Both brought in relevant factors that put the insult in context, although the two judgments presented very different views of the factual context. Such an approach is consistent with the first kind of contextualization found in Justice Wilson's opinions – rendering the accused's act intelligible to the trier of fact. Yet the emphasis on Thibert's "very human frailties which sometimes lead people to act irrationally and impulsively" is more focused on lowering the level of conduct expected of a man who is unable to accept that a partner has left the relationship. What is missing from the majority judgment is any attempt to engage in the second kind of contextualization – that is, contextualizing the defence itself. *Thibert* is a clear example of why these two types of contextual inquiry are not conceptually distinct. To contextualize the facts in a case, one must be aware of the social context of the defence at issue. This is why *Lavallee* was groundbreaking. Lavallee's experiences were interpreted through the lens of the gender inequality that had informed self-defence law.

Provocation has a long history of gender inequality, whereby men have successfully used the defence after killing a female partner who had been unfaithful or who was trying to leave the relationship.[77] The majority judgment in *Thibert* portrayed male violence in heterosexual relationships as an excusing factor, perpetuating the notion of women as the property of their husbands. Rather than questioning the paradigmatic account of the defence (as Justice Wilson did in *Lavallee*), the majority in *Thibert* used "context" in a way that entrenched the paradigmatic defence, including the arguably discriminatory assumptions embedded within it.

The approach taken by the dissent, by contrast, was consistent with Justice Wilson's consideration of the social context of violence against women. It was also consistent with her concern in *Hill* that the objective test for provocation not be simply watered down to empty it of any normative judgment about acceptable conduct and self-control. Whereas defences such as necessity and duress acknowledge fear and the desire to protect oneself or loved ones, provocation privileges rage and a lack of self-control as mitigating factors. As such, it is ripe for the kind of equality-informed evaluation made of self-defence in *Lavallee*.[78]

Constitutionalizing Moral Involuntariness: *R. v. Ruzic*

The second important development in defences relates to constitutionalization of the principle of moral voluntariness as a prerequisite for criminal fault. In the 2001 decision in *R. v. Ruzic,* the Supreme Court of Canada elevated the concept of moral involuntariness to a principle of fundamental justice under s. 7 of the *Charter.*[79] Marijana Ruzic, a resident of Belgrade in the former Yugoslavia, was charged with importing narcotics into Canada and possessing a false passport. She claimed that she had smuggled the drugs because she had been told that her family would be seriously harmed if she did not comply. She raised the statutory defence of duress and successfully argued that the elements of the defence requiring immediacy of the threats and presence of the threatener violated s. 7. Justice LeBel, for a unanimous Court, held that Ruzic was entitled to rely on the more generous common law defence of duress, which had no immediacy or presence requirements, on the basis that she was acting in a morally involuntary manner.

The Court entrenched normative involuntariness as a principle of fundamental justice protected by s. 7 of the *Charter* such that only morally voluntary acts can be punished by the criminal law, a principle that would seem to apply beyond excuse-based defences such as duress.[80] Justice LeBel held that a "person acts in a morally involuntary fashion when, faced with perilous circumstances, she is deprived of a realistic choice whether to break the law."[81] Much like a physically involuntary act, the accused's act under duress could not meaningfully be attributed to her because her "conduct is not, in a realistic way, freely chosen."[82]

It has been argued that this focus on voluntariness is based on a mechanistic account of human agency and thereby "acts as a normative veil, hiding the underlying assumptions about what emotions are legitimate or illegitimate, [and] what actions are good or bad."[83] Furthermore, the formulation of normative involuntariness in *Ruzic* is extremely broad, suggesting that conduct that is normatively involuntary can never be punished. This conceptual basis for defences is potentially broader than the concept of moral innocence that the Court rejected in *Ruzic*[84] on the basis that it was "undefinable and potentially far-reaching" in nature.[85]

What do the judgments of Justice Wilson tell us about the adoption of normative involuntariness as the conceptual basis for defences? At the very least, she focuses the application of the objective test on equality and on the notion that accused persons are rational actors making choices in what are often very difficult circumstances. Although those circumstances must be evaluated in light of the historical development and biases inherent in the defence in question, denying the accused's agency in deciding how to respond is not adequate. Given Justice Wilson's analysis in *Lavallee,* it is likely that she would have reached a result similar to that of the Court in *Ruzic,* abolishing the immediacy and the presence requirements of the duress defence of s. 17 of the *Criminal Code.* However, we know from *Perka* that Justice Wilson was concerned about basing defences on a concession to human frailty, a concept that is at the heart of normative involuntariness. Rather, we believe she would have focused on the rational decision made by the accused and would perhaps have asked whether Ruzic avoided a greater harm by committing the offence.

When *Lavallee* is read together with *Perka* and *Hill,* we discern an approach to criminal defences that is, on the whole, at odds with the mechanistic account of human behaviour[86] (*i.e.,* the accused had no real choice) inherent in the normative involuntariness concept. Justice Wilson did not shy away from the idea that accused persons were responsible for their actions, but she did not accept that the normative assumptions about acceptable human motivations built into our existing criminal defences are always just. In some cases, those assumptions are inaccurate or inconsistent with fundamental values such as equality.

Concluding Thoughts on Context and Criminal Defences

Contextualism, which has been called the "Supreme Court's new standard of judicial analysis and accountability,"[87] has come to pervade judicial decision making, at least to the extent that judges regularly appeal to context. Richard Devlin and Matthew Sherrard suggest that taking a contextual approach means that judges should "tailor their responsibilities to the realities of *systemic and intersectional inequality* in Canadian society."[88] The work of Justice Wilson in cases such as *Lavallee* has begun this process for criminal defences, but, as cases such as *Thibert* reveal, much work remains to be done. We hope that the Court's increased reliance on the concept of normative involuntariness will not impede its consideration of both forms of context discussed in this chapter, which, we believe, provide some principles to guide the ongoing development of the doctrine of criminal defences in an equality-promoting manner.

We do not mean to suggest that Justice Wilson's decisions provide a blueprint for substantive equality in the criminal law, which is a massive and perhaps impossible task in the context of our existing criminal justice system.[89] It would be inappropriate to read too much of our own critiques of substantive criminal law doctrine into her decisions, particularly given her apparent commitment to a cautious, incremental approach to developing the law. Nevertheless, her contributions in this area are worth considering, along with those of other recent members of the Court.[90]

As Rosemary Cairns Way has argued, the strict doctrinal dichotomy between subjective and objective fault, and particularly the early *Charter* trend toward constitutionalizing certain fault requirements, "masks the normative complexity of the allocation of blame."[91] The flip side of allocating blame is determining the scope of exculpation through the application of criminal defences, a task that involves equally complex normative judgments.[92] We see in Justice Wilson's contextual approach a willingness to wrestle with difficult normative issues in criminal law, at least to the extent of encouraging us to question the conceptual foundations of certain defences and the way that some defences may entrench existing inequalities. It will be up to the present Court to determine the extent to which this approach will influence future development of criminal law defences.

Acknowledgments

The authors thank Grant Hughes for his research assistance and the Manitoba Legal Research Institute for its support of this project. Thank you also to Benjamin Berger, Kim Brooks, Melina Buckley, and Jennifer O'Leary, who read drafts of this chapter and provided helpful feedback.

Notes

1 Bertha Wilson, "Will Women Judges Really Make a Difference?" (1990) 28 Osgoode Hall L.J. 507.

2 *Ibid.* at 521.

3 In *R. v. S. (R.D.),* [1997] 3 S.C.R. 484 [*R.D.S.*], the opinion of Justices McLachlin and L'Heureux-Dubé quotes Justice Cardozo on the impossibility of true judicial neutrality: "All their lives, forces which [judges] do not recognize and cannot name, have been tugging at them – inherited instincts, traditional beliefs, acquired convictions; and the resultant is an outlook on life, a conception of social needs ... We may try to see things as objectively as we please. None the less, we can never see them with any eyes except our own." B.N. Cardozo, *The Nature of the Judicial Process* (New Haven: Yale University Press, 1921) quoted in *R.D.S.* at para. 34.

4 See *e.g. Law v. Canada (Minister of Employment and Immigration),* [1999] 1 S.C.R. 497 at paras. 62-75 (on equality rights). The malleability of the "contextual approach" established in *Law* has been the subject of much critical commentary. See *e.g.* Sheilah Martin, "Balancing Individual Rights to Equality and Social Goals" (2001) 80 Can. Bar Rev. 299.

5 Lorne Sossin and Colleen M. Flood, "The Contextual Turn: Iacobucci's Legacy and the Standard of Review in Administrative Law" (2007) 57 U.T.L.J. 581; Robert Leckey, *Contextual Subjects: Family, State, and Relational Theory* (Toronto: University of Toronto Press, 2008) at 175-208.

6 J.E. (Ted) Fulcher, "Using a Contextual Methodology to Accommodate Equality Protections along with the Other Objectives of Government (with Particular Reference to the *Income Tax Act*): 'Not the Right Answer, Stupid. The Best Answer'" (1996) 34 Alta. L. Rev. 416.

7 Justice Wilson rejected a personalized objective test in contexts other than defences. In *R. v. Tutton,* [1989] 1 S.C.R. 1392, for example, a case in which parents were charged with manslaughter for failing to provide insulin to their diabetic child because they believed he had been healed by God, the issue was whether the *mens rea* for criminal negligence should be assessed on an objective or subjective standard. The Court split three to three, with Justice Wilson writing reasons in favour of subjective fault. She rejected the attempt by Justice Lamer to incorporate the personal characteristics of the accused into an objective standard of liability.

8 *R. v. Perka,* [1984] 2 S.C.R. 232 [*Perka*].

9 *R. v. Ruzic,* 2001 SCC 24, [2001] 1 S.C.R. 687 [*Ruzic*]. (Although *Ruzic* was a duress case, the case law indicates that the principle of moral or normative involuntariness applies to other defences as well.)

10 Benjamin L. Berger, "Emotions and the Veil of Voluntarism: The Loss of Judgment in Canadian Criminal Defences" (2006) 51 McGill L.J. 99.

11 *R. v. Lavallee,* [1990] 1 S.C.R. 852 [*Lavallee*].

12 *Perka, supra* note 8.

13 For a critique of the distinction between justifications and excuses, see Berger, *supra* note 10 at 104. Berger argues that all affirmative defences, whether conceptualized as excuses or justifications, have as their core a set of normative evaluations about the appropriate way to act.
14 See s. 34 of the *Criminal Code,* R.S.C. 1985, c. C-46 (self-defence); *R. v. Hibbert,* [1995] 2 S.C.R. 973 [*Hibbert*] (duress).
15 George Fletcher, *Rethinking Criminal Law* (Boston: Little Brown, 1978).
16 Necessity is conceptualized as a justification in, for example, the French and German legal systems, as well as in the American Law Institute's Model Penal Code. See Benjamin L. Berger, "A Choice among Values: Theoretical and Historical Perspectives on the Defence of Necessity" (2002) 39 Alta. L. Rev. 848 at paras. 28-35.
17 Wilson's consideration of equality in this case (and in others such as *R. v. Hill,* [1986] 1 S.C.R. 313 [*Hill*], where she pairs the notion with "individual responsibility") indicates a liberal formal equality approach that favours treating accused persons in the same manner. However, her later use of context in *Lavallee, supra* note 11, with its emphasis on the ongoing reality of violence against women and the failure of the law to respond to that reality, seems grounded in a vision of substantive equality.
18 Dudley and Stephens were sailors who were charged with the murder of a young member of their crew on the high seas and who claimed that they killed only under conditions of necessity – a shipwreck and near-certain starvation. The House of Lords rejected their claim of necessity and set very narrow parameters on the defence. *R. v. Dudley and Stephens* (1884), 14 Q.B.D. 273.
19 *Perka, supra* note 8 at para. 91.
20 *Ibid.* at para. 105.
21 Christine Boyle, "The Role of Equality in Criminal Law" (1994) 58 Sask. L. Rev. 203 at 213.
22 *Lavallee, supra* note 11.
23 See *R. v. Creighton,* [1993] 3 S.C.R. 3 [*Creighton*] (concerning unsuccessful claims of necessity arising out of poverty and homelessness).
24 *Hill, supra* note 17.
25 *Bedder v. DPP* (1954), 2 All E.R. 801 (C.A.).
26 The accused, a South Asian man, had stabbed to death the woman whom he intended to marry. Her son testified that she had told the accused "I am not going to marry you because you are a black man," just before he stabbed her. *R. v. Parnerkar,* [1974] S.C.R. 449 at 457.
27 *R. v. Daniels* (1983), 7 C.C.C. (3d) 542 (N.W.T. C.A.).
28 *Hill, supra* note 17 at para. 68.
29 *Ibid.* at para. 72.
30 See generally Camille Nelson, "(En)Raged or (En)Gaged: The Implications of Racial Context to the Canadian Provocation Defence" (2002) 35 U. Rich. L. Rev. 1007. While on the Ontario Court of Appeal, Wilson J. was the lone dissenter in favour of allowing provocation to go to the jury in a case where evidence indicated that the black accused had been called a "two-bit nigger punk" by the deceased. See *R. v. Olbey* (1977), 38 C.C.C. (2d) 390.
31 *Hill, supra* note 17 at 350.
32 *Lavallee, supra* note 11.
33 *Criminal Code,* R.S. 1985, c. C-46.
34 *Lavallee, supra* note 11 at 874.
35 *State v. Wanrow,* 559 P. (2d) 548 (Wash. Sup. Ct. 1977).
36 *Ibid.* at 559, quoted in *Lavallee, supra* note 11 at 875.
37 Christine Boyle has argued that "*Lavallee* may be the best-known example of an attempt to take an approach in which gender is not extracted out of the context." Christine Boyle, "The Role of the Judiciary in the Work of Madame Justice Wilson" (1992) 15 Dal. L.J. 241 at 246.
38 Isabel Grant, "The 'Syndromization' of Women's Experience" Part 4 in "A Forum on *Lavallee v. the Queen:* Women and Self-Defence" (1991) 25 U.B.C. L. Rev. 23 at 51-59.
39 Canadian Centre for Justice Statistics, "National Trends in Intimate Partner Homicides, 1974-2000" (2002) 22:5 Juristat 1 (reporting that women separated from their abusive partners were killed at the highest rate among spousal homicides).

40 Elizabeth A. Sheehy, "Causation, Common Sense, and the Common Law: Replacing Unexamined Assumptions with What We Know about Male Violence against Women or from *Jane Doe* to *Bonnie Mooney*" (2005) 17 C.J.W.L. 87.

41 We thank Benjamin Berger for his insightful comments on this aspect of our argument and for urging us to articulate more clearly our concern about conceiving of defences as concessions to *personal* human frailties.

42 Robert Hawkins and Robert Martin, "Democracy, Judging and Bertha Wilson" (1995) 41 McGill L.J. 1.

43 See also Wilson's judgment on intoxication in *R. v. Bernard,* [1988] 2 S.C.R. 833, which formed the basis of the Court's later decision in *R. v. Daviault,* [1994] 3 S.C.R. 63.

44 *Hill, supra* note 17.

45 In *R. v. Morgentaler,* [1988] 1 S.C.R. 30 at 166, Wilson J. was alone in viewing the criminal prohibition on abortion as a violation of women's liberty rights to "make fundamental personal decisions without interference from the state."

46 Danielle Pinard, "The Constituents of Democracy: The Individual in the Work of Madame Justice Wilson" (1992) 15 Dal. L.J. 81 at 91-92 (arguing that "one finds in Judge Wilson's work one preoccupation for the individual as a socially constructed being, and another for the welfare of the community as a whole").

47 See Marilyn MacCrimmon, "The Social Construction of Reality and the Rules of Evidence" in Donna Martinson *et al.,* "A Forum on *Lavallee v. R:* Women and Self-Defence" (1991) 25 U.B.C. L. Rev. 23 at 36-50.

48 See also Hester Lessard, "Equality and Access to Justice in the Work of Bertha Wilson *Symposium Proceedings*" (1992) 15 Dal. L.J. 35 at 60.

49 See Isabel Grant, "Exigent Circumstances: The Relevance of Repeated Abuse to the Defence of Duress" (1997) 2 Can. Crim. L. Rev. 331 (where the author examines the relevance of *Lavallee* in cases involving women who commit crimes under the duress of abusive male partners).

50 In one lower court decision, *R. v. Lalonde* (1995), 22 O.R. (3d) 275 (Gen. Div.), allowing a necessity defence to (welfare) fraud charges, the Court took into account the accused woman's experience of abuse at the hands of her former common law partner. Although the analysis is not well developed, the case has been described as significant for, among other reasons, recognizing the impact of battering as essential to contextualizing the "highly rigid doctrinal requirements of the defence of necessity." Sheila Noonan, "*Lalonde:* Evaluating the Relevance of BWS [battered woman syndrome] Evidence" (1995) 37 C.R. (4th) 110 at 111.

51 Andrée Coté, Diana Majury, and Elizabeth Sheehy, "Stop Excusing Violence against Women" (Position paper on the defence of provocation, National Association of Women and the Law, April 2000) [unpublished], online: <http://www.nawl.ca/ns/en/is-vaw.html#provocation>.

52 Bruce MacDougall, *Queer Judgments: Homosexuality, Expression, and the Courts in Canada* (Toronto: University of Toronto Press, 2000) at 154-65; N. Kathleen (Sam) Banks, "The 'Homosexual Panic' Defence in Canadian Criminal Law" (1997) 1 C.R. (5th) 371.

53 On the other hand, it has been argued that a provocation defence, infused with equality considerations, "may provide the sole vehicle ... for a contextual assessment of systemic racism when it plays a role in triggering violent responses." Nelson, *supra* note 30 at 1013-14.

54 MacDougall, *supra* note 52 at 154-65; Banks, *supra* note 52.

55 This approach was confirmed in *Hibbert, supra* note 14.

56 *Ruzic, supra* note 9.

57 *R. v. Thibert,* [1996] 1 S.C.R. 37 [*Thibert*].

58 *Hibbert, supra* note 14.

59 *Creighton, supra* note 23.

60 *Hibbert, supra* note 14 at para. 61.

61 *Ibid.* at para. 60.

62 At other times, he seemed to limit his comments to duress and necessity.

63 Chief Justice Lamer kept provocation analytically distinct from the other three defences, relying on Jeremy Horder for the distinction that provocation (partially) excuses a past

insult, albeit one in the very recent past, whereas the other three defences are aimed at avoiding future harm. *Ibid.* at para. 49, citing Jeremy Horder, "Autonomy, Provocation and Duress" (1992) Crim. L. Rev. 706 at 709.

64 *Hibbert, supra* note 14 at paras. 57, 61-62.

65 *Ibid.* at para. 58 [emphasis in original].

66 *R. v. Latimer,* 2001 SCC 1, [2001] 1 S.C.R. 3.

67 *Ibid.* at para. 34.

68 *Ibid.* at para. 33.

69 Rejecting a claim of necessity to trespass by homeless squatters, Lord Denning stated that, "if hunger were once allowed to be an excuse for stealing, it would open a way through which all kinds of disorder and lawlessness would pass." See *Southwark London Borough Council v. Williams,* [1971] 2 All E.R. 175 at 179 (H.L.).

70 *Thibert, supra* note 57.

71 *Ibid.* at para. 26.

72 *Ibid.* at para. 4.

73 *Hill, supra* note 17 at para. 19. Justice Wilson took a similar view in *Hill,* describing the objective test as ensuring that "there is no fluctuating standard of self-control against which accused are measured." *Ibid.* at para. 68.

74 *Thibert, supra* note 57 at para. 23.

75 See also *R. v. Stone,* [1999] 2 S.C.R. 290 (where, in a case that was framed as a "nagging wife" situation, the Supreme Court did not question the appropriateness of putting provocation to the jury where the accused man killed his estranged wife by stabbing her forty-seven times). For critical commentary, see Coté, Majury, and Sheehy, *supra* note 51 at 7-9.

76 *Thibert, supra* note 57 at para. 65.

77 Coté, Majury, and Sheehy, *supra* note 51.

78 Justice Wilson's opinion in *Lavallee* expanded the scope of self-defence. However, in *R. v. Penno,* [1990] 2 S.C.R. 865, she wrote an opinion that limited the scope of the intoxication defence (making it unavailable for a charge of impaired driving), which indicated her willingness to impose limits on defences where the social context and need for equality and individual responsibility lead to such a conclusion.

79 *Ruzic, supra* note 9.

80 The Court's analysis of moral involuntariness extended beyond excuses to include all affirmative defences. See Berger, *supra* note 10; Don Stuart, *Charter Justice in Canadian Criminal Law,* 4th ed. (Toronto: Carswell, 2005) at 109. See also Stephen G. Coughlan, "Duress, Necessity, Self-Defence and Provocation: Implications of Radical Change?" (2002) 7 Can. Crim. L. Rev. 147.

81 *Ruzic, supra* note 9 at para. 29.

82 *Ibid.* at para. 44.

83 Berger, *supra* note 10 at 110.

84 Coughlan, *supra* note 80.

85 *Ruzic, supra* note 9 at para. 41.

86 Berger, *supra* note 10 at 111.

87 Shalin M. Sugunasiri, "Contextualism: The Supreme Court's New Standard of Judicial Analysis and Accountability" (1999) 22 Dal. L.J. 126 at 129-30.

88 Richard F. Devlin and Matthew Sherrard, "The Big Chill? Contextual Judgment after *R. v. Hamilton and Mason*" (2005) 28 Dal. L.J. 409 at 413-14 [emphasis in original].

89 For a discussion of the extent to which equality continues to be an "under-utilized and under-valued" principle in substantive criminal law decisions from the Supreme Court, see Rosemary Cairns Way, "Incorporating Equality in the Substantive Criminal Law: Inevitable or Impossible?" (2005) 4 J.L. & Equality 203 at para. 37. See also Boyle, *supra* note 21; Christine Boyle and John McInnes, "Judging Sexual Assault Law against a Standard of Equality" (1995) 29 U.B.C. L. Rev. 341.

90 See *e.g.* Rosemary Cairns Way, "Culpability and the Equality Value: The Legacy of the Martineau Dissent" (2003) 15 C.J.W.L. 53 (arguing that the approach taken by Justice Claire L'Heureux-Dubé to assessing culpability is multi-dimensional, contextualized, and equality promoting in its rejection of the doctrinal dichotomy between subjective and objective

fault). See also Janine Benedet and Isabel Grant, "Hearing the Sexual Assault Complaints of Women with Mental Disabilities: Evidentiary and Procedural Issues" (2007) 52 McGill L.J. 515 at 548-51.

91 Cairns Way, *supra* note 90 at 55.

92 Berger, *supra* note 10.

9

"Finally I Know Where I Am Going to Be From": Culture, Context, and Time in a Look Back at *Racine v. Woods*

Gillian Calder

Carrier Sekani Family Services: Reclaiming Our Children

On 26 February 2004, the four clans of the Carrier Sekani First Nations[1] gathered for a Bah'lats[2] (often erroneously referred to as a "potlatch")[3] on their traditional territories in northern British Columbia. This was the first time in generations that all four clans had assembled for this traditional form of celebration. On this occasion, the Bah'lats marked the return of Carrier Sekani children who had been in foster care and who were coming home to meet their elders, extended families, and clan members, many for the first time. The Bah'lats was coordinated through Carrier Sekani Family Services (CSFS) and drew on traditional principles to meet the CSFS mandate of healing and empowering Aboriginal families. This ceremony, memorialized in documentary form,[4] showed the community taking direct responsibility for the health, social, and legal services of First Nations people residing in Carrier Sekani territory.[5]

This particular Bah'lats had several purposes. One was to celebrate the return of the children to their community. In this respect, the Bah'lats was a form of healing for the assault upon Aboriginal cultures that results from the removal of children.[6] A secondary reason was to demonstrate to the governments of British Columbia and Canada that Carrier Sekani traditions are still alive and well. Finally, the Bah'lats served to teach the children something they could not get in non-Native homes: knowledge of their traditions and systems of governance, communicated by elders as teachers in the presence of many witnesses who may be called upon in the future to verify the past.

In capturing the essence of the ceremony, the filmmakers focused on the stories of Carrier Sekani youth returning to the community.[7] One of these young people, Kelly, is interviewed before she enters the hall for the feast. Tucking her hair behind her ears and speaking with the unmistakable cadence of youth, she talks about her nervousness at attending her first "potlatch" and about how, at age twenty, she does not know much about her culture.

When asked why, she gently answers that she has lived in thirteen different foster homes since the age of two. Inside, she is greeted and welcomed into her clan; and we watch her look of disbelief as she meets family members, followed by her deep smile as she tells the interviewer, "Finally I know where I am going to be from."

Looking Back at *Racine v. Woods:* The Question

The goal of this chapter is to examine the impact of one child welfare decision on Canadian family law through the passage of time: Justice Bertha Wilson's reasons for a unanimous Supreme Court of Canada in the 1983 decision of *Racine v. Woods*.[8] In particular, I examine the Court's determination that it was in Leticia Woods' best interest to be adopted by her non-Aboriginal foster family instead of being returned to her Ojibway birth mother. I pay particular attention to how Justice Wilson's treatment of culture, race, aboriginality, and bonding is applied when examining the roles of social families and birth families. And I consider how Justice Wilson's treatment of these issues has played a role in the ongoing struggle for justice for Aboriginal families in the particular context of the placement of Aboriginal children outside of their communities.[9]

I began this chapter with a different First Nation, a different child, and a different moment in time to introduce a key lens that I want to bring to the analysis: how child welfare decision makers approach the issue of time. With attention to the relationship between law and time, this chapter examines Justice Wilson's oft-cited holding that, "when the test to be met is the best interests of the child, the significance of cultural background and heritage as opposed to bonding abates over time. The closer the bond that develops with the prospective adoptive parents the less important the racial element becomes."[10]

The significance of time within law is also implicated in the notion of justice upon which I rely to guide my analysis. I argue that, in the search for justice, among the difficult choices that face decision makers working in child welfare, the answer is not simply to make the least tragic choice at the moment of the decision. Justice demands an attentiveness not only to the child's immediate past and present, but also to her future; and her future includes the potential to develop new bonds and relationships and to cultivate an understanding of the culture and community that constitute her more distant past. I argue that the narrow understanding of time that informs child welfare decisions has played a role in perpetuating the colonialism that animates child welfare law in Canada today.[11]

In contrast, justice is furthered where the decision is informed by understandings of law, community, and time that are not solely the products of a dominant culture. In particular, a more robust understanding of these factors would help to avoid the injustices that, as I argue, have been perpetuated by a linear, liberal, and individual conception of time within the context of child welfare decisions. Giving priority to the narrative of a child's life that most closely reflects the story of progress toward autonomy runs the risk of ignoring other contested and complex conceptions of time and law through which social collectivities are lived.[12] I therefore conclude this discussion by querying how time itself played an important role in Justice Wilson's decision to sever the legal relationship between Leticia Woods and her birth family. I argue that, when viewed from a perspective that recognizes Aboriginal peoples as participants in, as opposed to subjects of, the justice system, the reasoning employed in *Racine v. Woods* is revealed as culturally bounded and limited. I thus begin my examination of the Court's decision with an acknowledgment that, as illuminated by a thicker notion of time and community, justice for Aboriginal children involves a healthy, stable, and loving present but also a recognition of the past and a future that promises the opportunity to know where they are from.

In what follows, I set out the story from *Racine v. Woods* against the backdrop of the history of Aboriginal child welfare in Canadian law, focusing primarily on the relationship between the residential school experience and the "sixties scoop" to present-day child welfare law. Second, I trace how *Racine v. Woods* has been followed in Canadian law and how it has been treated academically, including in Justice Wilson's own academic writing. I close with some attention to temporality, concluding that the best interests of the child test alone remains an inadequate legal test for judges and other decision makers charged with negotiating the tragic choices that characterize child welfare decisions.

The Context

The character of child welfare law is shaped by "different modes of implementing and justifying [the] fundamental alignment between the state and the family."[13] Child welfare law in Canada is based on the ideological assumption that families should bear both the responsibility and the cost of raising children.[14] This assumption has been particularly devastating for Aboriginal families. When Aboriginal child welfare arose, social work practice and judicial discourse constructed Aboriginal communities as economically and socially ravaged; thus, many Aboriginal families were seen to deviate from the dominant notion of a proper family and were therefore deemed unable to care for their children.[15] For this reason, situating *Racine v. Woods* in Canadian law begins with an understanding of the colonialist history of Aboriginal child welfare, which is characterized by repeated attempts on the part of the Canadian government to assimilate Aboriginal peoples, particularly in the twentieth century.

Despite recognition of the harm caused and the introduction of laws and policies that are more sensitive to the needs of Aboriginal children, families, and communities, "past government policies ... continue to have intergenerational effects, and many Aboriginal parents and communities now face great challenges in caring adequately for their children."[16] Two particular moments are significant. The first is the explicit policy of the federal government to "civilize" Aboriginal peoples through education, primarily through the mandatory attendance of Aboriginal children at residential schools. The second is the interference of child welfare systems in the lives of Aboriginal families, which occurred because the "standards of the dominant society" were employed to "judge traditional Aboriginal family and child care practices."[17]

In many parts of Canada, particularly in the north and the west, the *Indian Act* required that Aboriginal children attend residential schools, in a "conscious, deliberate and often brutal attempt to force Aboriginal people[s] to assimilate into mainstream society, mostly by forcing the children away from their languages, cultures and societies."[18] The residential school experience led to two levels of tragedy for Aboriginal children. The first was the immediate effects of the deplorable conditions and the devastating patterns of physical and sexual abuse present at many of the residential schools.[19] As adult survivors of residential schools began to disclose and document their experiences, criminal prosecutions and civil suits offered limited compensation and remedial support.[20] The second level of tragedy was more systemic and is beyond the ability of any legal system to redress: it is the breakdown of traditional Aboriginal methods of passing on customs of child-rearing and parenting. This breakdown left many Aboriginal parents without the benefit of their own parents, grandparents, and extended families' teachings about how to raise children.[21] Although impacts and survival strategies differed among the various First Nations across Canada, both of these levels of injustice manifest themselves in disproportionate poverty rates, high unemployment, high suicide rates, low education levels, high rates of substance abuse, disproportionate rates of incarceration,[22] lowered self-esteem, confusion of self-identity and of cultural identity,[23] and profound distrust of authority within many Aboriginal communities in Canada.[24]

The second significant moment is the interference of child welfare systems in the lives of Aboriginal families. Until the 1950s, provincial governments in Canada did not provide child welfare or other services to Aboriginal peoples, viewing the matter as falling under federal jurisdiction.[25] Even after the enactment of s. 88 of the *Indian Act,* which ensured that laws of general application in the province applied on reserve, provincial child welfare officials still felt some reluctance to respond to anything but the most difficult situations.[26] From the early 1960s through the 1970s, however, as residential schools began to close across the country, dominant society began to respond to the ways that Aboriginal families were raising their children by apprehending them in large numbers.[27] The result of what has become known as the "sixties scoop"[28] was a continued push to assimilation and an institutionalized vehicle for cultural genocide.

In many ways, the legacy of residential schools and of the sixties scoop remains present in the lives of Aboriginal peoples today. This legacy is manifest, for example, in the continued overrepresentation of Aboriginal children in government care. As Shauna Van Praagh writes, "[Y]oung members of communities [are] subject to particular – and racist – treatment, scrutiny, and criticism, [and] these children experience a disproportionately high level of contact with child welfare agencies; theorists, practitioners and politicians are grappling with the reasons and remedies for a situation in which too many children are removed from their parents in the name of protection."[29] In British Columbia, for example, Aboriginal children constitute less than 8 percent of the population but make up more than half of the approximately ten thousand children in care in the province.[30] In other provinces, such as Manitoba, where *Racine v. Woods* originated, current statistics reveal that almost 70 percent of the children in care are Aboriginal.[31] One means of understanding this continued trend is through an examination of how the best interests of the child test has been interpreted and applied in decisions involving the placement of Aboriginal children.

The Case Study

Against this partial history, the factual context of *Racine v. Woods* can be characterized as fairly typical of the child welfare landscape[32] and as another example of "the failure of structures and institutions of the dominant society to respect and recognize the importance of culture and traditions."[33] The child of an Aboriginal mother living with substance abuse was taken into foster care. When the foster parents applied to adopt the child against the birth mother's wishes, the Court faced the difficult question of who should care for the child. It chose the foster family. In this particular case, that meant choosing to leave the Ojibway child in the care of her social parents, one of whom was white and the other Métis, rather than returning her to her Ojibway birth mother.

Against the backdrop of a history of colonialism and assimilative goals, this decision can hardly be seen as a departure from the norm. However, the terms used to justify the decision are significant, and their impact is enduring. Writing for a unanimous Court, Justice Wilson articulated the tension as being between the importance of culture, heritage, and biology, on the one hand, and "psychological bonding" and stability, on the other. Rather than displaying overt colonialism, the Court expressed its sympathies for the mother;[34] yet it maintained that it must uphold the "best interests of the child," and in so doing, it found that "the significance of cultural background and heritage as opposed to bonding abates over time."[35] Drawing on an expert report, Justice Wilson cited the view that "this whole business of racial and Indian and whatever you want to call it all has to do with a parameter of time ... It's two women and a little girl, and one of them doesn't know her. It's as simple as that."[36]

Missing from this analysis is an acknowledgment that what courts so often face is how to determine the "least detrimental alternative,"[37] or indeed, how to choose between the tragic options with which families are faced. The complexity of the situation derives from the challenge of balancing the needs of individuals with the needs of communities when the health and security of one particular child is at issue – of how, in fact, to affirm that Aboriginal institutions in the fields of family and children's services are the way of the future without underestimating "the difficulties of turning ideals into reality."[38] Justice for Aboriginal peoples flows, I argue, from this more complicated understanding of what a just outcome can be.

The story in *Racine v. Woods* is, of course, much more complicated than is reflected by a reduction of the case to its most basic elements. On 4 September 1976, Linda Woods gave birth to Leticia Grace Woods in Portage la Prairie, Manitoba. At the time, Woods was in the process of divorcing her husband, Lloyd Woods, with whom she had two older children but who was not the father of Leticia. Linda Woods, "on her own admission," had a serious problem with alcohol that left her unable to care for her newborn infant.[39] On 20 October 1976, Leticia was apprehended by the Children's Aid Society of Central Manitoba (the "Society") pursuant to the child welfare legislation in place at the time and was placed in a foster home.

In February 1977, with Linda Woods' consent, Leticia was made a ward of the Society for an eighteen-month period. On 11 February 1977, she was placed in the foster home of Sandra Ransom. Ransom separated from her husband a few months later, and in September 1977, she and Leticia moved to the home of Allan Racine, whom she subsequently married. On 4 May 1978, when the wardship order expired, Leticia was returned to her mother with the full cooperation of the Racines. Although Linda Woods had not had contact with Leticia during the wardship, she had informed the Society that her sister was interested in adopting Leticia.

At Woods' invitation, the Racines came to visit Leticia twice during the first month that she was at her birth mother's home. On the second visit, with Woods' consent, they took Leticia home with them. The Racines believed that the relinquishment was permanent; however, Woods gave evidence that they were to have Leticia "just for a while" until she came for her.[40] Woods came for Leticia in October 1978 after permanently leaving Lloyd Woods in the wake of domestic violence. The Racines refused to give her up. They did not hear from Woods again until January 1982, when she launched an application for *habeas corpus*. In response, they applied for an order of *de facto* adoption.[41]

The Racines' application for adoption and Woods' application for custody were heard by Justice Krindle at an eight-day trial.[42] Krindle granted the adoption on the basis that Leticia had been cared for and maintained by the Racines for a period of three consecutive years, as stipulated in the *Child Welfare Act*.[43] As a *de facto* adoption could be granted only through a finding of abandonment, Justice Krindle also made the finding that Woods had abandoned Leticia between October 1978 and January 1982.[44] Ultimately, in her view, the Racines were well situated to deal with the special problems of raising an Indian child in a predominantly white environment, particularly given that Allan Racine was Métis.[45] It was thus in the best interests of Leticia to remain with the Racines. Linda Woods appealed to the Manitoba Court of Appeal, which overturned the adoption order, primarily on a different interpretation of the evidence, and made Leticia a ward of the Court with custody to the Racines.[46] The Racines appealed to the Supreme Court of Canada, where the decision of Justice Krindle was ultimately restored.

The result in *Racine v. Woods* is not surprising: it reinforced the centrality of the best interests of the child test as the paramount consideration while leaving the cultural bias of the test uninterrogated. The test continues to be applied with reference to the dominant standards of mainstream communities. It thereby "reinforc[es] the status quo by applying standards and tests which are not culturally relevant."[47] Although the Court contemplated the importance of seeing Leticia as an "Indian," it was reluctant to make that factor a dominant consideration. As many commentators on the decision have argued, liberal notions of the individual rights of the child trump concerns for community and cultural preservation.[48] However, applying the best interests of the child test within the context of the contested placement of an Aboriginal child with non-Aboriginal parents should involve a much more in-depth and nuanced examination of all the relevant factors.

Consideration of *Racine v. Woods:* In the Case Law

Racine v. Woods has had a lasting impact in judicial consideration, which has not been limited to adoption cases. Indeed, in Canadian law, it has been referenced 471 times during the last twenty-five years, including being followed twenty-eight times.[49] *Racine* is primarily cited for two main holdings, which are represented by two oft-quoted statements.

The first is Justice Wilson's holding that, "in an interracial context ... the law no longer treats children as the property of those who gave them birth but focuses on what is in their best interests."[50] In emphasizing that the best interests of the child test is not about the parents but about the children, she wrote, "[I]t is the parental tie as a meaningful and positive force in the life of the child and not in the life of the parent that the court has to be concerned about. As has been emphasized many times in custody cases, a child is not a chattel in which its parents have a proprietary interest; it is a human being to whom they owe serious obligations."[51] In finding that situations existed in law to enable the granting of a *de facto* adoption (the Court's ability to dispense with the biological parents' consent), Justice Wilson for the Court emphasized her view that the psychological parenting in the life of a child is a paramount consideration while ignoring the proprietary interests raised in the doctrine of *de facto* adoption itself. Thus, *Racine* serves as a precedent for the notion that, in child welfare law, the governing criterion is the best interests of the child, even when those interests are in conflict with those of the child's biological parents.[52]

The second key way in which *Racine v. Woods* has been followed in the case law in the years since 1983 centres on the quotation that is at the heart of this chapter: Justice Wilson's conclusion that, when the test to be met is the best interests of the child, the significance of culture as opposed to bonding lessens over time.[53] In the recent decision of *C.M.-C. v. Winnipeg (Child and Family Services, Central Area),* for example, the foster parents of three siblings applied for guardianship.[54] The children, all of whom were status Indians and Ojibway, had been apprehended from their mother, who played no part in the proceedings. The father of the children, who was from Ethiopia, was also not involved. The applicants took the position that an order of guardianship was in the best interests of the children, given the bonding that had developed during the nearly four years since the children had been placed with them. Their application was opposed by the Dakota Ojibway Child and Family Services on the basis that an order of guardianship to a non-First Nations family was not in the best interests of the children. With little analysis and, indeed, no discussion of the tragic choices faced by all the parties, the Court concluded that a bond had developed between the foster parents and the children. It granted the guardianship, relying on Justice Wilson's decision in *Racine v. Woods* for authority.

Similarly, in *(In the matter of) M.K.Kh.,* the Quebec Court of Appeal affirmed that it was in the best interests of a child, M.K.Kh., to remain in the custody of her non-Aboriginal foster family and to be declared eligible for adoption.[55] Although the Court acknowledged the importance of cultural identity and community ties, it decided that the child's best interests lay in staying with the only family that she had known. Again, the Court relied on Justice Wilson's decision in *Racine v. Woods*.[56] With primary attention focused on the present circumstances of the child, and with reference to the immediate past, the Court found that the foster family had been substituted for the birth family through the passage of time and by court orders.

In Her Words

Justice Wilson's judgment in *Racine* and, in particular, her holding that the importance of culture versus that of bonding abates over time has been the subject of considerable commentary in academic circles. One source for this commentary is Wilson herself, through the body of academic writing she left in addition to her judgments on both the Ontario Court of Appeal and the Supreme Court of Canada.[57] In an article written shortly after *Racine,* she addressed her reliance on a child's emotional ties and on psychological bonding in her articulation of the best interests of the child test.[58] Commenting on her own decision in *Racine,* she stressed the importance of psychological parenthood and of the related need for continuity.[59] In her view, the maintenance of the relationship between parent and child was of central importance to the psychological adjustment of children within the post-divorce family.

When *Racine v. Woods* is placed against the body of Justice Wilson's decisions as a whole and, in particular, against her family law decisions, two important themes become more apparent. The first is Justice Wilson's understanding of law as a moral imperative as opposed to a mere tool for pragmatic decision making.[60] This understanding is illustrated by her belief that the best interests of the child are paramount and by her optimism about the capacity of legal norms to protect children.[61] The second is her aspiration to ensure that individual family members behaved in accordance with standards of justice for individuals, regardless of their family status.[62] This, then, is highlighted by her view that the family that best guards the individuality of the child is in that child's best interests.

What is significant here is the attention that Justice Wilson paid in this judgment to the significance of the social family in an understanding of family: not permitting biology to be the sole trumping factor. However, it is only a particular understanding of the social family that is engaged. Justice Wilson's decision to grant a *de facto* adoption to the Racines had the effect of erasing another social understanding of family: one rooted in the collective kinship and extended family structure that Linda Woods and her sister offered.

In the Words of Others

A second source of commentary is other academic scholarship focusing directly on the issues raised in *Racine v. Woods.* This commentary ranges from challenges to the decision's evidentiary basis and critiques of it as a racist holding[63] to more liberal discussions of the case that acknowledge the importance of weighing racial and cultural issues against other factors.[64]

Here, several strands of critique stand out. First, *Racine* is often cited in academic material as a critical moment in the liberal understanding of best interests of the child and for the test's paramountcy in Canadian law dealing with children.[65] In particular, the case marks a shift from emphasizing the perspective of the parents toward stressing that of the child when applying the best interests analysis. The case is also seen as an authority for increased recognition of a child's relationship with his or her psychological parents.[66] *Racine v. Woods* is commonly cited as a moment in Canadian law when courts began to look increasingly to the behavioural sciences to provide answers and, often, to provide support for *status quo* assertions, primarily by non-biological parents.[67] More particularly, the case exemplifies the way in which Canadian courts are seen to downplay the significance of culture relative to that of stability, permanency, and bonding.[68]

Second, *Racine* is analyzed as an example of the failure of child welfare systems in Canada to give substantial recognition to the cultural differences of Aboriginal children in care.[69] Here, the central critiques can be found in the work of writers, including annie bunting and Marlee Kline, who pay attention to the ways in which the Ojibway child and her mother's claim to custody were abstracted from culture.[70] For these authors, judges who must rule on the case of an Aboriginal child who has been placed in a non-Native foster home for a significant period of time face a difficult and complex task.[71] These authors re-examine the case with attention to Aboriginal culture as a dynamic and contested process that is accessed rather than lived.[72] This re-examination means contesting the tendency of decision makers to construct the child as an abstract individual who is already out of culture and to separate their analysis of that child's best interests from concerns about the maintenance of her cultural connections.[73] When a child is constructed as conceptually separate from her culture, the judge renders unproblematic the actual removal of him or her from that culture.[74] For the authors who forward this critique, Justice Wilson's approach to the best interests of the child illustrates the potentially devastating consequences that flow from the incompatibility of liberal legal notions of law and childhood with the complexity of First Nations communities.[75]

Considering the Significance of Time

Ultimately, I want to contribute to this latter body of critical scholarship by looking at how a particular understanding of time informs the judgment's characterization of culture. What we know about child welfare law is that "histories of racism and colonialism are mapped onto individual children's narratives, even when decisions are silent on history."[76] We also know that the particular cultural and psychological needs of Aboriginal children run alongside their psychological needs for continuity in care and that they are tied to the future survival of communities.[77] The best interests of the child test, when attentive to these issues and complexities, cannot be bound by an individual, liberal, and linear notion of time. Nor can the judicial application of the test conceptualize culture as a unified, essentialist, and static body of practices and beliefs. Rather, in applying the test, judges must be more attentive to the varying ways that both identity and culture are "dynamic practice[s] of making and remaking meanings that are provisional, shifting and partial"[78] – fluid entities with which we interact, and hence that shape, particularly as a child matures.

Writing about the relationship between time and law, Gerald Postema confronts the relatively unchallenged practice of looking to past decisions to normatively guide present decision making in law and asks the reader of legal discourse to query why we start with the past.[79] Similarly, Paul Kahn's provocative study of the culture of law posits that the historicity of law is in fact its single most prominent feature.[80] My goal in looking back at *Racine v. Woods* is to ask a question that contemplates the future and confronts the assumption that, "[a]s with the residential schools and missionary homes, the underlying notion is that, with time, First Nations and Aboriginal peoples can somehow become less Indigenous; that, with time, Indigenality somehow becomes less constitutive and important; that with time, if First Nations and Aboriginal children are separated from their families and communities, they can be 'successfully assimilated.'"[81] I want to ask the following questions: Why, in thinking about the best interests of a child, does law privilege the current snapshot of the child? And when that child is born into an Aboriginal community, why is the impact of the future relationship with that community not given a greater weight in the decision-making process?

My critique of Justice Wilson's holding in *Racine v. Woods* is that the immediate past and present circumstances of this particular child were determinative. Giving priority to the biography of the individual over the history of the collective effectively erased the connections between the child and her community. This critique is not to deny the significance of environmental stability to the welfare of a child but is more a challenge to the presumption that leaving a child in her non-Aboriginal home in the short term will not lead to profound effects in the long term.[82] In focusing on the already established bond that had developed between Leticia and the Racines, Justice Wilson's determination of Leticia Woods' best interests froze her in time. Justice Wilson examined Leticia's life as she found it, without sufficient regard either to the possibility of an existing social or genetic bond to her birth mother or to the importance of her future interests in bonding with other members of her Aboriginal community. And, though Justice Wilson did not freeze time, her focus on the temporal limits of culture and her application of an uncontested linear notion of time led her to conclude that, as the years pass, cultural considerations abate.[83]

My argument here is not merely that I disagree with the result of the *Racine v. Woods* decision. More fundamentally, I am critical of the way in which the Court separated law and culture and set them up as monolithic dichotomous entities. Justice Wilson, and all the members of the Court who signed on to her reasons, had a responsibility, as Louis Wolcher asserts, to experience the event of deciding and to demonstrate that the problem itself was worthy of thought.[84] Wolcher writes, "[C]onformity to the spirit of law's task requires [decision makers] to acknowledge, more or less constantly, that they are tragic participants in the making [of] a world that is never more than a mixed blessing for those [of us] who must live in it."[85] Thus, my fundamental discomfort with the Court's reasons is not that, in outcome, the Court placed the child with the wrong family, but rather that, in failing to acknowledge the inherent tragedy of both choices for the child involved, it lost the opportunity for the reasons to transcend the moment.[86]

Justice Wilson told us clearly in 1983 that time was important in the best interests of the child test. Twenty-six years later, I think she is right; but in measuring the significance of time with both culture and community, she erred in not fully taking into account that, in applying the test, one should not ground the issues of cultural, community, and familial bonding in a notion of time that best suits the liberal autonomous citizen. In my view, the *Racine* decision accepts that the test itself is a natural product of the legal order, thereby leaving uncontested the constructed nature of all legal norms and institutions.[87] Furthermore, in prioritizing a linear approach to time over the notion that cultural concerns ebb and flow throughout lifetimes, the Court failed to recognize culture as a "contingent act of contesting and negotiating multiple meanings" rather than a passive following of "an integrated symbol or value system."[88] The judgment in *Racine v. Woods* needed to articulate that Aboriginal child welfare law is characterized by choices that implicate the present, the immediate past, the deep past, the future, and generations beyond the moment. For the outcome of the *Racine* decision to be just, it had to acknowledge that a determination of the task at hand was made impossible by the shortcomings of the conceptual tools available to the decision makers, including the best interests of the child test, law's commitment to carrying forward the past as an authoritative source of substantive norms,[89] the tragic histories of Aboriginal child welfare in Canada, the dynamic, fluid, and contingent nature of culture, Linda Woods' exclusion from the group of history's winners, who get to make law,[90] and Leticia Woods frozen before the Court as a seven-year-old child with only her immediate past and a thin description of her parents as a guide.

Arguably, my analysis could be reduced to a criticism of litigating these kinds of unanswerable and ultimately tragic questions through an inadequately situated set of legal tests. Similarly, my analysis could be subject to the challenge that, as the years passed, Justice Wilson may have shifted her own thought on these kinds of questions, particularly as she spent considerable time at the end of her career as a commissioner on the Royal Commission on Aboriginal Peoples.[91] What is certain, though, is that judges will continue to be called upon to determine these difficult issues, with real people before them facing varying levels of tragedies in the courtroom. In the face of this reality, decision makers dealing with the complex issue of Canadian Aboriginal child welfare law can learn from stories such as Kelly's.

By taking into consideration the past, the present, and the future, by recognizing the complex relationship between law, culture, and time, by rendering rich and thick reasons that pay attention to the dynamic and shifting nature of law's engagement with complicated questions of this nature, we can find the means to ensure that Aboriginal children in Canada are involved in the process of knowing where they are going to be from.

Acknowledgments

I am grateful to Kim Brooks, Sharon Cowan, Rebecca Johnson, Robert Leckey, and Hester Lessard for a provocative critique of this chapter in its early stages. Thanks also to Sharon Fox, Alison Latimer, Qian Mou, Palma Paciocco, and Megan Shaw for excellent research and editorial assistance, and to my Advanced Family Law seminar students at the University of Victoria in the spring of 2008, whose collective curiosities about this question pushed my analysis to a much more thoughtful place. A version of this chapter was given at "Law, Culture and the Humanities" in Berkeley, California, on 27 March 2008 and to the other authors of this volume at McGill University on 20 April 2008. Thank you to all participants for thoughtful engagement and important questions, with particular thanks to Kim Brooks.

Notes

1 The Carrier and Sekani First Nations are Athapaskan-speaking peoples who have occupied a vast territory in north-central British Columbia since time immemorial and who presently organize politically through the Carrier Sekani Tribal Council (CSTC). For more information on the CSTC, see, online: CSTC homepage <http://www.cstc.bc.ca/cstc/1/cstc+homepage>; Adam Warner, Travis Holyk, and Perry Shawana, *Whu Neeh Nee (Guiders of Our People) – Carrier Sekani First Nations Family Law Alternative Dispute Resolution Research Project,* online: <http://www.sfu.ca/cfrj/fulltext/adam.pdf>.

2 The Bah'lats, which is the governing structure of the Carrier Nation, guides the individual, community, and nation in all aspects of life, including teaching of the laws of the community.

3 Importantly, no Aboriginal community in British Columbia used the word "potlatch": it was an invented omnibus word employed by settler nations to describe what was viewed as a common set of practices. Douglas Cole and Ira Chaikin, *An Iron Hand upon the People: The Law against the Potlatch on the Northwest Coast* (Vancouver: Douglas and McIntyre, 1990) at 6.

4 P. Shawana, *Reclaiming Our Children: A Journey Home* (Prince George: Carrier Sekani Family Services and House of Talent Productions, 2004). As Kelly's story (given below) is taken solely from this documentary, it is important to remember that documentary film is "a form of artistic and politicized expression" that is "only as revealing as [the] interpreter is convinced." See Jessica M. Silbey, "Filmmaking in the Precinct House and the Genre of Documentary Film" (2005) 29:2 Columbia J. L. & the Arts 107 at 142, 172.

5 Warner, Holyk, and Shawana, *supra* note 1 at 4-5.

6 For a discussion of the storied history of the "potlatch," see Jo-Anne Fiske and Betty Patrick, *When the Plumes Rise: The Way of the Lake Babine Nation* (Vancouver: UBC Press, 2000), cited in John Borrows, *Indigenous Legal Traditions in Canada* (Ottawa: Law Commission of Canada, 2006) at 62, n. 187, online: Human Rights Catalogue <http://epe.lac-bac.gc.ca/100/206/301/law_commission_of_canada-ef/2006-12-06/www.lcc.gc.ca/pdf/2006-09-01-john%20burrows-en-final.pdf>.

7 Here the "film's images are an embodiment of a particular point of view ... shaped by the essential filmic storytelling devices of narrative and montage." Silbey, *supra* note 4 at 142.

8 *Racine v. Woods,* [1983] 2 S.C.R. 173 [*Racine*]. I acknowledge the work of Marie-Claire Belleau, Rebecca Johnson, and Christina Vinters (Chapter 12, this volume) for reminding me that, though this Supreme Court judgment was authored by Justice Wilson, it is also the holding of Ritchie, Dickson, Estey, and McIntyre JJ., the four other justices who signed on to it.

9 I am grateful to Alison Latimer, whose work to incorporate a thicker understanding of justice in the context of Aboriginal women in Canada has greatly influenced my thought.

10 *Racine*, *supra* note 8 at 187-88.

11 For a discussion of the notion that law carries forward the past in a linear process, see Paul Kahn, *The Cultural Study of Law: Reconstructing Legal Scholarship* (Chicago: University of Chicago Press, 1999) at 43-55.

12 For a discussion of the relationship between cultural conceptions of time and the organization and management of legal institutions, see Carol J. Greenhouse, "Just in Time: Temporality and the Cultural Legitimation of Law" (1989) 98 Yale L.J. 1631; Rebecca R. French, "Time in the Law" (2001) 72 U. Colo. L. Rev. 663.

13 Hester Lessard, "The Empire of the Lone Mother: Parental Rights, Child Welfare Law, and State Restructuring" (2001) 39 Osgoode Hall L.J. 717 at 724.

14 For a discussion of the history of child welfare law in Canada, and in particular the role of neo-liberalism in shaping the present debates, see *ibid.*

15 *Ibid.* at 741; Patricia A. Monture, "A Vicious Circle: Child Welfare and the First Nations" (1989) 3 C.J.W.L. 1 at 12-15.

16 Murray Sinclair *et al.*, "Aboriginal Child Welfare" in Nicholas Bala *et al.*, eds., *Canadian Child Welfare Law,* 2d ed. (Toronto: Thompson Educational, 2004) 199 at 199.

17 John J. Borrows and Leonard I. Rotman, *Aboriginal Legal Issues: Cases, Materials and Commentary,* 3d ed. (Markham, ON: LexisNexis, 2007) at 833.

18 *Ibid.* at 830, quoting A.C. Hamilton and C.M. Sinclair, *The Justice System and Aboriginal People: Report of the Aboriginal Justice Inquiry in Manitoba,* vol. 1 (Winnipeg: Queen's Printer, 1991) at 509.

19 Sinclair *et al., supra* note 16 at 203-4. See also s. 10 "Residential Schools" in *Report of the Royal Commission on Aboriginal Peoples: Looking Forward, Looking Back,* vol. 1, *False Assumptions and a Failed Relationship,* part 2, online: Indian and Northern Affairs Canada, <http://www.collectionscanada.gc.ca/webarchives/20071211055641/http://www.ainc-inac.gc.ca/ch/rcap/sg/sg28_e.html#99>.

20 Sinclair *et al., supra* note 16 at 204. For a discussion of the Government of Canada's final Indian Residential Schools Settlement Agreement and collective measures, see Resolution Sector, Indian and Northern Affairs Canada, "Overview of Resolution Sector," online: Indian and Northern Affairs Canada, <http://www.irsr-rqpi.gc.ca/index-eng.asp>.

21 Borrows and Rotman, *supra* note 17 at 832.

22 For a statistical overview of issues facing Aboriginal peoples in Canada, see Statistics Canada, "Overview 2007: Aboriginal Peoples," online: <http://www41.statcan.ca/2007/10000/ceb10000_000-eng.htm>.

23 See *e.g.* discussion of the impact on identity in Emily F. Carasco, "Canadian Native Children: Have Child Welfare Laws Broken the Circle?" (1986) 5 Can. J. Fam. L. 111 at 114; Philip Lynch, "Keeping Them Home: The Best Interests of Indigenous Children and Communities in Canada and Australia" (2001) 23 Sydney L. Rev. 501 at 519.

24 Borrows and Rotman, *supra* note 17 at 832.

25 Sinclair *et al., supra* note 16 at 216-17. This deprivation was based in part on the provincial interpretation of s. 91(24) of the *Constitution Act, 1867,* which gives jurisdiction over Indians and lands reserved for Indians to the federal government.

26 *Indian Act,* R.S. 1985, c. I-5.

27 Sinclair *et al., supra* note 16 at 206.

28 The term "sixties scoop" is attributed to Patrick Johnston, *Native Children and the Child Welfare System* (Toronto: James Lorimer, 1983).

29 Shauna Van Praagh, "Faith, Belonging, and the Protection of 'Our' Children" (1999) 17 Windsor Y.B. Access Just. 154 at 157, 180.

30 Justice Ted Hughes, *B.C. Children and Youth Review: An Independent Review of B.C.'s Child Protection System* (Victoria, 2007) at 49, online: <http://www.mcf.gov.bc.ca/bcchildprotection/pdf/BC_Children_and_Youth_Review_Report_FINAL_April_4.pdf>.

31 Manitoba Aboriginal Affairs Secretariat, *Aboriginal People in Manitoba* (Winnipeg: Service Canada, 2006) at 42, online: <http://www1.servicecanada.gc.ca/eng/mb/aboriginal-profile/aboriginals.pdf>.

32 I am grateful to Alison Latimer for her research and insight on this issue.

33 Monture, *supra* note 15 at 1.

34 Justice Wilson wrote, "While the Court can feel great compassion for the respondent, and respect for her determined efforts to overcome her adversities, it has an obligation to ensure that any order it makes will promote the best interests of her child." *Racine, supra* note 8 at 188.

35 *Ibid.* at 187.

36 *Ibid.* at 188.

37 This approach is described in Lessard, *supra* note 13 at 741-43.

38 This analysis is drawn from the *Report of the Royal Commission on Aboriginal Peoples: Gathering Strength,* vol. 3, c. 2 "The Family," s. 2.5 "Conclusion and Recommendations," online: Indian and Northern Affairs Canada, <http://www.collectionscanada.gc.ca/webarchives/20071218071240/http://www.ainc-inac.gc.ca/ch/rcap/sg/si6_e.html>. (Thank you to Hadley Friedland for raising this argument in her own work and bringing it to my attention in the context of mine.)

39 *Ibid.*

40 *Racine, supra* note 8 at 176.

41 *Ibid.*

42 *Woods v. Racine and Racine* (1983), 25 Man. R. (2d) 194 [*Woods*].

43 *Child Welfare Act, 1974,* S.M. 1974, c. 30 (also C.C.S.M., c. C80, s. 103(1) repealed 1985-86, c. 8, s. 87(1)).

44 *Woods, supra* note 42 at para. 13.

45 On Allan Racine as Métis, we see some attention paid by the courts to the presence of an Aboriginal parent in the family; yet we also see how courts can conflate notions of aboriginality. To be Métis and to be Ojibway are differing lived experiences.

46 *L.J.W. v. A.N.R.,* [1982] M. J. No. 59 (C.A.).

47 Monture, *supra* note 15 at 12.

48 See *e.g. ibid.* at 12. See also Samuel A. Bull, "The Special Case of the Native Child" (1989) 47 Advocate 523 at 527; Wesley Crichlow, "Western Colonization as Disease: Native Adoption and Cultural Genocide" (2002) 3 Critical Social Work, online: <http://www.uwindsor.ca/units/socialwork/critical.nsf/982f0e5f06b5c9a285256d6e006cff78/700f69db570bb04285256f01006bee13!OpenDocument>; Bernd Walter, Janine Alison Isenegger, and Nicholas Bala, "'Best Interests' in Child Protection Proceedings: Implications and Alternatives" (1995) 12 Can. J. Fam. L. 367 at 407.

49 On 12 April 2008, the author noted the Supreme Court of Canada decision on Quicklaw to show that the case was followed 28 times, distinguished 4 times, explained 17 times, mentioned 408 times, and cited in the dissent 14 times.

50 *Racine, supra* note 8 at 174.

51 *Ibid.* at 185.

52 See *e.g.* Nicholas Bala, "The Evolving Canadian Definition of the Family: Towards a Pluralistic and Functional Approach" (1994) 8 Int'l J.L. & Fam. 293 at 297; Claire Bernard, Robin Ward, and Bartha Maria Knoppers, "'Best Interests of the Child' Exposed: A Portrait of Quebec Custody and Protection Law" (1992) 11 Can. J. Fam. L. 57 at 58. For a recent decision that applies this analysis, see *L.M.O.(Re),* [2003] S.C.J. No. 423, 2003 SKQB 277.

53 See *e.g. Sawan v. Tearoe,* [1994] 1 W.W.R. 419 at paras. 40-41.

54 *C.M.-C. v. Winnipeg (Child and Family Services, Central Area),* [2006] M.J. No. 32, [2006] 2 C.N.L.R. 14.

55 *(In the matter of) M.K.Kh.,* [2004] J.Q. No. 5039, [2004] 2 C.N.L.R. 68.

56 *Ibid.* at paras. 11-12.

57 See *e.g.* Bertha Wilson, "Will Women Judges Really Make a Difference?" (1990) 28 Osgoode Hall L.J. 507; Bertha Wilson, "Women, the Family, and the Constitutional Protection of Privacy" (1992) 17 Queen's L.J. 5; Bertha Wilson, "Family Violence" (1992) 5 C.J.W.L. 137; Bertha Wilson, "Children: The Casualties of a Failed Marriage" (1985) 19 U.B.C. L. Rev. 245; Bertha Wilson, "The Variation of Support Orders" in Rosalie S. Abella and Claire L'Heureux-Dubé, eds., *Family Law: Dimensions of Justice* (Toronto: Butterworths, 1983) 35;

Canadian Bar Association Task Force on Gender Equality in the Legal Profession, *Touchstones for Change: Equality, Diversity and Accountability* (Ottawa: Canadian Bar Association, 1993).

58 Wilson, "Children," *supra* note 57.
59 *Ibid.* at 253.
60 Mary Jane Mossman, "The 'Family' in the Work of Madame Justice Wilson" (1992) 15 Dal. L.J. 115 at 121.
61 See Chapter 10, this volume.
62 Mossman, *supra* note 60 at 121.
63 Monture, *supra* note 15 at 13.
64 Christine Davies, "Native Children and the Child Welfare System in Canada" (1992) 30 Alb. L. Rev. 1200 at 1214; Ellen Anderson, *Judging Bertha Wilson: Law as Large as Life* (Toronto: University of Toronto Press for the Osgoode Society for Canadian Legal History, 2001) at 189-91.
65 See *e.g.* Nicholas Bala, "Family Law in Canada and the United States: Different Visions of Similar Realities" (1987) 1 Int'l J.L. & Fam. 1 at 33-34; D.A. Rollie Thompson, "Why Hasn't the Charter Mattered in Child Protection?" (1989) 8 Can. J. Fam. L. 133 at 148.
66 Bernard, Ward, and Knoppers, *supra* note 52 at 109; Nicholas Bala, "The Evolving Canadian Definition of the Family: Towards a Pluralistic and Functional Approach" (1994) 8 Int'l J. L. & the Family 293 at 296-97.
67 See *e.g.* David G. Duff and Roxanne Mykitiuk, "Parental Separation and the Child Custody Decision: Toward a Reconception" (1989) 47 U.T. Fac. L. Rev. 874 at 910; Robert Leckey, "Harmonizing Family Law's Identities" (2002) 28 Queen's L.J. 221 at 233.
68 Emily Grier, "Aboriginal Children in Limbo: A Comment on Re R.T." (2005) 68 Sask. L.R. 435 at 445-47.
69 See *e.g.* Keri B. Lazarus, "Adoption of Native American and First Nations Children: Are the United States and Canada Recognizing the Best Interests of the Children" (1997) 14 Ariz. J. Int'l & Comp. L. 255 at 280-81; Carasco, *supra* note 23 at 111. See also Robert Leckey, *Contextual Subjects: Family, State, and Relational Theory* (Toronto: University of Toronto Press, 2008) at 81-82.
70 annie bunting, "Complicating Culture in Child Placement Decisions" (2004) 16 C.J.W.L. 137; Marlee Kline, "Child Welfare Law, 'Best Interests of the Child' Ideology, and First Nations" (1992) 30 Osgoode Hall L.J. 375; Marlee Kline, "Complicating the Ideology of Motherhood: Child Welfare Law and First Nation Women" (1993) 18 Queen's L.J. 306. See also Lazarus, *supra* note 69 at 281-82.
71 bunting, *supra* note 70 at 162.
72 *Ibid.* at 146.
73 Kline, "Child Welfare," *supra* note 70 at 396.
74 Since *Racine,* numerous changes have been made in Canadian law to pay attention to the particular impact of child welfare systems on Aboriginal children. See *e.g.* BC's *Child, Family and Community Service Act,* R.S.B.C. 1996, c. 46, ss. 2(f) and 4; and the recent appointment of renowned Cree academic, lawyer, and judge Mary-Ellen Turpel-Lafond as BC's first Representative for Children and Youth.
75 Kline, "Child Welfare," *supra* note 70 at 423-24.
76 bunting, *supra* note 70 at 137-38.
77 *Ibid.* at 143, acknowledging the work of Marlee Kline.
78 Maneesha Deckha, "Is Culture Taboo? Feminism, Intersectionality, and Culture Talk in Law" (2004) 16 C.J.W.L. 14 at 25.
79 Gerald J. Postema, "On the Moral Presence of Our Past" (1991) 36:4 McGill L.J. 1153 at 1159-60. (I am grateful to Benjamin Berger for bringing this article and series of questions to my attention.)
80 Kahn, *supra* note 11 at 43.
81 Lynch, *supra* note 23 at 524.
82 *Ibid.* at 534.
83 I am grateful to Sharon Cowan for insights regarding this argument.
84 Louis E. Wolcher, "Universal Suffering and the Ultimate Task of Law" (2006) 24 Windsor Y.B. Access Just. 361 at 370. I acknowledge the importance of Hadley Friedland's "Tragic

Choices and the Division of Sorrow: Race, Culture and Community Traumatization in the Lives of Children" [unpublished] for my discussion here.

85 Wolcher, *supra* note 84 at 398.

86 See Chapter 12 at 231-32, this volume, for a discussion of the importance of the judicial task of rendering reasons, not the least of which is the opportunity a decision affords a judge to "imagine anew."

87 Kahn, *supra* note 11 at 30.

88 Deckha, *supra* note 78 at 27.

89 Kahn, *supra* note 11 at 43.

90 Wolcher, *supra* note 84 at 363.

91 See the examination of this phase of her life in Anderson, *supra* note 64 at 352-78. Thank you to Connie Backhouse and to Hester Lessard for discussions on this particular issue.

10
Challenging Patriarchy or Embracing Liberal Norms? Justice Wilson's Child Custody and Access Decisions

Susan B. Boyd

> Child custody is no longer a private matter; it is one that affects the whole community. What is in the best interests of our children is surely in the best interests of us all.
>
> – Bertha Wilson, "Children: The Casualties of a Failed Marriage"

During the late 1970s and the 1980s, the time frame during which Justice Bertha Wilson sat on the Ontario Court of Appeal and the Supreme Court of Canada, family law emerged as a field of public concern, and the contours of child custody and access law became increasingly contested.[1] This chapter reflects upon Justice Wilson's decisions regarding this legal matter, situating them within the context of shifting socio-legal norms relating to children, family, motherhood, and fatherhood.[2] These decisions numbered six at the Court of Appeal and one at the Supreme Court. In these seven cases, Justice Wilson wrote five dissents, reinforcing her reputation as a great dissenter.[3] Despite her modest judicial record in this area and the fact that she often spoke against the grain of majority judicial thinking, Justice Wilson's judgments provide a fascinating window into that period's changing norms on child custody law and process. They also reveal an inconsistent espousal of feminist critiques in this field.

In the 1970s, when Justice Wilson was appointed to the Ontario Court of Appeal, the fault-based system that had underpinned much of child custody law during the twentieth century was being challenged, as were assumptions about what constituted good mothering or fathering. The conjunction of a number of socioeconomic and cultural developments with the adoption of Canada's first divorce legislation resulted in a significantly higher rate of visible family breakdown. In the decade following the enactment of the first federal *Divorce Act* in 1970,[4] the divorce rate rose dramatically, doubling during the first year and nearly doubling again by the end of 1978.[5] Concurrently, the second wave of the women's rights movement became more visible and vocal, the lesbian and gay liberation movement was mobilized, and many married women and mothers entered the paid workforce. Whereas the external divide between "women's work" and "men's work" began to collapse, the sexual division of labour in the family remained largely intact, with women carrying more responsibility for children and housework even in marriages where both parties worked. Nevertheless, family law reform initiatives favoured a gender-neutral and no-fault orientation, and emphasized negotiation, cooperation, and agreement. Family law had started to shift away from its former preoccupation with preserving marriages to focus instead on preserving parent-child relationships and protecting vulnerable members of the family. The parent who did not assume primary responsibility for a child (usually the father) was increasingly viewed as having the legal right to participate as a parent in significant areas of the child's life, such as in decision making.[6] Social science and legal researchers began to centre on the benefits that fathers could provide for their children before, but especially after, parents separated, and the "father's revolution" began.[7]

Although the previous, more rigid, assumptions concerning the roles of men and women as gendered beings, workers, and parents began to break down, societal attitudes in the 1970s were inconsistent. For example, mothers and fathers who might previously have been considered deviant, notably lesbians and gays or adulterers of either sex, could now be awarded custody or access. However, women's behaviour – as mothers and as women – continued to be subjected to heavier scrutiny than that of men.[8] Movies such as *Kramer vs. Kramer* captured the public's imagination and prompted the impression that fathers increasingly assumed the care of young children, especially when mothers put their own interests first by entering the labour force or abandoning unfulfilling marriages.[9] Thus, the liberal spirit of the 1970s failed many mothers who went to court to seek custody.

The 1980s saw a more concerted effort to concentrate, in a gender-neutral manner, on the best interests of the child. But this also produced contradictory results. The equality discourse that characterized this decade, driven by the enactment of the *Canadian Charter of Rights and Freedoms,* made it difficult to legally recognize the sexual division of labour that still prevailed in most households.[10] Joint custody epitomized an approach to child custody that gave separating parents equal rights to their children, and children rights to a relationship with both parents. Fathers' rights groups argued forcefully for the inclusion of a joint custody presumption in the new *Divorce Act.* Although no such provision appeared, s. 16(4) clarified that judges could make joint custody orders. More significantly, a "maximum contact" and "friendly parent" provision was introduced in s. 16(10), espousing the principle that children should have as much contact with each spouse as was consistent with their best interests and directing judges to take into consideration the willingness of the parent seeking custody to facilitate such contact.[11] As the importance of children's contact with their fathers was increasingly emphasized, some questioned whether the goal of enhancing contact was in fact defining the best interests of the child, rather than the best interests of the child defining how much contact was appropriate.[12] Mothers began to claim that their voices were ignored, that their caregiving and organizational efforts in relation to children went unrecognized, and that their concerns about abuse toward themselves or their children were unduly dismissed.

Justice Wilson's custody and access decisions echo these contradictions. Some of her earlier decisions revealed an appreciation that one parent could use custody disputes as a way of continuing to wield power over the other. Yet other decisions displayed her considerable confidence in the capacity of new legal norms to prompt positive post-separation parenting behaviour toward those most vulnerable – the children.[13] Both stances mirrored important trends in the political and intellectual environment surrounding child custody law, including increased awareness of violence against women and how abuse can be prolonged in custody disputes, recognition of children's rights, emerging liberal views on sexuality, and the new emphasis on fatherhood and cooperative parenting. That these concerns sometimes played conflicting roles in her judgments reflects the fact that the trends themselves could be inherently contradictory. Her major custody decisions (*Kruger v. Kruger* and *Frame v. Smith*) demonstrate a faith in the capacity of parents to act in the interests of their children and the ability of legal norms to encourage such behaviour. Her decisions manifest her idealism, her social stance in a period of shifting norms, and the uneven impact of nascent feminist analysis of gendered power relations.

Challenging Bad Behaviour (by Men)

This section reviews five custody decisions in which Justice Wilson evinced some willingness to address the manipulative behaviour of fathers. I begin with two cases that she decided early in her career as the first woman on the Court of Appeal. In them, she looked beyond the substantive and jurisdictional issues raised by the fathers and did not shrink from assessing their behaviour as controlling and/or aimed at thwarting the mothers' claims. She also considered such conduct as a factor affecting the children's best interests.

In the first case, *Ishaky v. Ishaky*, decided in 1978, Justice Wilson upheld an interim order granting custody to the mother, who had been, as she termed it, under "enforced detention" in Israel as a result of the husband's legal manoeuvres.[14] She could have treated the case as a technical *forum conveniens* question; instead, she cut to its heart. The Ishakys were Israelis who had emigrated to Canada with their three children, but after eleven years, they returned to Israel with the two younger children. Shortly after arriving in Israel, Mr. Ishaky confiscated his family's passports and obtained an *ex parte* order from the Rabbinical Tribunal restraining his wife and children from leaving. He also commenced proceedings and sought to have Mrs. Ishaky declared a "rebellious wife" so that she would be deprived of maintenance in the event of divorce. He then returned to Canada to wrap up his business affairs. The eighteen-year-old child escaped from Israel, after which the husband obtained a further restraining order and laid criminal charges against the wife.

Meanwhile, Mrs. Ishaky commenced divorce proceedings through a solicitor in Ontario and sought interim custody. Mr. Ishaky responded by filing a motion for dismissal or stay of proceedings on the grounds that there was an ongoing Israeli action. The motions judge dismissed his application, granted interim custody to the wife, and ordered Mr. Ishaky to present the other child before the Court within seven days and to take all necessary steps to facilitate his wife's appearance. A further order restrained him from leaving Canada. He appealed.

Justice Wilson dismissed the appeal, finding that there had been sufficient evidence before the motion judge to provide him with a "very clear picture of this family" and to indicate what was in the best interests of the child, considering "the plight of the wife and child confined in Israel against their will, [and] the fact that Mr. Ishaky was perfectly content with the way in which his wife fulfilled her role as mother and objected only to her fulfilling it in Canada."[15] Although she conceded the bona fide nature of Mr. Ishaky's conviction that being raised in Israel would be best for his children, she also noted that this conviction "seemed to have impaired his judgement and blinded him to the terrible price he is paying for his obdurate attitude, namely the disruption of the family whose well-being he seeks to advance."[16] Justice Wilson suggested that his behaviour reflected an attitude characteristic of another era in which wives were viewed as their husbands' property.

The second case, *Petersik v. Petersik,* involved a father who had little contact with his wife and children during the two years in which he was away travelling.[17] In that time, the mother obtained an order granting her custody with reasonable access to the father. Upon his return, the father exercised access, and eventually his fourteen-year-old daughter moved in with him. The nine-year-old son chose to reside with his mother. The father filed for divorce and custody, making numerous allegations against the mother, including neglect and alcoholism. Justice Wilson granted a stay on an interim order giving custody to the father, citing the undesirability of shuffling children between parents throughout court proceedings. She also noted that there was no evidence that the mother had an alcohol problem.[18] In addition, she pointed out that the father's new common law partner "works full-time" and that the father "is, of course, also out all day at work," whereas the boy's mother was "at home and able to look after him."[19] This observation appeared to endorse the benefits of full-time female care, as well as the correlation between fatherhood and breadwinning: a commonly held notion in the history of child custody law, despite being somewhat shaken during the 1970s.[20] Justice Wilson might also have been acknowledging the mother's parenting as an important factor in this child's well-being.

Justice Wilson's history of dissent in custody and access cases began with the next case, *Glover v. Glover (No. 2),* in which a father had (allegedly) kidnapped his two children after the mother filed for divorce and custody.[21] Bell Canada had requested that the Court set aside an order compelling the father's brother-in-law to produce his telephone records so that the father's whereabouts might be determined. Whereas the majority focused on the confidentiality concerns of third parties and set the order aside, Justice Wilson noted that the husband was in contempt of several orders, including a custody order in favour of the mother. Since he could not be located, he could not be punished, making a "mockery" of the Court's process.[22] Although she agreed that no statutory authority existed to sanction the husband's behaviour, she would have held that the Court had inherent jurisdiction to so order. As in *Ishaky,* she would have cut through the technical issues to get at the substance of the proceedings.

The 1982 case of *Cooney v. Cooney,* in which the Court of Appeal affirmed a custody award to a father, also featured a dissent by Justice Wilson.[23] The parents had been high school sweethearts who had married very young and who worked in a family business operated by the mother's parents. The mother's relationship with her husband and her own mother had deteriorated after the death of her father in 1977. Justice Wilson's judgment indicates that both spouses had sought advice from a fellow employee about their marital difficulties. The mother subsequently entered into a relationship with him. Her own mother disapproved and sided with her son-in-law. The trial judge awarded custody to the father on the basis that the child was male and that "in future years the influence and guidance of a father may be equally if not more important than that of his mother."[24]

This paternal influence also seemed to persuade the Court of Appeal. The majority mentioned that the boy was doing well, saw a great deal of his maternal grandmother, and "seem[ed] to be a typical nine-year-old who likes skating, skiing and boating, all activities he can enjoy with his father."[25] They ultimately deferred to the trial judge's assessment of the witnesses but also indicated disapproval of the mother's new relationship, suggesting that she had prioritized it over her child's interests.[26]

Justice Wilson would have ordered a new trial for several reasons. First, she found that there was little evidence with respect to the child's best interests as opposed to spousal misconduct. Second, in hearing evidence concerning the mother's failure to give notification regarding her plan to take the child on vacation, the trial judge should have allowed her an opportunity to explain her actions. Third, the trial judge had placed undue weight on the mother's adultery. Justice Wilson emphasized that adultery did not constitute direct evidence that a mother was acting against a child's best interests. Referring to Justice de Grandpré's famous comment that "a wife who is 'well nigh impossible' as a wife may nevertheless be a wonderful mother,"[27] she stated, rather sharply, "We don't know whether Mrs. Cooney was 'a wonderful mother' or not but we do know that her husband as late as November of 1979, after the marriage had completely broken down, was writing to her and saying: 'I would never take Andrew away from you because I know you are a good mother and that you would never let any harm come to him.'"[28] Justice Wilson added, "Hell hath no fury like a person scorned!"[29]

She noted that "[t]his trial was a catharsis for the embattled parents but it told the trial judge little about the person who should have been 'front stage centre' in the minds of all the participants."[30] Justice Wilson objected to the way in which this custody case focused more on spousal misconduct such as adultery than on factors directly related to the child's interests – for example, the fact that the son had been "frightened and upset by one or two incidents where the husband used violence towards his mother in his presence."[31] A new trial was necessary to determine the child's "needs and which parent could best meet them, and, perhaps most important of all, how he related to each parent and where his emotional ties were."[32] Justice Wilson also appeared to recognize that the husband was being allowed to revenge himself upon his wife for her betrayal.[33] As in the previous cases, she proved willing to name problematic behaviour on the part of the father and to devise an appropriate legal remedy.

In the cases discussed above, Justice Wilson employed strong language; by contrast, her approach in her 1980 *Bezaire v. Bezaire* dissent seems cautious.[34] *Bezaire* is now regarded as a notorious case of a lesbian mother who lost custody to the father five years after she left an abusive marriage.[35] Much as she had in *Cooney,* Justice Wilson separated spousal conduct (in this case, sexual orientation) from ability to parent.

At the divorce trial, Gail Bezaire's lifestyle, rather than her husband's abuse, became the focus, even though she had counter-petitioned for divorce based on her husband's alleged acts of cruelty during the marriage. The trial judge dismissed her ground for divorce due to lack of corroborating evidence and granted the divorce on Mr. Bezaire's grounds: Gail's "homosexuality" (then a ground for divorce). In relation to the custody issue, considerable attention was paid to Gail's deprived childhood and the fact that she married at eighteen when she became pregnant. Referring euphemistically to the "strains on these two young people,"[36] the trial judge then focused on Gail's lesbianism, her relationships with women, and her participation in lesbian groups, noting that, though homosexuality of a parent was only one factor to be considered, "as far as this court is concerned, it is a negative factor."[37] In contrast, Mr. Bezaire's new family was portrayed as providing "a stable home, with a father figure, a mother figure, now a younger sister, with whom the children are enamored, and a fixed residence."[38] The fact that Mr. Bezaire had gone to jail rather than pay child support was not considered evidence of controlling behaviour.

Despite his negative assessment of Gail Bezaire, the trial judge initially proved reluctant to disturb her *de facto* custody of four years. He awarded her custody, but on strict conditions: that she obtain a residence, that Mr. Bezaire have extremely liberal access, and that she must obtain court approval before any other person resided with her – a condition clearly set with the goal of "negativing any open, declared, and avowed lesbian, or homosexual relationship."[39]

The father appealed the custody order and then applied to vary it on the grounds that the mother had breached the conditions by living in a "homosexual relationship." The trial judge granted the variation and ordered that the children be placed forthwith in the father's custody. The mother appealed. The Official Guardian got involved, resulting in new expert assessor reports. The majority upheld both the original order and the variation, thus dismissing the mother's appeal and making that of the father redundant. Justice Arnup highlighted "that the mother had been living from time to time in a lesbian relationship with two or three women in succession, and there was a good deal of evidence as to the effect of this upon the children."[40] But he also offered his much quoted thoughts on the relevance of homosexuality in a custody dispute:

> In my view homosexuality, either as a tendency, a proclivity or a practiced way of life, is not in itself alone a ground for refusing custody to the parent with respect to whom such evidence is given. The question is and must always be what effect upon the welfare of the children that aspect of the parent's make up and life-style has, and it will therefore be a question of evidence in that very case as to whether what has been shown to exist has or may tend to have effects adverse to the welfare of the children.[41]

Justice Wilson dissented in a brief judgment, noting that the assessment reports contained conflicting information and that the Official Guardian supported the mother's claim for the return of her children. She would have referred the custody issue back to the trial judge for the hearing of the new evidence. She was cautious, however, noting that it was impossible to speculate what effect, if any, fresh evidence would have on the trial judge. Although she did not state as much in her decision, the court-appointed psychiatrist had found some corroboration of Gail's allegations that the father had sexually abused the children.[42] It is impossible to know what impact this had on Justice Wilson, who would also have been aware of the allegations of cruelty made by Gail during the divorce trial. Justice Wilson also offered a view on the (ir)relevance of homosexuality that was somewhat stronger than the majority's: "I would like to add as an addendum to these reasons that in my view homosexuality is a neutral and not a negative factor as far as parenting skills are concerned."[43] In light of the majority decision, this statement would have been cold comfort to Gail Bezaire,[44] but it suggests that Justice Wilson would have liked to see a more balanced approach adopted in a new trial.

It seems shocking that the trial judge downplayed the domestic abuse in *Bezaire,* whereas he negatively emphasized Gail's lesbianism. At that time, however, awareness about domestic abuse was still low, and homosexuality had been decriminalized only a decade earlier. A study of divorce cases involving lesbians under the 1968 *Divorce Act* concluded that, "while adultery came to be viewed with a degree of judicial tolerance, homosexuality remained in the domain of deviant behaviour."[45] The few reported lesbian custody cases in Canada prior to *Bezaire* indicate that judges were particularly uneasy with mothers who were openly lesbian or who might "preach the joys of lesbianism."[46] Gail Bezaire did not fit the mould of a discreet lesbian. Justice Wilson's statement in *Bezaire* marked her as a judicial trendsetter in relation to "alternative" forms of parenting and as someone who was willing to challenge homophobic stereotypes in jurisprudence.

Normative Ideals for Parents

Justice Wilson's ability to see through the manipulative behaviour of fathers in the cases discussed above by no means meant that she became skeptical of all fathers. This section reviews her dissenting opinions in a famous joint custody case decided when she was still sitting on the Ontario Court of Appeal, and an equally well-known Supreme Court decision on remedies for access obstruction. Both dissents illustrate Justice Wilson's "high aspirations" for parenting relationships and her vision of the "symbolic role for law" in establishing standards of moral conduct.[47] Despite her careful and nuanced approach, these two decisions put her at odds with some feminist critique.

In the often-cited joint custody case of *Kruger v. Kruger,*[48] Justice Wilson made a strong statement in favour of the development of new custody remedies in the era of "friendly divorce."[49] Her dissent is said to have "foreshadowed the relatively recent shift, both judicial and statutory, towards awards of joint custody."[50] This shift has been criticized for its formalistic conception of equality, its bestowal of equal status on parents even when the mother is the primary caregiver, and its application of joint custody to inappropriate circumstances, such as where parents are in great disaccord.[51] For instance, where a father is awarded joint custody and is able to veto or dictate decisions in relation to children for whom he is not providing care, this award can be read as a continuation of his authoritative position within the family after the parents' separation.[52]

A closer look at *Kruger* shows that Justice Wilson's dissent was quite context- and fact-specific. In terms of legal context, at the time the case was decided, a traditional custody order endowed the custodial parent with a high degree of control and responsibility, including for decision making.[53] In contrast, though joint custody still gave one parent physical custody, the other received equal decision-making power and generous access.[54] As for the factual context, unlike other cases, *Kruger* arguably suggested such a high level of cooperation between the parents that feminist concerns about the impact of joint custody awards might be somewhat allayed. Both Mr. and Mrs. Kruger had attempted to surmount their significant differences as adults in order to shield the children from the consequences of their divorce. Justice Wilson relied on these facts to distinguish the case from *Baker v. Baker,* an earlier Court of Appeal decision that had denied a joint custody order to parents who were not willing or able to cooperate with each other.[55]

The parents in *Kruger* had achieved this considerable degree of cooperation despite their religious disagreement – often an easy recipe for conflict. Indeed, religion had played a significant role in the history of their marriage. A year after they were married (in 1964), problems arose due to the fact that, as the father admitted, "he was not a very good husband and father until he was converted to the Jehovah's Witness faith in July of 1973 ... [P]rior to that time he drank to excess, spent most of his free time with his drinking buddies, had an affair with another woman, and failed to realize the value of family relationships."[56] He apparently reformed as husband and father, and succeeded in establishing a good relationship with his children. He made mistakes, though, in his attempt to restore his relationship with Mrs. Kruger, who eventually wished to separate. Although they initially agreed that she and the children would stay in the matrimonial home, she eventually left, saying that health problems and harm to the children had resulted from the arrangement. When she told Mr. Kruger that she wanted to put the separation plan into effect, he changed his mind about letting her have custody. A Jehovah's Witness elder had advised him that the father, as the head of the household, should "exercise that headship and retain the children at [his] home."[57] Mrs. Kruger left the home alone in order to avoid making a scene.[58] Mr. Kruger was awarded interim custody pending trial, but the parents arranged that each should have the children for 50 percent of non-school hours. Each parent acknowledged the other's excellent parenting skills and expressed no reservations about the children being left in the other's care, with one key exception: Mr. Kruger insisted that he be in charge of their spiritual upbringing.

Tension had arisen between the parents because Mr. Kruger had indicated to the children that their mother was not behaving properly in the eyes of God. Although Mrs. Kruger was "extremely resentful" of this,[59] an expert found that she was still able to view her husband as a good parent and recommended that she be granted custody. The trial judge did so on condition that the children be brought up as Jehovah's Witnesses. She was willing to accede to this demand.

This relatively amicable post-separation relationship influenced Justice Wilson, as did the fact that "Mr. Kruger espoused the Jehovah's Witness faith with wholehearted zeal and sincerity."[60] In her dissent on appeal, in which she would have ordered joint custody, Justice Wilson emphasized the fact that Mrs. Kruger testified to her husband's bona fides in believing that a father had responsibility for the religious oversight of his family.[61] Being a woman of faith herself,[62] Justice Wilson may have been concerned that Mr. Kruger not be viewed negatively because of his religion.

Whereas the trial judge had assumed that one parent must receive full custody even if both demonstrated equal parenting capabilities, Justice Wilson thought that a joint custody order could be made. The majority did not disagree in theory but held that the facts in *Kruger* did not warrant imposition of joint custody: it was not clear whether the Krugers were agreeable to such an order – indeed, the facts revealed "considerable antagonism between the Krugers as former spouses ... notwithstanding their evident respect for one another as parents."[63] The kind of cooperation that the parents had achieved in the past and the type that would be essential under a joint custody order were two very different matters.[64]

The majority's skepticism about the success of joint custody under such circumstances accords with the cautious approach that many feminists adopt regarding joint custody. In contrast, Justice Wilson's embrace of this new normative development seemed to ignore the power imbalance that mothers often experience when negotiating custody disputes. The attention she had previously paid to power dynamics did not extend, in this case, to a consideration of the evidence that Mr. Kruger had engaged in potentially manipulative behaviour by devaluing Mrs. Kruger as unchristian.

Instead, Justice Wilson stated that "men and women who fall short as spouses may nevertheless excel as parents" and emphasized that concern for the child should be the paramount consideration.[65] She suggested that it was time for courts "to shed their 'healthy cynicism' and reflect in their orders a greater appreciation of the hurt inflicted upon a child by the severance of its relationship with one of its parents ... [I]n some circumstances it may be in the child's best interests not to choose between the parents but to do everything possible to maintain the child's relationship with both parents."[66] At odds with her decisions in cases such as *Ishaky*, Justice Wilson's dissent shows a surprising optimism about the possibility of cooperation, given the history of antagonism between the Krugers. She was perhaps overly sanguine about the notion that "[m]ost mature adults, after the initial trauma has worn off, are able to overcome the hostility attendant on the dissolution of their marriages or at the very least are capable of subserving it to the interests of their children," especially now that "the so-called 'friendly divorce' is one of the phenomena of our time."[67]

Indeed, many parents do overcome their conflicts to arrive at an arrangement regarding the children, as is evidenced by the fact that the vast majority of custody disputes are settled out of court.[68] However, some separating parents are never able to reach an agreement and must seek court arbitration. In these cases, it remains questionable whether judicially imposed orders for joint custody or shared or parallel parenting are advisable. Philip Epstein and Lene Madsen have commented critically on orders for parallel parenting (a recent variant of joint custody), saying that, "while perhaps well intentioned, parallel parenting is deeply flawed, reflecting less a concern with the best interests of children than judicial resistance to the imperative to 'choose' between parents, a narrow and formal conception of parental equality, and an unstudied faith in the ability to compel co-operation between hostile litigants."[69] Justice Wilson's dissent in *Kruger* flew in the face of such concerns. However context specific, it laid important groundwork in the embrace of joint custody as a normative ideal in Canadian law.

Justice Wilson's willingness to embrace forward-looking legal norms such as joint custody was later confirmed by her dissenting opinion in *Frame v. Smith*.[70] By the time that case reached the Supreme Court of Canada, child custody law had already been the subject of considerable public debate, prompted by the rise in fathers' rights and equality rights discourse, and by the discussion surrounding joint custody during the drafting of the "new" divorce legislation.[71] In the law reform debates, fathers' rights advocates alleged that vindictive or selfish custodial mothers were preventing fathers from seeing their children.[72] The decision must be viewed in light of these developments, which tend toward demonizing mothers who resist maximum contact between children and fathers.[73]

Frame v. Smith asked the Court whether a non-custodial father had a cause of action against the custodial mother and her new husband for interfering with his access rights. He claimed that the mother had done everything in her power to frustrate access, including making several moves, changing the children's surname and religion, claiming he was not their father, forbidding telephone conversations, and intercepting his letters. He asked for damages for out-of-pocket expenses of $25,000 and for general and punitive damages of $1 million and $500,000 respectively for severe emotional distress.

The majority of the Supreme Court recognized no cause of action, in part because multiplying lawsuits within the "family circle" would disrupt a child's familial and social environment[74] but also because any possible common law remedy had been superseded by legislative measures concerning custody and access. Justice Wilson, alone in dissent, held that the facts could give rise to a cause of action, not in tort, but for breach of fiduciary duty owed by a custodial parent to a non-custodial parent. She speculated that, had the case gone to trial, equitable compensation would allow recovery of both out-of-pocket expenses and a realistic sum for pain and suffering.[75] Mary Jane Mossman has observed that her approach boldly challenges the public-private divide, which restricts the role that law can play in private family relations.[76] However, Justice Wilson's approach in this case may not be that exceptional, since legal intervention in the private sphere occurs more readily when a family or family member transgresses behavioural norms.[77] Arguably, Justice Wilson regarded this mother's behaviour as well outside the normative expectations of good mothering, which, in modern custody law, involves a heavy responsibility to nurture a child's relationship with the father.[78] In penalizing such transgressions of cooperative parenting, her *Frame v. Smith* dissent is perhaps consistent with her earlier condemnation of fathers who had stepped outside the boundaries of proper behaviour.

Justice Wilson carefully articulated the competing interests in allowing a cause of action under these circumstances. She noted that interparental litigation is not in the child's best interest where it results in the destruction of the child's relationships with either parent.[79] But neither could it be "in the best interests of children to have custodial parents defy with impunity court orders designed to preserve their relationship with their non-custodial parents."[80] She found that extending tort law remedies would not be in children's best interests as it might provide weapons to malicious spouses. However, the remedy for breach of fiduciary duty could not be so distorted, because it would be available only in the limited family context of custody and access orders, circumstances under which the children are most vulnerable.[81]

Despite the common law's traditional reluctance to do so, Justice Wilson would have extended fiduciary duties to a wider range of persons, including custodial parents.[82] Her reasons included the "very substantial interest" that a non-custodial parent has in his (or her) relationship with the child, the confirmation of that relationship resulting from the access order, and the order's effect of putting the custodial parent in "a position of power and authority" and leaving the non-custodial parent more vulnerable.[83] In relation to that last point, she invoked the tropes of the selfish mother, albeit in gender-neutral terms: "The selfish exercise of custody over a long period of time without regard to the access order can utterly destroy the non-custodial parent's relationship with his child. The non-custodial parent (and, of course, the child also) is completely vulnerable to this."[84] She then cited the maximum contact, or friendly parent, provisions of the then new

Divorce Act, stating that the custodial parent was expected to act in good faith toward the non-custodial parent and the children, this being "one of the qualifications of a good custodial parent."[85] Wishing to create a strong incentive for custodial parents to recognize that their children were *entitled* to an ongoing relationship with the other parent, Justice Wilson said that "this cause of action will help to promote a healthy and beneficial relationship between a child and both parents."[86] Her assumption that a right of contact exists is notable since the maximum contact section specifies only that the extent of contact should be consistent with a child's best interests. This approach foreshadowed that of Justice McLachlin in *Young v. Young* and *Gordon v. Goertz.*[87]

Justice Wilson's gender-neutral language in *Frame v. Smith* ignored the fact that custody/access disputes rarely produce gender-neutral results: in the majority of cases during the 1980s, custody was awarded to the mother, with access to the father, reflecting the material realities of child care responsibilities. Her analysis of fiduciary duty must be examined in light of this actuality. In Chapter 5, Shannon O'Byrne points out that Justice Wilson's dissent set the stage for recognizing a man's claim for emotional distress. Her concern that "the custodial parent who denies access to the other parent is sacrificing the child's best interests ... to his or her own selfish interests"[88] can be seen both as demonizing mothers and as "zealous concern to protect the interests of men – this time as fathers."[89] That said, she set strict parameters for the operation of the fiduciary remedy: relief should be denied in cases where the non-custodial parent's conduct was contrary to a child's best interests, such as where she or he failed to pay spousal support or abused access rights.[90] She also found that "the cause of action for breach of fiduciary duty can proceed only if there is no risk that the support of the children will be impaired and no risk of a harmful conflict of loyalties arising in the children."[91] These conditions might be satisfied when the children were fully grown and self-supporting or when the relationship had been so severely damaged that a conflict of loyalties was unlikely to arise. Moreover, only a "sustained course of conduct designed to destroy the relationship" would trigger the cause of action.[92]

Justice Wilson also warned that, if a custodial parent genuinely believed that continued access by the other parent was not in the child's interests or was harmful to the child, she or he should not engage in ongoing wilful violations of the access order but rather should apply for variation or rescission of the order. The practicality of this advice is dubious, given that access is rarely denied to a parent and that effective supervision is (still today) difficult to arrange. Justice Wilson also arguably overlooked the possibility that, even where courts did not ultimately grant a remedy, a non-custodial parent could use this cause of action to harass the custodial parent with repeated actions.[93] As with her decision in *Kruger,* Justice Wilson appeared in *Frame v. Smith* to overlook some of the potentially serious ways in which fathers could use remedies in the custody and access field to manipulate their ex-partners or to maintain control. Finally, given that the failure of fathers to exercise access is a larger problem than blocking them from it,[94] the majority's refusal to extend a remedy seems more realistic and less punitive.

Challenging Patriarchy or Embracing Liberal Norms?

The cases analyzed in this chapter contain an inherent contradiction. On the one hand, Justice Wilson challenged the traditional familial ideology of male dominance over women and children. Several of her Ontario Court of Appeal decisions demonstrated her willingness to recognize the controlling behaviour of men and the need of women to leave unhappy marriages. In *Bezaire,* she took a courageous stance on lesbianism as a neutral rather than a prejudicial factor in custody disputes. In other cases, however, she promoted new legal approaches to custody and access that tended to empower men in the post-separation context. These trends can be seen as reinforcing a highly gendered post-divorce family unit in which women assumed the responsibilities of caregiving, whereas men retained legal control over the family. Because *Kruger* and *Frame v. Smith* are Justice Wilson's best-known decisions in this field, her main legacy is an embrace of liberal norms and formal equality that reinforce, rather than challenge, patriarchy.

In the early 1990s, Justice Wilson suggested that a "feminine" perspective might make a difference to judicial decision making in various fields,[95] and she identified family law as an area where feminist scholarship had already produced "first-rate analyses of the gender impact of law."[96] She also noted that, "in North America, the family has been the location of much of women's subordination," and, referring to the sexual division of labour in heterosexual families, she gestured toward feminist critiques on the problematic role of familial ideology in women's lives.[97] But these reflections did not precipitate a reassessment of how women's disproportionate responsibility for child care should influence joint custody awards or remedies for access obstruction. Thus, her earlier published views on child custody law remain intact: it would be preferable to move beyond the differential awards of "custody" and "access," which she believed caused fathers to gradually lose contact with their children, toward an approach that favours "divid[ing] custodial responsibility evenly between the two parents" through split custody, alternating or divided custody, or through joint or shared custody awards.[98] She lamented that the increased rate of family dissolution meant that "the number of children who currently come from broken homes is a social phenomenon without precedent."[99] In an effort to reduce the harmful effects of divorce, her dissent in *Frame v. Smith* indicated that she viewed the child's best interest as served through contact with "both parents" but did not offer any caveats regarding when it may not be so, notably in cases involving abuse.[100]

It is tempting to link Justice Wilson's liberal approach to her personal and professional history but ultimately impossible to know how influential various factors were in her custody decisions. She apparently had a "good" marriage with a husband who respected her and who shared housekeeping duties.[101] She did not have children, so she did not face the serious challenges of "balancing" a legal career with child care responsibilities.[102] Moreover, unlike Claire L'Heureux-Dubé, Justice Wilson never practised family law nor was a trial judge, an experience that can provide a rude awakening to the harsh realities of custody disputes. Like many, she was captured by the liberal feminist optimism of the 1970s and 1980s. She shared the desire to challenge the sexual division of labour by encouraging men to embrace the responsibilities of parenting, as women increasingly participated in the labour force. She hoped that positive legal norms about cooperation and sharing might promote the "friendly divorce" of the no-fault era. In this sense, she was ultimately a product of the law reform movement of her time. From the perspective of a feminist sensitive to the family law climate of the twenty-first century, however, it is difficult not to see Justice Wilson's dissents in *Kruger* and *Frame v. Smith* as a portent of the mother blaming to come.

Acknowledgments

Thanks are due to Jennifer Lee, Rachael Manion, and Kerri-Ann Reid for research assistance, to UBC's Hampton Research Fund for funding, to Kim Brooks for editorial direction, and to Gillian Calder and Robert Leckey for insightful comments.

Notes

1 Susan B. Boyd, *Child Custody, Law, and Women's Work* (Don Mills: Oxford University Press, 2003); Alison Harvison Young, "The Changing Family, Rights Discourse and the Supreme Court of Canada" (2001) 80 Can. Bar. Rev. 749.

2 This chapter examines disputes between separated parents. In Chapter 9 of this volume, Gillian Calder discusses Justice Wilson's custody decisions that arose in other contexts, such as the adoption case *Racine v. Woods,* [1983] 2 S.C.R. 173.

3 Marie-Claire Belleau and Rebecca Johnson, "Les Femmes juges feront-elles véritablement une différence? Réflexions sur leur présence depuis vingt ans à la Cour suprême du Canada" (2005) 17 Rev. Femmes & D. 27 at 30; see also Chapter 12, this volume.

4 *Divorce Act,* R.S.C. 1970, c. D-8.

5 Anne-Marie Ambert, *Divorce in Canada* (Toronto: Academic Press Canada, 1980) at 20-21.

6 Law Reform Commission of Canada, *Family Law* (Ottawa: Information Canada, 1976) at 48.

7 Anita Fineberg, "Joint Custody of Infants: Breakthrough or Fad?" (1979) 2 Can. J. Fam. L. 417; Janice Drakich, "In Search of the Better Parent: The Social Construction of Ideologies of Fatherhood" (1989) 3 C.J.W.L. 69.

8 Boyd, *supra* note 1 at c. 4.

9 Robert Benton, *Kramer vs. Kramer* (Culver City: Columbia Pictures Industries, 1979). *Kramer vs. Kramer,* which won the best picture at the Academy Awards for 1979, featured a workaholic father (Dustin Hoffman) who had to deal with parenting and domestic labour when his wife (Meryl Streep) left him. On the film's understanding of gender and child custody law, see David Ray Papke, "Peace between the Sexes: Law and Gender in *Kramer vs. Kramer*" (1995-96) 30 U.S.F.L. Rev. 1199.

10 *Canadian Charter of Rights and Freedoms,* s. 7, Part I of the *Constitution Act, 1982,* being Schedule B to the *Canada Act 1982* (U.K.), 1982, c. 11.

11 *Divorce Act,* R.S.C 1985, c. 3, s. 16.

12 See *e.g.* Jonathan Cohen and Nikki Gershbain, "'For the Sake of the Fathers'? Child Custody Reform and the Perils of Maximum Contact" (2001) 19 Can. Fam. L.Q. 121. Justice Beverley McLachlin's judgment in *Young v. Young,* [1993] 4 S.C.R. 3, effectively created a presumption that a significant amount of regular contact with the non-custodial parent is in the best interests of children.

13 Here I depart somewhat from Brian Dickson's assessment that she had a sense of the limits of the law. Dickson was, however, partly addressing the critique of Bertha Wilson for being a judicial activist, whereas I am concerned with her sense that new legal norms could change behaviour. See Brian Dickson, "Madame Justice Wilson: Trailblazer for Justice" (1992) 15 Dal. L.J. 1 at 8-9.

14 *Ishaky v. Ishaky,* [1978] O.J. No. 31, 7 R.F.L. (2d) 138 at para. 19 (C.A.).

15 *Ibid.* at para. 15.

16 *Ibid.* at para. 17.

17 *Petersik v. Petersik,* [1978] O.J. No. 2224 (C.A.).

18 *Ibid.* at para. 8.

19 *Ibid.* at paras. 3, 10.

20 Richard Collier, "'Waiting Till Father Gets Home': The Reconstruction of Fatherhood in Family Law" (1995) 4 Soc. & Leg. Stud. 5.

21 *Glover v. Glover et al. (No. 2),* [1980] O.J. No. 3677, 29 O.R. (2d) 401, 113 D.L.R. (3d) 174 (C.A.) [*Glover,* cited to O.J.].

22 *Ibid.* at para. 28.

23 *Cooney v. Cooney,* [1982] O.J. No. 3199, 36 O.R. (2d) 137, 132 D.L.R. (3d) 439 (C.A.) [*Cooney*].

24 *Ibid.* at para. 11.

25 *Ibid.* at para. 7 (per Cory J.A.).

26 *Ibid.* at para. 19.

27 *Talsky v. Talsky,* [1976] 2 S.C.R. 292 at 294.

28 *Cooney, supra* note 23 at para 35.

29 *Ibid.*

30 *Ibid.* at para. 30.

31 *Ibid.*

32 *Ibid.* at para. 29.

33 Ellen Anderson, *Judging Bertha Wilson: Law as Large as Life* (Toronto: University of Toronto Press for the Osgoode Society for Canadian Legal History, 2001) at 117-18.

34 *Bezaire v. Bezaire,* [1980] O.J. No. 1320, 20 R.F.L. (2d) 358 (C.A.) [*Bezaire* (C.A.)].

35 Susan Crean, *In the Name of the Fathers: The Story behind Child Custody* (Toronto: Amanita Enterprises, 1988) at 31-34; Kathleen A. Lahey, "On Silences, Screams and Scholarship: An Introduction to Feminist Legal Theory" in Richard F. Devlin, ed., *Feminist Legal Theory* (Toronto: Emond Montgomery, 1991) 47 at 57-59. After the Court of Appeal confirmed the custody award to the father, Gail Bezaire disappeared with her children for five years and was convicted in 1985 of taking children in contravention of a custody order: *R. v. Gail Bezaire* (1987), 2 W.C.B. (2d) 392 (Ont. Dist. Ct.) (Dymond D.C.J.).

36 *Bezaire v. Bezaire* (1979), 2 Fam. L. Rev. 51 at 51 (McMahon L.J.S.C.).

37 *Ibid.* at 54.

38 *Ibid.* at 56.

39 *Ibid.* at 57.

40 *Bezaire* (C.A.), *supra* note 34 at para. 5.

41 *Ibid.* at para. 18.

42 Lahey, *supra* note 35 at 58.

43 *Bezaire* (C.A.), *supra* note 34 at para. 26.

44 Crean, *supra* note 35 at 32.

45 Katherine Arnup, "'Mothers Just Like Others': Lesbians, Divorce, and Child Custody in Canada" (1989) 3 C.J.W.L. 18 at 23.

46 *K. v. K.* (1975), 23 R.F.L. 58 at para. 17 (Alta. Prov. Ct.) (Rowe Prov. J.).

47 Mary Jane Mossman, "The 'Family' in the Work of Madame Justice Wilson" (1992) 15 Dal. L.J. 115 at 138, 141.

48 *Kruger v. Kruger,* [1979] O.J. No. 4343, 25 O.R. (2d) 673, 104 D.L.R. (3d) 481 (C.A.) [*Kruger*].
49 *Ibid.* at para. 6.
50 Philip Epstein and Lene Madsen, "Joint Custody with a Vengeance: The Emergence of Parallel Parenting Orders" (2004) 22 Can. Fam. L.Q. 1 at 1.
51 See *e.g.* Anne-Marie Delorey, "Joint Legal Custody: A Reversion to Patriarchal Power" (1989) 3 C.J.W.L. 33; Sheila M. Holmes, "Imposed Joint Legal Custody: Children's Interests or Parental Rights?" (1987) 45 U.T. Fac. L. Rev. 300; Martha Shaffer, "Joint Custody, Parental Conflict and Children's Adjustment to Divorce: What the Social Science Literature Does and Does Not Tell Us" (2007) 26 Can. Fam. L.Q. 285.
52 Delorey, *supra* note 51 at 54.
53 *Kruger, supra* note 48 at para. 15 (Thorson J.A.).
54 *Ibid.* at para. 17, Thorson J.A., citing *Baker v. Baker* (1979), O.J. No. 4074, 23 O.R. (2d) 391, 95 D.L.R. (3d) 529 [*Baker*].
55 *Baker, ibid.*
56 *Kruger, supra* note 48 at para. 35 (Wilson J.A., dissenting).
57 *Ibid.* at para. 42.
58 *Ibid.* at para. 37.
59 *Ibid.* at para. 45.
60 *Ibid.* at para. 54.
61 *Ibid.*
62 See Anderson, *supra* note 33 (Bertha Wilson was active in the United Church).
63 *Kruger, supra* note 48 at para. 26.
64 *Ibid.*
65 *Ibid.* at para. 58.
66 *Ibid.*
67 *Ibid.* at para. 64.
68 Department of Justice, *Evaluation of the Divorce Act Phase II: Monitoring and Evaluation* (Ottawa: Canadian Department of Justice Bureau of Review, 1990) at 47 [*Evaluation of the Divorce Act*].
69 Epstein and Madsen, *supra* note 50 at 3; see also Anderson, *supra* note 33 at 113.
70 *Frame v. Smith,* [1987] 2 S.C.R. 99, [1987] S.C.J. No. 49. In Chapter 3 of this volume, Janis Sarra comments on this case.
71 See Boyd, *supra* note 1 at c. 5.
72 Susan B. Boyd and Claire F.L. Young, "Who Influences Family Law Reform? Discourses on Motherhood and Fatherhood in Legislative Reform Debates in Canada" (2002) 26 Studies in Law, Politics, and Society 43.
73 Susan B. Boyd, "Demonizing Mothers: Fathers' Rights Discourses in Child Custody Law Reform Processes" (2004) 6 Journal of the Association for Research on Mothering 52.
74 *Frame v. Smith, supra* note 70 at para. 9. (In its definition of "family circle," the majority seemed to include "the grandparents, and aunts and uncles of their children, to say nothing of close family friends.")
75 *Ibid.* at para. 82. Others have noted Bertha Wilson's creative use of common law remedies: see Chapters 3 and 6, this volume.
76 Mossman, *supra* note 47 at 146.
77 On the indeterminacy of the public-private divide, see Susan B. Boyd, ed., *Challenging the Public/Private Divide: Feminism, Law, and Public Policy* (Toronto: University of Toronto Press, 1997).
78 See *e.g.* Boyd, *supra* note 1; Helen Rhoades, "The 'No Contact Mother': Reconstructions of Motherhood in the Era of the 'New Father'" (2002) 16 Int'l J.L. Pol'y & Fam. 71.
79 *Frame v. Smith, supra* note 70 at para. 34.
80 *Ibid.* at para. 35.
81 *Ibid.* at para. 70.
82 In Chapter 3, this volume, Janis Sarra points out that Justice Wilson's dissent regarding fiduciary duty is perhaps the most often-quoted family law judgment in the commercial law context.

83 *Frame v. Smith, supra* note 70 at para. 65.
84 *Ibid.*
85 *Ibid.*
86 *Ibid.* at para. 71.
87 *Young v. Young,* [1993] S.C.J. No. 112, [1993] 4 S.C.R. 3; *Gordon v. Goertz,* [1996] S.C.J. No. 52, [1996] 2 S.C.R. 27. See also Boyd, *supra* note 1 at 132-33, 154.
88 *Frame v. Smith, supra* note 70 at para. 35.
89 Anderson, *supra* note 33 at 214.
90 *Frame v. Smith, supra* note 70 at para. 72.
91 *Ibid.* at para. 73.
92 *Ibid.* at para. 78.
93 See Jane Gordon, "Multiple Meanings of Equality: A Case Study in Custody Litigation" (1989) 3 C.J.W.L. 256; Sandra A. Goundry, *Final Report on Court-Related Harassment and Family Law "Justice"* (Ottawa: National Association of Women and the Law, 1998).
94 See *Evaluation of the Divorce Act, supra* note 68 at 11.
95 Bertha Wilson, "Will Women Judges Really Make a Difference?" (1990) 28 Osgoode Hall L.J. 507 at 515.
96 Bertha Wilson, "Women, the Family, and the Constitutional Protection of Privacy" (1992) 17 Queen's L.J. 5 at 11.
97 *Ibid.* at 13.
98 Bertha Wilson, "Children: The Casualties of a Failed Marriage" (1985) 19 U.B.C.L. Rev. 245 at 258.
99 *Ibid.* at 245.
00 See *e.g.* Rhoades, *supra* note 78; Miranda Kaye, Julie Stubbs, and Julia Tolmie, "Domestic Violence and Child Contact Arrangements" (2003) 17 Austl. J. Fam. L. 93.
01 Anderson, *supra* note 33 at 47.
02 *Ibid.* at 109. Anderson suggests that her spousal support decisions may not have sufficiently considered the fact that most younger women would have had young children, compromising their ability to become economically self-sufficient.

Part 3
Reflections

11
But Was She a Feminist Judge?

Beverley Baines

Justice Bertha Wilson "considers herself a moderate feminist."[1] This 1985 statement, reported in a national news magazine, appeared three years after Wilson's appointment to the Supreme Court of Canada.[2] Prior to this appointment, Justice Wilson sat on the Ontario Court of Appeal for seven years. With a decade of appellate adjudication behind her, she was no longer a novice on the bench. But was she a feminist judge?

Rosemary Hunter may have been the first to define a feminist judge.[3] She lists two criteria: gender and identity. Hunter is tentative about requiring a feminist judge to be a woman but categorical about identity, maintaining "that a feminist judge must identify her- (or him-) self as a feminist."[4] She suggests that self-identification might alleviate the essentialism of difference theory. However, self-identification is compromised if a judge changes her mind. For example, the 1985 report of Justice Wilson's self-identification as a "moderate feminist" was succeeded sixteen years later by the statement in her authorized biography that she "declines to identify herself as a feminist."[5] A change of this magnitude is significant. When did it take place? And does it follow that Justice Wilson was not accountable as a feminist thereafter? Or, to give another example, Justice Claire L'Heureux-Dubé, the second woman appointed to the Supreme Court of Canada, steadfastly refused to identify as a feminist until very late in her career on the bench. Does it follow that she was not accountable as a feminist for most of her judicial opinions?[6]

Such questions require resolution before self-identification can serve as a reliable measure of feminist adjudication. Rather than pursuing them in this chapter, however, I propose to shift the focus to sex equality. Unlike self-identification, which may reflect individual feminist idiosyncrasies, sex equality inspires most, if not all, Canadian feminists. Through this lens, we can attribute a feminist identity to a judge who presents herself as a proponent of sex equality.

In other words, sex equality refocuses the feminist question by analyzing who is a feminist judge from the perspective of interpretation rather than that of identity. Irrespective of whether a woman judge self-identifies as feminist, we can examine the meaning that she gives to the concept of sex equality in her judicial opinions. Inevitably, Supreme Court justices are called upon to interpret this concept in cases involving the *Canadian Charter of Rights and Freedoms* and statutory anti-discrimination laws, as well as in cases drawn from family, property, and criminal law contexts.[7] Therefore, I propose to ask the feminist question by exploring the concept of sex equality as it is manifest in Justice Wilson's decisions.

The first step is to situate sex equality in a theoretical context. Justice Wilson joined the Court at a time when feminist legal theory was beginning to develop in Canada. Just before the *Charter* was adopted, the Court had rendered two sex equality decisions that dismayed us all.[8] These two cases gave us good reason to reject the prevailing separate-but-equal concept of equality (also known as difference theory). As well, we worried that, even if the Court could be persuaded to change its approach, the judges would opt for the concept of formal equality (or sameness theory) to interpret the *Charter.* In contrast, most feminists subscribed to the concept of substantive equality (which invariably was depicted in terms of Catharine MacKinnon's theory of dominance and subordination). The desired change took some years to unfold, but ultimately the Court decided to adopt the rhetoric of substantive equality.[9] Since others have told the story of Justice Wilson's role in influencing this decision, I will refer only briefly to this aspect of her work.[10]

Instead, I intend to concentrate on three cases that led some feminists to question Wilson's commitment to substantive equality. Although these are not the only decisions critiqued by feminists, they represent distinctive areas of law. The first is *Pelech v. Pelech,* a family law case in which Justice Wilson wrote the majority judgment denying an ex-wife's application to vary a post-divorce maintenance agreement.[11] The second is an abortion case known as *R. v. Morgentaler* in which Wilson made no reference to the right to sex equality in s. 15(1) of the *Charter* when she concurred with the majority decision that the abortion provision in the *Criminal Code* infringed the right to security of the person protected in s. 7 of the *Charter.*[12] The third is a statutory rape case called *R. v. Hess; R. v. Nguyen* in which Wilson held for the majority that limiting the *Criminal Code* statutory rape provision to males did not infringe the right to sex equality in s. 15(1) of the *Charter.*[13] The feminists who criticize these three judgments all agree that Justice Wilson failed to declare that the impugned rules infringed substantive equality.

My objective is to explore the possibilities of resisting this critique. My resistance takes two forms. First, I suggest ever so gently that the critics might have missed something. That is, I review Justice Wilson's judgments in *Pelech,*

Morgentaler, and *Hess* for any signs of consistency with substantive equality, defined according to her critics by dominance theory. Perhaps they missed a signifier that has become more important with the passage of time. Essentially, this form of resistance involves revisiting dominance theory.

Second, I question the critics' preoccupation with dominance theory itself. More specifically, I ask whether recent developments in women's studies and queer theory offer a new perspective – I will call it "gender theory" for the sake of giving it a label – that might displace dominance theory as the prevailing approach to interpreting the concept of sex equality. An affirmative answer would be just the first step, however. The next step would involve applying this new gender theory to Justice Wilson's judgments in *Pelech, Morgentaler,* and *Hess.* Thus, I proceed with this second form of resistance by importing gender into the equality analysis.

Of course, the outcome of importing gender may be simply to replicate the findings of the feminist critics who applied dominance theory. Alternatively, it may be redemptive. In other words, one or more of Justice Wilson's three controversial judgments may be consistent with substantive equality when that concept is redefined in accordance with gender theory. Any such decisions should then qualify as feminist, her critics notwithstanding.

Background Jurisprudence

Before I embark on an analysis of Justice Wilson's three controversial cases, it seems only fair to mention some of her many positive contributions. I begin by noting that these three judgments constitute a very tiny fraction of the total number of cases that she decided. During the nine years that she sat on the Supreme Court of Canada, she was a prodigious jurist, participating in a significant number of cases. According to research published for the first time in this volume, Marie-Claire Belleau, Rebecca Johnson, and Christina Vinters report that Justice Wilson participated in 551 "significant" decisions, authoring as many as 179 opinions.[14] Out of a total of 179, only three controversial judgments is infinitesimal – a mere 1.7 percent – a percentage that would be even lower if we measured them against all the decisions in which she participated, irrespective of whether she wrote the judgments herself.

Moreover, qualitatively speaking, Justice Wilson's judgments in *Charter* and other cases are important to feminists because she initiated the Supreme Court of Canada's contextual approach to rights analysis. For example, in 1983, she dissented in a rape case *(R. v. Konkin),* maintaining that the complainant's sexual conduct after the rape was irrelevant because it showed her trauma, rather than whether the accused was guilty of the offence.[15] Later, in 1986, Wilson concurred in a *Charter* religious freedom case *(R. v. Big M Drug Mart),* advocating that primacy be given "to an effects based test of constitutional harm because of its importance in addressing systemic inequalities."[16] Also in 1986, she dissented in a *Charter*-age discrimination case *(McKinney v. Board of Governors of the University of Guelph)* on the grounds that mandatory retirement harmed not only workers lacking private pension schemes, but also women workers in the organized sector who had not been able to accumulate adequate pension credits because "of the high incidence of interrupted work histories due to child bearing and child rearing."[17] These cases illustrate that Justice Wilson repeatedly contextualized issues, not only because adding more voices to the legal narrative reveals and corrects imbalances, but also because it "changes how we understand what is happening in a legal dispute."[18]

Continuing her campaign for contextual analysis, Justice Wilson successfully formalized this approach in three *Charter* cases decided in 1989, although regrettably none happened to be sex equality cases. In the first of these *(Andrews v. Law Society of British Columbia),* Wilson wrote that equality must be assessed according to "the context of the group in the entire social, political and legal fabric of our society."[19] In the second case *(R. v. Turpin),* she described the equality rights provision in s. 15 of the *Charter* as "remedying or preventing discrimination against groups suffering social, political and legal disadvantage in our society."[20] In the third case *(Edmonton Journal v. Alberta),* she extended the application of contextual analysis from equality rights to the right to freedom of expression when she wrote that expression might have "a greater value in a political context than it does in the context of disclosure of the details of a matrimonial dispute."[21] Therefore, not only does contextual analysis expose the "systemic nature of inequality,"[22] but also it is suited to revealing assumptions that underlie the abstract analysis of other *Charter* rights.

Feminists should also approve of Justice Wilson's contributions to the "cultural meaning of womanhood."[23] For example, concurring in a pornography case *(R. v. Towne Cinema Theatres Ltd.),* Wilson injected the idea that the pornographic portrayal of women is the portrayal of human beings who are being dehumanized.[24] As another example, in a prostitution case *(Reference re ss. 193 and 195.1(1)(c) of the Criminal Code (Man.))* in which Wilson dissented with Justice L'Heureux-Dubé, she maintained that criminalizing prostitution infringed the freedom of expression of prostitutes, who should be portrayed not as victims, but as economic actors with expression rights.[25] Probably the best known example, however, is the battered woman's case *(R. v. Lavallee),* in which Wilson wrote for the majority that the "definition of what is reasonable must be adapted to circumstances which are, by and large, foreign to the world inhabited by the hypothetical 'reasonable man.'"[26] This judgment, in which the battered woman was acquitted of murder on the grounds of self-defence because Wilson refused to apply the male model of reasonableness – refused, in other words, to abstract gender from context – stands as a very rich source of messages about womanhood.[27]

Finally, there are the women's cases in which Justice Wilson participated but did not write her own judgment. To illustrate, many of these involved statutory human rights legislation that prohibited sex discrimination in employment. For instance, she joined a unanimous Court in redefining sex discrimination to include pregnancy discrimination *(Brooks v. Canada Safeway),* a reversal of the Court's decision to the contrary written a decade earlier *(Bliss v. Canada (A.G.)).*[28] In another example, she joined a unanimous Court in recognizing that sexual harassment is sex discrimination *(Janzen v. Platy Enterprises Ltd.).*[29] In a third instance, she joined a unanimous Court to uphold an affirmative action (or employment equity) remedy for women working in non-traditional jobs for a national rail transportation company *(Action Travail des Femmes v. Canadian National Railway Co.).*[30]

Of course, it is the existence of this women-centric jurisprudence that makes it all the more difficult to understand the three controversial cases. If Justice Wilson had not rendered so many decisions that found feminist approval, the three controversies would not be so glaring. In fact, I want to point out that one of the three judgments is not so egregiously controversial. *Morgentaler* is rightly the subject of feminist critique because Justice Wilson did not invoke equality rights to decriminalize abortion. However, it is also rightly the subject of feminist approval because she supported decriminalization, albeit on grounds other than sex equality. Moreover, in doing so, she won more feminist approval by being the only judge to emphasize liberty rather than security of the person. Therefore, subject to this caveat about her abortion judgment, I want to examine these three noteworthy cases that offended feminists, first by revisiting dominance theory and then by importing gender theory to challenge it.

Revisiting Dominance Theory

Are there any indications that Justice Wilson took the then prevailing substantive equality theory of dominance and subordination into account when she rendered her controversial judgments in the family law *(Pelech),* abortion *(Morgentaler),* and statutory rape *(Hess)* cases? Catharine MacKinnon was the most forceful exponent of dominance theory from her earliest writings. Dominance theory treats sexuality as inherently subordinating of women. MacKinnon writes that "sexuality organizes society into two sexes – women and men – which division underlies the totality of social relations."[31] Nor does sexuality just create difference; rather, sexuality, or more specifically, sexualizing women, is what men do to keep women subordinated. Not only is sexuality "a form of power," but also, like heterosexuality, it "institutionalizes male sexual dominance and female sexual submission."[32] To put it succinctly, "sexuality is the linchpin of gender inequality."[33]

To be consistent with MacKinnon's theory of dominance and subordination, Justice Wilson must recognize that to be a woman is to be permanently and always subordinated and oppressed. If that is too strong a statement, it is not an exaggeration to say that women are subordinated and oppressed whenever they are sexualized, which is surely true of the contexts in which all three of Wilson's controversial judgments arise – family law, abortion, and statutory rape. Therefore, let's examine each of these judgments in turn.

Pelech

Pelech is one of a trilogy of family law maintenance variation applications heard together by the Supreme Court of Canada.[34] Each presented a slightly different set of facts. In *Pelech,* for which Justice Wilson wrote the majority judgment, an ex-wife sought to vary a maintenance agreement that had provided for a lump-sum settlement thirteen years earlier. The agreement was made post-divorce with legal advice having been provided to both parties. The agreement was incorporated into a court order, and it did not apply to the two children, whose custody was awarded to the ex-husband. The ex-husband paid the maintenance as agreed. His financial situation improved significantly over the intervening years, whereas Mrs. Pelech's health and financial situation deteriorated until she had to seek social assistance. The trial judge found that her health problems predated the marriage and did not stem from the marriage or from the behaviour of her ex-husband during that period.

In *Richardson v. Richardson,* which is the second of the trilogy of cases, the application to vary the agreement was brought during the divorce proceedings.[35] Although the agreement was for one year's payment of maintenance to Mrs. Richardson, the wife, who had custody of the child, it became obvious during that year that she could not find employment. She went on social assistance. Accordingly, she brought the application to vary the maintenance agreement during the divorce proceedings.

The third of the trilogy cases is *Caron v. Caron.*[36] It involved a separation agreement that contained a clause providing for cessation of maintenance payments to the wife if she remarried or cohabited. This separation agreement was incorporated into the divorce decree (nisi). After the divorce, when Mrs. Caron cohabited with a man, her ex-husband ceased to make maintenance payments. As a result, she was forced to go on social assistance. Mrs. Caron applied for a variation of the divorce decree (nisi) to have her ex-husband resume his maintenance payments.

In all three cases, the ex-wives had their applications to vary the maintenance agreements denied. At the Supreme Court of Canada, the same six judges – five men and Justice Wilson – decided all of these cases. Wilson wrote the majority judgments in all three. Justice La Forest denied her unanimity, writing concurrences in *Pelech* and *Caron,* and dissenting in *Richardson.* According to Justice Wilson and four of her brother judges, the prevailing state of the law was in disarray on the issue of when maintenance agreements could be varied. They clarified the law, holding that, wherever possible, settlements reached with the advice of independent legal counsel should be respected. The test for intervention is stringent – a court should intervene only if there is "a radical change in circumstances flowing from an economic pattern of dependency engendered by the marriage."[37]

Justice Claire L'Heureux-Dubé was not a member of the Court when the family law trilogy of cases was heard, but she was there for the next significant case involving an application to vary a maintenance agreement *(Moge v. Moge)*.[38] In fact, she wrote the majority judgment in this case, and it is clear that she disagreed with the approach that Justice Wilson had espoused in the trilogy.[39] L'Heureux-Dubé's judgment is the epitome of feminist dominance theory.[40] She referred to the feminization of poverty, the continuing economic disadvantages of one spouse (meaning the wife), the reaping of economic advantages by the other (meaning the husband), problems faced by a spouse who is not in the labour force, *e.g.* loss of seniority and missed promotions, and the exacerbation of labour-force problems caused by the child care responsibilities of a single parent after the divorce.

L'Heureux-Dubé distinguished the test derived from the trilogy cases, saying it was not applicable to non-consensual situations where no final agreement had been reached between the parties. However, her disapproval of the trilogy test, which she characterized as following the self-sufficiency model, was apparent. According to her, this model had the potential to financially penalize women by creating a break from their financial dependence on their spouses before the conditions for self-sufficiency had been met. She subscribed instead to the compensatory model of support, which holds that, after divorce, spouses must still contribute to support payments according to their abilities. If a former spouse suffers continuing economic disadvantages because of the marriage and its dissolution, whereas the other spouse reaps economic advantages, the compensatory model requires long-term support or an alternative settlement.

Even if we accept Justice L'Heureux-Dubé's characterization of the choice of approaches as one between the self-sufficiency model and the compensatory model,[41] rhetoric aside, is it self-evident that the compensatory model is more consistent with feminist dominance theory? The answer is "yes" if dominance is, like compensatory support, unending. However, if the point of identifying systemic male dominance (*viz.* the feminization of poverty) is not only to remedy, but also to end, women's subordination, the compensatory model may not be the only answer. Another response may involve focusing on developing self-sufficiency or, as Justice Wilson put it, on taking "responsibility for their own lives and their own decisions."[42] It is true that the self-sufficiency model imports the real danger of premature termination of support, but a danger attaches to the compensatory model as well – that perpetual support and subordination may reinforce each other.

Thus, my review of Justice Wilson's family law trilogy judgments leaves me with a question for which I have no conclusive answer: do circumstances exist in which the ethic of self-sufficiency could be responsive to dominance theory's identification of the feminization of poverty? To put it differently, feminists who subscribe to dominance theory are right that Justice Wilson did not use the rhetoric of dominance and subordination. In contrast, Justice L'Heureux-Dubé excelled at this form of articulation. However, such rhetoric is not everything. The ethic of self-sufficiency on which Wilson relied may provide another approach to addressing the oppression that post-divorce maintenance regimes may otherwise sustain. Without more, therefore, feminist dominance theorists should not assume that the ethic of self-sufficiency has no role to play in countering subordination.

Morgentaler

Morgentaler presented a *Charter* challenge to the constitutionality of the prohibition on abortion in the *Criminal Code*.[43] Procuring an abortion was a crime except when three doctors (known as the therapeutic abortion committee) certified that the life or health of the woman was endangered and a fourth doctor carried out the procedure in an accredited hospital. Dr. Morgentaler was charged with this crime when he set up a private clinic to perform abortions without complying with the specified conditions. The seven-person Court split five to two, with the majority holding that the abortion prohibition violated the right to security of the person protected by s. 7 of the *Charter*. In fact, the Court issued four separate judgments, three by male judges, each of whom wrote for one other male judge (bonding?), and one by Justice Wilson writing alone.

Justice Wilson opened her judgment with the following statement: "At the heart of this appeal is the question whether a pregnant woman can, as a constitutional matter, be compelled by law to carry the foetus to term."[44] She agreed with the four male judges who held that the onerous requirements imposed on obtaining abortions exposed pregnant women to a threat to their physical and psychological security, hence violating their right to security of the person protected by s. 7 of the *Charter*.[45] However, that did not end the matter for Justice Wilson as it did not answer the further question that she said must be asked: would a hypothetical prohibition on abortion that posed no threat to security of the person be constitutionally valid? For Wilson, the answer lay in the right to liberty, which is also protected by s. 7 of the *Charter*. Thus, much of her judgment was devoted to asking whether the s. 7 right to liberty gives "the pregnant woman control over decisions affecting her own body."[46]

Her answer was in the affirmative, based on her unique interpretation of the s. 7 right to liberty as guaranteeing to individuals (women as well as men) "a degree of personal autonomy over important decisions intimately affecting their private lives."[47] In applying this interpretation to the social and ethical decision of whether to carry a fetus to term or to abort, Justice Wilson wrote, "It is probably impossible for a man to respond, even imaginatively, to such a dilemma not just because it is outside the realm of his personal experience (although this is, of course, the case) but because he can relate to it only by objectifying it, thereby eliminating the subjective elements of the female psyche which are at the heart of the dilemma."[48] Not surprisingly, she concluded that the "right to reproduce or not to reproduce ... is properly perceived as an integral part of modern woman's struggle to assert *her* dignity and worth as a human being."[49]

Feminists approve of the outcome of this case. They accept the value of Justice Wilson's innovative interpretation of the right to liberty in this context, and many even attach some legitimacy to the reasoning that led Wilson to concede that the state could limit late-stage abortions in order to protect the fetus. However, some feminists object to her failure to invoke the right to sex equality protected under s. 15 as the grounds for declaring the abortion prohibition unconstitutional.[50] But does this mean that she failed to apply dominance theory?

I suggest that Justice Wilson's rhetoric reveals the application of dominance theory. However, she applied this theory in the context of the s. 7 right to liberty rather than in the context of s. 15 sex equality rights. Diana Majury has argued cogently that substantive equality is not about assessing women against men: rather, it supports differences by "recreating society and societal structures."[51] Justice Wilson not only demanded that we recognize the significance of the right to reproduce or not to reproduce, she also insisted that we treat it as an integral part of women's experiences. She contextualized reproduction as an issue of the "modern woman's struggle to assert her dignity and worth as a human being."[52] Portrayed as an issue of inequality that does not need a comparator group, it is part of contemporary women's "struggle to recreate societal structures to include their needs and aspirations."[53] Majury concludes, and I agree, that Justice Wilson's opinion in this case "is one of the best and strongest articulations of a substantive equality analysis that we have had from the Court to date."[54]

Moreover, since Canada is a federal state, Justice Wilson may have made the appropriate decision to apply the right to liberty in decriminalizing abortion. Restrictions on abortion have not disappeared: they have simply shifted from the federal criminal law jurisdiction to the provincial health and hospital jurisdiction. Accordingly, abortions are limited by provincial restrictions on access to, and funding for, this medical procedure. I have argued elsewhere that these debilitating provincial constraints should be declared unconstitutional, using the right to sex equality in s. 15 of the *Charter*.[55]

Hess

Hess was actually two cases *(R. v. Hess* and *R. v. Nguyen)* heard together on appeal to the Supreme Court.[56] Both concerned statutory rape, which was then defined in the *Criminal Code* as a male person having sexual intercourse with a female person who was under the age of fourteen.[57] All seven members of the Court, including the three women justices, agreed that this provision could not be reconciled with the principles of fundamental justice in s. 7 of the *Charter,* because it was an absolute liability offence ("whether or not he believes that she is fourteen years of age or more").[58] However, the justices split five to two on the question of whether the government could justify this violation.

More specifically, Justice Beverley McLachlin dissented (with Justice Gonthier concurring), maintaining that the protection of female children from premature sexual intercourse and pregnancy justified making statutory rape a strict liability offence. That is, strict liability put the burden where it should be – on the male accused. In writing for the majority, which included Justice L'Heureux-Dubé, Justice Wilson accepted the objective of protecting female children but rejected the contention that absolute liability met the minimal impairment test. She noted that no evidence was presented about the deterrent effect of absolute liability. Since the government did not meet the s. 1 justification test, these cases were sent back for new trials in which due diligence, not absolute liability, would be the requisite standard.

The feminist legal scholars who commented on Justice Wilson's opinion in *Hess* and *Nguyen* paid little to no attention to her interpretation and application of ss. 7 and 1 of the *Charter.*[59] Nor did they object to the outcome of these cases. Instead, they were vehemently critical of the way in which she applied s. 15 of the *Charter.* Ironically, Wilson began her comments on s. 15 by stating that the appeals had already been disposed of under s. 7 and that it was "not, strictly speaking, necessary" to address s. 15.[60] In other words, her comments about s. 15 were *obiter.* However, she recognized that it might be "useful" for her to address this section since Justice McLachlin was forced to do so, having found that the provision violated s. 7 but was saved under s. 1.[61] In particular, Wilson wanted to express her disagreement with McLachlin's conclusion that the statutory rape provision infringed s. 15.[62]

I maintain that this background provides an important context to Justice Wilson's remarks about s. 15. If we read her comments as responsive to what Justice McLachlin wrote rather than standing on their own, they are consistent with dominance theory. On the other hand, if we analyze what Wilson wrote in the abstract, it is impossible to reconcile her remarks about s. 15 with dominance theory. Her critics opted for the second approach and concluded that her observations about s. 15 set sex equality theory back to its pre-*Charter* dark ages.

To elaborate, Justices Wilson and McLachlin differed over whether the statutory rape provision violated the right to sex equality under s. 15 of the *Charter*. McLachlin found that it did because the offence could be committed only by males and the victim could only be female. In contrast, Wilson refused to find that the provision violated sex equality, writing that, in the context of criminal law, a distinction based on sex may legitimately be made where, as a matter of biological fact, the offence can be committed by one sex only.

Since the *Criminal Code* defined statutory rape as sexual intercourse,[63] and sexual intercourse as "penetration to even the slightest degree,"[64] Justice Wilson pointed out that only males over a certain age are in fact capable of penetrating another person. She reasoned that it would be absurd to suggest that the provision discriminates against males, since only men could be perpetrators. A comparable absurdity would be to suggest that a provision prohibiting self-induced abortion is discriminatory because it is limited to females. Noting that older women could and did have sex with boys under fourteen, Justice Wilson said it was up to the legislature to decide whether they too should be punished. In fact, other forms of penetration such as sodomy and buggery were already dealt with in separate sections of the *Criminal Code*.

In contrast, Justice McLachlin, dissenting, wrote that the statutory rape provision did violate men's sex equality rights, discriminating against them by burdening them in a way that women were not. Not surprisingly, however, she was of the view that the government could justify violating s. 15 just as it had justified violating s. 7 of the *Charter* on the grounds of protecting female children and because only males can cause pregnancies. Since men are always older than their victims in the offence of statutory rape, McLachlin believed that attributing responsibility to them for the sexual intercourse having taken place would not be irrational.

Feminist critics focused on what they saw as a reversion to biology in Justice Wilson's decision. In Christine Boyle's words, Wilson's approach was "criticized as a step back from the line of authority which focuses on persistent disadvantage as a guide to when there is an infringement of section 15."[65] Earlier, Hester Lessard had taken a similar position, maintaining that "one would have expected the emphasis in *Hess* to have been on whether men are a socially disadvantaged group."[66] Both Boyle and Lessard refer to Isabel Grant and William Black's elaboration of how an analysis of disadvantage might have been applied in *Hess* and *Nguyen*.[67] Effectively, these critics insisted on the necessity of recognizing disadvantage as an inherent component of a s. 15 analysis. Disadvantage is viewed as essential to dominance theory and hence to substantive equality.

My contention is that Justice Wilson agreed with these critics. She invoked the biological definition of statutory rape to make the point that it was not sufficient to sustain a claim for the infringement of s. 15. For her, biological distinctions alone could never be discriminatory and hence could never violate the right to sex equality in s. 15. It is hard to see how feminists could disagree with her. In contrast, Justice McLachlin's position was that biological distinctions were sufficient to make a case for discrimination and hence a violation of the right to sex equality in s. 15. To put it differently, men do not need to be disadvantaged to claim s. 15 equality rights. Hers was the formal equality approach.

We should have understood the meaning of Justice Wilson's insistence on biological distinctions as not being sufficient to claim discrimination. She did not mean that men could not claim the benefit of s. 15. Rather, her argument was that men must show social disadvantage to claim equality rights under the section. Anything less should not count as a substantive equality argument.

Importing Gender Theory

Thus far, I have argued (I hope successfully) that Justice Wilson's controversial decisions in *Pelech, Morgentaler,* and *Hess* can be construed as consistent with dominance theory. This theory informs substantive equality analysis and signals that women – whether judges, lawyers, scholars, or students – can be perceived as feminists even if they do not self-identify as such.

Dominance theory is not the only game in town, however. A recent challenge comes from women's studies and queer theorizing about the relationship between the concepts of sex and gender.[68] Despite some claims to the contrary, feminist legal theorists (and judges for that matter) have tended to collapse the distinction between sex and gender. True, they identify sex primarily as the biological distinction between women and men, whereas they conceptualize gender primarily as the socially constructed traits or roles encapsulated by the words "feminine" and "masculine." However, the distinction effectively collapses when the legal meaning of sex equality is interpreted. The courts require, and the lawyers provide, a melding of the biological distinctions (does the law make a distinction based on sex?) with those that are socially constructed (does the sexed law discriminate?).

In contrast, contemporary women's studies and queer theory refuse to treat sex and gender as synonymous. In these theories, as Mary Anne Case explains, "the two terms have long had distinct meanings, with gender being to sex what masculinity and femininity are to male and female."[69] Case argues for disaggregating the concept of gender from sex, on the one hand, and from sexual orientation, on the other. Her argument for disaggregation is based on American cases that differentially treat individuals who "diverge from the gender expectations for their sex – when a woman displays masculine characteristics or a man[,] feminine ones."[70] American case law regards discrimination against a female as sex discrimination, whereas for a male, "his behavior is generally viewed as a marker for homosexual orientation and may not receive protection from discrimination."[71]

For Case, this differential legal treatment "has important implications for feminist theory" because "it marks the continuing devaluation, in life and in law, of qualities deemed feminine."[72] The danger that she identifies is the "danger of substituting for prohibited sex discrimination a still acceptable gender discrimination."[73] Case explores the issues raised by the continuing devaluation of the feminine and the acceptability of gender discrimination in the context of American employment decisions. However, I want to ask whether this has any resonance with Justice Wilson's family law maintenance variation judgment in *Pelech*. When Wilson upheld the finality of the original maintenance agreement, did she attribute feminine or masculine characteristics to the ex-wife by invoking the ethic of self-sufficiency? Although the dominance theory critique assumes masculinity, I am not so sure. Recall my concern that dominance theory appears to remedy, but not end, subordination, whereas the ethic of self-sufficiency conceptualizes empowerment as a strategy for overcoming subordination.

I could try to put this differently by asking the following questions: Does dominance theory accept gender discrimination? Does dominance theory have any redeeming features? According to Meredith Render, the answer may lie in deconstructing the theory (which she labels as sexual subordination theory).[74] Indeed, as Render explains, feminist and queer theorists have already deconstructed dominance theory, moving away from and rejecting "the premise that sexualization itself inherently or uniquely subordinates women."[75] As well, feminist and queer theorists have deconstructed the category of sex (which Render labels gender but by which she means biological females and males), claiming that it "is never a relevant category but is instead entirely socially constructed."[76] Render reports that these two deconstructivist moves by feminist and queer theorists have not left a vacuum, but rather they have "*intersected* – in such a way as to present an androcentric-assimilation model of female liberation."[77]

Render is critical of this androcentric model, arguing that it fails to address and in fact reinforces "existing misogynistic ideas about feminized women."[78] She situates her critique in the context of sexual harassment where the androcentric model has made it difficult for harassment doctrine "to meet the needs of an increasingly unidentifiable category of victims."[79] Similarly, we might ask what would happen if the androcentric model were transposed to the contexts of abortion and statutory rape. If deconstructionist scholarship is right to challenge the premise that sexuality subordinates women, and to challenge the retention of the category of biological sex, what remains for the doctrine of sex equality to address?

Was Justice Wilson ahead of her time when she refused to use sexual subordination (or dominance theory or the right to sex equality) as the basis for holding that the abortion prohibition was unconstitutional, albeit finding it unconstitutional for other reasons? Was she ahead of her time when she refused to use the category of biological sex as the basis for holding the statutory rape provision unconstitutional?

I am not a big fan of prescient adjudication, and so my point has not been to use the arguments from recent feminist and queer theory to laud Justice Wilson. Rather, my point has been to use her controversial judgments to provoke a discussion about the premises that inform the doctrine of sex equality. Do we conflate the concepts of sex and gender, assertions to the contrary notwithstanding? Should we disaggregate gender from sex, not only to address issues raised by queer theory, but also to address issues of concern to feminists and women? Is dominance theory still relevant to the legal meaning of sex equality? Does a distinction based on sex, meaning biological sex, always discriminate? These are all questions that Justice Wilson struggled with in one context or another. They have not disappeared, and we must struggle with them too.

Conclusion

Studies of Justice Bertha Wilson's jurisprudence (there are surprisingly few) invariably refer to two statements that she made about the significance of gender. The first invites us "to appreciate the common humanity of men and women. We are human beings first and foremost, and only secondarily male and female."[80] The second poses the question "will women judges really make a difference?"[81] When I read these two statements together, I began to wonder whether they were consistent. After all, the second statement appeared seven years after the first; perhaps it signalled a major change in Justice Wilson's perspective on sex and gender. In addition, since both appeared in lectures delivered by Wilson, I wondered how, if at all, they were reflected in her judicial opinions.

After reviewing her three controversial judgments and trying to situate them in both dominance theory and contemporary gender theory, I concluded that Justice Wilson was consistent in both her judgments and the two statements quoted above. If we take the first statement at face value, she self-identified as a humanist who refused to deny the relevance of the category of sex. Asking whether women judges will really make a difference is not inconsistent with this self-identification. In the family law maintenance variation case *(Pelech),* Wilson implicitly constructed a humanist strategy for the ex-wife. In the abortion case *(Morgentaler),* she made a point of explicitly attributing human dignity to pregnant women facing the dilemma of abortion, even though the accused in the case was a medical doctor. Finally, in the statutory rape cases *(Hess* and *Nguyen),* she could see no way to deny the relevance of the category of sex, given the legislative definition of rape as penetration.

Should we ask more of her? Yes, as I would like to know the answers to two further questions. First, did she mean that sex as a biological category would always exist, and if so, why would the category still exist? Second, can we disaggregate gender from sex, and if so, should we? In the context of this second question, I keep wondering if I want to reconceptualize femininity, and if so, does it portend the necessity to reconceptualize other gendered traits such as submission?

Finally, to return to the question that opened this chapter – was Justice Wilson a feminist judge? – my conclusion is that, by the standards of her time, she was. She played a leading role on the Court with respect to the promotion of substantive equality, and her three controversial decisions can be reconciled with dominance theory. Although more reflection is required to determine conclusively whether these same three decisions are consistent with contemporary gender theory, there is some likelihood that they are. Ultimately, my objective has been to conceptualize feminism as a challenging and dynamic theoretic that can be used to analyze the judgments of woman judges irrespective of whether they self-identify as feminist.

Acknowledgments

Early versions of this chapter were presented at the "International Seminar on Women in Legal Careers and in Justice" at the University of Buenos Aires Faculty of Law (April 2007) and at the "Gender and Judging IRC" of the Law and Society Association at Humboldt University (July 2007). I would like to acknowledge the helpful comments of Marie-Claire Belleau, Rebecca Johnson, Sally Kenney, Beatriz Kohen, Erika Rackley, Ulrike Schultz, Hilary Sommerlad, and Margaret Thornton. I would also like to acknowledge the research assistance of Shannon Nelson (funded by a grant from the Law Foundation of Ontario) and of Amy Kaufman of the Queen's University Faculty of Law.

Notes

1 Sandra Gwyn, "Sense and Sensibility" *Saturday Night* (July 1985) 13 at 19.

2 Justice Wilson was appointed on 4 March 1982 and retired 4 January 1991. Six women have since been appointed to the Supreme Court: Justice Claire L'Heureux-Dubé, appointed 15 April 1987 and retired 1 July 2002; Justice Beverley McLachlin, appointed 30 March 1989, became Chief Justice 7 January 2000; Justice Louise Arbour, appointed 15 September 1999 and resigned 30 June 2004; Justice Marie Deschamps, appointed 7 August 2002; Justice Rosalie Abella, appointed 30 August 2004; and Justice Louise Charron, appointed 30 August 2004. Currently, four women – Chief Justice McLachlin and Justices Deschamps, Abella, and Charron – sit on the nine-member Court.

3 Rosemary Hunter, "Can Feminist Judges Make a Difference?" (2008) 15 Int'l J. of the Legal Profession 7 at 8.

4 *Ibid.* at 9.

5 Ellen Anderson, *Judging Bertha Wilson: Law as Large as Life* (Toronto: University of Toronto Press for the Osgoode Society for Canadian Legal History, 2001) at 14.

6 See Constance Backhouse, "The Chilly Climate for Women Judges: Reflections on the Backlash from the Ewanchuk Case" (2003) 15 C.J.W.L. 167 at 180, ns. 62, 76, 187. (Backhouse does not provide the date for when each woman changed her feminist identification, noting at 187, n. 76 only that "it seems clear that Wilson J. was not as forthcoming in claiming feminism as was L'Heureux-Dubé J.")

7 *Canadian Charter of Rights and Freedoms,* Part I of the *Constitution Act, 1982,* being Schedule B to the *Canada Act 1982* (U.K.), 1982, c. 11.

8 *Canada (A.G.) v. Lavell,* [1974] S.C.R. 1349; *Bliss v. Canada (A.G.),* [1979] 1 S.C.R. 183 [*Bliss*].

9 See *Andrews v. Law Society of British Columbia,* [1989] 1 S.C.R. 143 [*Andrews*]; *Law v. Canada,* [1999] 1 S.C.R. 497. See also Beverley Baines, "Law v. Canada: Formatting Equality" (2000) 11 Const. Forum Const. 65.

10 See *e.g.* Christine Boyle, "The Role of the Judiciary in the Work of Madame Justice Wilson" (1992) 15 Dal. L.J. 241; Hester Lessard, "Equality and Access to Justice in the Work of Bertha Wilson" (1992) 15 Dal. L.J. 35; Anderson, *supra* note 5.

11 *Pelech v. Pelech,* [1987] 1 S.C.R. 801 [*Pelech*].

12 *R. v. Morgentaler,* [1988] 1 S.C.R. 30 [*Morgentaler*]. *Criminal Code,* R.S.C. 1985, c. C-46.

13 *R. v. Hess; R. v. Nguyen,* [1990] 2 S.C.R. 906 [*Hess; Nguyen*].

14 See Chapter 12, Table 12.1 at 234.

15 *R. v. Konkin,* [1983] 1 S.C.R. 388.

16 Lessard, *supra* note 10 at 48, quoting *R. v. Big M Drug Mart,* [1985] 1 S.C.R. 295.

17 *McKinney v. Board of Governors of the University of Guelph,* [1990] 3 S.C.R. 229 at 415.

18 Lessard, *supra* note 10 at 61.

19 *Andrews, supra* note 9 at 152.

20 *R. v. Turpin,* [1989] 1 S.C.R. 1296 at 1333.

21 *Edmonton Journal v. Alberta,* [1989] 2 S.C.R. 1326 at 1355.

22 Lessard, *supra* note 10 at 63.

23 Boyle, *supra* note 10 at 243.

24 *R. v. Towne Cinema Theatres Ltd.,* [1985] 1 S.C.R. 494 at 523.

25 *Reference re ss. 193 and 195.1(1)(c) of the Criminal Code (Man.),* [1990] 1 S.C.R. 1123 at 1206.

26 *R. v. Lavallee,* [1990] 1 S.C.R. 852 at 874.

27 See Boyle, *supra* note 10 at 255.

28 *Brooks v. Canada Safeway,* [1989] 1 S.C.R. 1219, overruling *Bliss, supra* note 8.

29 *Janzen v. Platy Enterprises Ltd.,* [1989] 1 S.C.R. 1252.

30 *Action Travail des Femmes v. Canadian National Railway Co.,* [1989] 1 S.C.R. 1114.

31 Catharine A. MacKinnon, "Feminism, Marxism, Method, and the State: An Agenda for Theory" (1982) 7 Signs 515 at 516.

32 *Ibid.* at 533.

33 *Ibid.*

34 *Pelech, supra* note 11.

35 *Richardson v. Richardson,* [1987] 1 S.C.R. 857 [*Richardson*].

36 *Caron v. Caron,* [1987] 1 S.C.R. 892 [*Caron*].

37 *Pelech, supra* note 11 at 851; *Richardson, supra* note 35 at 866; *Caron, supra* note 36 at 897. Robert Leckey, "What Is Left of *Pelech*?" in Jamie Cameron, ed., *Reflections on the Legacy of Justice Bertha Wilson* (Markham, ON: LexisNexis, 2008) 103 at 110, notes that Justice Wilson's judgment in *Pelech* "aims to shift maintenance from the moral to the economic realm."

38 *Moge v. Moge,* [1992] 3 S.C.R. 813.

39 Feminist legal scholars also critiqued Wilson's decisions in the trilogy. See Chapter 16 at 307-10, this volume; Martha J. Bailey, "*Pelech, Caron,* and *Richardson*" (1989-90) 3 C.J.W.L. 615; Brenda Cossman, "A Matter of Difference: Domestic Contracts and Gender Equality" (1990) 28 Osgoode Hall L.J. 303; Diana Majury, "Unconscionability in an Equality Context" (1991) 7 Can. Fam. L.Q. 123; Martha Shaffer and Carol Rogerson, "Contracting Spousal Support: Thinking through Miglin" (2003) 21 Can. Fam. L.Q. 49.

40 Yet it too is the subject of feminist critique. See *e.g.* Colleen Sheppard, "Uncomfortable Victories and Unanswered Questions: Lessons from Moge" (1995) 12 Can. J. Fam. L. 283.

41 Justice Beverley McLachlin (now chief justice) wrote a concurring judgment in *Moge* in which she referred approvingly to both models, refusing to choose between them. Similarly, when she wrote for the unanimous Court in *Bracklow v. Bracklow,* [1999] 1 S.C.R. 420, McLachlin again relied on both models. Earlier, in "Spousal Support: Is It Fair to Apply New-Style Rules to Old-Style Marriages?" (1990) 9 Can. J. Fam. L. 131, she outlined two models of marital breakdown, referring to them as the union for life model and the joint venture model.

42 *Pelech, supra* note 11 at 850.

43 *Morgentaler, supra* note 12.

44 *Ibid.* at 161.
45 See *ibid.* at 162-63.
46 *Ibid.* at 163.
47 *Ibid.* at 171.
48 *Ibid.*
49 *Ibid.* at 172 [emphasis in original].
50 See *e.g.* Moira McConnell, "Abortion and Human Rights: An Important Canadian Decision" (1989) 38 Int'l & Comp. L. Rev. 905; Shelley A.M. Gavigan, "*Morgentaler* and Beyond: Abortion, Reproduction, and the Courts" in Janine Brodie, Shelley A.M. Gavigan, and Jane Jenson, eds., *The Politics of Abortion* (Toronto: Oxford University Press, 1992) 117 at 127.
51 Diana Majury, "The Charter, Equality Rights, and Women: Equivocation and Celebration" (2002) 40 Osgoode Hall L.J. 297 at 320.
52 *Morgentaler, supra* note 12 at 172.
53 *Ibid.*
54 Majury, *supra* note 51 at 320.
55 See Beverley Baines, "Abortion, Judicial Activism and Constitutional Crossroads" (2004) 53 U.N.B.L.J. 157.
56 *Hess; Nguyen, supra* note 13.
57 *Criminal Code, supra* note 12, s. 146(1), which provided, "Every male person who has sexual intercourse with a female person who (a) is not his wife, and (b) is under the age of fourteen years, whether or not he believes that she is fourteen years of age or more, is guilty of an indictable offence and is liable to imprisonment for life."
58 *Ibid.*
59 See Boyle, *supra* note 10; Christine Boyle, "The Role of Equality in Criminal Law" (1994) 58 Sask. L. Rev. 203; Andrea York, "The Inequality of Emerging Charter Jurisprudence: Supreme Court Interpretation of Section 15(1)" (1996) 54 U.T. Fac. L. Rev. 327; Lynn Smith, "The Effect of Charter Equality Rights on Minorities and Women" in Gérald-A. Beaudoin, ed., *The Charter: Ten Years Later* (Cowansville, QC: Éditions Yvon Blais, 1992) 141; Donna Greschner, "Aboriginal Women, the Constitution and Criminal Justice" (1992) 26 U.B.C. L. Rev. 338; Isabel Grant and William Black, "Equality and Biological Differences" (1990) 79 C.R. (3d) 372.
60 *Hess; Nguyen, supra* note 13 at 927.
61 *Ibid.*
62 See *ibid.*
63 *Criminal Code, supra* note 12 at s. 146(1).
64 *Ibid.* at s. 3(6): "For the purposes of the Act, sexual intercourse is complete upon penetration to even the slightest degree, notwithstanding that seed is not emitted."
65 Boyle, "The Role of Equality," *supra* note 59 at 205.
66 Lessard, *supra* note 10 at 57 (adding that the expected emphasis would also have been "on what the experiences of men and women in determining their sexual lives has been, and on whether the statutory rape offence perpetuates or ameliorates historical and social inequalities between men and women").
67 Boyle, "The Role of Equality," *supra* note 59 at 206, and Lessard, *supra* note 10 at 58, both invoking the arguments by Grant and Black, *supra* note 59 at 376.
68 See *e.g.* Judith Halberstam, *Female Masculinity* (Durham: Duke University Press, 1998); Jean Bobby Noble, *Masculinities without Men: Female Masculinity in Twentieth-Century Fictions* (Vancouver: UBC Press, 2004).
69 Mary Anne Case, "Disaggregating Gender from Sex and Sexual Orientation: The Effeminate Man in the Law and Feminist Jurisprudence" (1995-96) 105 Yale L.J. 1 at 2.
70 *Ibid.*
71 *Ibid.*
72 *Ibid.* at 3.
73 *Ibid.*
74 Meredith Render, "Misogyny, Androgyny and Sexual Harassment: Sex Discrimination in a Gender-Deconstructed World" (2006) 29 Harv. J.L. & Gender 99.
75 *Ibid.* at 101.

76 *Ibid.* at 102.
77 *Ibid.* at 103 [emphasis in original].
78 *Ibid.*
79 *Ibid.*
80 Bertha Wilson, "Law in Society: The Principle of Sexual Equality" (1983) 13 Manitoba L.J. 221 at 225.
81 Bertha Wilson, "Will Women Judges Really Make a Difference?" (1990) 28 Osgoode Hall L.J. 507.

12

I Agree/Disagree for the Following Reasons: Convergence, Divergence, and Justice Wilson's "Modest Degree of Creativity"

Marie-Claire Belleau, Rebecca Johnson, and Christina Vinters

> Certainly, the legislature is the more effective instrument for rapid or radical change. But there is no reason why the judiciary cannot exercise some modest degree of creativity in areas where modern insights and life's experience have indicated that the law has gone awry.
>
> – Bertha Wilson, "Will Women Judges Really Make Difference?" 1990

> Creativity (krē'ātiv'itē) *n.* 1. the state or quality of being creative. 2. the ability to transcend traditional ideas, rules, patterns, relationships, or the like and to create meaningful new ideas, forms, methods, interpretations, etc.; originality, progressiveness, or imagination. 3. the process by which one utilizes creative ability.
>
> – Random House Webster's *Unabridged Dictionary,* 2d (2001)

In the 1990 Betcherman Lecture at Osgoode Hall Law School, Justice Bertha Wilson posed the now famous question whose resonance has been felt and explored in many corners of the globe: "Will women judges make a difference?"[1] One might respond to this question with the observation that, whatever one's conclusion on the effect of gender, *this* woman judge did indeed make a profound difference. But the inevitable rejoinder arises: what *kind* of difference?

This second question could be answered in a variety of ways. A jurisprudential approach might explore the substance of her opinions and consider the ways in which she shaped our understandings and interpretations of the *Canadian Charter of Rights and Freedoms,* producing groundbreaking decisions, many of which have left a lasting imprint on Canadian law. A biographical approach might explore the factors that contributed to the character of this woman in her role of judge. A personal approach might speak of the impact Justice Wilson had on those who watched her shoulder the burden of being the first woman on the Supreme Court, bearing the multiple and contradictory hopes and dreams of Canadian women.

In this chapter, we follow in the tradition of those who might take an empirical approach, seeking to discover or document patterns of difference manifest in her judgments. Here, we consider some of the empirical data on the Supreme Court in the hope of better understanding the difference Justice Wilson made, a difference we see articulated in her Betcherman Lecture comments about the importance of judges exercising a "modest degree of creativity."

In this exploration of Wilson's judicial creativity, we will not attend to the substance of the rich jurisprudence she produced. The texture and subtlety of many of her written opinions are the subject matter of other chapters. Here, we consider Justice Wilson's jurisprudential contributions in a completely decontextualized fashion, without reference to the social or political importance of their subject or the power of any one of her written texts. Instead, we have reduced those contributions to a number of quantifiable variables, asking only about her practices of voting (whether she voted with or against the majority) and her forms of participation (distinguishing the opinions she wrote from those she signed).[2]

The irony of taking this approach – of decontextualizing the judge who placed the concept of *context* back into the judicial lexicon – is not lost on us. However, the question we pursue here is not a substantive one endeavouring to say something about the kinds of claims Justice Wilson might have supported or opposed. The question here is as follows: what can the pattern of her voting and participation practices tell us, when considered apart from the social and political contexts in which the particular cases were decided? We suggest that empirical attention to "results and reasons," and to the categories of majority, concurrence, and dissent, can give us additional insight into judicial creativity and the shape of the difference that Justice Wilson participated in making.

Our analysis proceeds in three sections. First, we identify some of our background assumptions about the nature of the work that judges do, the way creativity is made manifest in that work, and the terminology through which sites of creativity are acknowledged. We also address some of the challenges in quantitative analysis of judicial work. Second, we share some statistics on the work of Justice Wilson. Third, we place those data in context, situating Wilson's statistics alongside those of the other judges with whom she worked. Finally, we conclude with some observations about Justice Wilson's "modest degree of creativity."

The Work of a Judge

Although political scientists have produced a fairly significant body of empirical research on courts and judges,[3] legal scholars have conducted less research of this kind. Recent years have seen an increase in Canadian empirical legal scholarship,[4] but we think it fair to say that some caution remains within the legal community about (perceived) attempts to reduce the processes of legal decision making to a number of quantifiable variables. In large measure, the wariness, we believe, is linked to concerns about approaches that take insufficient account of the complexity of judicial decision making, with its textured weaving together of result and reason. We thus explicitly set out some of our presumptions about legal decision making, presumptions that often go unarticulated but that should be made explicit in the context of our empirically based approach to Justice Wilson's contributions.

First, the work of a judge is to settle a claim or dispute by reaching an outcome that is generally expressible in the starkest of binary terms: someone "wins" and someone "loses." Will this woman go to jail or walk free? Will a child remain with his or her parents or be placed in another's care? Will a patent be granted or not? Will insurance coverage allow for monetary recovery? Does a director have a fiduciary duty? The job of the judge is "to decide."

In reaching a decision, the judge must reconcile the contradictory demands of predictability and responsiveness to change.[5] The ideal of universal application of legal principles can blind law to the demands of the particular case, just as attention to the particular can threaten the stability of law itself. Each case poses a new context for the unavoidable working out of these contradictory pulls. The judge must employ creativity in each new context in order to find solutions to the inescapable tensions in justice's demands for stability and responsiveness. Here, she asks two questions: Is this case analogous to or unlike others? How are the facts of the case to be understood against the background of similar situations? Creativity is mustered in the cause of producing some outcome – *a result.*

The resulting judgment – the yes or no – may in important ways be experienced as a performative utterance, a speech act (in the sense described by J.L. Austin).[6] But there is of course more, because, in this space of decision making, it is not enough for the judge simply to speak the words "yes" or "no." The judge must also give *reasons.* The reasons tell us *how* the judge's thinking process proceeded from the facts to the outcome. The reasons tell us *why* certain outcomes are desirable, justifiable, or inevitable.[7] The reasons explain why evidence must be thrown out in a given case, how children are or are not legal subjects, and why some injuries can occur without obligations on the part of others to help.

In providing reasons, the judge cannot avoid participating in the stabilization or reimagination of the world in which we live.[8] Each moment of judgment, of decision making, confronts the judge with the need to imagine anew.[9] Such imaginings do not, we might add, necessarily entail change. The need to reimagine can certainly result in decisions that affirm the status quo, that inscribe anew our commitments to the past, or that resist prevailing winds of change. But creativity is required in the business of constructing both a result and the reasons given for that result. The combination of result and reason constitutes the unique fabric of the judicial text, a text that is very much a construction, an achievement, something struggled for and made. Like other constructions of the creative spirit (poetry, art, music), the legal judgment is something that can be assessed, admired, pilloried, used, or rejected. This is the horizon that confronts every trial judge, whether operating in criminal, family, or tax court.

Appellate judges are faced with additional challenges. Here, several judges must come together to collectively apply their insight and imagination to the problem. *A group* must construct both reason and result. After deliberation, appellate judges may be of one mind, or they may disagree over results, over reasons, or over both. That the resulting judgment is an achievement rather than a discovery is particularly evident when one considers other legal traditions where appellate decision making is negotiated in different ways. In France, for example, appellate judges can and do disagree during deliberations, but the details of disagreement are protected by *le secret du délibéré*. The published reasons do not reveal the identities of the judges who supported the decision (or of those who dissented). The resulting decision is published as a unanimous and anonymous judgment of "the Court," even if it is the decision of a bare majority.[10] That is, the published reasons reveal nothing of the particular judicial personalities involved: disagreement among the actual judges is effaced in the moment of articulating the decision. This does not mean that dissent does not occur. Rather, it means that the creativity required in arriving at a particular judgment is exercised in a manner that is not visible. The judgment that is produced will be expressed in a non-authorial voice. It is "the Court" that speaks.

The Supreme Court of Canada sometimes publishes opinions that look very much like those produced by its French counterpart, signed only by "the Court." Consider, for example, *Reference re Secession of Quebec*[11] or *Tremblay v. Daigle*.[12] Writing under this *nom de plume* allows the Court to steer clear of attaching specific judicial identities to cases in contexts where that identity might be used to undercut the unanimity of result. However, such cases are the exception, rather than the rule. In the Canadian legal tradition, judicial deliberations are conducted as much in secret as they are in France, but there is no requirement that opinions be unanimous and anonymous. Although unanimity on an appellate court is always possible, and may be desirable, the stability of law does not require that all judges share one view. Where judges differ, a case may generate a variety of opinions; result and reason are not bound together for the appellate court as they are for the judge sitting alone. With an increased variety of possibilities open to the judges, the sites for modest creativity are similarly expanded.

A word on terminology is in order here. Where unanimity does not exist, but more than half the judges support a particular outcome, the resulting decision is inscribed as a *majority*. A *dissenting* opinion is one that reaches a different result. Where a judge agrees with the result reached by the majority in outcome but differs as to the reasons, her opinion is called a *concurrence*. Though in the English language the word "concur" means "to agree," in law, a concurrence is a form of disagreement. This is more evident to francophone readers of Canadian judgments than to their English-speaking counterparts: the English words "dissent" and "concurrence" translate into *dissidences sur les résultats* and *dissidences sur les motifs*. This linguistic marking more clearly exposes the distinction between result and reason. It also puts emphasis on the dissenting nature of both concurrences and dissents. The central point for the empirically minded is that, for the purposes of statistical analysis, the distinction between a dissent and a concurrence can be problematic: it straddles the categories of majority and dissent. If one is concerned primarily with the result in a case, a concurrence can be counted with the majority. But if one's concern is with the reasons given, a concurrence can instead be counted as a dissent.

Yet more complications face the empiricist attempting to account for the opinions in *plurality* judgments. In some situations, a case produces a number of opinions, none of which can be said to have captured a majority. In such situations, there may be a clear majority as to the *result* in the case. However, there are no majority *reasons* against which to read the multiple concurring and dissenting opinions. If there is no majority against whom a judge can set herself in opposition, her concurrence is less a form of disagreement than an articulation of one of several possible stances in a context where a stable centre has not yet formed. Although one can label this opinion as a concurrence, it may be a different beast from a concurrence articulated alongside a clear majority. It may well be that not all concurrences should be treated alike. Certainly, an empirical approach to judicial opinions may need to account for the ways judges exercise their creativity in the context of highly divisive plurality judgments. In the section that follows, we consider the work of Justice Wilson, taking into account the distinctions between reason and result, and the various types of opinions through which judicial creativity can be expressed.

Focusing on Justice Wilson

During her time at the Supreme Court, Justice Wilson participated in 551 decisions, which are captured in Table 12.1.[13] This table identifies the forms that Justice Wilson's participation took in those 551 judgments. Here, we

Table 12.1

Justice Wilson at the Supreme Court (4 March 1982 to 4 January 1991)

	Number	Percent
Wrote for unanimous court	41	7.4
Wrote majority	22	4.0
Wrote dissent	41	7.4
Wrote concurrence	35	6.3
Wrote partial dissent	10	1.8
Wrote concurrence in plurality	30	5.4
Subtotal	*179*	*32.3*
Signed unanimous	213	38.5
Signed with majority	79	14.3
Signed with dissent	17	3.1
Signed with concurrence	9	1.6
Signed with partial dissent	0	0.0
Signed concurrence in plurality	7	1.3
Subtotal	*325*	*58.8*
Took no part in judgment	1	0.2
"The Court"	48	8.7
Subtotal	*49*	*8.9*
Total	**553**[1]	**100.0**

1 The total number of opinions is 553, though the total number of cases in which Justice Wilson took part is 551, as she signed two opinions for two cases. These were, first, *R. v. A,* [1990] 1 S.C.R. 995, in which nine judges participated. Wilson signed the majority opinion (six judges) written by Cory J. and additional concurring reasons by Sopinka J. (four judges). McLachlin J. wrote a dissent for herself and Lamer J. In the second case, *N.B.C. v. Retail Clerks' Union,* [1984] 1 S.C.R. 269, Wilson J. signed the *per curiam* reasons of Chouinard and the additional reasons of Beetz, Estery, McIntrye, Lamer, and Wilson JJ., written by Beetz J. Chouinard and Dickson JJ. did not join in the additional reasons. In both cases, Wilson J. signed a majority and a concurring opinion, affirming results but open to two sets of reasons.

have distinguished the cases in which she wrote from those in which she signed the opinions of others. Further, we have divided the cases according to the type of opinion in which she participated (unanimous, majority, dissenting, concurring, or partially dissenting). We have also distinguished two categories of concurring opinions: those written against the backdrop of a majority opinion and those written when there was no clear majority (that is, in the context of a *plurality* opinion where *no* one opinion can be said to reflect the law on a given point). We distinguished them to differentiate the two types of engagement from each other (working against a majority versus struggling as a group to constitute a majority).

The table makes visible the diversity of ways in which appellate judges participate in the decision making of the Court, through authoring and

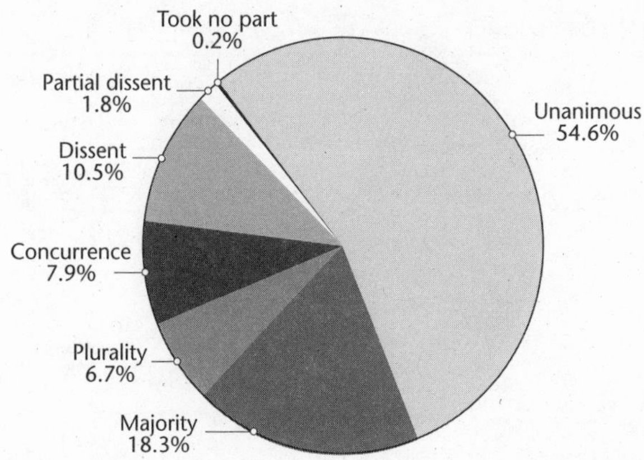

Figure 12.1 Judgments in which Justice Wilson took part, 1982-91

signing a variety of different kinds of opinions. Some things are immediately visible. First, Justice Wilson was a signatory to 302 unanimous opinions in the 551 cases she heard (41 that she herself wrote, 213 that were authored by other judges, and 48 under the name of the Court). That is, nearly 55 percent of the time, she shared the views of her colleagues. Her forms of participation in decision making are presented in Figure 12.1.

Unanimity is the dominating form of Justice Wilson's participation in decision making. And when she was not writing with a unanimous court, she was likely to be writing with the majority (having written twenty-two majority opinions and signed another seventy-nine). If one considers her participation in both unanimous and majority judgments, she agreed with the majority opinion in nearly 73 percent of the cases she heard.

But the next question is, of course, what to make of her participation in concurring opinions. Are they to be counted with majority or dissenting opinions? Here, the nature of empirical research requires clarity about how information is to be categorized. If one is interested in looking at the extent to which Justice Wilson agreed with her colleagues, one might group together unanimous, majority, concurring, and plurality judgments. In each of these, Wilson shared the majority's position on the result of the case. If one takes this approach, strictly speaking, she supported the majority in 87 percent of the cases she heard and disagreed with the result in less than 13 percent.

If, however, one is interested in difference or in creative divergence from the majority (on reasons as well as on results), another approach must be taken. If one conceptualizes a minority opinion as stemming from the creative possibilities inherent within the moment of decision, yet requiring expression outside the corners of the majority opinion, the dissents and concurrences need to be grouped together, leaving a rate of disagreement that is twice as high – that is, in the range of 27 percent.

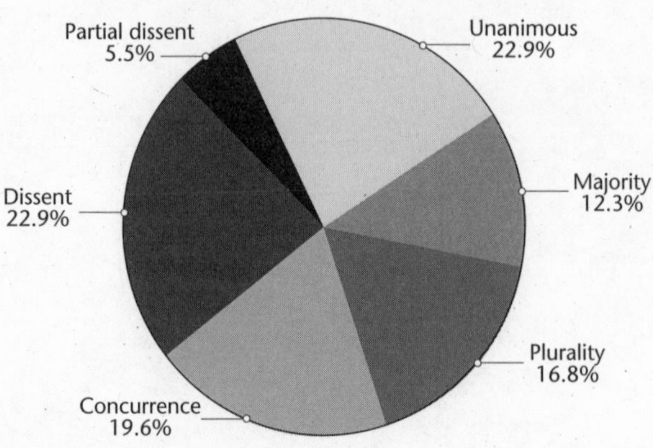

Figure 12.2 Judgments written by Justice Wilson, 1982-91

At this point, it is worth noting that Figure 12.1 blends together authored and signed opinions. Peter McCormick, however, reminds us that distinguishing minority opinions a judge wrote from those a judge signed is worthwhile: the propensities for these two modes of support do not tend to echo one another.[14] Thus, it is useful to consider the authored and signed opinions separately.

In Figure 12.2, we have a graphical distribution of the 179 cases in which Justice Wilson authored an opinion. The different trends are immediately visible. Whereas Figure 12.1 painted the portrait of a judge engaging primarily in the practice of agreement, Figure 12.2, capturing only her written opinions, depicts a judge in significant divergence from the majority.

First, note that, though unanimity remains an important category (she authored the unanimous opinion of the Court in forty-one cases), this form of participation is now counterbalanced by an equivalent number of dissenting opinions (she also authored forty-one dissents). But her most frequent form of authorship was the concurrence (sixty-five in total, of which thirty were produced in the context of plurality judgments). Graphically, we can see that Justice Wilson wrote for the majority (unanimous and not) 35 percent of the time.

Again, if one focuses only on results, one might place the concurrences together with the majority opinions. From that perspective, Wilson shares the majority's opinion 71 percent of the time. But if one considers the reasons for those decisions, a very different picture emerges. Concurrences are then counted alongside dissents, and Wilson joins the majority only 35 percent of the time. What Figure 12.2 shows us is a judge who, when she diverged from the majority, was likely to author an opinion and was more likely to do so on the reasons than on the results.

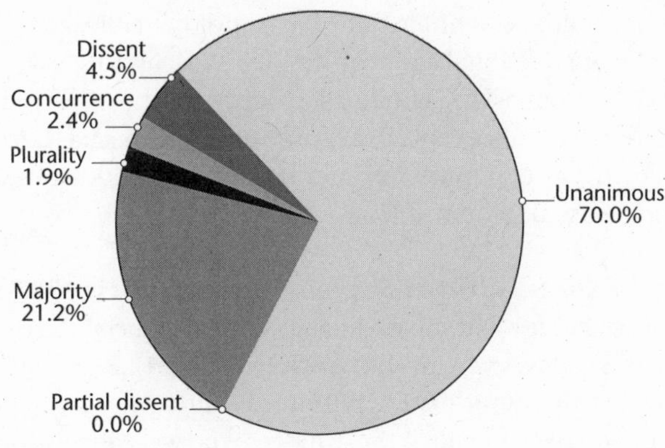

Figure 12.3 Judgments signed by Justice Wilson, 1982-91

If we focus exclusively on the signed judgments, the pattern shifts significantly. Figure 12.3 captures the opinions to which Justice Wilson was a signatory. Here, we see a portrait of a judge in agreement with the majority. She signed 213 authored (those written under the name of a judge) unanimous opinions and 48 opinions issued on behalf of the Court – a total of 70 percent of her signed opinions. If we add to this the majority opinions she signed, the total expands to over 90 percent. She signed relatively few concurring opinions (nine concurrences and an additional seven concurrences in plurality). However, if the focus is on results, and we add those cases to those with a majority outcome, the proportion of cases in which she agreed with the majority rises to over 95 percent. That is, if we consider divergence only in the form of dissent as to outcome, we see that she signed the dissents of others in less than 5 percent of the cases. Nonetheless, even with the more robust definition of dissent (combining concurrences and dissents), she signed on to the opinions of other judges who expressed disagreement in less than 10 percent of her "signing" cases. In short, when she was not writing her own opinions, her practices of judgment were largely convergent with the majority.

In view of the numbers, we can conclude that an understanding of Justice Wilson's creativity requires a consideration of the categories of unanimity and concurrence. Wilson largely agreed with her colleagues. When she could, she joined them. When she joined them, she frequently signed on unequivocally. When her view differed from that of the majority, however, she was likely to express that difference in the context of a written opinion and more likely than not to express it in the form of a concurrence – a disagreement not about the result, but about the reasons for the result.

In this regard, does she differ from the rest of her colleagues? Difference is an unavoidably relational concept, and it is difficult to speak of sameness or difference without asking about the practices of the other judges. To say more about Justice Wilson and the forms in which she exercised a modest degree of creativity, one must consider her judicial work alongside that of the other judges with whom she sat.

Difference in Context: Other Supreme Court Judges, 1982-91

How did other judges participate in the work of judicial decision making while Justice Wilson served on the bench? In Table 12.2, we have listed the fifteen judges with whom Justice Wilson sat during her tenure on the Supreme Court. We have included those judges who were already on the Court when she was appointed (Justices Beetz, Chouinard, Dickson, Estey, Lamer, and McIntyre), as well as those who arrived after her (Justices Cory, Gonthier, La Forest, Le Dain, L'Heureux-Dubé, McLachlin, Sopinka, and Stevenson). It is important to acknowledge that there are some clear limits to the comparative work one can do with the data captured in Table 12.2. For one thing, the table does not reflect a stable time period. Though each of these judges served with Wilson, they did not all sit together. Le Dain, for example, retired five years before McLachlin was appointed. And only (Chief) Justice McLachlin is still a sitting justice and still in the process of hearing new cases.

When one considers Table 12.2, then, it is important to remain conscious that it portrays the differences in the decision-making practices of multiple judges situated over overlapping yet different streams of time. One might, indeed, suggest that the table is more like a potpourri or compilation album than a site for rigorous statistical analysis. And yet, such compilations can give us a useful context within which to start a discussion about forms of judicial participation and about questions that might arise when one takes an empirically oriented approach to judicial decision making. The numbers here, though far from *predictive* or *explanatory,* can give us a sense of how to better understand Justice Wilson's contributions – of how to locate her patterns of creativity alongside those of her judicial colleagues.

For each judge listed in Table 12.2, we have included information equivalent to that which we provided earlier about Justice Wilson in Table 12.1. That is, the numbers given in each column correspond to all of the cases in which each judge sat, separating unanimous from divided cases and divided cases into the various forms that the judge's participation could take (*i.e.,* joining the majority, dissenting, and concurring opinions). The first row of data reflects the overall average of all the judges included in this table. Because we are interested here in questions of creativity and difference, we have organized the judges from most to least likely to differ with the majority as evidenced by the numbers in column five, the column that captures each judge's divergence from the majority.

Table 12.2

Participation by Supreme Court of Canada justices in judgments (written and signed), reported decisions, 1982-2007

1		2	3	4	5	6	7	8
Average		325	298	56.6	42.8	25.7	15.0	35.8
		Number of cases		Percentage of non-unanimous				
Justice	Date of appointment	Unanimous[1]	Non-unanimous	Took part in majority	Differed from majority	Took part in concurring[2]	Took part in dissent	Took part in writing non-unanimous
L'Heureux-Dubé ♀	15/04/1987	340	531	35.6	63.3	31.5	28.1	42.7
Wilson ♀	04/03/1982	302	250	40.4	59.6	32.4	23.2	55.2
McLachlin ♀	30/03/1989	472	555	53.1	46.1	23.6	19.6	43.8
La Forest	16/01/1985	306	467	54.8	45.2	30.4	12.0	38.8
Lamer	28/03/1980	397	502	54.9	45.0	29.1	13.4	44.5
Sopinka	24/05/1988	207	382	54.2	44.8	25.7	17.3	46.1
McIntyre	01/01/1979	407	183	55.8	43.7	23.5	16.4	37.2
Stevenson	17/09/1990	27	70	57.1	42.9	28.8	14.3	25.7
Beetz	01/01/1974	490	134	57.5	41.6	29.1	11.1	22.4
Dickson	26/03/1973	486	229	59.4	40.5	27.9	12.2	39.3
Estey	29/09/1977	384	107	61.7	37.4	17.8	17.8	42.1
Gonthier	01/02/1989	404	506	62.6	35.2	21.3	12.5	17.2
Chouinard	24/09/1979	289	86	65.1	34.9	20.9	12.8	16.3
Cory	01/02/1989	267	397	68.0	31.0	19.4	9.8	35.5
Le Dain	29/05/1984	97	70	68.6	30.0	24.3	5.7	30.0

1 This column includes a judge's participation in opinions written under the name of "the Court."
2 This category includes concurrences delivered in the context of plurality judgments.

Before asking questions about the various judges' forms of participation, we draw attention to the second and third columns: unanimous and non-unanimous cases. These columns capture the total number of cases in which each of the judges participated but separate them into those that produced a unanimous judgment (whether authored by a particular judge or written in the name of the Court) and those that resulted in some form of disagreement (producing at least two written opinions). Although it is certainly true that every judge has the power to turn a potentially unanimous decision into a divided one through the act of saying "no" (whether according to result or reasons), the first two columns tell us little about an individual judge's proclivity to do so. Rather, they give us some sense of the magnitude of disagreement between the members of the bench during each judge's tenure. To say that Justice Dickson, for example, heard 486 unanimous and 229 divided cases says nothing about the position he took on any one of those divided cases. It does tell us, however, that during Dickson's time, the Court produced more unanimous than divided decisions. During Justice Lamer's years, on the other hand, the Court produced more divided than unanimous decisions. These first two columns thus provide some context against which to better understand the forms of participation in which the individual judges engaged.

Of the fifteen judges listed in the table, seven participated in more unanimous than divided cases (Justices Wilson, McIntyre, Beetz, Dickson, Estey, Chouinard, and Le Dain). For the other eight judges, the pattern is reversed: they participated in more divided than unanimous cases. Justice Wilson's appointment to the Supreme Court coincided with the adoption of the *Charter,* a development that required the judges to grapple with the interpretation and implementation of a new constitutional document. Wilson indeed appears positioned at a watershed, at the tipping point of a shift from more to less unanimity. Although dissent as a phenomenon is a firmly entrenched part of our legal tradition, Table 12.2 shows evidence of the larger ebbs and flows of dissenting practice that seem to be the product of something more than the propensities of individual judges. The first two columns serve as a reminder that judicial disagreement, though persistent, is variable in intensity over time.[15]

The next four columns indicate the judges' decision-making patterns in the divided cases in which each participated. Column four gives the proportion of cases in which the judge agreed with the majority. So, for example, one can see that, in the divided cases, Justice Wilson sided with the majority just over 40 percent of the time. This is significantly lower than the average rate of "with the majority" decisions of 56 percent. Indeed, only Justice L'Heureux-Dubé was less likely to agree with the majority. Column five expresses the same information but from the flip side – that is, the rate at

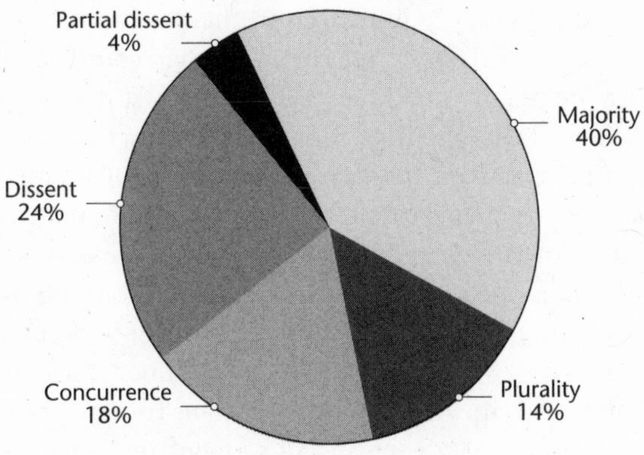

Figure 12.4 Distribution of non-unanimous judgments in which Justice Wilson took part, 1982-91

which each judge differed from the majority. This is a global disagreement number, incorporating both concurrences and dissents.

Columns six and seven disaggregate the global disagreement, giving us a sense of the judges' modest creativity by considering the extent to which they participated in disagreement in its convergent and divergent forms. How often was the judge disagreeing on the results (dissent) and how often on the reasons (concurrence)? One might note, for example, that Justice Estey's disagreements are split fairly evenly between concurrences and dissents. Justice Le Dain, on the other hand, was far more likely to express disagreement in the form of a concurrence than in a dissent. Figure 12.4, rounding percentages to the nearest whole number, represents Justice Wilson's participation in the non-unanimous decisions.

Where there was any level of disagreement on the Court, Wilson, we can see, was less than likely to be found with the majority. In fact, 60 percent of the time, she disagreed with the majority. She disagreed both through concurrence *and* through dissent. Indeed, no one listed in Table 12.2 was more likely than Justice Wilson to be concurring, and only Justice L'Heureux-Dubé was more likely to be found in dissent. In the context of divided cases, Wilson was more likely than not to see something that differed from the majority view.

Such a conclusion does leave us feeling compelled to acknowledge the presence of the elephant in the room. Table 12.2 lists fifteen judges, from most to least likely to differ with the majority. The first three are also the first three women judges appointed to the Supreme Court of Canada. This raises obvious questions about the relationship of gender, judgment, and dissent, questions that we will not consider here at any length.[16] We note only that, as Justice Wilson pointed out in the Betcherman Lecture, these questions are complicated ones. Certainly, Canadian court watchers, though acknowledging the heightened propensity of the first female judges to dissent, have also noted that the three women did not act together or seem to share common perspectives. Indeed, on substantive legal questions, each seemed as likely to disagree with her female as with her male colleagues.[17]

The magnitude of the shared dissenting practice makes it hard not to suspect that gender is operating in some fashion here, but the ways in which it might be operating are far from simple. However, whether or not it is possible to draw any conclusions about "the gender question" from the numbers in Table 12.2, they do demonstrate *some* things about Justice Wilson. First, they show us that dissenting and concurring practices were a very important part of her judicial work and important expressions of her modest degree of creativity. Second, the final column in Table 12.2 directs our attention to authorship, providing us with a glimpse at a further dimension of Wilson's creativity, one that gives an ironic inflection to the word "modest." The table focuses largely on questions of majority, dissenting, and concurring participation without distinguishing practices of voting from those of writing. The final column tells us about the volume of authorship in the divided cases. It summarizes the proportion of times that the judge authored an opinion, be it majority, dissenting, or concurring. In this final column, Justice Wilson's position is most striking. The average rate at which judges authored opinions is 35 percent. Wilson authored opinions in 55 percent of the non-unanimous cases in which she participated. This is significant, both in terms of proportional participation and sheer numbers. Between 1982 and 1999, the *Supreme Court Reports* published 1,028 divergent opinions (concurrences and dissents). Justice Wilson alone authored 116 of those opinions. That is, although she was but one of twenty-eight judges who passed through the Court during those years, she authored 11 percent of all divergent written opinions produced over a seventeen-year period. When considering these numbers, one cannot help but hear the echo of those first- and second-generation feminists who asserted that, to be successful, women had to work twice as hard.

Conclusion: Justice Wilson – Difference and Modest Creativity

Let us return, then, to the question of creativity. We opened this piece with the Random House Webster's dictionary definition of creativity, a definition that reminds us to attend not only to "the ability to transcend traditional ideas" but also to "the process by which one utilizes creative ability." Empirical data provide one avenue for the exploration of Justice Wilson's jurisprudence. The numbers enable us to take a step back from the narrative details and make it possible to view the scope of her work in its entirety, including the patterns and trajectories of her decisions and the forms of her participation during her tenure on the Supreme Court. Such an approach enables us to ask further questions about the processes through which Wilson exercised her judicial creativity.

The information gathered in the tables and figures above helps to make visible additional dimensions of the work in which Justice Wilson engaged and the processes through which her creativity emerged. Her creativity can of course be explored through her judgments and through biography. Empirical data can also assist in such a venture, helping us to see new patterns, to consider various ways of understanding judicial creativity, and to reflect on the ways that judges are figures acting in a flow of time. They can confirm what we think, change our perspective, leave us baffled, or open new avenues of inquiry.

The numbers outlined in this chapter document Justice Wilson's strong desire to express her point of view. This comes across particularly clearly in the large discrepancy between her high rate of writing separate opinions and her much lower rate of signing them. Wilson often agreed with her colleagues about outcomes. But the numbers do support the widely held opinion of Justice Wilson as a fearlessly independent judicial pioneer. Her view of matters was very likely to differ from that of the majority (regardless of whom that majority was composed), and when it did, she felt strongly enough about that difference to produce written reasons explaining her perspective.

A study of Justice Wilson's "numbers" also shows us how she encouraged a different outlook about common results. By demonstrating that a concurrence is an important kind of dissenting voice, she nurtured a dialogue not just about *what* the law should do, but also about *why* and *how* the law should do it. Even without attending to the substance of Wilson's creativity in this analysis, we can see a sweeping overview of her propensity for innovatively interweaving modern insights with the law in areas where she judged that the law had gone awry. The statistics also provide some tools for examining the concurrence as a locus of judicial creativity. The concurrence can be a vehicle for judges to swathe out new paths through blocked territory to commonly desired destinations. This is a space for creativity as judges seek to hold on to common outcomes but to attend to multiple ways of getting there and to consider space for alternative routes.

We can see that, for Justice Wilson, reasons were of tremendous importance. Of course, they lie at the heart of judicial work; they are crucial for the stabilization of law. Reasons sketch possibilities for the future. Wilson's insistence on written reasons may tell us something of her sense of the potential of law. That she so frequently felt compelled to write concurring opinions says *something* about her. For her, expressing a different point of view seems to have been worth the effort, even if her opinions were not to be taken up by the others. This is clear simply by virtue of the number of separate opinions she generated.

Regardless of whether one views Justice Wilson's decision making through the lens of gender, one must acknowledge the importance of authorship in her practices of judicial participation. In saying this, we do not wish to fetishize or overemphasize the importance of judicial authorship. Judges collectively participate in the production of judicial opinions in ways that are more and less visible, and the act of "voting" cannot be minimized, since it is, in large measure, what determines whether any written decision stands as the *law* or as the dissenting articulation of a path not taken. Even with this caveat, an examination of Justice Wilson against her peers clearly demonstrates that her modest degree of creativity was exercised largely in the context of the opinions that she authored. In particular, the expression of her creativity through the practice of writing concurrences is a locus ripe for future exploration.

Acknowledgments
We wish to thank our research assistants Julie Banville, Christine Joseph, Anik Lamontagne, and Sarah-Dawn Schenk. We are grateful to the Social Sciences and Humanities Research Council of Canada and the law firm of Borden Ladner Gervais for supporting our research.

Notes

1 Bertha Wilson, "Will Women Judges Really Make a Difference?" (1990) 28 Osgoode Hall L.J. 507.

2 The numbers we use here are from our own database of Supreme Court cases, gathered and coded by a number of student researchers, as part of a research project funded by the Social Sciences and Humanities Research Council.

3 Peter McCormick, *Supreme at Last: The Evolution of the Supreme Court of Canada* (Toronto: James Lorimer, 2000); Virginia Hettinger, Stephanie A. Lindquist, and Wendy Martinek, *Judging on a Collegial Court: Influences on Federal Appellate Decision Making* (Charlottesville: University of Virginia Press, 2006); Lee Epstein *et al.*, *The Supreme Court Compendium: Data, Decisions, and Developments,* 3d ed. (Washington, DC: Congressional Quarterly, 2003).

4 See *e.g.* Thaddeus Hwong, *A Quantitative Exploration of Judicial Decision Making in Canadian Income Tax Cases* (Ph.D. Dissertation, Osgoode Hall Law School, 2006), online: The Court <http://www.thecourt.ca/resources/thaddeus-hwong>; Christine M. Joseph, "All but One: Solo Dissents on the Supreme Court of Canada" (2006) 44 Osgoode Hall L.J. 501; Daved Muttart, *The Empirical Gap in Jurisprudence: A Comprehensive Study of the Supreme Court of Canada* (Toronto: University of Toronto Press, 2007); Moin A. Yahya and James Stribopoulos, "Does a Judge's Party of Appointment or Gender Matter to Case Outcomes? An Empirical Study of the Court of Appeal for Ontario" (2007) 45 Osgoode Hall L.J. 315.

5 Peter Fitzpatrick, *Modernism and the Grounds of Law* (Cambridge: Cambridge University Press, 2001).

6 J.L. Austin, *How to Do Things with Words* (Cambridge, MA: Harvard University Press, 1962).

7 As the unanimous Court recently said in *R. v. Walker,* 2008 SCC 34 at para. 19, quoting *R. v. Sheppard,* [2002] 1 S.C.R. 869 at paras. 15, 24: "Reasons for judgment are the primary mechanism by which judges account to the parties and to the public for the decisions they render ... Interested members of the public can satisfy themselves that justice has been done, or not, as the case may be."

8 For a fuller discussion of this point, see Marie-Claire Belleau and Rebecca Johnson, "I Beg to Differ: Interdisciplinary Questions about Law, Language and Dissent" in Logan Atkinson and Diana Majury, eds., *Law, Mystery and the Humanities: Collected Essays* (Toronto: University of Toronto Press, 2008) 145.

9 James Boyd White, *The Edge of Meaning* (Chicago: University of Chicago Press, 2001).

10 Wanda Mastor, *Les opinions séparées des juges constitutionnels* (Paris/Aix-en-Provence: Economica/Presses universitaires d'Aix-Marseille, 2005).

11 *Reference re Secession of Quebec,* [1998] 2 S.C.R. 217.

12 *Tremblay v. Daigle,* [1989] 2 S.C.R. 530.

13 We have not included oral judgments in these numbers. The focus here is on cases issued with written reasons sufficient to enable us to identify the outcome, who participated in the decision making, and the type of decision generated.

14 Peter McCormick, "'With Respect ... ' – Levels of Disagreement on the Lamer Court 1990-2000" (2003) 48 McGill L.J. 89 at 100. According to McCormick, joining a separate opinion occurs only, on average, three-fifths as often as writing one.

15 Court watchers document that periods do occur in which the Court as a whole feels more or less pressure to speak with a unanimous voice or at least to ensure that what dissent exists is articulated in a more constrained fashion. Interestingly, in recent years, both Canadian and American scholars have remarked on a tendency to reduced dissent. See Christopher Guly, "Beverley McLachlin: 'A Model Judge'" *Canadian Lawyer* 30:6 (June 2006) 16; Reynolds Holding, "In Defence of Dissent" *Time Magazine* 169:9 (26 February 2007) 44.

16 For a more extended discussion of the gendered dimensions of this question, see Marie-Claire Belleau and Rebecca Johnson, "Les femmes juges feront-elles véritablement une différence? Réflexions sur leur présence depuis vingt ans à la Cour suprême du Canada" (2005) 17 C.J.W.L. 37.

17 F.L. Morton, Peter H. Russell, and Troy Riddell, "The Canadian *Charter of Rights and Freedoms:* A Descriptive Analysis of the First Decade, 1982-1992" (1995) 5 N.J.C.L. 1. The researchers chart the judges on two axes: criminal law issues (left or right) and "court party" or "social justice" issues (left or right). The three female judges end up in three different quadrants. See also McCormick, *supra* note 3.

13
A Way of Being in the World

Lorna Turnbull

The photograph of Bertha Wilson that Justice James MacPherson of the Ontario Court of Appeal described in the eulogy he gave at Wilson's funeral on 8 May 2007 is reproduced on the following page. He noted that she had inspired a whole generation of women law students, lawyers, and judges. He emphasized the important and formative role she had played in the lives of her law clerks, quoting Margaret Atwood: "Learning ... involves a kind of laying on of minds; what you learn from your teachers is not merely a body of knowledge but a way of thinking, and, beyond that, a way of being in the world."[1]

Certainly, Bertha Wilson's law clerks would have particular insights to share about her as a teacher and a mentor, but her ability to be a teacher, not merely of knowledge, but of how to be in the world, reached many more than the twenty individuals who clerked for her. This chapter examines Wilson as a role model to the many whose lives she touched simply by being who she was and where she was: the first woman justice of the Supreme Court of Canada. It is written from the point of view of one who knew her only from afar.

The story told here is just that, a story. It is personal; it is my story. Mary Jane Mossman has noted in this volume that life stories contain silences, and certainly there is much that I do not know about Wilson.[2] The story I tell here will be partial, focused on the details that seemed to resonate with me, overlooking those that someone else would find more compelling.

In the feminist praxis of using narrative to underpin or illustrate larger academic ideas, I explore understandings of role models through my own story about Wilson. As Rebecca Johnson notes in "Blurred Boundaries," "personal experience seems fine in autobiography and memoir, but it does not fit comfortably in traditional legal discourse."[3] Like Johnson, I am weaving personal stories, both Wilson's and my own, with the traditional scholarly discourse of role model theory, although I have chosen not to use the clever italicized stylistic device that she employed.

Figure 13.1 Justice Bertha Wilson in Aurora, Ontario, at the home of James and Gladys MacPherson with three students celebrating their call to the bar, 25 April 1991. Photograph by James MacPherson.

An important detail that made Wilson so compelling to me as a role model was our shared Scottish roots. Historian Arthur Herman has said that being Scottish "is more than just a matter of nationality or place of origin or clan or even culture. It is also a state of mind, a way of viewing the world and our place in it."[4] He argues that Scots created the basic ideals of modernity:

> As the first modern nation and culture, the Scots by and large have made the world a better place. They taught the world that true liberty requires a sense of personal obligation as well as individual rights. They showed how modern life can be spiritually as well as materially fulfilling. They showed how a respect for science and technology can combine with a love for the arts; how private affluence can enhance a sense of civic responsibility; how political and economic democracy can flourish side by side; and how a confidence in the future depends on a reverence for the past. The Scottish mind grasped how, in Hume's words, "liberty is the perfection of civil society," but "authority must be acknowledged essential to its very existence"; and how a strong faith in progress also requires a keen appreciation of its limitations.[5]

Many of these attributes are reflected in the portrayals and analyses of Justice Wilson contained in the chapters of this book, and these traits were something I sensed more than two decades ago when reading about her inspired me to go to law school. Perhaps through this piece, I can make some sense of our shared Scottish approach to making the world a better place. Perhaps I can also make sense of the ways Wilson touched my life, viewing these many connections as more than mere chance.

A mentor is commonly understood to be a person who provides advice and support to a protege through an interactive relationship. A mentor invests vast amounts of time and energy in fostering the development and success of the protege. Wilson was not a mentor to me. A wealth of research has examined mentors and the importance of the mentoring relationship for career development.[6] It is widely believed that women's equality will be enhanced as women gain improved access to suitable mentors.[7] More recent theories have suggested that career development occurs, not only through the guidance of mentors and sponsors higher up in a professional or organizational hierarchy, but also through the network of developmental relationships that individuals create for themselves to enhance their career paths. In particular, role models are thought to be important in individual career development, just as the evidence demonstrates that they are crucial to individual growth and development more generally.[8] For me, Wilson was a formative role model.

If role models are important to professional development, how do women manage when they have so few women upon whom to pattern themselves?[9] Certainly, the number of women at the upper echelons of the legal profession has not been historically large and has failed to keep pace with the rate at which women are entering and graduating from law school.[10] Even in the twenty-first century, women continue to leave the profession at rates alarming enough to provoke repeated study.[11] With fewer suitable role models, women may face the arduous cognitive task of translating male role model behaviour into conduct that works for them.[12] Furthermore, because law as a profession is masculine, it demands that women undergo intrapsychic changes and alienation from aspects of the feminine self so as to adopt their professional identities.[13] For women, integrating the dominant identity of a legal professional with their own marginal female identity leaves them on the edges of both, living in and partaking of two realities, affirming or invalidating neither. Although a woman who simply wants to follow the dominant model may be able to sublimate her minority identity and rely on male models, one who wishes to maintain her feminine identity has a particular need for models, to see that integration is possible.[14]

Donald Gibson proposes a definition of role models that is particularly apposite in the context of this chapter, which seeks to highlight the important learning that I gained from Bertha Wilson. Gibson notes that the notion of role model contains two key concepts. The first is that of "role." With respect to this, Gibson states that individuals tend to identify with those who occupy important social roles. Furthermore, the focuses of identification are most likely to be those with whom they already share some similarities and whom they are motivated to emulate. The emphasis contained within this concept is on the motivational and self-definitional aspects of the role model. Gibson's second concept is that of "modelling" – the psychological matching of cognitive skills, character traits, and patterns of behaviour between the individual and the model. The attraction to the role model is driven by a desire to learn new skills or norms, with the emphasis on the learning aspects.[15]

In 1985, after graduating from Queen's University with a B.A. Honours in Psychology (my thesis examined sex-role stereotyping), I was at a loss concerning where I might fit in the world. The Canadian-born child of Scottish immigrants who had lived some of her life in Europe, I had chosen to return to Canada because I thought it a place where I would have more opportunities, where diversity was welcomed, and where I could realize my fullest potential. I had considered medicine, motivated by a youthful desire to help people. Rejection, accompanied as it was by the explanation that, though I may have had all the personal attributes to make a fine physician (in fact, I was told that, had I scored any higher, I would be Mother Teresa), I lacked the academic qualities (having managed to maintain only an 87 percent average in my first two years of university), left me cynical. I also considered business, naively imagining that I could put my psychology training to good use in the human resources department of some corporation. A six-month internship in a large multinational consulting company quickly persuaded me that human resources mattered little compared to financial resources and that women were welcome in business only if they were willing to pick up the partners' dry cleaning. I spent the next six months working at Marks and Spencer, the fine British department store, which had a presence in Canada during the eighties, while I contemplated whether to go to grad school to become a clinical psychologist or to law school. An article in *Saturday Night* cleared up any lingering questions I had about where to use my talents.

The article caught my attention because of its clever title ("Sense and Sensibility") and because the caption on the first page proclaimed that "Bertha Wilson is exceptional on the Supreme Court of Canada not only because she's a woman but also because she views the law as a force for social change." The article went on to report, "[I]t is not only her sex that makes her special. It's her sense and sensibility, a kind of practical sensitivity tinged with Scottish asperity, enriched but by no means defined by her genes."[16] I could just imagine what she was like and how she approached her awesome task. She would be much like my mother and my grandmother, both of them practical, generous Scottish women who were always prepared for hard work. What struck me most in that article, and has stayed with me ever since, were the lines quoted from the speech Wilson gave on the occasion of her appointment to the Ontario Court of Appeal. She spoke of her research practice at Osler, Hoskin & Harcourt[17] and of the dangers of losing sight of the spirit and larger dimensions of law: "Perhaps the unusual nature of my practice has helped me to retain this perspective, and to remember that people and the law are inextricably intertwined, and the role of the profession is essentially to serve the needs of the people."[18] Wilson saw that the Supreme Court, with the newly entrenched *Canadian Charter of Rights and Freedoms,* would "decide the kind of society Canadians want to live in."[19] I could not resist and began my legal education in September 1986.

Gibson's definition of role models recognizes that they are a cognitive construction based upon the attributes of certain people perceived by an individual to be similar to herself. The role model relationship is typically one-sided and based upon the perceptions of the individual. The act of identification creates the model, regardless of any actions on the part of the model or any relationship between the individual and the model. By occupying valued social positions or illustrating valued characteristics, the role model helps the individual to define and develop her self-concept or to direct her behaviour toward achieving what the model has achieved.[20] Psychologists and sociologists, who have explored conceptual ideas about the self for nearly a hundred years, have shown that these notions of self-definition and creation are well founded.[21]

Wilson recognized them too and expressed great uneasiness at the notion that she might be perceived as a role model. She said that, as talk began in early 1982 about who would replace Justice Martland on the Supreme Court, she fervently hoped that she would not be asked. She was getting too old to face another new beginning; yet she knew that, if she were asked, "there wasn't a choice. Too many women were counting on [her]."[22] And she was right. Her appointment on 4 March 1982 was heralded as a "great day for women in the country" by Solicitor General Robert Kaplan. Lucie Pepin, president of the Advisory Council on the Status of Women, said, "I think it is really sensational. I am so pleased ... [S]he will bring a different perspective ... [S]he is a very capable and good judge. Women will feel more secure as they establish their rights under the constitution for at last they have representation in the highest court in the land."[23]

Most of those who were quoted in the news reports of the day commented on the importance of having a woman on the Court, particularly with the advent of the entrenched *Charter.* Canadian Bar Association President Paul Fraser proclaimed that there were now "women in every level of the judicial system, making the role of women in the administration of justice appropriately complete." More realistically, Conservative MP Flora MacDonald noted that women still represented only 4 percent of federal judicial appointments and that, though Wilson's appointment may have made a crack in the male bastion after 115 years, it could only be regarded as a beginning. Her colleague MP Walter McLean said that "it must only be seen as a first step because of the very real danger it will be seen as only a token appointment. With 52 percent of the population of the country women, one doesn't want to think it is all over. With the number of women entering the legal profession today they will want equal consideration in the future."[24] Minister of Justice Jean Chrétien must have shared McLean's insight. Federal mines minister Judy Erola, who was also the minister responsible for the status of women, had lobbied along with health minister Monique Begin, the only other woman in Cabinet, for Wilson's appointment in the face of opposition from Prime Minister Pierre Trudeau. It was Chrétien who is reported to have said to Trudeau, "Well Boss, the girls are right, I think it is time for a woman otherwise we will have problems."[25]

After her appointment, women from across the country contacted Wilson to rejoice in her achievement, yet she found herself unable to rejoice with them. She felt that she simply could not meet all of the expectations of all the well-wishers and the women who had worked so hard to get her there.[26] She believed women should have equal opportunities and equal pay for work of equal value, but she knew that changes in the law come slowly and incrementally, and that if she brashly went about trying to change everything all at once, she would fail to live up to her judicial obligations of impartiality and independence.[27]

Role model theory suggests that Wilson's reticence about being a role model is not relevant. What is important is the cognitive activity of an individual in choosing and observing the role model rather than the behaviour of the model herself.[28] Choosing and attending to a role model is an active process that may entail focusing on differing attributes of a variety of models, either concurrently or over time as the individual uses these to develop a sense of her ideal self or a range of possible selves. Role models allow us to imagine what we could become, what we would like to become, and what we wish to avoid becoming.[29] Self-development occurs through a process of acquiring and then achieving or resisting these possible selves. It is the individual who decides which selves are possible or impossible and whether or not a given possible self has been achieved. Integrating learning from a variety of others is a critical task of forming a cohesive identity.[30]

Role models also provide motivation and inspiration. If the model's success seems attainable, it will inspire, motivating others to strive for similar success, suggesting goals to be achieved along the way, and building confidence.[31] Through the selection of role models, the construction of possible selves, and the setting of goals and planning of behaviours, individuals can be viewed as active producers of their own development.[32] Experimenting with possible selves is an important way for an individual to acquire a new identity. A significant element of agency is involved in this identity construction as individuals devote greater attention to certain models and revise their choice of models based upon their own experimentation with those models and the feedback they receive regarding their modelled behaviour. Progress through life or career transitions takes place in a series of iterative cycles as the individual becomes accustomed to, and increasingly familiar with, the adopted identity.[33]

Role models are selected from a variety of potential candidates. The target may be someone with whom the individual interacts frequently or may be someone distant in the sense that she is not actually present but is observed through the media, for example. Potential models may even be found among historical, fictitious, or celebrity figures. Some commentators have suggested that, for self-definition or competence development, distant models may be less influential than those with whom an individual directly interacts.[34] Research also suggests, however, that the greater the perceived similarity between the individual and her role model, the more influential the model will be for the individual. Role models are specific and individually significant and relevant, but they are also social, as they are constructed by individuals based upon social comparisons. Each individual is free to construct any variety of possible selves, but the pool of possible selves is shaped by the individual's own social, cultural, and historical context, by the models, images, and symbols presented in the media, and by an individual's immediate social experiences.[35]

It is of course a cultural cliché to observe that men and women of outstanding achievement, those whom Penelope Lockwood and Ziva Kunda term "superstars," can serve as role models.[36] Lockwood and Kunda found that individuals were most likely to make comparisons where the model was relevant – that is, where similarities existed between the self and the model, especially in age, race, gender, or personality. Similarity of circumstances also makes a potential model relevant.[37] Lockwood and Kunda identified the ideal model as somewhat older and at a more advanced career stage than the individual; furthermore, the model will have achieved what the individual hopes for herself, outstanding but not impossible success in an enterprise at which she wishes to excel.[38]

So perhaps it is no surprise that Wilson immediately appealed to me and inspired me to apply to law school. She was a superstar, she had reached what I saw as the pinnacle of a legal career, and she was the first woman to do so. Her background resonated with me. Although forty years my senior, and in a position I should never presume to aspire to, she was an unassuming and sensible woman who showed an incredible sense of duty and who believed that the function of the profession was to serve the needs of the people. Perhaps the law had a place for me.

Attending law school is the first step in the transition to becoming a professional. The socializing effects of law school have been extensively scrutinized and critiqued.[39] Students are effectively learning a new identity, which they must try to integrate with their own self-concept. However, the new identity should not come at the expense of being true to oneself.[40] It is often difficult to retain the high ideals and aspirations that originally propelled one to become a lawyer. Having a role model such as Wilson, along with two of my professors and a couple of classmates, allowed me to hold to my ideals, remember the people whom the law should serve, and imagine myself becoming a force for change.

When meeting new friends in law school, I was not at all shy about telling the story of how the *Saturday Night* article about Wilson had motivated me to attend. I even allowed that I might aspire to becoming a judge. This quickly earned me the nickname "Madam Justice Turnbull." I was both embarrassed and flattered. How presumptuous of me to imagine that such an honour could ever be mine. Yet, if I worked hard and proved myself, might I not some day merit such an appointment? The judicial possible self stayed with me throughout my formal training. Because possible selves are provisional, individuals have considerable freedom to define and redefine them.[41] I decided to complete the bar course and be called to the bar immediately after law school, despite my intention to proceed to graduate work and pursue a career in academia, keeping my judicial possible self alive. I knew that judicial appointments required at least ten years of membership in a provincial law society, and I wanted the clock to start ticking. Of course, I have been a member of a law society for seventeen years now and am happily ensconced in my academic career. The closest I came to judicial activity was serving as the chief justice of the Supreme Court of Osgoode Hall during first-year mooting exercises.

Wilson's appointment to the Supreme Court was still relatively fresh during my years in law school, and there was no shortage of professors who were eager to offer their thoughts on her work. Not all the comments were laudatory, and those who criticized her often did so because they perceived that she overstepped the boundaries of the legal questions in issue. Throughout all of her decisions, I could see that Wilson remembered the people behind the legal questions. Later commentators have observed this trend over the corpus of Wilson's decisions. Alan Watson has wondered if her lively understanding of the human condition and strong concern for civil, humane society was shaped by the enduring influence of the Scottish Enlightenment tradition. He admits that proving any causal relationship between that tradition and the "Scottish character" is impossible. However, he observes that the universal education policies that were the product of the Enlightenment may well have made privileged Scots aware of the situation of disadvantaged members of their communities as they encountered each other in school. His commentary regarding the influence of the Enlightenment on Wilson's decision making shows how Wilson found that, if the application of a rule led to harsh justice, the "proper course to follow is to examine the rule itself rather than affirm it and attempt to ameliorate its ill effects on a case by case basis."[42] Wilson does this, notes Watson, in a scholarly way, making constant reference to academic literature. I always found her judgments exciting and inspiring to read, and her pragmatic and compassionate viewpoint made sense to me.

Wilson took a broad and principled approach to the judicial task, always remembering the spirit and larger dimensions of the law. In the context of the *Charter,* she wrote, "The challenge for the courts then is to develop norms against which the reasonableness of the impairment of a person's rights can be measured in a vast variety of different contexts ... These norms must reflect to the maximum extent possible the political idea of a free and democratic society. Could there be a broader mandate for judicial creativity?"[43] In *Morgentaler,* which came down in my last year of law school, she treated a woman facing the decision of whether to have an abortion "as a whole person rather than as a body with peculiar physical and psychological needs."[44] She remained conscious of the context in which legal questions arose and endeavoured to make principled decisions within that context. As Hester Lessard suggests, there is a trend in Wilson's work to "ensure that the conceptual complexities of rights discourse ultimately remain grounded in the realities of specific human lives and needs. The enumerated and unenumerated 'others' of equality discourse will only become 'us' if the law begins to speak in multiple voices."[45] Wilson herself commented, "[I]t is so much easier to come up with a black and white answer if you are unencumbered by a broader context which might prompt you, in Lord MacMillan's words, to temper the cold light of reason with the warmer tints of imagination and sympathy."[46] Clearly, inclusion of people was her hallmark.

My admiration and respect for Justice Wilson grew when, during my second year of law school, I had the privilege of meeting her in person. One of my classmates was married to the Executive Legal Officer of the Supreme Court, and I was invited to dinner one evening in their home with Bertha and John Wilson. I was completely overawed, but their gracious manner put me at ease. I told her how reading about her in *Saturday Night* had moved me to enter law school. I especially mentioned her view that the law and the people were inextricably intertwined and that the law could be a force for social change. I told her I was looking forward to seeing women achieve equality under the *Charter.* Predictably, she warned me not to get carried away with transformative dreams but to remain focused on the incremental nature of legal change and to work where the opportunities presented themselves. She reminded me of how important it was to live up to the highest ideals of the profession, to maintain my integrity, and to be of service. We also chatted about Scottish roots, the area of Scotland where my family lived, and the double-decker buses that connected the villages around the loch. I told her of riding the top deck of the bus with my Gran and loudly singing "Oh, ye canny push your granny off a bus." I felt completely at ease and understood. And once again, I felt inspired, not just by her accomplishments or her vision and insight, but by the warm and gracious person she was.

I was also impressed by her relationship with John. They were both evidently very intelligent, and they delighted in each other's wit. Their companionable manner and deep mutual respect were obvious, even on one meeting. Of course, I had read of their relationship in the *Saturday Night* article. It was described as being both a "thoroughly old-fashioned marriage and a supremely modern one." John acknowledged that "for years she went where I went and looked after me, now it is her turn."[47] I hoped that I might have a similar relationship, not one like my parents' where my mother had followed my father and looked after him until, after twenty-three years and seven moves covering nearly twenty thousand kilometres, he decided to end the marriage.

Bringing closure to my progress into the legal profession, Madam Justice Wilson was the recipient of the honorary Doctor of Laws degree conferred during my call to the bar ceremony in 1991. Addressing the special convocation of the Law Society, she spoke about the importance of having a sound theoretical grounding in law, of being well read beyond law, and of remaining aware of the broader social and philosophical context within which legal issues arise. She also called on all the newly admitted lawyers to remember that they were members of a profession with obligations to give back to the community.[48] This was a careful speech, in many ways less inspiring than the Betcherman Lecture she had given just months before. But for me, it was a perfect bracket on the end of my formal legal training. That night, I met Bertha Wilson for the second and last time. I had dinner at the home of the same friend who had invited me to meet her when I was in law school. It was a celebratory event. There were at least a dozen of us, including my mother and my partner. We took photographs. We spoke of our plans for the future. We vowed to make a difference.

Recent research shows that individuals work on the development of their self-concept throughout their lifetime, not solely in their early years. Increasingly, theorists recognize the self as malleable rather than stable and reason that the possible selves provide for a changing and complex self-concept. Nonetheless, these same selves provide an authentic or stable core in the sense that they represent the individual's persistent hopes and fears as well as his or her potential future achievements, given appropriate social conditions. Hazel Markus and Paula Nirius have developed the notion of a "working self-concept," where the possible selves are seen as the personalized cognitive carriers of some of the dynamic aspects of personality.[49]

Gibson suggests that young individuals attend to global role models – single models who manifest all, or most of, the attributes to which they aspire. In many ways, Wilson served as such a model for me during the early years of my life in law. Over time, as the individual matures and the self-concept becomes more defined, she will increasingly attend to a few specific attributes of multiple role models, or even to the negative aspects of models.[50] All individuals are equally likely to observe role models, but young people feel most capable of actually accomplishing or preventing their possible selves. Gibson suggests that this may spring from their lack of realism, noting that young people also make the least effort toward achieving their most hoped-for possible self.[51]

By contrast, it has been shown that, for older individuals, possible selves are greater motivators for actual behaviour. As we age, the range of possible selves narrows and becomes more closely tied to the current self. The possible selves are also well elaborated and thus more instrumental in organizing and energizing the actions of the individual.[52] Older individuals are also more likely to have increased confidence in their self-concept and are less likely to rely on global positive models, attending instead to specific traits or behaviours.[53]

For myself, later in life, I still rely on several significant role models, those who represent, at least superficially, rather divergent possible selves. Perhaps these somewhat dissimilar women resonate for me because they share character traits that I value. Several are also professional models in the sense that they are women in law. Two are professors who teach and write and interact with students in ways that I admire. Two are judges. Several are close relatives or friends who have devoted their lives to the greater good. Of course, some are also wonderful mentors who have asked me the piercing questions that have helped to shape my path and who have encouraged me honestly but enthusiastically when the path was difficult.

One of these role models also served the important function of showing me how one could be both an accomplished member of the justice profession and a mother, something I aspired to for myself but which few of my other models demonstrated.[54] Wilson had also been important in that regard, although she was not a mother. When I found myself overwhelmed with the demands of three very young children and trying to launch an academic career, I reminded myself that she had not entered law school until she was thirty-one, so surely I still had time to build a career as a law teacher. (As it happened, I did not hold a tenure-track position until I was nearly the same age.)

Among all of my professional role models, their personal attributes as much as their prodigious accomplishments make them meaningful for me. Those personal attributes have also made my mother, my aunt, and my grandmother important in shaping my aspirations about who I want to be. At the end of the day, I have concluded that it is *how* to be in the world, not *what* to be, that matters most.[55] I know this from the women in my family, all three of them strong, generous people who have devoted their lives to the service of others less fortunate. And I know it from the monumental women in law whom I have chosen as role models because of the values of equality and fairness, concern and compassion that they have lived out in their professional lives. These personal attributes of Wilson make her present for me, many years after I last met her and even after her death.

The kind of person she was allowed me to learn from her how to be in the world. She was a Canadian by choice because she cherished the free and open society with its rich mosaic of creeds, cultures, and customs. After retiring from the Supreme Court, she chose to continue to serve the less fortunate by chairing the Canadian Bar Association Task Force on Gender Equality in the Legal Profession and serving on the Royal Commission on Aboriginal Peoples. She was courageous.[56] She had a formidable intellect. She was deeply compassionate. She knew about the human condition because she cared to know. She said in the *Saturday Night* article that it was just as important for a judge to know about people as it was to know about the law and that when she was a minister's wife in a coastal village in Scotland, she learned about people: "I became intimately involved with the drama of the daily lives of these people, their joys and their sorrows and, at sea, their terrible tragedies. I discovered how complicated people are, how lonely proud people are, how dependent on the rest of us old people are and how most of us are locked up tight inside ourselves, much of the time, pretending to be something we are not."[57]

It seems to me that Wilson was never locked up tight inside herself. She was fully and authentically herself, living and serving from the core of who she was. In the eulogy he gave at her memorial service, Justice James MacPherson called her a hero:

> By 1991, she had become a hero, especially to a generation of women law students and young lawyers. At a personal level, I see this vividly in a ... photograph that has been in our home for eighteen years ... My wife was a graduate that day. Justice Wilson came to celebrate. The picture shows Justice Wilson seated in a chair and three young women, in their ... robes, standing around her. The faces of the three women, all looking down at Justice Wilson, are infused with joy and pride.
>
> Eighteen years later, one of those women is a law professor at University of Manitoba, another is a lawyer at the African Canadian Legal Clinic in Toronto who has argued in the Supreme Court of Canada, and the third has been a refugee lawyer in Canada and internationally with the United Nations

> High Commission for Refugees. Justice Wilson showed these women the way, she inspired them. She did the same for an entire generation of women law students, lawyers and, today, judges.[58]

I believe that what Justice MacPherson says is true and that Wilson has been an inspiration to a whole generation of women in law. My story is just one – one that, given this opportunity, I immediately wanted to tell. I wanted everyone to know how inspiring Wilson had been and also how, in some serendipitous way, she had touched my life directly at key junctures. In that way, it has been a wonderful story to tell, and it is an honour to pay some tribute, however small, to someone I regard as a great woman. But it has also been very difficult to tell. First, role models can never be perfect. My older, more critical, and explicitly feminist self is challenged by some of the ways Wilson could not bear all the weight of expectation we put upon her as a "first." My older, more tolerant self immediately recognizes how impossible that would have been. Of course, my idealistic twenty-year-old self also failed to live up to all the aspirations prompted by my view of Bertha Wilson. Second, Wilson was an extremely private person, a fact quite probably stemming from the Scottish Presbyterian idea that one ought not to draw attention to oneself.[59] My own Scottish Presbyterian roots have propagated the same notion in me, making it very difficult to talk about how influential Wilson has been in my life because, of necessity, I must also talk of myself.

This story, which describes the circle of Wilson's influence in my life, must end with one last circle. I have lived my life in law for twenty-two years, since I began my law studies at the University of Ottawa. Now, as an associate professor and an associate dean, I hear from some of the young women in my faculty that they view me as a role model. As was the case for Wilson, it matters little whether I wish it to be so. But I think of Wilson and hope that I might offer these young women even half the inspiration she was to me. I wear the mantle seriously:[60] I hope, like Wilson, that what they learn from me is not merely a body of knowledge but a way of thinking and, beyond that, a way of being in the world.

Acknowledgments

The author wishes to acknowledge the support of Kim Brooks and the Social Sciences and Humanities Research Council for this volume and for the opportunities for the contributors to work collaboratively; Mary Jane Mossman, Rebecca Johnson, Jaime Cameron, Janine Benedet, and all the other commentators for suggestions on how to handle this non-legal essay; Adele Domenco for painstaking editing work; and Frederick for listening to the endless angst as I struggled to find the voice to express important ideas that left me feeling unusually vulnerable.

Notes

1 Text of Justice MacPherson's eulogy [on file with the author].

2 See Chapter 16 at 297, this volume.

3 Rebecca Johnson, "Blurred Boundaries: A Double Voiced Dialogue on Regulatory Regimes and Embodied Space" (2005) 9 Law Text Culture 157 at 158.

4 Arthur Herman, *How the Scots Invented the Modern World* (New York: Three Rivers Press, 2001) at vii. Herman goes on to say, "[T]his Scottish mentality was a deliberate creation, although it was conceived by many hands. It is a self-consciously modern view, so deeply rooted in the assumptions and institutions that govern our lives today that we often miss its significance, not to mention its origins. From this point of view, a large part of the world turns out to be 'Scottish' without realizing it" *(ibid.).*

5 *Ibid.* at 428-29.

6 See *e.g.* Donald E. Gibson, "Role Models in Career Development: New Directions for Theory and Research" (2004) 65 J. Vocational Behaviour 134 at 135, 137. By contrast, research on role models in careers is more limited.

7 See Dean Jobb, "Women Lawyers in Law Firms Need Mentors: McLachlin" *Lawyers Weekly* (21 March 2003) 1. Chief Justice Beverley McLachlin repeated that message in her remarks at the panel discussion for the Canadian Bar Association's National Women Lawyers Forum and Standing Committee on Equity, 14 August 2007, Calgary, Alberta. See also the recommendations made in Canadian Bar Association Task Force on Gender Equality in the Legal Profession, *Touchstones for Change: Equality, Diversity and Accountability* (Ottawa: Canadian Bar Association, 1993), for which Justice Bertha Wilson acted as chair.

8 See Gibson, *supra* note 6 at 134, 135.

9 See Elizabeth Douvan, "The Role of Models in Women's Professional Development" (1976) 1 Psychology of Women Quarterly 5 at 5; John Hagan and Fiona Kay, *Gender in Practice: A Study of Lawyers' Lives* (Oxford: Oxford University Press, 1995); Jean McKenzie Leiper, *Bar Codes: Women in the Legal Profession* (Vancouver: UBC Press, 2006) at 15.

10 See Danielle E. Reid, "Six Who Have Made a Difference: Mentors and Role Models for Women Lawyers" *New Jersey Lawyer* 171 (17 September 1995) 11. Reid notes that, whatever their styles, these top lawyers are visible to an increasing number of women in law. They have made a difference by breaking down barriers, serving as symbols, or directly advancing other women's careers *(ibid.).* Still, the higher one looks in the hierarchy, the fewer the women. This results in fewer models and mentors, and, relative to men, it keeps down the number of women who are moving up, because of significant attrition in women's legal careers.

11 See *Consultation Report: Retention of Women in Private Practice Working Group,* online: Law Society of Upper Canada <http://www.lsuc.on.ca/media/retentionofwomen.pdf>.

12 See Gibson, *supra* note 6 at 149. Feminists have criticized the notion of role models when it is used to justify the hiring of marginalized persons on utilitarian grounds (*i.e.,* tokenism) rather than on the merit of the individual. This reasoning encourages the view that these individuals are inferior candidates. It also allows members of the majority to shirk any responsibility for the marginalized among them on the basis that they now have their own role models. See Anita L. Allen, "On Being a Role Model" (1990-91) 6 Berkeley Women's L.J. 22 at 33. See also Christine M. Koggel, "A Feminist View of Equality and Its Implications for Affirmative Action" (1994) 7 Can. J.L. & Jur. 43 at para. 29.

13 See Leiper, *supra* note 9 at 3; Douvan, *supra* note 9 at 12.

14 See Douvan, *ibid.* at 14, 15, 17. She notes that Freud's early female followers faced the same challenges. In an interview for the *Law Times,* Linda Rothstein maintained that, unlike men, women are looking for models who are not infallible because women have always been juggling all the other roles in their lives: "Women are looking for a sense of how to appear in control, confident, and competent, without necessarily assuming all the typical testosterone-driven manifestations of [infallibility]." Quoted in David Gambrill, "Look beyond Own Firm for Mentors" *Law Times* (18 February 2002) 1, 2. See also Leiper, *supra* note 9 at 7.

15 See Gibson, *supra* note 6 at 136.
16 Sandra Gwyn, "Sense and Sensibility" *Saturday Night* (July 1985) 13 at 13, 14.
17 See Chapter 1, this volume, for a description of her vital role at Osler during the fifties, sixties, and seventies.
18 Quoted in Gwyn, *supra* note 16 at 17.
19 *Ibid.* at 14. *Canadian Charter of Rights and Freedoms,* Part 1 of the *Constitution Act, 1982,* being Schedule B to the *Canada Act 1982* (U.K.), 1982, c. 11.
20 See Gibson, *supra* note 6 at 136, 139.
21 See *ibid.* at 140. Theorists who have studied self-concept over the century include William James, Sigmund Freud, Carl Rogers, and Daniel Levinson. See Hazel Markus and Paula Nirius, "Possible Selves" (1986) 41 American Psychologist 954 at 955, 56.
22 Quoted in Gwyn, *supra* note 16 at 18.
23 Richard Devlin, A. Wayne MacKay, and Natasha Kim, "Reducing the Democratic Deficit: Representation, Diversity, and the Canadian Judiciary, or Towards a 'Triple P' Judiciary" (2000) 38 Alta. L. Rev. 734 at 764, citing Sydney Sharpe, *The Gilded Ghetto: Women and Political Power in Canada* (Toronto: Harper Collins, 1994) at 96-97.
24 *Ibid.*
25 *Ibid.*
26 See Bertha Wilson, "Will Women Judges Really Make a Difference?" (1990) 28 Osgoode Hall L.J. 507; Gwyn, *supra* note 16 at 19.
27 See Gwyn, *ibid.* at 19; Wilson, *supra* note 26 at 507.
28 See Donald E. Gibson, "Developing the Professional Self-Concept: Role Model Construals in Early, Middle and Late Career Stages" (2003) 14 Organization Science 591 at 606.
29 See Gibson, *supra* note 6 at 141; Susan Cross and Hazel Markus, "Possible Selves across the Life Span" (1991) 34 Human Development 230 at 231, 232; Markus and Nirius, *supra* note 21 at 954. Perceiving similarities with a positive role model, as Wilson was for me, is inherently satisfying, as such a comparison can result in feelings of competence and self-efficacy. Gibson, *supra* note 6 at 144-45. It is also possible to learn and grow from negative models, but the focus of this chapter is on Wilson as a positive role model.
30 See Gibson, *supra* note 28 at 593; Gibson, *supra* note 6 at 147; Cross and Markus, *supra* note 29 at 233.
31 See Gibson, *supra* note 6 at 139, 149; Cross and Markus, *supra* note 29 at 232; Penelope Lockwood and Ziva Kunda, "Superstars and Me: Predicting the Impact of Role Models on the Self" (1997) 73 Journal of Personality and Social Psychology 91 at 93, 101.
32 See Markus and Nirius, *supra* note 21 at 955.
33 See Herminia Ibarra, "Provisional Selves: Experimenting with Image and Identity in Professional Adaptation" (1999) 44 Administrative Science Quarterly 764 at 782-84.
34 See Gibson, *supra* note 6 at 142, 148.
35 See Markus and Nirius, *supra* note 21 at 954.
36 Lockwood and Kunda, *supra* note 31 at 93.
37 *Ibid.* at 92.
38 *Ibid.* at 102.
39 See generally Catherine Weiss and Louise Melling, "The Legal Education of Twenty Women" (1988) 40 Stan. L. Rev. 1299; Steven C. Halpern, "On the Politics and Pathology of Legal Education (Or, Whatever Happened to That Blindfolded Lady with the Scales?)" (1982) 32 J. Legal Educ. 383; Mary Jane Mossman, "Feminism and Legal Method: The Difference It Makes" (1987) 3 Wis. Women's L.J. 147 at 163-65; William M. Sullivan *et al., Educating Lawyers: Preparation for the Profession of Law* (San Francisco: Jossey-Bass, 2007).
40 See Herminia Ibarra, "Making Partner: A Mentor's Guide to the Psychological Journey" (2000) 78 Harv. Bus. Rev. 146 at 149.
41 See Cross and Markus, *supra* note 29 at 233.
42 Alan Watson, "The Scottish Enlightenment, the Democratic Intellect and the Work of Madame Justice Wilson" (1992) 15 Dal. L.J. 23 at 27. Hester Lessard also noted the Scottish influence in "A Tribute to Bertha Wilson, Justice of the Supreme Court of Canada, 1982-1990" (1991) 1 C.L.E.L.J. vii at x.

43 B. Wilson, "The Charter of Rights and Freedoms" (1985-86) 50 Sask. L. Rev. 169 at 171.
44 Lessard, *supra* note 42 at viii.
45 *Ibid.* at xii.
46 Wilson, *supra* note 26 at 520-21.
47 Gwyn, *supra* note 16 at 16.
48 See Bertha Wilson, "Remarks Given at the Call to the Bar Ceremony and on Being Awarded the Degree of Doctor of Laws" (1991) 25 Law Soc'y Gaz. 103.
49 Markus and Nirius, *supra* note 21 at 966.
50 See Gibson, *supra* note 6 at 150.
51 Gibson, *supra* note 28 at 593.
52 See Cross and Markus, *supra* note 29 at 249.
53 See Gibson, *supra* note 28 at 606.
54 Increasingly, women are looking for role models who live such a full life (*i.e.,* as mothers and as workers), rejecting earlier female role models because they do not relate to the life choices they make. See Ida O. Abbott, "Women in Law Firms: Redefining Success" (2004) 30 Law Practice 35 at 37; Gibson, *supra* note 6 at 146. By contrast, however, models who appear to have achieved "superwoman" status as employed mothers can make more ordinary women feel incompetent. See Lockwood and Kunda, *supra* note 31 at 91.
55 Lorraine Code remarks on the importance of the way of being in the world: "I refer intentionally to character models rather than role models in order to emphasize ... that unlike roles, these ways of being are not to be assumed and cast aside casually and randomly. Character models are instances of possible ways of being." Quoted in Koggel, *supra* note 12 at para. 29.
56 She was willing to make a difference in the face of scathing attacks, such as the REAL Women complaint to the Canadian Judicial Council. See Ellen Anderson, *Judging Bertha Wilson: Law as Large as Life* (Toronto: University of Toronto Press for the Osgoode Society for Canadian Legal History, 2001) at xiii, xv. See also Robert E. Hawkins and Robert Martin, "Democracy, Judging and Bertha Wilson" (1995) 41 McGill L.J. 1.
57 Quoted in Gwyn, *supra* note 16 at 16.
58 Justice MacPherson's eulogy, *supra* note 1.
59 See Gwyn, *supra* note 16 at 14.
60 bell hooks, *Yearning: Race, Gender and Cultural Politics* (Boston: South End Press, 1990) at 229, expressed this profound responsibility eloquently: "I know that having many young [black] women looking at me, not just at my work, but at how I am living my life – my habits of being, and seeing me as an example, as someone charting the journey, has made me work harder to get my life together. Knowing that they are watching me, seeing what's going on with my psyche, my inner well-being, has changed many of my priorities. I am less self indulgent."

14
Ideas and Transformation: A Reflection on Bertha Wilson's Contribution to Gender Equality in the Legal Profession

Melina Buckley

Bertha Wilson shaped my understanding of the transformative possibilities inherent in the law and the legal profession. She served as a touchstone for me, as she undoubtedly did for many women who came to law in the early era of the *Canadian Charter of Rights and Freedoms*. I celebrated her appointment to the Supreme Court of Canada when, as a young single mother, I thought my aspirations to become a lawyer little more than a distant dream and at times an impossible one. My introduction to her legal reasoning came during first-year constitutional law in reading her concurring reasons in *R. v. Big M Drug Mart Ltd.* – a judgment that, for me, remains to this day a cherished statement of the potential of constitutional rights.[1] My introduction to Bertha Wilson the person came shortly after she retired from the bench when she agreed to serve as the chair of the Canadian Bar Association's (CBA) Task Force on Gender Equality in the Legal Profession. I was one of the CBA employees assigned to assist the task force and eventually served as its project director.

This chapter is a personal reflection on Bertha Wilson's role as task force chair and her contribution to the discourse on gender equality in the legal profession. In her biography, Ellen Anderson recounts this period of Wilson's post-judicial life in a lively and engaging manner.[2] Here, I would like to provide a more intimate account of the task force process, the report, and its aftermath, situating my analysis within a discussion of the power of ideas as an agent in processes of change and transformation. In taking on leadership of the task force, Wilson began with the premise that gender inequality in the legal profession was an ethical and a legal issue of fundamental importance to our society. Illegality was the dominant theme, and therefore she saw the solution to be primarily one of elucidating the legal and ethical responsibilities of the profession toward its own members. Once these ideas were well understood, Wilson believed, members of the legal profession would respond in good faith and take the necessary steps to ensure equality and justice in its ranks.

Wilson's approach to the task force was consistent with her extensive body of judgments through which she attempted to make established categories more inclusive and responsive to the diversity of needs within the Canadian community and to put into place an analytic framework that was fully receptive to equality claims.[3] For example, in *Big M Drug Mart,* Wilson concurred with the majority in holding that legislation that provided for Sunday as a compulsory day of rest violated freedom of religion protected in s. 2 of the *Charter.* In her concurring reasons, she focused on the proper analytic framework to a *Charter* case. She held that, in determining whether legislation or other governmental act was constitutional under the *Charter,* a court should consider only its effect and not the underlying governmental purpose:

> While it remains perfectly valid to evaluate the purpose underlying a particular enactment in order to determine whether the legislature has acted within its constitutional authority in division of powers terms, the *Charter* demands an evaluation of the impingement of even *intra vires* legislation on the fundamental rights and freedoms of the individual. It asks not whether the legislature has acted for a purpose that is within the scope of the authority of that tier of government, but rather whether in so acting it has had the effect of violating an entrenched individual right. It is, in other words, first and foremost an effects-oriented document.[4]

Wilson explained that this approach was required for the sake of both "consistency and analytic clarity,"[5] and in particular to distinguish *Charter* analysis from the traditional constitutional law analysis that had had such a deadening effect on the application of the *Canadian Bill of Rights.* She was also of the view that placing the analytic focus on the effect of legislation impugned under the *Charter* rather than on its purpose would impose a less heavy evidentiary burden on the plaintiff: "Once the plaintiff can point to an actual or potential impingement on a protected right, it will not matter that the underlying legislative purpose is subject to conjecture."[6] The purpose of legislation becomes relevant only in considering whether a rights infringement can be justified under s. 1 of the *Charter.* This clarity of thought and singular emphasis on the effects of unconstitutional government actions on claimants would be highly welcome today, given the obfuscation that has clouded *Charter* analysis, particularly in s. 15 equality rights claims.[7]

Wilson's early and consistent emphasis on effects-based analysis in the *Charter* context blossomed into a robust equality-based analysis that expanded the abstract notion of equality by tying it to substantive notions of full participation in society.[8] This approach is also evident in her stewardship of the gender equality task force and, in particular, in her emphasis on the need for the legal profession to transform itself in order to redress social-structural conditions of inequality and to ensure that women, and other previously excluded groups, could become full participants. As a judge, she focused on clearly enunciating the principles that should guide conduct. She brought this same approach to her work as chair of the task force.

I too am a fervent believer in the transformative possibilities of ideas, but I have come to understand that the power of ideas must be coupled with robust processes of engagement if they are to achieve substantive change. This is one of the lessons that I learned through my experience with the gender equality task force and, in particular, through my engagement with Bertha Wilson and subsequent reflections on her approach to chairing this initiative.

Task Force Process

The CBA had committed to undertaking an inquiry into gender inequality in the legal profession in 1989, but it was Bertha Wilson's retirement from the bench and speedy acceptance of the invitation to chair this initiative in the spring of 1991 that galvanized the association to begin to work in earnest. Interest in, and momentum behind, the task force completely dwarfed the available resources at the CBA. Two staff members were responsible for the early stages of the task force planning[9] including drafting the terms of reference, managing the process for selecting task force members, and assisting in fundraising efforts. Initially, Wilson had envisioned being a one-person commission akin to Rosalie Abella's inquiry into employment equity.[10] Undoubtedly, she wished we had had government-sized resources for the study as well! However, the CBA was committed to its traditional mode of operation – a blue ribbon committee – and so she gracefully and actively participated in the selection process including requesting that specific individuals be appointed.[11]

The task force was officially launched at the 1991 CBA annual meeting in Calgary to much fanfare. At the first brief meeting, Wilson elaborated her vision of how it would work and asked that each task force member assume the responsibility for a specific sector of the profession. Everyone agreed that there was no need to prove that gender discrimination existed within the legal profession since that had already been demonstrated in previous studies; the focus was to be on solutions. Wilson felt strongly that the solutions should be tailored to the various legal practice environments so that the managing partners of large law firms, the heads of corporate legal departments, the law deans, chief judges, and justices, and so on could each find practical suggestions for dealing with sex discrimination in their specific context.

All task force members were charged with the responsibility to gather information, undertake consultations, and take other necessary steps so that they could bring to the table recommendations for inclusion within the report.[12] The central topic of discussion at this meeting was the extent to which the task force should solicit representations from individuals and groups concerning the experience of gender discrimination. Differing views were expressed about the relative importance of seeking out these narratives, and it was eventually agreed that some steps would be taken toward this end – not for the purpose of establishing discrimination, but to obtain views concerning potential solutions to the problems experienced.

The task force's work was severely hampered throughout the first year of its two-year mandate by lack of resources. Despite strong efforts, fundraising met with disappointing results, and it became clear that the CBA had underestimated the revenue required to properly fund a project of this scale. To make matters worse, the CBA's energies were largely focused on the extensive process of constitutional renewal that led to the proposed constitutional amendments contained in the Charlottetown Accord, which was eventually rejected in a national referendum. Staff turnover further restricted the support available to the task force; eventually, primary responsibility devolved to me and was added to my other extensive duties. There was money enough only for a few meetings of the task force, and each was more uncomfortable than the one before as the CBA was called to account for the sorry state of affairs. I still have nightmares about sitting across the table from an irate, cold, and yet polite Bertha Wilson while I gamely tried to make the best of a bad situation. Certain disaster was averted only by the dedication of the task force and members of the provincial working groups and by our collective ingenuity in finding ways to move forward without resources. We were spurred on by the strong, vocal support and interest of women lawyers and judges across Canada and by the huge sense of responsibility generated by their expectations. A fairly broad program of research and consultation was initiated, although these efforts were hindered by the delays caused by the lack of resources.

The task force meetings were somewhat awkward and stilted. Bertha Wilson was such a dominant force that the very knowledgeable members were reticent to fully express themselves. As a result, many important discussions took place outside of the formal meetings. Wilson was tireless and would easily have worked non-stop through a full-day meeting unless a task force member shyly asked for a pause. Only upon these polite requests did she sit back and take a deep breath. Despite the strain of straitened circumstances, time pressures, and infrequent meetings, a positive dynamic evolved as the results of the research and consultation began to trickle in. Occasionally, a light moment would transpire – as, for example, when we jokingly considered banning golf as a manifestation of the old boys' club and Wilson reacted with a melodramatic horror that was clearly elicited from deep within her Scottish bones.

The turning point on the financial front came at the August 1992 annual meeting in Halifax, when Bertha Wilson went public about the lack of financial support and human resources made available to the task force. In her inimitable style, she pulled no punches: "All of us who are working on this project view the Canadian Bar Association as having a special responsibility to provide leadership in this very sensitive area of gender equality. It is an ethical as well as a legal issue of fundamental importance to our society ... Will our profession be a protagonist in the drama of women's advancement or merely a Greek chorus?"[13] The financial and support issues plaguing the task force were joined by criticisms that it was unrepresentative of the diversity of the legal profession and that its membership should be expanded to include representatives of visible minorities, women with disabilities, lesbians, and Aboriginal women. Both Wilson and the CBA initially resisted these calls on the fairly practical grounds that the few resources would be stretched even further and that integrating new members would be difficult since the project was well under way. However, in October 1992, when the CBA was directly challenged on this point at the task force's national conference in Toronto, CBA President Paule Gauthier, Q.C., readily agreed, and two new members, Sharon McIvor and Judge Corrine Sparks, were appointed within a month.[14] Rather than slowing momentum as originally feared, the two were readily integrated and made an enormously positive contribution to the group dynamic and the report. In particular, perhaps because of her judicial status, Sparks was willing to be direct in discussions with Wilson, thereby opening up the conversation and removing some of the impediments to the full exchange of ideas.

The critical period in the task force's work began with the national conference in late October 1992 and continued through a series of face-to-face meetings including three two-day national consultations[15] and a private meeting between Bertha Wilson and task force member Patricia Blocksom with a group of lesbian lawyers held in conjunction with the annual meeting of the National Association of Women and the Law in Vancouver in early 1993. In my view, these joint meetings were profound experiences that had a transformative impact on task force members, including Bertha Wilson. It was through these sessions that gender discrimination issues were fully contextualized. The barriers faced by women in the legal profession stopped being abstract concerns and became the real problems of real people. The closest analogy that I can find is the striking contrast between reading the text of a play and having it brought to life for you on stage.

Although Wilson had initially undervalued these meetings, she was fully engaged in the exchanges that took place. She was extremely well prepared for each session, asking perceptive questions and listening intently to the presentations. She shone in her capacity to acknowledge the speakers and her ability to convey her appreciation for the courage and generosity it took for them to share their experiences. Their faces glowed in the warmth of this reception and recognition, and the glow was a powerful force that had its own presence in the room. These long moments are etched in my memory, and I have reflected on them over the years, seeking to fully understand the power of personal stories of equality rights violations and how to integrate these narratives into change processes, particularly in legal forums.

By this stage, the task force initiative was fully funded, and the research and consultation programs were near completion. Now came the delicate negotiation over the writing of the report. It was clear to me that Bertha Wilson had originally planned to write the report herself and to base it on the input of the task force members in each of their areas of responsibility. This report structure, with one chapter dedicated to each legal practice environment, had been set by her at the outset and was never up for discussion. By this time, it was obvious that she would not have the time to write the report, in light of her onerous responsibilities as member of the Royal Commission on Aboriginal Peoples. It was equally apparent that the other members of the task force had neither the time nor the inclination to write up their own sections of the report. I experienced this phase as a personal struggle with Wilson, as she would not give me the mandate to proceed with the writing despite the significant time restraints (only a few months remained). In addition, she resisted the CBA's determination that the report be provided in time for filing at the August 1993 annual meeting. In her view, the strictures of the CBA timelines should be cast aside, given the enormous amount of time wasted during the first year of the project due to the CBA's poor planning. This ongoing conflict continued until close to the report's deadline.

The CBA held firm for a number of reasons. The most important of these, and the one that motivated me, was the fact that the incoming CBA President, Cecilia Johnstone, Q.C., was deeply committed to gender equality in the legal profession and was set to be an energetic champion of the report.[16] It was clear to us within the CBA that, if the task force did not table its report on time, the historic moment would pass, and the report would be likely to gather dust.

The breakthrough came at the April meeting of the task force, which Wilson was unable to attend due to ill health. This was to be the meeting at which general directions were given for the contents of the report. In fact, the first full and unconstrained conversation among members occurred during the meeting, which emboldened me to propose a specific process for the writing and review of the report – Wilson could author whichever sections she chose, I would write the remainder of the first draft, basing it on input from task force members, and everyone would comment freely upon the result. My proposal was accepted by default: there was simply no one else available to do the job. Two painful and tortuous months ensued as I tried to eke out the time from an overburdened schedule to begin to write.

A few weeks after I was given the go-ahead, by our May meeting, I had a shoddily written partial report, and the task force members were very nervous. I was given one last chance and somehow pulled a full report out of thin air within a few weeks, we sighed a collective sigh of relief, and focused on making it the best report we could under enormous time restraints.

A few moments remain as clear to me today as they were almost fifteen years ago when they occurred in 1993. First and foremost was Bertha Wilson's careful lawyerly consideration of the issues and her clarity of purpose. She came to the last task force meeting with an introduction and specific amendments to propose – notably the controversial recommendations dealing with a law firm's duty to accommodate lawyers with family responsibilities by reducing billable hour targets.[17] She read them from her clear and careful cursive script as if reading a judgment from the bench. We were all enthralled and some of us barely held back from clapping at the beauty of what she had to say. Second, I remember going to Wilson's home early one July morning to pick up her editorial suggestions on what was nearly the penultimate draft of the report. She met me in her kitchen, wearing a turquoise velour housecoat and sporting a girlish smile expressing real joy that the report was nearly completed. Her jubilance was a striking contrast to the early, sour castigations and an ample reward for the many long days and nights of work.

The Report: Touchstones for Change

The task force report, *Touchstones for Change: Equality, Diversity and Accountability,*[18] documents the nature of barriers to legal education and entry into the profession faced by women and highlights the fact that these barriers are particularly severe for women who suffer multiple discrimination, including racialized women,[19] lesbians, and those with disabilities. The report also identifies the forms of discrimination experienced by women lawyers, including segregation in employment opportunities that results in "pink" files and "blue" files as well as streaming of women into specific sectors of the profession; barriers to career development and advancement that result in the "glass ceiling" and the "steel door"; sexual harassment, gendered assessments, and other problems related to workplace environment and culture; and the lack of accommodation of family responsibilities. *Touchstones for Change* made 228 recommendations with a view to addressing these barriers and working toward substantive equality for women within the legal profession. The recommendations were tailored to the various sectors of the profession including law schools, private practice, government legal departments, corporate legal departments, the judiciary, law societies, and the CBA.

Bertha Wilson gave the report its title and its unifying themes of equality, diversity, and accountability. She set out these themes in the introduction and conclusion, thereby illuminating the underlying ideas that she believed should motivate the profession in implementing the large number of detailed recommendations made by the task force. Wilson believed that the CBA initiative came at an auspicious time for a call to change because the legal profession was in a "period of indecision and doubt" and was already in the process of "moral and intellectual stocktaking." In her view, lawyers were asking themselves questions about whether they were too "commercialized" and at risk of becoming high-priced technicians, in it only for the money:

> It was into this period of indecision and doubt that the Task Force was born and it is not surprising that the women who entered the profession in numbers sufficient to create a so-called critical mass were able to bring to it the new energy and vitality that the feminist movement has generated. Here was a real opportunity to give voice to a different perspective on the legal profession, a perspective that took no account of vested interests because the new recruits had none. They had never been part of the power structure to which the profession had felt it must adapt. They had no feeling of being trapped by the pervasive values of the clientele and they started to think about the answers to the questions their male colleagues were asking.[20]

These important and intertwined questions had to be considered in the framework of recognizing the accountability and responsibility attendant upon self-governance. Accountability was thus the central idea, or "touchstone," that would guide the transformation of the legal profession into a fully inclusive one. Wilson explained the touchstone in these words: "We cannot have self-regulation without accountability and we cannot have accountability without openness. This much seems clear. As members of the profession we must know the policies by which our profession is governed because we are accountable for them, every last one of us. This is what it means to be a member of a self-governing profession."[21] Wilson made it clear that she saw women and other "newcomers" as a positive force that would regenerate the legal profession and act as a counter against the decline in legal standards. Women would not be passive within this transformative process; rather, they would be both the cause and effect of beneficial change. This was a win-win-win situation: women would benefit by being fully included in an important and powerful profession; the community would be better served by a legal profession that was more representative; and the profession as a whole would profit through this revitalization. In support for this thesis, she quoted Justice Abella's comment that "[t]his change can be the profession's greatest strength if it acknowledges and draws on the concerns, aspirations and talents of its newest recruits."[22]

Another touchstone, or norm, was substantive equality. Wilson outlined the ways in which the legal profession was not "environmentally friendly" to women and argued that these barriers could be overcome through a clear commitment to equality. Toward this end, she reminded lawyers of the legal definition of equality, which was to be the animating force underlying processes of change. Wilson expounded the legal norm of substantive equality in some detail in the introduction, and this theme was woven in throughout the report. I quote her exposition on equality at some length because it formed the central theme, which Wilson hoped would strike a chord with lawyers and judges:

> Overcoming these barriers represents women lawyers' struggle for equality with men in the pursuit of their careers. But what do we mean by equality? I believe that the Supreme Court of Canada answered this question in *Andrews v. Law Society of British Columbia*. It made it clear that when we speak of equality we are addressing inequality because the *purpose* of human rights legislation is to eliminate inequality. This is why an abstract concept of equality is meaningless ...
>
> The Supreme Court of Canada accordingly rejected an abstract concept of equality under section 15 of the Charter and focused instead on the remedial aspect, the achieving of equality through the elimination of existing inequality. The Court, in stressing the remedial aspect, focused on the historic reality of disadvantaged groups in our society ...
>
> One of the barriers faced by women lawyers in virtually all sectors of the profession is the failure to accommodate the child-bearing and child-rearing functions of women. If performance is assessed, for example, as it is in large law firms, on the basis of billable hours, pregnant women or women discharging child care responsibilities will inevitably receive a lower assessment. Most firms do not perceive this as a form of discrimination because they insist on applying an abstract concept of equality, namely that the same number of billable hours should be expected from everyone. It is only when one recognizes that the purpose of the equality guarantee is to redress inequality that one appreciates the need to examine the *context* in order to see whether discrimination and inequality are present. They clearly are in the billable hours example, because the application of the billable hours criterion to measure a lawyer's contribution to the firm has an adverse impact on pregnant women and on women with child-rearing duties to perform. They cannot achieve the same number of billable hours as their male colleagues. They are, in effect, penalized because of their gender. The billable hours criterion is an example of *adverse effects discrimination* under our human rights legislation.[23]

Wilson's elucidation of equality and the example of how billable hour targets resulted in adverse effects discrimination was based on Chief Justice Dickson's reasons in *Brooks v. Canada Safeway Ltd.*[24] In *Brooks,* Dickson examined the social context of pregnancy and found it to be something that benefited the whole of society; therefore, he concluded that a policy that imposed costs exclusively on women was an example of sexual discrimination. Wilson extended this reasoning and stated that the same must be true of women's child-rearing responsibilities. She highlighted that discrimination against women lawyers of child-bearing age and those discharging child-rearing responsibilities must be redressed for gender equality to be achieved within the legal profession.[25]

Through the touchstone of diversity, Wilson explained the scope of the transformation required for the legal profession to become fully inclusive, bearing in mind the multiple forms of discrimination operating within both it and Canadian society as a whole:

> The Task Force has been told by minority groups all across the country that our profession has been, since its inception, a white, male, elitist one. In the past three decades women have succeeded in breaking through the gender barrier in significant numbers but many other barriers remain. Your Task Force has asked itself therefore: what should the face of the legal profession look like as it enters the 21st century? Should it continue as a white elitist profession or should it reflect the Canadian diversity?[26]

For Wilson, ensuring that all minority groups had their proper place in our country and profession was simply a natural evolution of historical processes, but more importantly, she also saw this as a matter of justice and fairness. She emphasized that "Women of Colour, Aboriginal women, disabled women, lesbian women all have had experiences of life that differ profoundly from those of the dominant Canadian culture and each group brings a unique and different perspective to our understanding of life and the law."[27] These profound differences had to be recognized and accommodated. Wilson pulled no punches in this regard when she inscribed,

> The Task Force believes that the goal of the profession should be diversity. It believes that all "voices" should be heard and all "perspectives" presented. There is no such thing as a neutral perspective. This is the message that came to us loud and clear:
>
> > A *white* view of the world is not neutral.
> > A *masculine* view of the world is not neutral.
> > A heterosexual view of the world is not neutral.[28]

Wilson urged that this traditional view had to be challenged in order for the profession to become inclusive: "We must discard the white, male, heterosexual image of the lawyer and welcome 'the other' to our profession."[29] She emphasized that this should be a real welcome: "[W]omen and women's minority groups [should] be fully accepted not with timid tolerance but in the sure knowledge that their enthusiastic acceptance is only just and fair."[30]

Again, Wilson leaned upon the theme of illegality to galvanize action. She argued that continued inaction could not be tolerated in a country as boastful of its human rights record as Canada. Hearkening back to her introductory subject of professionalism, Wilson drew the three ideas of accountability, equality, and diversity together in this way: "It would be ironic indeed if the legal profession were using its self-governing status not for the public's protection but for its own. It would be unthinkable if it were using its monopoly to violate the law which it is dedicated to uphold."[31] Although Wilson relied upon the power of ideas to animate the legal profession, she did not completely ignore the challenge facing its members. She recognized that the profession was steeped in tradition and therefore slow to change. She laid the groundwork for her challenge to the profession by referring to Lord Buckmaster's famous comment on the snail's pace of change in the legal profession: "I would beg of your Lordships not to delay consent until time will have robbed it of all its graciousness and what today might be a free and dignified act of justice will become tainted with the meanness and the cowardice of expediency."[32] She closed her introduction to the report by asking, "Will the reforms the Task Force advocates in this Report be implemented as a free and dignified act of justice? Is the profession ready for equality of opportunity for all women – white women, Women of Colour, Aboriginal women, women with disabilities, lesbian women? Or will their male colleagues make them wait another fifty years until time will have robbed their consent of its graciousness and tainted it with the meanness and cowardice of expediency?"[33]

Wilson authored the chapter on gender equality in the judiciary and made a number of recommendations dealing with the judicial appointment process, compulsory training for judges in both gender and racial issues, judicial discipline, and so on. She bemoaned the fact that the Canadian judiciary "remained generally aloof" regarding issues of gender bias in the justice system, especially as compared to that of the United States where many of the chief justices had taken the lead in studying gender bias and developing programs to eliminate it.[34] However, her most important and unique contribution dealt with the issue of discrimination in the judiciary. This section contains a brief but sensitive and moving portrayal of women's experience on the bench in which she conveyed the disheartening occurrences and alienation that had confronted female judges. Wilson attributed some of the instances of discrimination against women judges and lawyers to individual male behaviour. However, she also noted a more discernable pattern of inequality with respect to the treatment of women judges in some courts, particularly as it related to the assignment of cases:

> Some women judges complained that they were not permitted to sit on sexual assault cases on the ground that they were not capable of exercising the required degree of objectivity. Those women judges were usually younger, recently appointed, and perceived by their male colleagues to be "radical feminists." As has been pointed out by many writers on gender issues, a "radical feminist" in the eyes of some men may simply be a woman who believes in equality, publicly asserts that belief and attempts to achieve it. Because the existing norm has always been and still is the norm of inequality, equality must inevitably seem radical to some in that it is a total rejection of inequality. It does, indeed, go to the very "root" of it![35]

In her postscript to the report, Wilson emphasized the challenge of reform. She noted that the task force had had a unique opportunity to conduct an overview of the legal profession in Canada. It had had many "intimate glimpses" of the people who were joining the profession, who were leaving the profession, and who were concerned about the profession. She concluded, "All are aware that reform is required."[36] But reform would not come easy, and the difficulties inherent in transformation could create a sense of despair and lead to acceptance of the existing situation as inevitable: "This is precisely the attitude we encountered among many of the lawyers we spoke to, male and female. They had lost any sense of agency or power in their profession. They didn't even feel any anger about it, only resignation and reconciliation to 'a liveable life under the shadow' of existing legal culture."[37] She was somewhat distraught at having been repeatedly told, especially by young persons, that they did not believe that the profession could or would change. This sense of loss of power and despair was very troubling to her. In response to this cynicism, she felt that the task force was providing a more hopeful alternative vision of the legal profession. She closed the report by referring to a favourite Lord Denning quote: "It is all very well to paint justice blind, but she does better without a bandage round her eyes. She should be blind indeed to favour or prejudice, but clear to see which way lies truth: and the less dust there is about the better."[38] And so she concluded: "We hope that the Task Force has helped to remove some of the dust."[39]

The Aftermath

Touchstones for Change, which was much anticipated, created a huge stir warranting front-page coverage in the national media and even its own editorial cartoons. In her address to the CBA National Council when the report was tabled, Wilson boldly stated that the achievement of equality would require twenty years but that this incremental process would be sustained by the vision of an ethical, fair profession and by the spectre of loss of the privilege of self-regulation. This underlying approach was very much driven by Bertha Wilson's vision: her impeccable ethical sense and her strong belief that her ethical world view was shared by the legal profession at large. She was clearly anticipating cooperation from the profession, not confrontation.

Touchstones for Change was both hailed as an important milestone and catalyst for change and decried in many quarters. Even some who supported the overall objective of improving the status of women in the legal profession felt that it was too negative and should have focused on "positive" reasons for change. It was argued, for example, that the task force should have highlighted the "hidden brain drain" of losing women from the profession and the economic rationale supporting equality and diversity in the workplace rather than expounding on the nature of discriminatory practices throughout the profession. Many found the wording or tone too strong and therefore "offensive." Although some resistance was anticipated, it is fair to say that task force members and senior bar leaders were dismayed by the virulence of the critique. The legal profession did not readily accept the task force's "judgment"; nor did members of the judiciary. Some of the report's accomplishments and substance got lost in the debate that surrounded it.

The swiftest and harshest reactions were to Wilson's own findings about discrimination on the bench. These findings were publicly repudiated by Chief Justice Allan MacEachern in British Columbia, as well as her close friend Chief Justice Antonio Lamer. The harsh criticisms and rejection of findings by senior judges chilled the climate for reception of the report generally. Those of us engaged in promoting discussion of it took to wearing the military-style suits in vogue at that time. The severe cuts and brass buttons seemed to offer some protection from the tirades we experienced in some quarters. It took several years for the CBA to review, debate, in some cases amend, and eventually adopt, the large number of recommendations at its national meetings, which were held only twice a year. Although some have recounted this process as difficult and even traumatic, I found it to be an important venue of engagement and overall an educational one. The CBA's debate concerning the report created an important public space for discussion of equality and discrimination. There were occasional low moments, to be sure. However, open discussion set the stage for substantive change to a greater degree, whereas silent, polite acceptance of the report would have relegated it to the dust heap.

Wilson was fairly pragmatic regarding the debate about some of the task force's recommendations – including the ones dealing with the billable hour targets and the requirement to accommodate lawyers with family responsibilities, which she had championed. She remained of the view that, in order to effect long-term change, the profession simply needed more education about discrimination. However, the reaction to her findings and recommendations on the judiciary caused her much more personal grief. Anderson sums up her discussions with Wilson:

> If asked, Wilson will say that she personally encountered only isolated instances of discrimination instigated by particular individuals during all her years in the legal profession. When she became involved in the task force she was surprised and even shocked by the extent of the problems faced by other women because her own career did not illustrate persistent or systemic discrimination. For Wilson the whole experience became enormously painful. Her own work on the Gender Equality study was in her own estimation, ironically, an unequivocal and deeply personal experience with gender discrimination.[40]

To the disappointment of many, Wilson did not actively participate in the promotion of the report or in its implementation. In a sense, her perspective was judge-like. She had issued her reasons and was content to sit back behind the bench and leave it to the parties responsible to take appropriate action. She told her biographer that she was reasonably content with the pace of reform.[41] Her vision of the role of the task force was simply to point the way, and she felt certain that it had "helped remove some of the dust."[42]

Reflections

The task force report's alternative vision of the profession and Wilson's three touchstones of equality, diversity, and accountability have stood the test of time. They continue to provide guidance, albeit indirectly, as lawyers, judges, and legal organizations work toward transforming the legal profession to eradicate discrimination and become fully inclusive.[43] The lesson that I have drawn from my reflections on Bertha Wilson's approach to the work of the task force is that, though ideas and ideals inform processes of change and can even lead them, they are not self-executing. The light can go on when an individual fully grasps the concept of substantive equality, and this transcendent moment is a powerful and animating one. But all of the lessons in the world on legal principles, duties, and responsibilities are insufficient. All of the task force members, Wilson included, began their work with a strong commitment to equality and some level of knowledge of the discrimination faced by women in the profession. Yet, it was the process of hearing the lived experiences of a diverse group of women that changed them. The challenge remains how to capture the sparkling transformative essence of the narrative to motivate the degree, breadth, and number of changes required to achieve substantive equality. I learned much from working with Bertha Wilson and in my reflections on the task force experience. I now know that we must do more than "remove the dust" – we must also create and sustain the spark.

Notes

1 *R. v. Big M Drug Mart Ltd.*, [1985] 1 S.C.R. 295 [*Big M Drug Mart*]. *Canadian Charter of Rights and Freedoms,* Part 1 of the *Constitution Act, 1982,* being Schedule B to the *Canada Act 1982* (U.K.), 1982, c. 11.

2 Ellen Anderson, *Judging Bertha Wilson: Law as Large as Life* (Toronto: University of Toronto Press for the Osgoode Society for Canadian Legal History, 2001).

3 Hester Lessard, "Equality and Access to Justice in the Work of Bertha Wilson" (1992) 15 Dal. L.J. 35 at 48.

4 *Big M Drug Mart, supra* note 1 at para. 158.

5 *Ibid.* at para. 160.

6 *Ibid.* at para. 162.

7 For discussions about the problematic limitations of current s. 15 analysis, see the essays in Fay Faraday, Margaret Denike, and M. Kate Stephenson, eds., *Making Equality Rights Real: Securing Substantive Equality under the Charter* (Toronto: Irwin Law, 2006).

8 Lessard, *supra* note 3 at 54.

9 Terence Wade and Robin Geller.

10 Judge Rosalie Silberman Abella, Commissioner, *Report of the Commission on Equality in Employment* (Ottawa: Minister of Supply and Services Canada, 1984).

11 Keen to have a male managing partner on the task force, Wilson recommended Alec Robertson, Q.C., of Vancouver. She also recommended Professor John Hagan, who had carried out extensive research into the structure of the legal profession and law form dynamics.

12 The initial division of labour was the judiciary (Wilson), large law firms (Alec Robertson), small law firms and the CBA (Sophie Bourque), corporate counsel (Patricia Blocksom), faculties of law (John Hagan), and the practice of family law (Daphne Dumont).

13 Quoted in Anderson, *supra* note 2 at 336.

14 Sharon McIvor took on the specific responsibility of investigating the situation of Aboriginal women within the profession and contributed overall to the task force's report and recommendations. Judge Corrine Sparks focused on the situation of women of colour.

15 The three consultations were with representatives of law-related women's groups, the chairs of the CBA provincial and territorial working groups established to work with the task force, and law deans and representatives of law societies from across Canada.

16 Johnstone had been active on this front for many years and was instrumental in initiating the task force. She chaired the Alberta Working Group established under the auspices of the task force, actively supported the task force throughout its mandate, made implementation of the report her priority as CBA president, and continued to contribute to progress in this area until her appointment to the Alberta Court of Queen's Bench in 1996.

17 These recommendations were as follows: 5.18: "The Task Force recommends that law firms set realistic targets of billable hours for women with child rearing responsibilities pursuant to their legal duty to accommodate"; 5.19: "The Task Force recommends that, as part of the same legal duty to accommodate, the reduced target of billable hours should not delay or affect the eligibility for partnership nor affect normal compensation"; and 5.20: "The Task Force recommends that law firms evaluate lawyers on a basis that gives due weight to the quality of time expended rather than exclusively to the quantity of the time expended." Canadian Bar Association Task Force on Gender Equality in the Legal Profession, *Touchstones for Change: Equality, Diversity and Accountability* (Ottawa: Canadian Bar Association, 1993) at 99 [*Touchstones*].

18 *Ibid.*

19 Pursuant to one of the *Touchstones for Change* recommendations, the CBA subsequently established a Working Group on Racial Equality in the Legal Profession, which presented its reports *The Challenge of Racial Equality: Putting Principles into Practice* and *Virtual Justice: Systemic Racism and the Legal Profession* (a dissenting report written by the working group's co-chair Joanne St. Lewis) in February 1999.

20 *Touchstones, supra* note 17 at 1.

21 *Ibid.* at 2.

22 R.S. Abella, "Women in the Legal Profession" (1983) 12 Law & Soc'y Gaz. 315 at 322, quoted in *Touchstones, supra* note 17 at 2.

23 *Touchstones, ibid.* at 2-3 [emphasis in original]
24 *Brooks v. Canada Safeway Ltd.*, [1989] 1 S.C.R. 1219.
25 *Touchstones, supra* note 17 at 3.
26 *Ibid.* at 3-4.
27 *Ibid.* at 4.
28 *Ibid.*
29 *Ibid.*
30 *Ibid.*
31 *Ibid.*
32 Quoted in *ibid.* at 5.
33 *Ibid.*
34 *Ibid.* at 191.
35 *Ibid.* at 194.
36 *Ibid.* at 272. Wilson referred to Nellie McClung's 1914 comments about the "wonderful plans she and women like her" had for Canada's future: "We would rewrite our history. We would copy no other country. We would be ourselves, and proud of it. How we scorned the dull brown Primer from which we had learned Canadian history! Written as it was from the top down with no intimate glimpses of the people at all." Gwen Matheson, ed., *Women in the Canadian Mosaic* (Toronto: Peter Martin, 1976) at 17, quoted in *Touchstones, supra* note 17 at 272.
37 *Touchstones, ibid.*
38 *Jones v. National Coal Board* (1957), 2 Q.B. 44 at 64, quoted in *ibid.* at 273.
39 *Ibid.*
40 Anderson, *supra* note 2 at 349.
41 *Ibid.* at 351.
42 *Touchstones, supra* note 17 at 273.
43 See *e.g.* the essays in Elizabeth Sheehy and Sheila McIntyre, eds., *Calling for Change: Women, Law, and the Legal Profession* (Ottawa: University of Ottawa Press, 2006). Many of these originated as papers presented at the conference "Re-imagining Touchstones: The Wilson Report Ten Years On and Counting; Re-visiting the Issues and Re-thinking the Questions," held at the University of Ottawa, Faculty of Law, Ottawa, March 2004.

15

Taking a Stand on Equality: Bertha Wilson and the Evolution of Judicial Education in Canada

Rosemary Cairns Way and T. Brettel Dawson

The last two decades have seen significant shifts in conceptions of judging in Canada, catalyzed, many would argue, by the demands inherent in the interpretation and application of the *Canadian Charter of Rights and Freedoms*.[1] One manifestation of this shifting conception of judging is the institutionalization of pervasive, comprehensive, and continuing education on "social context" for Canadian judges overseen by the National Judicial Institute (NJI).[2] Support for social context education exists at the highest levels of the judiciary.[3] Justice Iacobucci, then a member of the Supreme Court of Canada and vice-chair of the NJI, named the program "one of the outstanding jewels in the Crown of judicial educational accomplishments,"[4] and international interest in the project is widespread.[5] In our view, judicial education addressing diversity, equality, and social context reflects an acknowledgment that judges' identities, experience, and world views are significant to the act of judging and that impartial judgment requires contextualized analysis.[6] In short, acceptance of social context education signals the acceptance of a particular vision of judging and the judicial role.[7]

As we near the second decade of the twenty-first century, it is easy to forget the tremendous legal upheaval occasioned by entrenched constitutionalized rights and, in particular, the seismic shift in conceptions of judging triggered by the equality guarantee. Bertha Wilson's illustrious career as legal professional, judge, and public intellectual mapped and mirrored some of the most significant legal changes of the twentieth century – to the practice of law (the entry of women), to the practice and theory of judging (the contextual method), to the legal profession (the recognition of its role in perpetuating discrimination), and to the relationship between Aboriginal peoples and the justice system (the public naming of the ongoing systemic discrimination reinforced and legitimated by the legal system). The role she played in all of these changes was characterized by a humility combined with principle, tempered by realism, and infused with courage.

In this chapter, we concentrate on one aspect of her remarkable career – her public commitment to reconceptualizing the judicial role and her concomitant public stance on judicial education, a strategy for change that is consistent with both her intellectual humanism and her pragmatic realism. We focus on two extra-judicial moments relatively late in her career: her Betcherman Lecture "Will Women Judges Really Make a Difference?"[8] and her recommendation, as chair of the Canadian Bar Association Task Force on Gender Equality in the Legal Profession, that judges be required to attend sensitivity courses on gender and racial bias.[9] These two moments tell us a great deal about Bertha Wilson's understanding of what it means to judge, what it means to be a "woman judge," and what public responsibilities inhere in the judicial office. They also place her at the centre of a passionate but discreet debate within the judiciary, now mostly resolved, regarding the appropriate scope of judicial education. Nevertheless, the questions Wilson asked about judging and the significance of identity to the judicial role continue to challenge us today.

The 1990 Betcherman Lecture

On 8 February 1990, when Justice Wilson delivered the fourth annual Barbara Betcherman Memorial Lecture, in which she spoke publicly about the connections between gender and the judicial role, her candour was both unusual and, for many, unsettling.[10] At that time and in that context, her willingness to investigate publicly the relevance of her identity as a woman to her capacity to judge was breathtakingly courageous: "Justice Wilson spoke for over an hour in that dry, precise, largely uninflected, tone that is so personal to her. At the end of the speech the room erupted into a standing, cheering ovation. I have never seen an argument of such breadth and subtlety communicated with such direct and simple force."[11]

The invitation to deliver the lecture asked Justice Wilson to discuss the "particular perspectives women might bring to the role of judging and to consider these perspectives in relation to the traditional requirement that judges be both independent and impartial."[12] The speech, given only ten months before her resignation from the Supreme Court of Canada,[13] was that of a fully matured jurist with a consolidated conception of judging exemplified by decisions such as *R. v. Morgentaler*,[14] *Edmonton Journal v. Alberta (A.G.)*,[15] and the decision she was working on at the time, *R. v. Lavallee*.[16] Wilson was fully aware of the risks of public speaking, having been named in a complaint to the Canadian Judicial Council (CJC) following her 1983 speech examining the principle of sexual equality.[17]

Perhaps not surprisingly, the Betcherman Lecture is characterized by caution and is carefully structured and judicious in both its commentary and conclusions. The fact that it was delivered (and reported on) rather than its actual content may have been primarily responsible for provoking a "firestorm of controversy."[18] Justice Wilson begins by admitting that the weight of public expectations that accompanied her appointment to the Supreme Court was both unrealistic and difficult to bear, given the incremental nature of legal change and the constraints of judicial office. She continues with a wide-ranging but mainly descriptive discussion of impartiality, neutrality, the role of the judiciary, and developments in feminist scholarship. Adverting to her topic, she suggests that one's view on the potential impact of women judges will probably depend on whether one is confident about the neutrality and impartiality of existing legal rules.[19] In perhaps the most controversial and widely discussed part of the speech, she concludes that "a distinctly male perspective is clearly discernible" in certain areas of the law, resulting in legal principles that are "not fundamentally sound."[20] Her comments on criminal law foreshadow her opinion in *Lavallee,* released three months later: "Some aspects of the criminal law in particular cry out for change; they are based on presuppositions about the nature of women and women's sexuality that, in this day and age, are little short of ludicrous."[21]

The speech reflected trends in academic, philosophical, and legal developments stimulated by the promise of the *Charter.* Wilson noted a national interdisciplinary conference "Equality and Judicial Neutrality" (the Banff Conference)[22] examining the "socialization of judges to equality issues."[23] In the conference keynote address, Rosalie Abella, then chairperson of the Ontario Labour Relations Board, spoke about the equality guarantee: "Section 15 of the *Canadian Charter of Rights and Freedoms* is the most important legislative change in this generation. It is also the most complicated. Every single one of us has something to learn about equality and most of us have a great deal to learn. Unless the legal and judicial professions admit to this pedagogical need, we will be a profound disappointment to the public, most of whom, from their less advantaged life-styles know far better than we the urgent need for an equality law."[24]

The pedagogical need Abella identified reflected her view that judges were, inevitably, "armed not only with relevant legal texts, but with a set of values, experiences and assumptions that are thoroughly embedded."[25] In her opinion, the progressive potential of the equality guarantee was inextricably linked to acknowledging the existence of these embedded perspectives and to developing a new analytical approach to judging.

The Banff Conference presaged legal developments that undermined the "old story" that judges were merely neutral ciphers. By the late 1980s, the Supreme Court had clarified two key aspects of its approach to the *Charter,* both with significant implications for the judicial role. First, the document was to be given a large and liberal interpretation,[26] guided by "respect for the inherent dignity of the human person, commitment to social justice and equality, accommodation of a wide variety of beliefs, respect for culture and group identity, and faith in social and political institutions which enhance the participation of individuals and groups in society."[27] Second, in *Andrews v. Law Society of British Columbia,* the Court adopted a substantive approach to the equality guarantee.[28] Broadly understood, *Andrews* requires a particular approach to judging – judging that is attentive to impact, to social condition, and to disadvantage, and that imagines an ameliorative role for law.

These legal developments were accompanied by the increasing attention paid by academics, lawyers, and the media to the notion that judicial identity was relevant to decision making. The fact that judges were predominantly white, able-bodied, heterosexual, wealthy men did not escape the attention of critical scholars.[29] Feminists argued that so-called neutral principles in fact systemically privileged male interests, pointing out that, when decision makers were overwhelmingly male, neutral decision making inevitably reflected the male point of view. Diversity and representativeness were increasingly seen as significant to the judicial appointments process, although a lively debate focused on the precise benefits of diversifying the bench. Wilson adverted to these questions in her lecture, drawing on contemporary feminist scholarship to explore the ways in which women judges could "make a difference." In particular, Carol Gilligan's groundbreaking book *In a Different Voice* had opened a conceptual space, acknowledged by Wilson, to wonder what the law and its doctrines might look like if women's voices were included.[30]

Justice Wilson explored broader questions as well: Was the value of diversity based on an assumption about how women or people of colour would interpret the law? Was such an assumption stereotypical? Or realistic? Was it based on a belief regarding the inherent value of diverse perspectives and the likelihood that a homogeneous bench would reflect a relatively homogeneous perspective? Or was it about public perceptions of the bench? In the lecture, the significant question is how a woman judge, committed to the ideal of impartiality, can and should respond to the existence of a dominant male perspective in the law. Can this perspective be counteracted by the injection of a female perspective? Or does the nature of the judicial process itself present "an insuperable hurdle" to such "judicial affirmative action." Bertha Wilson's answer is measured. Although the legislature remains the most appropriate place "for rapid or radical change," there is no reason why the judiciary cannot exercise some "modest degree of creativity in areas where modern insights and life's experience have indicated that the law has gone awry."[31] Recognizing that, "in some respects, our existing system of justice has been found wanting ... [and] the time to do something about it is now,"[32] Wilson concluded, "It is so much easier to come up with a black and white answer if you are unencumbered by a broader context."[33]

Wilson believed that change was the responsibility of all judges and that judicial education could play a key role in breaking down discriminatory barriers by providing a setting through which judges could learn about equality analysis, explore the role of context in judging, and examine their own world views. She "heartily endorsed" the CJC's decision to include "gender issues in their summer seminars for judges."[34] But she went further, saying, "[This initiative] is a significant first step towards the achievement of true judicial neutrality. But it is only a first step and there is a long way to go."[35]

The speech was remarkably candid and action-oriented. Wilson was prepared to publicly challenge an uncritical commitment to neutrality, to publicly acknowledge the existence of gender bias, to publicly muse on the relevance of identity to judging, and to publicly suggest that the commitment to unexamined neutrality had contributed to the perpetuation of inequality by the legal system. Not surprisingly, her words provoked another complaint to the CJC, which, like the first, was quickly dismissed. The speech that occasioned the first complaint, a 1983 discussion of sexual equality, examined the social institutions that contributed to the existence of inequality. Wilson's discussion of the church, an institution of enormous personal significance, identifies the "distinct masculine bias" in key doctrinal concepts, the role of canon law in perpetuating women's inequality, the overwhelming predominance of male ministers, rabbis, priests, and bishops, and the impact of the male-only interpretation of sacred texts. Describing a "feminist revolution which has precipitated a crisis of confidence," Wilson notes the existence of a new professional – the "female theologian," who, for the first time in history, is offering a genuine feminine viewpoint and critique.[36] Wilson is speaking from personal experience, commenting on her involvement in a small study group that discussed the effect of male dominance on church doctrine. The example illuminates her optimism regarding the power of study and self-reflection, an optimism that was also reflected in her public endorsement of mandatory judicial education programs on gender and race. It is to that pragmatic recommendation that we now turn.

The CBA Task Force on Gender Equality and *Touchstones for Change*

The CJC mandated "comprehensive, credible and in-depth" social context education in March 1994, a decision that reflected at least fifteen years of dynamic evolution in the law and within the judiciary. This section explores the pragmatic precursors to that resolution – the compelling evidence that the legal system perpetuated systemic discrimination and that the judiciary was not immune from discrimination, and the formalized calls for institutional accountability in the form of targeted judicial education. Bertha Wilson played a significant role in this process through her work on the task force report, *Touchstones for Change: Equality, Diversity and Accountability.*[37]

In the timeline of this larger narrative, the task force report and Bertha Wilson's public call for mandatory judicial education on gender and race appear as almost immediate predecessors to the CJC's support for social context education. The report appears to be the tipping point, the moment when social context education changed from a divisive controversial idea to an imperative.

Between 1987 and 1993, at least eight major studies examined the experience of women, Aboriginal people, and members of visible minority communities with the legal system.[38] Many of these reports called for professional and judicial education, often termed "sensitivity training." For example, the Royal Commission on the Donald Marshall Jr. Prosecution recommended that, *inter alia,* "Judicial Councils support courses and programs dealing with legal issues facing visible minorities, and encourage sensitivity to minority concerns for law students, lawyers and judges."[39] The *Report of the Aboriginal Justice Inquiry of Manitoba* recommended that "federal, provincial and municipal governments, individually or in concert, with the assistance and involvement of Aboriginal people, establish formal cross-cultural educational programs for all those working in any part of the justice system who have even occasional contact with Aboriginal people."[40] These inquiries focused on the experience of litigants, accused persons, and other stakeholders in the justice system. The CBA task force turned the lens inward on the experiences of women in the legal profession. Bertha Wilson agreed to chair the task force in the spring of 1991, and the final report was tabled at the CBA annual meeting in August 1993. The report, unequivocal in its assertion that gender discrimination permeated all aspects of the profession,[41] concluded that "discrimination existed in barriers to employment opportunities and representation, career advancement, a lack of accommodation for family responsibilities and sexual harassment."[42] In Chapter 14 of this volume, Melina Buckley offers a fascinating analysis of the task force rooted in her experience as project director. In this section, we focus on the examination of gender bias within the judiciary.

The report found that women were underrepresented as judges on every court in Canada, whether measured as a percentage of the population in general or as a percentage within the legal profession. In 1982, 4 percent of the federally appointed judiciary consisted of women. In 1985, when s. 15 was proclaimed in force, the number of women had increased to 5.6 percent.[43] By 1990, it stood at 9 percent, including three women at the Supreme Court of Canada (currently four). Ontario statistics demonstrated that the underrepresentation could not be attributed to a lack of qualified candidates but rather derived from the application of apparently neutral selection criteria that placed women at a disadvantage. Almost half of the women judges who responded to a confidential survey reported experiencing discrimination in the workplace. Women judges were assigned disproportionately more family law cases and disproportionately less high-profile criminal or corporate work, regardless of their pre-appointment experience. In addition, they felt lonely and isolated on the bench, primarily because the long-standing male culture excluded them from the collegiality necessary to make the cloistered judicial life personally manageable.[44]

According to Wilson's biographer, the judicial sections of the report provoked an immediate response from then Chief Justice Lamer, who was very concerned about the suggestion of intrajudicial discrimination:

> Lamer put enormous pressure on Wilson to disclose which judges were complaining and which judges were offending. She refused to do so. Of course she could not break her promise of confidentiality to the women who had confided in her only on condition that they not be identified; moreover she believed it would be damaging to the Canadian Bar Association if she revealed any of the sources of her information. And Wilson was sharply criticized for keeping silent; the assumption (much more palatable than facing up to the fact of the discrimination in the judiciary which she had reported) was that if she could produce no evidence, the discrimination did not really exist.
>
> Stymied by Wilson's principled stubbornness, Lamer attempted an independent investigation of his own. He wrote directly to every federally appointed judge and invited them to tell him about any "bias or unequal treatment at the hands of judges." He got no response.[45]

Two of the fifteen recommendations specific to the judiciary are significant for our purposes:

> 10.6: That sensitivity courses for judges on gender and racial bias be made compulsory not only for newly appointed judges but for all judges;
> 10.8: That the Canadian Judicial Council or the National Judicial Institute consider possible means of bringing women judges together to discuss matters of special interest to them and ensure that funding is made available for this purpose.[46]

This endorsement of judicial education raised questions: Would education "make a difference" to judging and the judicial role in Canada? Would it be acceptable to the judiciary? Would "sensitivity training" amount to inappropriate advocacy? In fact, the task force report considered the relationship between judicial independence and judicial education and concluded that there was no conflict. Bertha Wilson suggested that, if necessary, training could be provided exclusively by other judges, although she commented, "I must say, however, that I have never heard judges resist instruction in judgment-writing on the ground that it was delivered by those non-judges especially schooled in the art of the English language."[47]

In the 1993-94 CJC annual report, Chief Justice Lamer acknowledged the task force recommendations:

> Canada's federal judiciary, like every institution in every country and jurisdiction, is under increasing scrutiny and pressure ...
>
> On such issues as gender and racial equality within the courts, and accountability, the judiciary has been criticized and found wanting. Opinions within the Council vary on these matters. I am conscious that progress in each of these areas has been uneven, varying by province, by court and at times by individual judge.
>
> More important, I am aware that when a report such as *Touchstones for Change* ... criticizes the judiciary and the Council itself for insensitivity to the concerns of women, we have a responsibility to either disprove that criticism or demonstrate how we are responding. In any case, we are bound to consider the matters seriously.[48]

In the following section, we examine what emerged as a result of that consideration.

The Judicial Education Context

Bertha Wilson's recommendations on judicial education were made during a period of reorganization in the structure of Canadian judicial education when change was possible. An examination of the annual reports of the CJC between 1987 and 1994 reveals increasing attentiveness to issues of equality and discrimination as an aspect of judicial accountability. In the preface to the 1987 report, the council's chair, Chief Justice Dickson, noted an increasing public expectation of openness in important institutions, an expectation that reflected the way in which the *Charter* had "turned the spotlight of public opinion more strongly on the courts."[49] In 1988-89 the report commented on the "feeling among some Canadians – mostly women – that some judges do not take sexual assault and sexual abuse seriously enough."[50] That same year, Council decided that its own educational programs, held annually and organized by the Education Committee, should consider "gender-related" issues: "Among other things, it is clear from the complaints record that there is much controversy over sentencing in sexual assault cases. In addition, the *Canadian Charter of Rights and Freedoms* has given sexual equality new prominence as an issue before the courts. The new sessions are intended to help judges see how gender impacts on cases that come before them so they can respond with sensitivity as well as justice."[51] The report for the following year noted the response to the seminars: "Sessions on gender-related issues were held for the first time at [the annual seminars]. These issues continue to provoke controversy, and the Council intends to make consideration of them a regular feature of its seminars. Indeed, while participants have a choice among most topics, all will attend a half-day session on gender-related issues at the 1990 seminar."[52] It was at this point that the NJI was established as an independent judge-led not-for-profit corporation to provide overall leadership in judicial education. The need for a national coordinating body to supply leadership in judicial education had been identified by the Canadian Judicial Centre Project convened in 1985 by the minister of justice and the chief justice of Canada. Its chair, Justice W.A. Stephenson, had concluded that "existing Canadian [judicial education] programs show uneven coverage with significant gaps and deficiencies, duplication and a lack of coordination ... [W]hat is lacking in Canada is any national coordination of resources, any effective means of exchanging information, and any adequately funded long-range planning capacity."[53] The mandate of the new Canadian Judicial Education Centre (later renamed the National Judicial Institute) was to assist courts in the development of programs, to develop and deliver national educational programs, to provide technical and organizational services to the courts, and to inform the Canadian judiciary about legal developments. Added later was a mandate to assist with judicial education projects in other countries.[54]

In its fledgling years, the NJI developed targeted educational materials dealing with gender bias, race, and family violence.[55] However, equality-focused education remained at the margins. The courses that dominated the NJI's agenda were centred on skills training (computer use, complex trials, case management, judgment writing) or on substantive law updates. Sessions on gender issues or cross-cultural awareness tended to be stand-alones and were viewed as add-ons or as catering to "special interests." Independently of the NJI, the Western Judicial Education Centre (WJEC) offered a series of seminars between 1984 and 1994 specifically focused on "providing education relating to problems with the administration of justice of primary concern to the community."[56] Major conferences on gender equality, the delivery of justice to Aboriginal people, and racial, ethnic, and cultural equity were grounded in an acknowledgment of systemic discrimination.[57] However, the programs were highly controversial, particularly among the federally appointed judiciary. The WJEC was viewed as a provincial court initiative, overwhelmingly attended by provincial court judges, and as the brainchild of the committed, creative, and maverick judge-educator Justice Douglas Campbell.[58]

It was in this context, including shifting attitudes toward judicial education, that the task force recommendations were made. Recognizing the importance of a coherent response, the CJC established a special committee on equality in the courts in September 1993. The committee's role was "to develop suggestions ... as to how to eliminate inequality in the courts, if any, by reason of gender or any other basis."[59] In March 1994, as one of its first acts, the committee recommended, and Council unanimously approved, the development of "comprehensive, in-depth, credible education programs on social context issues which includes gender and race."[60] The ambiguity of the resolution and its reliance on a newly coined phrase – "social context"[61] – might have suggested that this was more public relations gesture than actual commitment. However, and to its credit, the judiciary did eventually make good on its public commitment to social context education in a manner that was careful, cautious, pragmatic, and incremental. Responsibility for implementing the 1994 resolution was vested in the NJI. The education program that resulted was built around a commitment to an inclusive vision of the law and judicial process consistent with *Charter* values. Crucially, it pioneered new forms of education to address this "new subject," and, in so doing, it played an important role in continuing and deepening the discussion about contextual judging urged by Bertha Wilson.

The NJI established the Social Context Education Project (SCEP) with funding from the Department of Justice. The first steps focused on developing a conceptual framework. Two senior legal academics were commissioned to assist in identifying objectives, and a number of key ideas emerged. First, social context education needed to be mainstreamed as "an ongoing part of judicial education, in the same way that there is ongoing education about substantive law or criminal justice issues."[62] Second, the program was to be grounded in Canada's commitment to equality,[63] one that represented a "significant shift from the past"[64] and created a need for sustained education. Third, the initiative was to be approached as a long-term process, intended to "make discussion of social context issues automatically part of the landscape"[65] and aligned with the overall objectives of judicial education – fairness, impartiality, and consistency with legal principles.[66]

To implement this vision, the NJI appointed a National Coordinator (an academic) and two judges to serve as special directors. A national advisory committee was convened with membership drawn from judges, academics, and the community. Very early on, the project organized a judicial consultation to discuss the initiative with judges. The May 1997 consultation was the first national meeting ever attended by judges from every province and all levels of court. Asked to identify the ways in which persistent disadvantage and inequality manifested in their courtrooms, judges named *groups* (poor people, single mothers, Aboriginal peoples, young offenders, unrepresented litigants, recent immigrants, the disabled, same-sex couples) and *issues* (spousal abuse, sexual assault, credibility assessment, custody, systemic racism, low literacy). Additionally, participants emphasized the importance of senior leadership and localized programming that reflected regional and provincial priorities.

What resulted was a decentralized concept in which the role of the SCEP was to coordinate, share ideas and resources, assist with the identification of relevant expertise, and provide an overall intellectual infrastructure for the initiative. To ensure that local judges had the skills they needed, the SCEP organized faculty development programs for judges undertaking planning and facilitation roles. These programs covered substantive social context and adult education skills. During Phase 1 of the SCEP, court-based education committees in every province developed introductory full-court conferences on social context themes. By 2001 each province had held a social context seminar. In Phase 2, the focus shifted to a more intensive process of faculty development with judges interested in developing their skills as judicial educators in the area of social context. Each participating judge developed an education module, which was delivered in his or her court education programs or as part of the NJI national seminars. At the time of writing, the project encompasses the continual updating and development of a standing social context curriculum, development and dissemination of education resources, and ongoing integration of social context issues into NJI courses and processes.

The new subject matter of social context required a new form of judicial education, one that took principles of adult education seriously, that encouraged critical self-awareness, and that enabled participants to practise applying new ideas and methods to practical problems. The SCEP addressed social inequalities relating to gender, race, sexual orientation, Aboriginal justice issues, disability, poverty, and social condition. It was built around themes reflecting the judicial role, including fairness, decision making, impartiality, and equality. It was judge-led and community-connected. However, participation in the programs was voluntary. Very early on, Chief Justice Lamer (as chair of the NJI Board of Governors) rejected the notion of mandatory programming,[67] an idea that had been recommended by Bertha Wilson in *Touchstones for Change*. Wilson's position probably reflected her view that the matter needed urgent, sustained, and serious attention as well as her sincere concern that judges would not attend if the programs were optional. However, the decision against mandatory programming was probably the only option palatable to the judiciary in Canada at that time – and, hence, it was an essential element in ensuring the program's success. Mandatory programming could have been seen as inconsistent with judicial independence. In addition, some might have perceived a decision to make the education mandatory as an admission that judges needed remediation in this area and that others could provide it to them. So fundamental are these concerns that all judicial education in Canada – both then and now – remains voluntary. Judicial education programs must assiduously avoid any sense that they offer a platform to influence or direct the judiciary, an idea encapsulated in the NJI's *Twenty Principles of Judicial Education* as the principle of "non-prescriptiveness."[68] Social context education must not advance a particular point of view and, most particularly, not the agendas of special interest groups, however they are defined. Rather, it must identify and examine issues from a range of perspectives, must be of high quality, relevant to the judicial task, and designed to foster dialogue. Additionally, and equally importantly, it must be consistent with the requirements of judicial independence while upholding respect for *Charter* values.

Social context education, as defined and shaped by Canadian judges, was not sensitivity training but rather an examination of the fundamentals of the judicial role regarding which varying perspectives existed; it addressed difficult and contentious legal and social issues; it asked questions that did not have "right" answers (eliminating the reassuring comfort of settled jurisprudence); it brought into focus the people in the courtroom and their varying backgrounds, capacities, and expectations of the judicial process; and finally, it necessarily brought the person and perspectives of the judge into the frame. Social context education brought judicial education to "the coalface," the rough and ready point at which life and law intersect or, less prosaically, at which the abstractions of law tumble into concrete, complex, often wrenching, and necessarily choice-laden realities of daily life in courtrooms across the country. Social context education was not about the status quo: rather, it was about improving justice in those courtrooms.

Contextual Judging by Contextual Judges

What are the possibilities and risks entailed in the conceptions of judging and judicial education championed by Bertha Wilson? What does it mean to be a judge – and a woman judge – in the twenty-first century? What does it mean for judges to have – and use – context (including their own identity or experience) in fulfilling their judicial roles? Conversations in Canada about judges and judging have shifted enormously in the period since Justice Wilson's Betcherman Lecture.[69] The relevance of context to decision making is universally acknowledged, as these remarks by Chief Justice McLachlin demonstrate: "Context, policy and philosophy have always been a part of judging. What the *Charter* has done is to bring this kind of thinking out of the closet ... Judges now openly acknowledge that before they make decisions that affect peoples' lives or government policy, they must have some understanding of the circumstances or context of the problem before us and the implications of deciding one way or another."[70]

We believe that social context education has played an observable role in these changes and that Justice Wilson's support of expanded judicial education addressing social context is an important part of her enduring legacy. Social context education recognized that context is an element in judicial process. By linking social context to the judging process, the SCEP catalyzed expanded understandings of judging itself and began what has been an ongoing transformation beyond black letter law. An example of this can be seen in the following comment made by a judicial participant in a Phase 2 SCEP program: "The law is not applied in isolation – it is applied by people to people and thus, the days of 'black letter law' if they ever existed, are no longer sufficient to provide judges with the tools to properly carry out their functions."[71]

Although decision making that attends to the social context of the dispute is increasingly accepted and expected, a related question concerns the relevance of the judge's identity to the decision-making process. This issue was central in the 1997 decision in *R. v. S. (R. D.)*.[72] In that case, Justice Corinne Sparks, the first black woman to be appointed to the bench in Canada, made comments in a youth court proceeding involving divergent testimony from a black youth and a white police officer concerning an event that occurred in an area known for racial tensions. In her oral ruling, after finding reasonable doubt and acquitting the youth, Judge Sparks remarked, "I am not saying that the Constable has misled the court, although police officers have been known to do that in the past. I am not saying that the officer overreacted, but certainly police officers do overreact, particularly when they are dealing with non-white groups."[73] The Crown (supported by the Canadian Police Association) filed an appeal claiming that the judge had created a reasonable apprehension of bias. The Supreme Court issued multiple opinions and, by a plurality, dismissed the appeal. However, the judges split on which "side of the line" the remarks fell. A minority held that Sparks demonstrated bias and stereotyped all police officers, whereas two of the majority judges considered her remarks "unfortunate, unnecessary, or close to the line." The other judges disagreed, characterizing the comment as "an entirely appropriate recognition of the facts in evidence in this case and of the context within which this case arose – a context known to Judge Sparks and to any well-informed member of the community."[74] These judges went further, stating that judges should bring their diverse experiences and perspectives with them to the bench: "[J]udges in a bilingual, multiracial and multicultural society will undoubtedly approach the task of judging from their varied perspectives. They will certainly have been shaped by, and have gained insight from, their different experiences, and cannot be expected to divorce themselves from these experiences on the occasion of their appointment to the bench. In fact, such a transformation would deny society the benefit of the valuable knowledge gained by the judiciary while they were members of the Bar."[75] The judges noted that "[t]he reasonable person is cognizant of the racial dynamics in the local community, and, as a member of the Canadian community, is supportive of the principles of equality."[76] This recognition is consistent with Rosalie Abella's comments at the Banff Conference[77] as well as with Justice Lynn Smith's more recent claim that "it is not only acceptable, but expected that judges' own perspectives and experiences will enter into the judgment process ... [I]mpartiality requires a decision-maker to be conscious of his or her own perspective, and to be open to other points of view."[78]

The challenge inherent in the recognition of individual perspective is that of reconfiguring "impartiality" as "situated."[79] Once context and identity are brought into judging, abstracted universalized norms are displaced. In turn, "judge" and "judging" are no longer universal or abstracted quantities. Yet, what bearing does gender (or other diversity) appropriately have on judging, the theme that informed much of Wilson's musing in the Betcherman Lecture? It is not uncommon to hear women judges (or women lawyers) deny that their gender has any bearing on their work or their life experience. Mary Jane Mossman's historical work on the first women lawyers traces the recurring idea that women were admitted to the profession on the same terms as men and, by implication, to do the same job(s) in the same way.[80] The recent obituary for Dame Augusta Wallace (the first woman to become a judge in New Zealand) quoted her view that, "whether you are male or female and any shape or size," the real test in law "is your ability to compete with your fellow practitioners."[81] Similar remarks were attributed to Margaret Hyndman, Canada's first female King's Counsel. A *Maclean's Magazine* profile published in 1949 noted that, "no petticoat careerist," she was "a little stout" and an excellent host at dinner parties. Her femininity established, the profile quoted her as stating, "Only the fact that I am a lawyer matters. That I am a woman is of no consequence" and advising other women to "forget your sex and expect no quarter."[82] Certainly, no one could quarrel with the comments of either Wallace or Hyndman as statements regarding the importance of competence (as well as the endless struggle for women to be taken seriously in their legal careers). However, the claim that being a woman "is of no account" and that all judges are admitted "on the same terms" is precisely what Bertha Wilson, another legal pioneer, challenged judges to explore.

In our view, and presaged by Bertha Wilson, it remains pressing and permissible for (women) judges to identify and ask questions about how gender may make a difference. We believe that judges (of both genders) need to focus on the specificities of experience in both fact finding and legal interpretation. We think this needs to start with women judges (and judges with other diverse identities) simply because, if they do not ask these questions, who will? Of course, judges need to look beyond questions of gender in order to take various inequalities into account.[83] Our experiences and "offline conversations" suggest that female judges are beginning to exert the influence of their growing numbers by questioning (and changing) the approaches of a male judiciary. However, and for a range of reasons, this is happening quietly and episodically.

Another image of a "journey here" is germane, one of constraints experienced and, over time, thrown off.[84] There are indications that Wilson herself moved from resisting recognition of gender disparity in her professional life toward acknowledging it and urging structural changes. In interviews with her biographer, she described her work on the CBA task force as, "ironically, her first unequivocal and deeply personal experience of gender discrimination."[85] Was this belated realization and acknowledgment because she had not realized how exceptional she was? Or was it because she discovered that some of the negative experiences she encountered on the bench were not unique? Wilson asked whether female judges would (or should) act affirmatively to make a difference. The answers may lie in sheer numbers or in individual courage, but they will require (women) judges to reflect carefully on the connections between judicial process and change.

Bertha Wilson asked us to examine the links between life and law and between judging and social context. Hers was a principled understanding of the judicial task, the public interest, and the reality of a diverse society in which systemic inequalities constrain human experience. In our view, the legacy of the Betcherman Lecture, the task force report, and social context education for Canadian judges is the opening of a conversation about judging and judicial education that continues today. We conclude with her words: "If women lawyers and women judges through their differing perspectives on life can bring a new humanity to bear on the decision-making process, perhaps they *will* make a difference. Perhaps, they will succeed in infusing the law with an understanding of what it means to be fully human."[86]

Notes

1 *Canadian Charter of Rights and Freedoms,* Part I of the *Constitution Act, 1982,* being Schedule B to the *Canada Act 1982* (U.K.), 1982, c. 11.

2 Rosemary Cairns Way was the first coordinator of the Social Context Education Project (SCEP) at the National Judicial Institute (NJI) during its initial phase (January 1997-July 1999). Brettel Dawson replaced her in July 1999 and coordinated the second phase of the SCEP (1999-2003) before becoming academic director of the NJI.

3 In 1994 the Canadian Judicial Council (CJC) supported judicial education programs on "social context issues ... including gender and race," which were "comprehensive, in-depth and credible." The CJC has continued to endorse the education programs. Most recently, in 2005, the CJC supported "credible, in-depth and comprehensive" social context education as an ongoing part of judicial education. CJC, *Resolutions* [on file with the CJC].

4 Frank Iacobucci, "The Broader Context of Social Context" (Remarks from the Social Context Education Faculty and Curriculum Design Program 1, Part 2, 2001) [unpublished, on file with the authors].

5 For example, an optional Social Context Symposium held in 2004 as part of the "Canada Conference: Judicial Education in a World of Challenge and Change" organized for the "Second International Conference of the Training of the Judiciary," Ottawa, attracted some 75 percent of the three hundred conference delegates drawn from eighty countries.

6 See *e.g.* Beverley McLachlin, "Judicial Neutrality and Equality" (paper presented at "Aspects of Equality: Rendering Justice," Hull, Quebec, 4-5 November 1995 [unpublished, on file with the authors]. Lynn Smith, "Contextual Judging" (paper presented at the "Canada Conference: Judicial Education in a World of Challenge and Change: Second International

Conference on the Training of the Judiciary" Ottawa, 31 October-5 November, 2004) [unpublished, on file with the authors] [Smith, "Contextual Judging"]. See also a related version of this address published as "Judicial Education on Context" (2005) 38 U.B.C. L. Rev. 569.

7 The process of tracing the penetration of education into Canadian courtrooms is complex. Formal acceptance may not translate into actual practices. There is no shortage of concerned academic discourse on directions in, for example, Canadian equality jurisprudence. See *e.g.* Sheila McIntyre and Sanda Rodgers, eds., *Diminishing Returns: Inequality and the Canadian Charter of Rights and Freedoms* (Toronto: Butterworths, 2006); *Rewriting Equality/Récrire l'égalité,* special issue (2006) 18 C.J.W.L., containing the first six decisions of the Women's Court of Canada, which attempt to work out what a constitutional theory of equality should look like.

8 Bertha Wilson, "Will Women Judges Really Make a Difference?" (1990) 28 Osgoode Hall L.J. 507.

9 Canadian Bar Association Task Force on Gender Equality in the Legal Profession, *Touchstones for Change: Equality, Diversity and Accountability* (Ottawa: Canadian Bar Association, 1993) [*Touchstones*].

10 Wilson, *supra* note 8.

11 Brian Bucknall, "Letter to the Editor," *Toronto Star* (24 February 1990).

12 Ellen Anderson, *Judging Bertha Wilson: Law as Large as Life* (Toronto: University of Toronto Press for the Osgoode Society for Canadian Legal History, 2001) at xiii.

13 *Ibid.* at 325. Wilson's letter of resignation to Justice Minister Kim Campbell was dated 21 November 1990.

14 *R. v. Morgentaler,* [1988] 1 S.C.R. 30.

15 *Edmonton Journal v. Alberta (A.G.),* [1989] 2 S.C.R. 1326.

16 *R. v. Lavallee,* [1990] 1 S.C.R. 852. In the following comment, Justice Wilson specifically linked the speech with the decision: "It was when I was writing that [speech] and thinking about it that I realized that there were quite a number of aspects of the law that needed to be rethought from a gender perspective and that [*Lavallee*] was one, that was a chance to begin doing it by looking at the defence of self-defence and how it was essentially male-oriented. And I thought to myself, now here is a chance to give some leadership to what I have said in my speech ... [T]he more I thought that the more I realized how many areas that needs to happen [to]." Quoted in Anderson, *supra* note 12 at 219.

17 Bertha Wilson, "Law in Society: The Principle of Sexual Equality" (1983) 13 Manitoba L.J. 221. The complaint, launched by REAL Women, was quickly dismissed. See Anderson, *supra* note 12 at xv-xvi.

18 Anderson, *ibid.* at xii.

19 Wilson, *supra* note 8 at 511.

20 *Ibid.* at 515.

21 *Ibid.*

22 Although Justice Wilson did not attend the conference, it is clear that she fully endorsed its objectives and recommendations.

23 Sheilah Martin and Kathleen Mahoney, eds., *Equality and Judicial Neutrality* (Toronto: Carswell, 1987) at iii.

24 Rosalie Silberman Abella, "The Dynamic Nature of Equality" in Martin and Mahoney, *ibid.* 3 at 3.

25 *Ibid.* at 8-9.

26 *Law Society of Upper Canada v. Skapinker,* [1984] 1 S.C.R. 357 at para. 10.

27 *R. v. Oakes,* [1986] 1 S.C.R. 103 at para. 64.

28 *Andrews v. Law Society of British Columbia,* [1989] 1 S.C.R. 143.

29 See *e.g.* Isabel Grant and Lynn Smith, "Gender Representation in the Canadian Judiciary" in Ontario Law Reform Commission, *Appointing Judges: Philosophy, Politics and Practices* (Toronto: Ontario Law Reform Commission, 1991) 57; Errol P. Mendes, "Promoting Heterogeneity of the Judicial Mind: Minority and Gender Representation in the Canadian Judiciary" in Ontario Law Reform Commission, *ibid.,* 91.

30 Carol Gilligan, *In a Different Voice: Psychological Theory and Women's Development* (Cambridge, MA: Harvard University Press, 1982). See also Carrie Menkel-Meadow, "Portia in

a Different Voice" (1985) 1 Berkeley Women's L.J. 39; Carrie Menkel-Meadow, "The Comparative Sociology of Women Lawyers: The 'Feminization' of the Legal Professions" (1986) 24 Osgoode Hall L.J. 897; Leslie Bender, "*A Lawyer's Primer on Feminist Theory and Tort*" (1988) 38 J. Legal Educ. 3; T. Brettel Dawson, *Estoppel and Obligation* (LL.M. Thesis, Osgoode Hall Law School, 1987) at Chapter 8: "Principles, Pragmatism and Paradigm Shift" [unpublished].

31 Wilson, *supra* note 8 at 516.

32 *Ibid.* at 521.

33 *Ibid.* at 520.

34 *Ibid.* at 517. See text *infra* at note 48.

35 *Ibid.*

36 Wilson, *supra* note 17 at 227-28.

37 *Touchstones, supra* note 9.

38 See *e.g.* Manitoba Association of Women and the Law, *Gender Equality in the Courts* (Winnipeg: Manitoba Association of Women and the Law, 1988); Law Society of British Columbia, *Gender Equality in the Justice System* (Vancouver: Law Society of British Columbia, 1991); Michael Jackson, *Locking up Natives in Canada: A Report of the Canadian Bar Association Committee on Imprisonment and Release* (Ottawa: Canadian Bar Association, 1988); Nova Scotia, Royal Commission on the Donald Marshall Jr. Prosecution, *Digest of Findings and Recommendations,* vol. 8 (Halifax: Queen's Printer, 1989); Task Force on the Criminal Justice System and Its Impact on the Indian and Metis People of Alberta (Cawsey Task Force), *Justice on Trial: Task Force on the Criminal Justice System and Its Impact on the Indian and Metis People of Alberta* (Edmonton: Cawsey Task Force, 1991); Manitoba, Public Inquiry into the Administration of Justice and Aboriginal People, *Report of the Aboriginal Justice Inquiry of Manitoba: The Justice System and Aboriginal People,* vol. 1 (Winnipeg: Queen's Printer, 1991) (Commissioners C.M. Sinclair and A.C. Hamilton), online: <http://www.ajic.mb.ca/volume.html> [Manitoba Public Inquiry]; *Touchstones, supra* note 9; Canadian Panel on Violence against Women, *Changing the Landscape: Ending Violence – Achieving Equality* (Ottawa: Minister of Supply and Services, 1993).

39 Royal Commission on the Donald Marshall Jr. Prosecution, *supra* note 38 at 26.

40 Manitoba Public Inquiry, *supra* note 38 at 661.

41 *Touchstones, supra* note 9.

42 *Ibid.* at vii.

43 According to figures provided by the Office of the Federal Commissioner for Judicial Affairs, the percentage of women on the federal bench for the period 1980-2008 was as follows: 1980, 3 percent; 1982, 4 percent; 1985, 5.6 percent; 1990, 9 percent; 1993, 13 percent; 1999, 21 percent; 2003, 26 percent; 2008, 31 percent. See online: <http://www.fja-cmf.gc.ca/appointments-nominations/judges-juges-eng.html>.

44 *Touchstones, supra* note 9.

45 Anderson, *supra* note 12 at 349.

46 *Touchstones, supra* note 9 at 285. In fact, an inaugural meeting of women judges (which was open to men judges as well) was held under the auspices of the Canadian chapter of the International Association of Women Judges in November 1995. The conference was called "Aspects of Equality: Rendering Justice."

47 *Ibid.* at 191. The specific reference was probably to the one-week intensive seminar on judgment writing established in 1981 and offered each year by the Canadian Institute on the Administration of Justice.

48 CJC, *Annual Report, 1993-94* (Ottawa: CJC, 1994) at v-vi.

49 CJC, *Annual Report, April 1, 1987-March 31, 1988* (Ottawa: CJC, 1988) at v.

50 CJC, *Annual Report, 1988-89* (Ottawa: CJC, 1989) at 12.

51 *Ibid.* at v.

52 CJC, *Annual Report, 1989-90* (Ottawa: CJC, 1990) at 3. The Council summer education sessions continued until 1993. Presumably, the sessions were discontinued because of the growth and development of the NJI.

53 *Ibid.*, Executive Summary at i.

54 National Judicial Institute Letters Patent (Canada, Minister of Consumer and Corporate Affairs, 18 April 1988).
55 A video and supporting materials on gender bias were prepared during the first year of the NJI's operations. Until 1998 these were included in the information package sent to newly appointed judges. A video-based educational module titled "Judicial Awareness: Race, Culture and the Courts" was completed in 1993 as were two video-based educational modules on spousal assault and child sexual abuse. See *Annual Report, 1992-93* (Ottawa: NJI,1994) at 5.
56 The work of the WJEC is described in Douglas Campbell, "The Process of Developing and Delivering Social Context Education: Statement of Activities (1988-1994) and the Next Phase," 31 March 1994 [unpublished, on file with the author].
57 The programs were "Sentencing: The Social Context: Part I" 1989; "Sentencing: The Social Context: Part II" 1990; "Equality and Fairness: Accepting the Challenge" 1991; "Seminar on Racial, Ethnic and Cultural Equity" 1992; and "Seminar on Gender Equality in Judicial Decision-Making" 1994.
58 Justice Campbell was appointed to the Federal Court of Canada in 1995. He continues to be actively involved in judicial education internationally.
59 CJC, *Annual Report, 1993-94, supra* note 48 at 25.
60 Decisions of the CJC, other than those published on its website, <http://www.cjc-cmc.gc.ca>, are not public documents. No specific citations are available for this or other social context resolutions.
61 We recognize the complexity and significance of naming. We assume that "social context" was a compromise term designed to avoid prelabelling the program as "gender or race sensitivity training" and thereby arousing immediate resistance by judges. Even so, some judges quickly coined the initiative as "charm school for judges."
62 Katherine Swinton, *Report to the National Judicial Institute on Social Context Education for Judges* (Ottawa: NJI, 1996) [unpublished, archived at the NJI].
63 Lynn Smith, *Statement of Needs and Objectives for Continuing Judicial Education on the Social Context of Judicial Decision Making* (Ottawa: NJI, 1996) [unpublished, archived at the NJI].
64 *Ibid.* at 2.
65 *Ibid.* at 6.
66 *Ibid.* at 7.
67 Given this decision and our earlier reference to his concern about Wilson's findings in *Touchstones for Change,* it is perhaps necessary to point out that Lamer CJ. is on record as supporting the social context education initiative. He commented that "the Project is designed to make those who participate in it better judges by making them more aware of the broader social, economic, cultural and political context within which we judges function in a society as diverse as Canada." Antonio Lamer, Transcript, NJI Seminar for Members of the CJC, March 1998 at 1 [unpublished, on file with the author].
68 NJI, *Twenty Principles of Judicial Education in Canada,* October 2006 [unpublished, on file with the authors].
69 See *e.g.* Elizabeth Sheehy, ed., *Adding Feminism to Law: The Contributions of Justice Claire L'Heureux-Dubé* (Toronto: Irwin Law, 2004).
70 Beverley McLachlin, "Canada's Coming of Age" (2003) 19 Sup. Ct. L. Rev. 368 at 368.
71 Correspondence with the authors, 2002.
72 *R. v. S. (R.D.),* [1997] 3 S.C.R. 484.
73 *Ibid.* at para. 29.
74 *Ibid.* at para. 30.
75 *Ibid.* at para. 38.
76 *Ibid.* at para. 48.
77 See Abella, *supra* note 24 at 3.
78 Smith, "Contextual Judging," *supra* note 6 at 15.
79 See *e.g.* Hilary Astor, "Mediator Neutrality: Making Sense of Theory and Practice" (2007) 16 Soc. & Leg. Stud. 221; Jennifer Nedelsky, "Embodied Diversity and the Challenges to Law" (1997) 42 McGill L.J. 91.

80 Mary Jane Mossman, *The First Women Lawyers: A Comparative Study of Gender, Law, and the Legal Professions* (Oxford: Hart, 2006). See also Joan Brockman, *Gender in the Legal Profession: Fitting or Breaking the Mould* (Vancouver: UBC Press, 2005).

81 Quoted in Diana Dekker, "Dame Augusta Wallace: Judge a No Nonsense Role Model" *Dominion Post* [New Zealand] (17 April 2008) B7.

82 McKenzie Porter, "The Legal Lady" *Maclean's Magazine* (15 July 1949) 15 at 23, reproduced in T. Brettel Dawson, ed., *Women, Law and Social Change,* 5th ed. (North York: Captus Press, 2009 xvii at xix.

83 See Marilyn J. Waring, *In the Lifetime of a Goat* (Wellington, NZ: Bridget Williams Books, 2001); revised and expanded Canadian edition *1 Way 2 C the World*: *Writings 1984-2006* (Toronto: University of Toronto Press, 2009).

84 It seems clear that power and status in the profession continue to align along gender lines. See *e.g.* Fiona M. Kay and Joan Brockman, "Barriers to Gender Equality in the Canadian Legal Establishment" (2000) 8 Fem. Leg. Stud. 169; Mary Jane Mossman, "Legal Education as a Strategy for Change in the Legal Profession" in Elizabeth Sheehy and Sheila McIntyre, eds., *Calling for Change: Women, Law and the Legal Profession* (Ottawa: University of Ottawa Press, 2006) 179; Mary Jane Mossman, "Engendering the Legal Profession: The Education Strategy" in Ulrike Schultz and Gisela Shaw, eds., *Women in the World's Legal Professions* (Oxford: Hart, 2002) 77; Jean McKenzie Leiper, *Bar Codes: Women in the Legal Profession* (Vancouver: UBC Press, 2006).

85 Anderson, *supra* note 12 at 349.

86 Wilson, *supra* note 8 at 522 [emphasis in original].

16
Bertha Wilson: "Silences" in a Woman's Life Story

Mary Jane Mossman

Telling the Stories of Women in Law

> Whether we are aware of it or not, our culture gives us *an inner script by which we live our lives*. The main acts for the play come from the way our world understands human development; the scenes and key characters come from our families and socialization ... and the dynamics of the script come from what our world defines as success or achievement.
>
> – Jill Ker Conway, *When Memory Speaks: Reflections on Autobiography* [emphasis added]

This quotation from Jill Ker Conway's book about the art of telling life stories provides a good introduction to my reflections on Justice Bertha Wilson's life. As Conway argues, a society's culture, and especially its gendered expectations for men and women, shapes meanings for our experiences and influences how we tell our life stories. For men, the "overarching pattern for life comes from adaptations of the story of the epic hero in classical antiquity," in which life is an odyssey and the hero must overcome trials and tests through "courage, endurance, cunning and moral strength."[1] By contrast, as Conway explains, women who began to enter the professions in the late nineteenth century were required to rewrite the traditional gender script, in a context in which there were no precedents for their lives: "Many stories of women's struggle for education and successful battles with discrimination might well have fitted the [epic hero] model of a life devoted to the unremitting quest for success ... [However], pioneer women professionals were [often] silent about their ambitions and recounted their lives as though their successes just happened to them, rather like the soprano's chance meeting with the tenor in the first act of an opera ... What are we to make of such silences?"[2] Conway's question about "silences" suggests a need to be attentive to Wilson's life story, that of a pioneer woman professional in the late twentieth century, to understand how she "negotiated the problem of self-awareness and [broke out of] the internalized code a culture supplies about how [a woman's] life should be experienced."[3]

Yet, regardless of Conway's assertions about the need to be attentive to gender in life scripts, Wilson herself never wished to be considered a *woman* lawyer, despite the reality of difficulties that she seems to have encountered in her work as a professional "woman pioneer."[4] Moreover, as reported by Wilson's authorized biographer Ellen Anderson, Wilson firmly eschewed the label "feminist."[5] By contrast, she was much more forthright about her identity as a Scottish immigrant to Canada. Yet, in reflecting on her immigrant status, Anderson includes not only Wilson's geographic transplantation, but also her admission to the culture of male exclusivity in the legal profession and the judiciary: "For Bertha Wilson, avowedly not a feminist, immigration to Canada was the big event in her life – an event which had far greater weight than the fact of her gender. Wilson has sustained a perpetual sense of herself as a multiple immigrant, first grafting herself onto the Scottish root stock of her new country, *then repeatedly transplanting herself into what had been traditionally male preserves and finding new ways to flourish.*"[6] As this passage suggests, Anderson merges Wilson's identity as a woman pioneer in law *within* her immigrant status, an interesting variation on the concept of "silences" that Conway identifies as typical of the life stories of pioneer women professionals.

In addition, this merging of gender and immigrant identities resonates with Ursula Franklin's explanation for the failure to acknowledge gender on the part of (some) women in the professions. Significantly, Franklin adopts an immigration metaphor to describe why women who first entered professions so often expressed no interest in challenging gender bias. As she explains, just as immigrants are loath to criticize the government that permitted their entry, so women pioneers in the professions cannot be expected to criticize their new milieu: instead, they "seek conformity in language and habit, absorb the new culture, and defend the new system."[7] Given this, the silences in Wilson's story suggest a need for further probing. Certainly, because Wilson was one of a small minority of women lawyers in Ontario during the 1960s,[8] her gender was always noticeable; as she herself remembered many years later, whenever she entered the Osler, Hoskin & Harcourt boardroom for consultations with corporate clients, "[t]here was no question that their faces fell."[9] As a result, Wilson was *always* negotiating the gender factor, even as she adopted a variety of strategies to ignore it, circumvent it, or overcome it. As her 1993 contribution to the Canadian Bar Association (CBA) Task Force on Gender Equality in the Legal Profession later revealed, moreover, it seems likely that she had a keen sense of the impact of the gendered "cultural script" on women lawyers in Canada, in spite of her earlier silences.[10]

In reflecting on the gender factor in Wilson's life, I focus on three of her early decisions, "hard cases" with which I regularly grapple in my teaching. In examining them, I want to speculate about how they may be related to Wilson's ideas about gender and law, and whether her experiences as a pioneer woman in law may be reflected in her responses to the issues in these cases. Two of the decisions come from the Ontario Court of Appeal: *Re Rynard* involved the interpretation of a will;[11] *Becker v. Pettkus* (later upheld by the Supreme Court of Canada) dealt with a woman's claim to share in accumulated property at the end of a cohabiting relationship.[12] The third case is the *Pelech* trilogy in the Supreme Court of Canada, which involved the role of the Court in reviewing applications for variation of separation agreements that had been privately negotiated by the parties.[13] *Re Rynard* is essentially a property case, *Becker v. Pettkus* concerns family property, and the *Pelech* trilogy is a family law decision. Since all three decisions attracted academic criticism, they remain difficult to teach; but they also permit some interesting analyses of relationships between law and gender. In this context, I want to speculate about *how* Wilson's experiences as a pioneer woman in law may have shaped her perspectives on gender issues, albeit in a context of silences.[14]

Property Law: Being a Woman and a "Lawyer's Lawyer"

> You will find that the study of law is quite different from any other subject you've taken on ... You have to reason it through and make it part of your own intellectual experience ... You can plumb the depths of your intellectual capacities and achieve the joy and satisfaction in knowing that you've really got it ... It's more than just a subject; *it's a growing experience.*
>
> – Bertha Wilson, 1990

Anderson's biography of Wilson reveals that, from the beginning, she thrived on the intellectual challenges presented to students at Dalhousie Law School. She was one of six women in a class of fifty-eight when she graduated in 1957, receiving the Smith Shield for her moot court performance, a prize, and a scholarship to do graduate work at Harvard in property law and nuisance. However, Dean Read discouraged Wilson from accepting the Harvard scholarship, advising her that "[t]here will never be women academics teaching in law schools, not in your day."[15] She articled in Halifax with F.W. Bissett, Q.C., a sole practitioner who worked almost exclusively in low-end divorce law and criminal work, including prostitution cases; and she was called to the bar in Nova Scotia in 1958. Almost immediately, as a result of her husband's new career opportunity, the Wilsons moved to Toronto. After consulting the telephone book for Toronto law firms, Wilson obtained an interview and then an articling position at the Osler firm on the clear understanding that her services would terminate when she was called to the bar in Ontario.[16]

However, Wilson's research and organizational skills, which became apparent early on, resulted in the firm's invitation to remain at Osler, where she eventually created its highly regarded research department and her defining role as "the in-house lawyer's lawyer."[17] In this role, Wilson provided advice to other lawyers at the firm on a wide range of client files, created a meticulous database of precedents and legal opinions, and assisted in developing the litigation arguments in cases such as *Leitch Gold Mines v. Texas Gulf Sulphur.*[18] In addition, however, she gradually developed a wills and estates practice, and became involved in establishing a section on charities for the CBA (Ontario) as well as a magazine, the *Philanthropist.*[19] In this practice, Anderson reported, Wilson's gender was advantageous in assisting the wives of corporate executives with the preparation of wills, some of whom preferred to discuss their wishes with a woman. In addition, Anderson asserted that it was Wilson who "recognized that because husbands and wives do not necessarily have the same testamentary intentions, their will instructions should therefore be taken separately."[20]

A few years after her 1975 appointment to the Ontario Court of Appeal, Justice Wilson rendered the decision in *Re Rynard,*[21] an application to interpret the will of Margaret Rynard; it was also about the interpretation of a principle of property law, the rule in *Shelley's Case* (1581).[22] This is a hard case to teach, not only because of its highly technical legal principles, but also because it is difficult to explain why a hoary old principle such as the rule in *Shelley's Case* remains part of Ontario law in the twenty-first century. In reflecting on this case, I want to explore how Wilson's research acumen, her expertise concerning the "private" law of wills and estates, and her attention to the ethical context of women's will making may all be manifest in her approach to the issues in *Re Rynard.*

Re Rynard was an appeal from a decision of Justice Walsh concerning the interpretation of Margaret Rynard's will. When Rynard died in 1934, she left her modest estate, mainly a farm, to her husband and thereafter to her two sons. After her husband's death in 1960, her sons (who were also executors of the estate) applied for a motion for construction of the will, focusing particularly on clauses 3, 4, and 5. Clause 3 of the will provided a life estate in the farm to her son Kennedy Rynard, subject to the payment of two annuities; clause 4 stated, *inter alia,* that the "balance shall go to the heirs of my son Kennedy." Taken together, these two clauses created the classic language that attracts *Shelley's Case:* where A takes an estate of freehold, and in the same grant, an estate is limited to "A's heirs" in fee, the words "to the heirs" are words of limitation, and not words of purchase.[23] As a result, the application of the rule in *Shelley's Case* and the doctrine of merger in relation to clauses 3 and 4 meant that Kennedy Rynard received the estate in fee simple; and his heirs received nothing. As Justice Wilson noted, "[T]his language was perfectly intelligible to conveyancers in the days of Edward II!"[24]

Yet, the will contained a further challenge: clause 5 declared that its conditions should prevail, notwithstanding anything to the contrary in the will. This clause carefully limited Kennedy's ability to sell or mortgage his interest, stating that the testatrix wished to ensure that he had a means of livelihood but to prevent the farm being seized or attached by creditors. The clause further stated that, if Kennedy were to contravene these conditions, his interest would terminate, and the estate would pass to his brother, Dr. Bernard Rynard. The interpretation of clause 5 created a major challenge, however, because the rule in *Shelley's Case* is a rule of law, not a rule of construction, and thus applies without regard to the intention of a testator; indeed, as counsel for Kennedy stated, "It may, and frequently does, fly in the face of the testator's intention."[25] Thus, in spite of Margaret Rynard's clear instructions in clause 5, Kennedy's counsel asserted that the clause could not prevent the application of *Shelley's Case,* thereby resulting in a fee simple for Kennedy and nothing for the heirs.

In assessing this argument, Justice Wilson referred to Lord Davey's analysis of the rule in *Van Grutten v. Foxwell,* an 1897 House of Lords decision,[26] and concluded that application of the rule in *Shelley's Case* can occur only after analyzing a threshold issue of construction: that is, in using the words "to his heirs," did the testator intend to refer to the "whole line of inheritable issue of the tenant for life" or, by contrast, "simply the children or next of kin of the tenant for life"? In the former instance, the rule would apply, and Kennedy would receive a fee simple; in the latter case, however, since the rule would not apply, Kennedy would receive only a life estate.[27] Thus, Justice Wilson reviewed the trial judge's conclusion that s. 31 of the *Wills Act* defined how the word "heirs" should be interpreted so as to avoid the application of *Shelley's Case* to Margaret Rynard's will. Rejecting this interpretation, she held that there was no suggestion that the purpose of s. 31 was to repeal, either expressly or impliedly, the rule in *Shelley's Case.* In reaching this conclusion, she carefully reviewed the history of primogeniture in English law, a number of nineteenth-century cases interpreting the word "heirs," and statutory developments in the United Kingdom relating to the rule.[28] Then, proceeding to clause 5, Justice Wilson concluded that Kennedy received only a determinable fee simple (rather than a fee simple absolute),[29] emphasizing Margaret Rynard's clear intention that Kennedy's estate might determine before his death on the occurrence of specified events:

> I do not believe that the testatrix, when she used the word "heirs" in cl. 4, could have intended to refer to the whole line of inheritable issue of Kennedy when in the next clause she went on to specify the circumstances in which he would be deprived of his life estate and it would pass to his brother. There is no doubt about the fact that she intended her son Kennedy's life estate to be determinable [according to the concluding sentence of clause 5]. And, in my view, by giving cl. 5 paramountcy over cl. 4, she succeeded in doing so.[30]

Thus, following examination of several cases concerning the application of *Shelley's Case* to determinable estates, Justice Wilson held that Kennedy Rynard's interest was a determinable life estate, to which the rule in *Shelley's Case* did not apply. As a result, Kennedy received only a life estate, determinable in accordance with clause 5, with a fee simple remainder to his heirs. Technically, this conclusion meant that the reference to "heirs" in the will constituted words of purchase, not words of limitation.[31]

Clearly, the reasoning in this case required an ability to apply highly technical (and utterly antiquated) principles of estates law, as well as an understanding of the complicated doctrinal history of common law property principles. As a result, *Re Rynard* usefully demonstrates for students how legal language must always be interpreted within doctrinal complexity; the bottom-line message is that real perils are attached to "do it yourself" wills! Yet, there are more fundamental issues too. For example, the rule in *Shelley's Case* requires some understanding of the historical context of feudalism and of how judicial decisions about competing interests in this historical context have shaped modern principles of property law. Indeed, since some explanations for *Shelley's Case* emphasize its significance in promoting dominant economic interests in feudal society, *Re Rynard* offers an opportunity to examine critiques concerning the use of current property law principles to perpetuate such interests.[32]

More significantly, since there was no case precisely on point,[33] Justice Wilson's conclusion that repeal of *Shelley's Case* was a matter for the legislature has been criticized as a lost opportunity for judicial repeal.[34] Nonetheless, it is important to note that Justice Wilson's decision, with all of the technicalities of ancient principles, precisely implements the wishes of the testatrix, Margaret Rynard; as noted, Rynard had made great efforts to enable her son Kennedy to have the farm as a means of support, while also ensuring that he could not destroy its intended purpose. From the perspective of feminist theory, Justice Wilson's decision arguably accorded agency to Margaret Rynard in relation to her intentions regarding her property and her children's well-being.[35] By contrast, application of the rule in *Shelley's Case* would have undermined Margaret Rynard's efforts entirely, granting Kennedy Rynard an unfettered fee simple estate, which, in accordance with her fears, he might well have later lost.

More importantly, though judicial repeal of the rule in this case would also have accomplished Margaret Rynard's objectives, *a decision that the rule was no longer valid would not have accorded the same kind of recognition to* her *wishes.* Clearly, this suggestion is highly speculative on my part, although it gains some credibility in the context of Wilson's experience in practice, not only because the legal reasoning reveals the expertise of a fine "lawyer's lawyer," but also in relation to her commitment in legal practice to ensuring that women were able to make wills that fully reflected their own individual wishes. Indeed, I sometimes speculate that Justice Wilson wanted, perhaps unconsciously, to promote the carefully considered intentions of Margaret Rynard; thus, in the face of a rule that denied significance to (anyone's) intention, she carved an exception, in the absence of direct precedent, out of the "threshold issue of construction" to implement Margaret Rynard's wishes, precisely and firmly. In this context, *Re Rynard* seems to confirm Conway's suggestion that we need to pay attention to silences in the lives of women who first gain entry to male professions and to explore how they may "[break] the internalized code a culture supplies about how [a woman's] life should be experienced."[36]

Families and Property: Private Lives and Public Policy

> [It is true] that in North America the family has been the location of much of women's subordination. For instance, much of women's experience of inequality, degradation and subjugation has been perpetrated by the institution of the family and by their loved ones behind closed doors.
>
> – Bertha Wilson, 1991

Wilson made these comments in a 1991 speech about the constitutional protection of privacy, which she delivered in Hong Kong. In it, she explored connections between constitutional guarantees of equality and women's family roles; she made a number of other similar presentations on family law issues during her career.[37] Perhaps her interest in family law arose because her mid-1970s appointment to the Ontario Court of Appeal coincided with a period of public discussion and legislative hearings about reforms concerning family property and spousal support in Ontario, which followed the enactment of the new federal *Divorce Act* in 1970. As the new *Family Law*

Reform Act of 1978 stated, title to property at marriage breakdown was subject to a division of "family assets"; in this way, marriage breakdown triggered the possibility of changes in title to property owned by each of the spouses.[38] According to Anderson, "Wilson believed that the new laws reflected a profound shift in social consensus and accordingly that the courts had a duty to enforce this duly authorized legislation."[39] Indeed, a number of her family law decisions in the Court of Appeal and in the Supreme Court of Canada reveal her efforts to grapple with these complex issues of private rights and public policy. And even though Justice Wilson was increasingly involved in *Canadian Charter of Rights and Freedoms* decisions, cases that engaged her in legal struggles "as large as life itself,"[40] I want to explore how some of these non-*Charter* family law decisions reveal, sometimes through their silences, how gender and law intersected in Wilson's life and work.

Justice Wilson's decision for a unanimous Court of Appeal in *Becker v. Pettkus* clearly reflects an understanding of the "profound shift in social consensus" introduced by the provincial family law statutes in the late 1970s.[41] This decision confirmed an equitable remedy for women in cohabiting relationships, even though the recently enacted provincial legislation clearly applied *only* to married couples. Because this case was appealed to the Supreme Court of Canada, which upheld Wilson's decision, it has become well known for establishing the availability of the constructive trust to remedy unjust enrichment in cohabiting relationships.[42] Nonetheless, it was Justice Wilson's decision in the Ontario Court of Appeal (relying on the 1975 dissenting opinion of Justice Laskin in *Murdoch v. Murdoch* in the Supreme Court[43] and the Court's later decision in *Rathwell v. Rathwell,*[44] produced just a few months before Justice Wilson's decision in *Becker v. Pettkus*) that first recognized cohabitees' entitlement to an equitable share of accumulated property at the end of a cohabiting relationship: "This may be an opportune moment to mention that, as far as the application of the law under review is concerned, nothing, in my opinion, hinges on the fact that the appellant and respondent were not legally married. I would respectfully adopt the approach taken by Lord Denning, MR [in *Cooke v. Head* and *Eves v. Eves*] to the effect that the principles of resulting and constructive trust are equally applicable to common law spouses."[45] Undoubtedly, Justice Wilson's expertise concerning principles of equity grounded her ability to design a creative solution in this case, but it is possible that some facts regarding Rosa Becker also resonated with her, shaping the nature of her judicial solution.

Rosa Becker and Lothar Pettkus, both immigrants to Canada in the early 1950s, formed a relationship in Montreal and pooled their financial resources. Since Becker paid most of their expenses for several years, Pettkus was able to save his earnings to purchase a farm south of Montreal some years later. Significantly, the title to both this property and a second farm in eastern Ontario was in Pettkus' name alone. Although Becker apparently raised the possibility of marriage while they were still living in Montreal, Pettkus responded that he wanted to wait until they were better acquainted. Thus, after moving to these successive farm properties, the couple worked together for nearly twenty years, developing successful beekeeping operations and related activities. As the trial transcripts later indicated, Becker made substantial contributions of both funds and labour; indeed, as Anderson reported, Pettkus agreed in his evidence at trial that "the business would not have become so prosperous if she had not contributed her labour for nothing."[46] Nonetheless, the trial judge concluded that Becker's financial support prior to the purchase of the first property was in the nature of "risk capital invested in the hope of seducing the younger defendant into marriage," and he discounted her labour and financial contributions on the farm properties.[47]

On appeal to the Ontario Court of Appeal, Justice Wilson concluded that the trial judge had "grossly underestimated" the value of Becker's contributions.[48] However, the choice of an appropriate remedy required careful consideration, having regard to the decisions of the Supreme Court of Canada in *Murdoch* and *Rathwell*.[49] Justice Wilson would have been well aware that, when a majority of the Court had denied Irene Murdoch a share in the property held in her husband's name at the end of their twenty-five-year marriage, stating that her work was merely the "work done by any ranch wife,"[50] the decision had been greeted with public outrage. As a result, *Murdoch* became the catalyst for legislative schemes concerning spousal property entitlement at marriage breakdown in all common law provinces in Canada during the late 1970s.[51] In early 1978, the Supreme Court of Canada revisited the issue in *Rathwell*, and several judges granted Mrs. Rathwell's claim on the basis of the constructive trust remedy identified in the dissenting opinion in *Murdoch*.[52] In applying these principles to Rosa Becker, Justice Wilson held that Becker's contributions of financial support and labour for almost twenty years constituted unjust enrichment, warranting the remedy of constructive trust. Thus, stating that "equality is equity," she held that Becker was entitled to a beneficial one-half interest in the property held in Pettkus' name; her decision was substantially upheld in the appeal to the Supreme Court of Canada in 1980.[53]

Both the use of principles of unjust enrichment and the remedy of constructive trust in the family law context have attracted ongoing academic criticism,[54] even though Canadian jurisprudence concerning family property has also been lauded by family law scholars in other common law jurisdictions.[55] In thinking about this case in relation to gender issues and Wilson, however, I conclude that *Becker v. Pettkus* may represent more than an innovative use of the principles of equity to address gender inequality in spousal relationships. I think it possible that Rosa Becker's status as a hard-working woman who was also an immigrant may have been significant for Wilson too. In a 1985 interview with *Saturday Night*, Wilson explained that she firmly resisted calls to promote feminist views, particularly because they would render her biased and make her "totally useless as a judge." More specifically, however, the article noted an "edge in [Wilson's] voice when it comes to well-heeled militants at the wheels of BMWs." Wilson remarked, "I do think the [feminist] movement has focused too much on the middle class and that the women who *really have problems nowadays* – waitresses, shopgirls, factory workers – tend to get short-changed. Nor do I believe in putting down men. I think both sexes are complementary, and one of the things that's most exciting is to see men and women working out new roles for themselves, in a family context."[56] In the context of *Becker v. Pettkus,* it is not hard to imagine that Justice Wilson regarded Rosa Becker as one of the women "who *really have problems nowadays*"; as a working-class immigrant woman with few skills, Becker had obviously laboured very hard to become financially established, relying on a partnership with Pettkus, both as family and as economic security. In responding to Becker's plight with a creative legal solution, Justice Wilson was identifying *her* commitment to gender equality for the most needy women in Canadian society. In doing so, she engaged in judicial reform in this case, even though the legislature had expressly declined to extend family property principles to cohabitees. Arguably, this was a case in which the facts of Rosa Becker's life story as an immigrant woman motivated Wilson to adopt equity to achieve justice.

Thus, just as her decision in *Re Rynard* promoted Margaret Rynard's intentions with respect to her estate, so Justice Wilson's decision in *Becker v. Pettkus* ensured that Rosa Becker's expectations with respect to her contributions of labour and funds to family property were realized. At the same time, the gender issues were much more apparent in *Becker v. Pettkus,* so that it is tempting to conclude that Wilson's commitment to gender had become more overt during the years between *Rynard* and *Becker v. Pettkus*. Any such claim, however, must take account of her judgment a few years after Becker's case in the Supreme Court of Canada's *Pelech* trilogy, concerning the spousal support provisions of the 1968 *Divorce Act.*[57] In this case, involving three women in varying degrees of financial destitution, Justice Wilson's reasoning failed to ameliorate their circumstances when she rejected applications to change the terms of the private agreements they had earlier negotiated with their former spouses; in each case, the women had abandoned any future entitlement to spousal support in their agreements. Adopting principles that promoted autonomy and finality for spouses at the end of a relationship, Justice Wilson narrowly defined the circumstances in which judicial intervention could vary the terms of private agreements in the interests of fairness.[58]

The facts of these cases were not in dispute. In *Pelech v. Pelech,* on appeal from British Columbia, the spouses had been married for fifteen years and had two children.[59] Mr. Pelech ran a business, and Mrs. Pelech worked as a bookkeeper and receptionist. At separation, both obtained legal advice and eventually signed an agreement; under its terms, Mrs. Pelech received a lump sum of spousal support, payable over thirteen months, in full satisfaction of her entitlement. At the time of the agreement, she was thirty-seven years old. Unfortunately, following the divorce, her physical and mental state deteriorated, and she was unable to work, so she began to use her divorce settlement to support her financial needs; by 1982, this fund was depleted, and she applied for welfare. In the meantime, Mr. Pelech's business had continued to prosper, and his net worth had grown from $128,000 at the time of the agreement to $1.8 million fifteen years later in the early 1980s. Thus, when Mrs. Pelech applied to vary the terms of the separation agreement, the trial judge ordered Mr. Pelech to pay her $2,000 per month, to avoid having her become a charge on the "public purse." The British Columbia Court of Appeal reversed the trial decision, confirming that the parties were bound by their agreement. As noted, the Supreme Court of Canada upheld the decision of the appellate court in British Columbia; thus, Mrs. Pelech remained a welfare recipient.

In *Richardson v. Richardson,* the parties separated in 1979 after twelve years of marriage.[60] Mr. Richardson was a police officer in Ottawa, and his wife had worked as a clerk-typist for the federal government. She stopped work after the birth of their second child. Following their separation, she moved to North Bay to live with her parents and to look for work; by that date, she was forty-six years old. Each parent obtained custody of one child, and they reached a settlement at a pre-trial conference, which provided that Mr. Richardson would pay spousal support for a year. The spouses also agreed that he would assume their debts; in return, she released her equity in the matrimonial home (the debts and her equity in the home were approximately equal). When Mrs. Richardson was unable to find employment and was receiving welfare, she applied for a variation of the agreement; the trial judge imposed a further obligation of spousal support on Mr. Richardson, but the Ontario Court of Appeal overturned this decision. The appellate court's decision was upheld by Justice Wilson's decision in the Supreme Court of Canada, although Justice La Forest dissented from the majority decision.[61]

The *Pelech* trilogy received significant academic criticism, particularly for its failure to take account of gender inequalities in family law bargaining and for its focus on formal rather than substantive equality in spousal relationships. For example, the trilogy assumed that men and women at the end of spousal relationships were equally able to sustain themselves financially and that their abilities to negotiate separation agreements were also equal: a classic case of formal, rather than substantive, equality. As the critics noted, assumptions about equality of bargaining power in the negotiation of a separation agreement may preclude an examination of the substantive processes of contract negotiation between former spouses.[62] In addition, formal equality fails to recognize systemic disadvantages, including family structures and workplace arrangements, which may prevent one parent (usually the mother) from achieving autonomy and financial independence at the end of a marriage. Specifically, by contrast with men, women may have fewer educational qualifications or skills and less workplace experience because of their child-bearing and child-caring responsibilities.[63] As a result, the *Pelech* trilogy creates challenges for family law teachers: what is the rationale for Justice Wilson's emphasis on formal gender equality in the trilogy, by contrast with her use of equity in *Becker v. Pettkus*?

In my view, the explanation for these differing approaches is quite complex. Hearkening back to her comments about the "profound shift in social consensus" introduced by the new provincial family law regimes of the late 1970s, Justice Wilson accepted a need to permit spousal relationships and their obligations to end. In addition, she accepted that the 1968 *Divorce Act* rendered the decision to end a relationship, subject to a few overriding considerations, as one for spouses to make and for the state to respect; as she said, "[The spouses] made the decision to marry and they made the decision to terminate their marriage. Their decisions should be respected."[64] Indeed, a few years earlier, Wilson had analyzed in detail the implications of the new family law reforms, particularly in relation to property, concluding that the state had delegated responsibility to spouses "to regulate by means of a previous consensual arrangement" the financial consequences of their decision to separate.[65] According to Wilson, moreover, this legislative trend to less state intervention in divorce represented "legislative recognition, in line with prevailing social attitudes, that there should be greater individual autonomy" at divorce.[66]

Yet, though such views undoubtedly influenced Justice Wilson's emphasis on individual autonomy in the trilogy decisions, it is crucial to take account of her belief in *the state's corresponding duty to support dependent family members*. Indeed, it is arguable that her reasoning in the trilogy was firmly grounded in a belief in another "shift in social consensus" of the late 1970s: one in which responsibility for dependent family members swung from the "former family" to "the state." As early as 1983, in one of her first Supreme Court of Canada cases, Justice Wilson had joined the dissenting judgment of Justice Lamer on this issue, upholding the need for finality and a "clean break" for spouses at marriage breakdown, after the enactment of the 1968 *Act:*

> [T]he evolution of society requires that one more step be taken in favour of the final emancipation of former spouses. To me, aside from rare exceptions the ability to work leads to "the end of the divorce" and the beginning of truly single status for each of the former spouses. I also consider that the "ability" to work should be determined intrinsically and should not in any way be determined in light of factors extrinsic to the individual, such as the work force and the economic situation ... *A divorced spouse who is*

> *"employable" but unemployed is in the same position as other citizens, men or women, who are unemployed. The problem is a social one and it is therefore the responsibility of the government rather than the former husband.* Once the spouse has been retrained, I do not see why the fact of having been married should give the now single individual any special status by comparison with any other unemployed single person.[67]

Perhaps because this 1983 decision revealed a split between the majority and dissenting views, provincial appellate courts then tended to develop different approaches to the issue. Indeed, when Wilson contributed a paper on issues about variation of support orders to a family law conference in 1983, she clearly outlined the policy issues facing courts with respect to whether families or the state should assume primary responsibility for financial dependence at marriage breakdown. After reviewing a number of lower court decisions that reached quite diverse conclusions on this issue, she concluded that judges were "groping for the right principles and the right policies."[68] Just a few years later, her views crystallized in the *Pelech* trilogy in the Supreme Court of Canada.

The trilogy decision examined how some appellate courts in Canada respected and fully enforced the finality of private agreements, whereas others routinely reviewed such agreements and intervened whenever it seemed necessary to achieve fairness; in addition, the decision identified a number of intermediate approaches.[69] However, *in keeping with her view that societal, rather than familial, support was appropriate for dependency at marriage breakdown,* Justice Wilson held that only in limited circumstances should courts review privately negotiated family agreements, clearly siding with the proponents of "finality" rather than those advocating "fairness":

> Absent some causal connection between the changed circumstances and the marriage, it seems to me that parties who have declared their relationship at an end should be taken at their word ... They should thereafter be free to make new lives for themselves without an ongoing, contingent liability for future misfortunes which may befall the other ... Accordingly, where an applicant seeking maintenance or an increase in the existing level of maintenance establishes that he or she has suffered a radical change in circumstances flowing from an economic pattern of dependency engendered by the marriage, the court may exercise its relieving power. Otherwise, the obligation to support the former spouse should be, as in the case of any other citizen, *the communal responsibility of the state.*[70]

As is evident, Justice Wilson's judgment assumes that individual dependency will be alleviated by "the communal responsibility of the state." Although her assumption was not unreasonable, the *Pelech* trilogy coincided with governmental policies in the late 1980s that substantially cut social programs, thus eliminating much of the social safety net that was needed to realize her goal in practice. As a result, many former spouses (mainly women) plunged into poverty, unable to become self-sufficient post-separation: the phenomenon of the "feminization of poverty."[71] Later Supreme Court decisions, after Justice Wilson had resigned from the Court, have continued to (re)define the responsibilities of former spouses for the financial well-being of dependent family members[72] and also to (re)define the validity of principles of autonomy and finality in family law bargaining.[73] Yet, as Justice Wilson had suggested more than two decades earlier in a conference paper, it is arguable that, even now, "[w]e are [still] groping for the right principles and the right policies."[74] Thus, from Wilson's perspective, the *Pelech* trilogy may have appeared to be less about equality in spousal relationships and more about the possibility of implementing a collective societal responsibility for dependent family members – as part of a shifting consensus about the role of the state at separation or divorce. In this context, governmental policies that created the "post-separation family," one in which *spousal relationships* end, but all their *obligations* continue, eventually succeeded in undermining the trilogy philosophy endorsed by Justice Wilson.

Rethinking the Silences in Justice Wilson's Life Script

> Reality has changed. Indeed, it is because reality has changed that contemporary feminism has made such an impact. [The 1960s and 1970s constituted] a period of wide-spread social ferment characterized by a tremendous sensitivity to discrimination and injustice in all its forms. It was an environment in which the concept of sexual equality took root and flourished.
>
> – Bertha Wilson, "Law in Society: The Principle of Sexual Equality"

Justice Wilson made these comments at a 1983 symposium in Winnipeg; in her presentation, she reviewed the reports of the Royal Commission on the Status of Women (1970) and the Canadian Advisory Council on the Status of Women (established in 1973).[75] As in her 1990 Osgoode Hall Law School lecture,[76] there is evidence in her Winnipeg presentation of her support for gender equality in law and of her recognition of the impact of feminism in reforming law in women's interests. In this context, moreover, Wilson appears supportive of both women's equality and feminism. More significantly, her commitment to gender equality as a matter of professionalism was plainly evident in her later work with the CBA task force report.[77] Thus, her support for gender equality issues was clearly expressed at a number of different times, both while she was a judge and afterward. In addition, as my reading of these three hard cases reveals, Wilson's ideas continued to evolve, not necessarily in a linear fashion. In the end, it is possible that her commitment to gender equality was part of a larger, more idealist conception of "humanity" (ungendered), a view that she suggested in her lecture at Osgoode: "If women lawyers and women judges through their differing perspectives on life can bring a new humanity to bear on the decision-making process, perhaps they *will* make a difference. Perhaps they will succeed in infusing the law with an understanding of what it means to be fully human."[78] In this context, both men and women have obligations to strive to make law fully human: "law as large as life." However, if we read Wilson's life story in relation to the problems she encountered as a woman pioneer in law, some silences remain regarding these ideals; undoubtedly, she must often have faced frustration and disappointment, although, to her credit, she did not abandon the ideals. In reflecting on this conundrum, I think that we may not fully appreciate "Wilson the woman" so long as we focus mainly on the legal reasoning of "Wilson the judge"; and we need to explore her non-*Charter* decisions more carefully as well. Although Justice Wilson described her view of "law as large as life,"[79] and the Anderson biography clearly demonstrates how her legal decisions often reflected this commitment, Wilson the woman experienced at least some discontinuity with the ideals she professed, both as a lawyer and as a judge. How should we understand the silences in her life story?

This is a large question, and an important one. In my view, a key factor was her self-identified role as a lifelong "student of the law," a role she recommended to new lawyers in her remarks to the 1991 call to the bar ceremony in Toronto: "As the volume of fresh information constantly increases [lawyers] continue to spend ever longer hours just to keep up to date, and *the discipline of regular study* ... that we have acquired ... at Law School ... will later stand us in good stead. [F]or the responsible practitioner of the future wide reading and study outside the narrow perimeter of the law is vital."[80] As Anderson's biography attests, Wilson practised this advice diligently throughout her career; she remained a student of the law, committed to hard work, dedicated to research, and receptive to new ideas and new ways of thinking. Particularly as she moved from the research department at Osler to the judiciary, and especially to the Supreme Court of Canada, Wilson increasingly came into contact with people and ideas outside the normal boundaries of private practice in a large Toronto law firm and beyond the constraints of private litigation. In such a context, her curiosity about new perspectives and her willingness to engage with difficult challenges encouraged her to engage in a "work in progress," particularly as a member of the judiciary.

In my assessment, moreover, we also need to consider how Wilson worked, for most of her career, in a male legal world, one in which she claimed that she always felt a need to prove herself, over and over again.[81] In such a context, as Carrie Menkel-Meadow suggests in relation to other early women in law, Wilson's survival, as well as her success, may have depended on her ability to "[act] like men" – or at least on paying scant attention to gender.[82] Thus, even though she may have held strong personal views about gender equality, her own experiences were not always congruent with her philosophy, and she may not have had many opportunities to work with women peers and colleagues. In this context, of course, there are important silences about her judicial appointments: how did a woman, self-described as shy, mainly devoted to legal research, lacking much involvement with clients, and with almost no litigation experience, achieve appointment to the Ontario Court of Appeal and then to the Supreme Court of Canada? Even if, as Carol Sanger argues, women were entitled to enjoy success in the public sphere "only if fame was bestowed upon them, *not if they seized and relished it themselves,*"[83] it seems that Wilson's judicial appointments, like the soprano's chance meeting with the tenor in Conway's analysis, probably did not "just happen." Indeed, there are some important silences about the significance of male lawyers, well-connected members of the "old boys' club" at Osler and elsewhere, who probably championed Wilson's appointment to the Court of Appeal and then to the Supreme Court of Canada.[84]

Thus, as one reflects on the relationship between gender and law in the life story of Bertha Wilson, these silences remain both curious and crucial to understanding her as a pioneer woman lawyer and judge. As Gerda Lerner argued several decades ago, we need to understand how such women "function[ed] in [a] male-defined world *on their own terms.*"[85]

Acknowledgments

Professor Mossman acknowledges with thanks the excellent research assistance provided by Catherine Hayhow, class of 2008, Osgoode Hall Law School, and helpful comments from Beatrice Tice, Chief Law Librarian, University of Toronto Faculty of Law.

Notes

1 Jill Ker Conway, *When Memory Speaks: Reflections on Autobiography* (New York: Alfred A. Knopf, 1998) at 7.

2 *Ibid.* at 15-16 [emphasis added].

3 *Ibid.* at 17.

4 There are several examples in Ellen Anderson, *Judging Bertha Wilson: Law as Large as Life* (Toronto: University of Toronto Press for the Osgoode Society for Canadian Legal History, 2001), although Anderson is careful not to ascribe these problems to Wilson's gender: in relation to Wilson's time at the law firm of Osler, Hoskin, & Harcourt, see 59-65 and 70-71; for the Ontario Court of Appeal, see 87-88; and for the Supreme Court of Canada, see 127. Moreover, according to Anderson, "Wilson was no Pollyanna. She was scrupulously fair in warning women law students what to expect in their future careers; 'I really did believe and used to say to the women ... all your life as a woman you are proving yourself, you are

proving yourself again, every fresh group, every advancement that you get, proving yourself again, that you can do it. *And you get tired of it.'"* *Ibid.* at 200 [emphasis added].

5 *Ibid.* at 197.

6 *Ibid.* at 135 [emphasis added]. (In addition, Anderson noted that Wilson was not just the first woman but also the first immigrant of working-class parents appointed to the Supreme Court of Canada.

7 Ursula Franklin, "Will Women Change Technology or Will Technology Change Women?" reprinted in Ursula M. Franklin, *The Ursula Franklin Reader: Pacifism as a Map* (Toronto: Between the Lines, 2006) 243 at 249.

8 Wilson was called to the bar in Ontario on 25 June 1959, as "Bertha Wernham, Mrs. Wilson," and the list of women admittees shows her as number 203; however, many women (particularly married women) did not practise law, so the numbers in active practice were still quite small.

9 Quoted in "Wilson to Lead Status of Women Probe" *London Free Press* (20 August 1991).

10 Canadian Bar Association Task Force on Gender Equality in the Legal Profession, *Touchstones for Change: Equality, Diversity and Accountability* (Ottawa: Canadian Bar Association, 1993) [*Touchstones*].

11 *Re Rynard* (1980), 31 O.R. (2d) 257 [*Re Rynard*].

12 *Becker v. Pettkus* (1978), 19 OR (2d) 105. The decision was later appealed and upheld in the Supreme Court of Canada: see *Becker v. Pettkus,* [1980] 2 S.C.R. 834 [*Becker*].

13 *Pelech v. Pelech,* [1987] 1 S.C.R. 801 [*Pelech*]; *Richardson v. Richardson,* [1987] 1 S.C.R. 857 [*Richardson*]; *Caron v. Caron,* [1987] 1 S.C.R. 892 [collectively *Pelech* trilogy].

14 Since this assessment makes some effort to link Bertha Wilson, the woman, with Justice Wilson, a member of the Ontario Court of Appeal and the Supreme Court of Canada, I generally refer to her as Wilson when I am discussing her as a woman in law and as Justice Wilson when I am examining her reasons for judgment in the cases.

15 Anderson, *supra* note 4 at 48. See also Christian Wiktor, ed., *Dalhousie Law School Register* (Halifax: Dalhousie Law School, 1983) at 39, 203.

16 Anderson, *supra* note 4 at 48-55.

17 *Ibid.* at 58.

18 *Ibid.* at 65-69: *Leitch Gold Mines v. Texas Gulf Sulphur* (1968), 1 O.R. 469 (Wilson worked with John Arnup on this litigation).

19 Anderson, *supra* note 4 at 62-63.

20 *Ibid.* at 59.

21 *Re Rynard, supra* note 11.

22 *Wolfe v. Shelley* (1581), 1 Co. Rep. 93b, 76 E.R. 206 (K.B.) [*Shelley's Case*]. The concepts applied in *Shelley's Case* derived from the fourteenth century and were closely connected to principles of feudalism.

23 *Re Rynard, supra* note 11 at 261-62. (Words of purchase identify the recipient of an interest, whereas words of limitation describe the estate conveyed.)

24 *Ibid.*

25 *Ibid.* at 260.

26 *Van Grutten v. Foxwell,* [1897] A.C. 658.

27 *Re Rynard, supra* note 11 at 261-62.

28 *Ibid.* at 262-63.

29 She also considered and rejected the application of the doctrine of repugnancy. See *ibid.* at 264-65.

30 *Ibid.* at 265.

31 *Ibid.*

32 For an excellent critique of *Re Rynard* in relation to the doctrinal principles of *Shelley's Case,* as well as a cogent argument that Justice Wilson should have judicially repealed the *Shelley's Case* rule in *Re Rynard,* see Bruce Ziff and M.M. Litman, "Shelley's Rule in a Modern Context: Clearing the 'Heir'" (1984) 34:2 U.T.L.J. 170. The authors also conducted a survey of Canadian lawyers specializing in estates practices, which indicated that even many legal specialists do not always recognize the technical language that attracts the rule.

33 As Justice Wilson stated, "*I have found no case on point* but the approach [in *Armstrong*] commends itself to me and compels me to the conclusion, applying ordinary principles of construction, that the testatrix has effectively limited Kennedy Rynard's interest to a determinable life estate. This being so, it is not open to the Court to apply the rule in *Shelley's Case* so as to convert his determinable life estate into a fee simple absolute" [emphasis added]. See *Re Rynard, supra* note 11 at 267; the case referred to is *Re Armstrong,* [1943] O.W.N. 43.

34 See Ziff and Litman, *supra* note 32.

35 For one example, see Anne Bottomley, "Self and Subjectivities: Languages of Claim in Property Law" in Anne Bottomley and Joanne Conaghan, eds., *Feminist Theory and Legal Strategy* (Oxford: Blackwell, 1993) 56. Significantly, in her 1990 lecture at Osgoode Hall Law School, Wilson suggested that the principles of property law were "so firmly entrenched and so fundamentally sound" that there was no real need for the perspective of women judges; by contrast, she argued that "some aspects of criminal law ... cry out for change." See Bertha Wilson, "Will Women Judges Really Make a Difference?" (1990) 28 Osgoode Hall L.J. 507 at 515.

36 Conway, *supra* note 1 at 17.

37 Bertha Wilson, "Women, the Family and the Constitutional Protection of Privacy" (Paper presented at the "Conference on Human Rights," Hong Kong, June 1991). See *e.g.* Bertha Wilson, "Children: The Casualties of a Failed Marriage" (1985) 19 U.B.C. L. Rev. 245; Bertha Wilson, "Family Violence" (1992) 5 C.J.W.L. 137.

38 The 1968 *Divorce Act* was subsequently repealed and replaced by the *Divorce Act, 1985,* R.S.C. 1985, c. 3, which became effective in 1986; in addition, the 1978 *Family Law Reform Act,* R.S.O. 1980, c. 152, in Ontario was later repealed and replaced by the *Family Law Act,* R.S.O. 1990, c. F. 3, in 1986. By the time the second wave of family reforms occurred, Justice Wilson was a member of the Supreme Court of Canada.

39 Anderson, *supra* note 4 at 101.

40 Looking back at her career shortly after her resignation from the Court, Wilson suggested, in a 1990 speech to law students at Queen's University, that the *Charter* had crystallized her long-standing views about law: "The Charter ... had put law into the kind of perspective in which I have always seen it – as large as life itself – not a narrow legalistic discipline in which inflexible rules are applied regardless of the justice of the result, but a set of values that we, as a civilized and cultured people, endorse as the right of all our citizens." Quoted in *ibid.* at 383-84. Justice Wilson also used this phrase at her retirement ceremony on 4 December 1990: see Bertha Wilson, "Retirement Ceremony of the Honourable Bertha Wilson, Supreme Court of Canada" (1991) 25:1 L. Soc'y Gaz. 6 at 18. Other speakers included Antonio Lamer C.J.; Hon. Kim Campbell, Minister of Justice; Hon. Howard Hampton, Attorney General of Ontario; Wayne Chapman, President, Canadian Bar Association; and James Spence, Treasurer, Law Society of Upper Canada. *Canadian Charter of Rights and Freedoms,* Part 1 of the *Constitution Act, 1982,* being Schedule B to the *Canada Act 1982* (U.K.), 1982, c. 11.

41 See *Becker, supra* note 12 (Ont. C.A.).

42 For a comprehensive overview, see Berend Hovius, "Property Division for Unmarried Cohabitees in the Common Law Provinces" (2003-4) 21 Can. Fam. L.Q. 175.

43 *Murdoch v. Murdoch,* [1975] 1 S.C.R. 423, 41 D.L.R. (3d) 367 [*Murdoch*].

44 *Rathwell v. Rathwell,* [1978] 2 S.C.R. 436 [*Rathwell*].

45 *Becker, supra* note 12 at 112 (Ont. C.A.).

46 Anderson, *supra* note 4 at 103; and see *Becker, supra* note 12 at 108-9 (Ont. C.A.).

47 Since Becker had left the relationship once before the final separation, taking cash and some beehives containing forty bees, the trial judge characterized this arrangement as a "settlement of their financial affairs," even though Becker had returned the hives, the bees, and about half the cash when she returned after this initial separation. *Becker, ibid.* at 105-8.

48 *Ibid.* at 108.

49 See *Murdoch, supra* note 43; *Rathwell, supra* note 44.

50 *Murdoch, supra* note 43 at 376 (D.L.R.).

51 See *e.g.* Law Reform Commission of Canada, *Studies on Family Property Law* (Ottawa: Information Canada, 1975).

52 See *Murdoch, supra* note 43; *Rathwell, supra* note 44.

53 *Becker, supra* note 12 (S.C.C.).

54 See *e.g.* Ontario Law Reform Commission, *Report on the Rights and Responsibilities of Cohabitants under the Family Law Act* (Toronto: Ontario Law Reform Commission, 1993); Mitchell McInnes, "Unjust Enrichment and Constructive Trusts in the Supreme Court of Canada" (1996-98) 24-25 Man. L.J. 513; John McCamus, "Restitution on Dissolution of Marital and Other Intimate Relationships: Constructive Trust or Quantum Meruit?" in J. Neyers, M. McInnes, and S. Pitel, eds., *Understanding Unjust Enrichment* (Oxford: Hart, 2004) 359.

55 See *e.g.* Simone Wong, "Constructive Trusts over the Family Home: Lessons to Be Learned from Other Commonwealth Jurisdictions" (1998) 18 L.S. 369; Marcia Neave, "Living Together: The Legal Effects of the Sexual Division of Labour in Four Common Law Countries" (1991) 17 Monash U.L. Rev. 14.

56 Sandra Gwyn, "Sense and Sensibility" *Saturday Night* (July 1985) 13 at 19 [emphasis added].

57 See *Pelech* trilogy, *supra* note 13. *Divorce Act*, R.S.C. 1970, c. D-8.

58 See also Bertha Wilson, "The Variation of Support Orders" in Rosalie Abella and Claire L'Heureux-Dubé, eds., *Family Law: Dimensions of Justice* (Toronto: Butterworths, 1983) 35.

59 See *Pelech, supra* note 13. See also M.J. Mossman, *Families and the Law in Canada* (Toronto: Emond-Montgomery, 2004) at 542.

60 See *Richardson, supra* note 13. See also Mossman, *supra* note 59.

61 *Richardson, supra* note 13 at 873. In particular, Justice La Forest emphasized the deterioration of Mrs. Richardson's work skills during the time she remained at home to care for her two children (at 886-87).

62 See Diana Majury, "Unconscionability in an Equality Context" (1991) 7 Can. Fam. L.Q. 123; Marcia Neave, "Resolving the Dilemma of Difference: A Critique of 'the Role of Private Ordering in Family Law'" (1994) 44 U.T.L.J. 97.

63 See *e.g.* Martha J. Bailey, "*Pelech, Caron* and *Richardson*" (1989-90) 3 C.J.W.L. 615; Carol J. Rogerson, "The Causal Connection Test in Spousal Support Law" (1989) 8 Can. J. Fam. L. 95; Nicholas Bala, "Domestic Contracts in Ontario and the Supreme Court Trilogy: A Deal Is a Deal" (1988) 13 Queen's L.J. 1. See also Susan Moller Okin, *Justice, Gender and the Family* (New York: Basic Books, 1989). In Wilson, "Women," *supra* note 37, Wilson acknowledged, without further comment, that the trilogy had attracted criticism.

64 See *Pelech, supra* note 13 at 851.

65 Bertha Wilson, "State Intervention in the Family" in Rosalie Abella and Melvin Rothman, eds., *Justice beyond Orwell* (Montreal: Les Éditions Yvon Blais, 1985) 353 at 360.

66 *Ibid.* at 358.

67 *Messier v. Delage*, [1983] 2 S.C.R. 401 at 426 [emphasis added].

68 Wilson, *supra* note 58 at 67.

69 Specifically, Justice Wilson reviewed the "private choice" approach, adopted by the Ontario Court of Appeal in *Farquar v. Farquar*, (1983) 35 R.F.L. (2d) 287; the use of the "court's overriding power to achieve fairness," adopted by the Manitoba Court of Appeal in *Newman v. Newman* (1980), 19 R.F.L. (2d) 122; and the "middle ground" approach used in *Webb v. Webb* (1984), 39 R.F.L. (2d) 113.

70 *Pelech, supra* note 13 at 851-52 [emphasis added].

71 See Rogerson, *supra* note 63; Brenda Cossman, "Family Feuds: Neo-liberal and Neo-conservative Visions of the Reprivatization Project" in Brenda Cossman and Judy Fudge, eds., *Privatization, Law and the Challenges to Feminism* (Toronto: University of Toronto Press, 2002) 169.

72 See *Moge v. Moge*, [1992] 3 S.C.R. 813; *Bracklow v. Bracklow*, [1999] 1 S.C.R. 420. See also Carol J. Rogerson, "Spousal Support after *Moge*" (1996-97) 14 Can. J. Fam. L. 289; Carol J. Rogerson, "Spousal Support Post-*Bracklow:* The Pendulum Swings Again?" (2001) 19 Can. Fam. L.Q. 185.

73 See *Miglin v. Miglin*, [2003] 1 S.C.R. 303; *Hartshorne v. Hartshorne* (2004), 236 D.L.R. (4th) 193 (S.C.C.).

74 Wilson, *supra* note 58 at 67.
75 Bertha Wilson, "Law in Society: The Principle of Sexual Equality" (1983) 13 Man. L.J. 221 at 222-23.
76 Wilson, *supra* note 35.
77 See *Touchstones, supra* note 10.
78 Wilson, *supra* note 35 at 522 [emphasis in original].
79 Anderson, *supra* note 4 at 45.
80 Bertha Wilson, "Remarks Given at the Call to the Bar Ceremony and on Being Awarded the Degree of Doctor of Laws" (1991) L. Soc'y Gaz. 102 at 104.
81 See Anderson, *supra* note 4.
82 Carrie Menkel-Meadow, "The Comparative Sociology of Women Lawyers: The 'Feminization' of the Legal Profession" (1986) 24 Osgoode Hall L.J. 897 at 899-900.
83 Carol Sanger, "Curriculum Vitae (Feminae): Biography and Early American Women Lawyers" (1994) 46 Stan. L. Rev. 1245 at 1257 [emphasis added].
84 See *e.g.* Beverly B. Cook, "Women Judges: A Preface to Their History" (1984) 14 Golden Gate U.L. Rev. 573 at 575.
85 Gerda Lerner, *The Majority Finds Its Past: Placing Women in History* (New York: Oxford University Press, 1979) at 148.

Contributors

Elizabeth Adjin-Tettey is an Associate Professor at the University of Victoria, Faculty of Law, where she has been teaching since 1998. She has also taught at the University of Windsor and Carleton University. Her main areas of expertise include torts and remedies. Professor Adjin-Tettey is also a strong advocate for social justice, and her current research interests include critical race and feminist analysis of law as well as insurance law. She is a co-author of *Remedies: The Law of Damages* (2008).

Beverley Baines is a Professor at Queen's University, Faculty of Law, where she teaches in the areas of public and constitutional law. Professor Baines is also the current Head of the Department of Women's Studies at Queen's University, and she teaches law and public policy in the School of Policy Studies. She recently published *The Gender of Constitutional Jurisprudence* with Ruth Rubio-Marin. Her research interests continue to focus on women's equality rights, most recently as they appear to conflict with religious freedom in contexts such as family arbitration in Ontario, the crime of polygamy, and Quebec's proposed new sex equality provision.

Marie-Claire Belleau is a Professor at Laval University, Faculty of Law. She has an LL.B. from Laval and a D.E.A. from Paris II. She pursued her graduate work at Harvard Law School, where she received both her LL.M. and S.J.D. Frequently invited to teach abroad (Spain, Belgium, France), she has wide-ranging interests and expertise in legal theory, family mediation, and judicial decision-making processes, and in particular, judicial dissent and judicial discretionary power. Her research interests also span the history of legal thought, comparative law, feminist legal theory, identity theory, and critical legal studies.

Janine Benedet is an Associate Professor at the University of British Columbia, Faculty of Law, where she teaches criminal law, labour law, and the regulation of sexual offences. Her areas of research include sexual violence against women, such as sexual assault, pornography, prostitution, and sexual harassment. Prior to joining the UBC faculty in 2005, she was an associate in labour and employment law at a Toronto law firm and a faculty member at Osgoode Hall Law School. She is a member of the bars of both Ontario and British Columbia.

Susan B. Boyd is a Professor at the University of British Columbia, Faculty of Law, and also holds the Chair in Feminist Legal Studies at the University of British Columbia. She works in the fields of family law and feminist legal studies. She recently co-edited *Reaction and Resistance: Feminism, Law, and Social Change* (2008); *Poverty: Rights, Social Citizenship, and Legal Activism* (2007); and *Law and Families* (2006). She is the author of *Child Custody, Law, and Women's Work* (2003). Her current research focuses on the shifting conceptions of motherhood in family law in relation to the fathers' rights movement and expanding legal definitions of parenthood and family.

Kim Brooks is an Associate Professor at McGill University, Faculty of Law, and is the H. Heward Stikeman Chair in the Law of Taxation. She teaches in all areas of taxation; however, her primary research interests lie in the areas of corporate and international tax and include tax policy.

Melina Buckley is a lawyer and legal policy consultant working primarily in constitutional and human rights law, access to justice, and dispute resolution. Between 1991 and 1993, she served as Project Director to the Canadian Bar Association (CBA) Task Force on Gender Equality in the Legal Profession. She is counsel to the CBA in its test case litigation on the constitutional right to civil legal aid and has represented intervenors in several cases at the Supreme Court of Canada, including *Symes, Meiorin, Little Sisters, Via Rail,* and *Christie.* She holds a Ph.D. in law from the University of British Columbia.

Rosemary Cairns Way is an Associate Professor at the University of Ottawa, Faculty of Law, where she recently completed a five-year term as Vice-Dean. She graduated with the gold medal in law from the University of Western Ontario and clerked at the Supreme Court of Canada. In 1997, she became the initial national coordinator of the Social Context Education Project at the National Judicial Institute. She has continued her association with the National Judicial Institute since returning to the Faculty of Law in 2000. Her current research is focused on the infusion of equality values into judicial education, law school pedagogy, professional responsibility, and the substantive criminal law.

Gillian Calder is an Assistant Professor at the University of Victoria, Faculty of Law. Since her appointment in July 2004, Professor Calder has taught courses and related seminars in constitutional and family law. Her current research interests include law's regulation of women, work, and family; the provision of social benefits through Canadian law; feminist, constitutional, and equality theories; and the relationship between performance and law.

T. Brettel Dawson is an Associate Professor at Carleton University, Faculty of Law. She teaches in the areas of women and the legal process and socio-legal research methodology. Chair of the department between 1994 and 1999, she was the English language co-editor of the *Canadian Journal of Women and the Law* in 1991-92 and 1994-96. She is also Academic Director at the National Judicial Institute (Canada) and was previously the Coordinator for Social Context Education at the institute. She has continuing responsibility for social context integration in judicial education along with projects involving curriculum and pedagogy development. She is also involved in international judicial reform.

Angela Fernandez is an Assistant Professor at the University of Toronto, Faculty of Law, where her research and teaching interests include contracts, legal history, and the legal profession. Professor Fernandez completed a combined LL.B. and B.C.L. in the National Program at the Faculty of Law, McGill University, in 2000. In 2000-1, she served as law clerk to Justice Michel Bastarache of the Supreme Court of Canada. She completed her LL.M. at Yale Law School in 2002, and her dissertation, *Spreading the Word: From the Litchfield Law School to the Harvard Case Method,* was awarded a J.S.D. degree by Yale Law School in 2007.

Isabel Grant is a Professor at the University of British Columbia, Faculty of Law. She received her law degree from Dalhousie University and her LL.M. from Yale University, after which she was a law clerk to Justice Willard Estey at the Supreme Court of Canada. Her primary research interests include substantive criminal law and mental health law. She has published widely in the areas of homicide and violence against women. Recently, she published a paper on the criminalization of the non-disclosure of one's HIV status and two papers (with Janine Benedet) on the sexual assault of women with mental disabilities.

Rebecca Johnson is an Associate Professor at the University of Victoria, Faculty of Law, where she teaches criminal law, law-and-film, and business associations. Before completing her LL.M. and S.J.D. at the University of Michigan, she was a law clerk to Justice Claire L'Heureux-Dubé at the Supreme Court of Canada. Her research interests generally involve issues of intersectionality and particularly the discourses and practices of power operating at the intersection of law and popular culture. Her current research project considers reason and emotion in the judicial dissent.

Larissa Katz is an Assistant Professor at Queen's University, Faculty of Law, where her current research and teaching interests include property, intellectual property, law and development, and the theory of rights and obligations. Professor Katz obtained her LL.B. from the University of Alberta in 2000 and her LL.M. from Yale Law School in 2004. Prior to accepting an academic position, she clerked for Justice Charles Gonthier at the Supreme Court of Canada and practised international corporate and securities litigation with Sullivan & Cromwell LLP in New York.

Claire L'Heureux-Dubé's legal career spans over fifty years. A judge in the Quebec Superior Court and the Quebec Court of Appeal, she was the second woman, the first from Quebec, to be appointed to the Supreme Court of Canada, where she was best known as a staunch champion of social justice. She has been the President of the Quebec Association of Comparative Law, the Chairman of the Canadian section of the International Commission of Jurists, the International President of the International Commission of Jurists, and the Chair of the Steering Committee of the Maison de justice de Québec. She received the Margaret Brent Women Lawyers of Achievement Award, became an Honorary Member of the

American College of Trial Lawyers, was granted the Companion of the Order of Canada, and was made a Grand Officer of the National Order of Quebec.

Moira L. McConnell is a Professor at Dalhousie University, Faculty of Law, where she teaches contract law and a variety of courses related to international marine and environmental law. She obtained her LL.B. from Dalhousie Law School and her Ph.D. in law from the University of Sydney (Australia), where she also lectured. She was an articled clerk to Justice Wilson at the Supreme Court of Canada (1984-85). Currently, she is also a special advisor to the Director of the International Labour Standards Department, International Labour Office of the International Labour Organization, and works on a variety of projects with a broad range of organizations, governments, and academic institutions. She has published widely in the fields of public and private international law, corporate law and governance, administrative and constitutional law, environmental law, maritime law and policy, and human rights law.

Mary Jane Mossman is a Professor at Osgoode Hall Law School of York University, where she teaches family law, property law, and issues of gender equality and the law. Widely published in these areas, Professor Mossman also researches legal aid and access to justice, social assistance, and the history of women in the legal profession. Her most recent book is *The First Women Lawyers: A Comparative Study of Gender, Law and the Legal Professions* (2006).

Shannon Kathleen O'Byrne is a Professor and former Associate Dean of Research and Graduate Studies at the University of Alberta, Faculty of Law, where she teaches contracts law, corporations law, and judicial remedies. Professor O'Byrne has published and delivered papers on a wide variety of topics, and her work has been cited by courts across the country, including the Supreme Court of Canada. Additionally, she has been recognized for her teaching skills, receiving both the Tevie H. Miller Teaching Excellence Award and the AC Rutherford Award for Excellence in Undergraduate Teaching from the University of Alberta in 2002.

Debra Parkes is an Associate Professor at the University of Manitoba, Faculty of Law. She obtained her LL.B. from the University of British Columbia in 1997 and her LL.M. from Columbia University in 2001. Her teaching and research interests include criminal law, constitutional law (with a focus on equality and social and economic rights), employment and labour law, and penal law and policy. Professor Parkes is the President of the Canadian Law and Society Association and a member of the Manitoba Bar.

Janis Sarra is a Professor at the University of British Columbia, Faculty of Law, and is the Director of the National Centre for Business Law. She served as Associate Dean of the Faculty of Law until 2007, and in 2004, she was awarded the title of Distinguished University Scholar for her scholarship in corporate and securities law. She is the author of numerous books, reports, and articles on corporate law, financial services law, and insolvency law. Her most recent books include *Rescue! The Companies' Creditors Arrangement Act* (2007); *Business Organizations: Principles, Policy and Practice* (2007), with R. Yalden *et al.; The 2007*

Annotated Bankruptcy and Insolvency Act, co-authored with G. Morawetz (2006); and *Securities Law in Canada, Cases and Commentary,* co-authored with M. Condon and A. Anand (2005).

Beatrice Tice is an Associate Professor and Associate Dean for Library and Information Services at the University of California, Irvine's newly founded Faculty of Law. After receiving her law degree from Stanford Law School in 1989, Professor Tice spent over nine years in practice as a litigator with several large southern California law firms. She received her M.L.I.S. with a Special Certificate in Law Librarianship in 2000 and since then has worked in academic law libraries, including serving as the Chief Law Librarian at the University of Toronto, Faculty of Law, from 2004 until June 2008. Professor Tice's research interests include the influence of legal publishing practices on the development of the rule of law.

Lorna Turnbull is an Associate Professor at the University of Manitoba, Faculty of Law, and a graduate of Queen's University, the University of Ottawa, and Columbia University. She has taught and published in both law and women's studies. She recently published *Double Jeopardy: Motherwork and the Law,* which is recognized nationally and internationally as "essential reading" on motherhood and law. For most of her life, Professor Turnbull has also been involved in social development at the grassroots level. She has served as part of an advisory group on gender equality claims being litigated before Canadian courts and is currently working with the UN Platform for Action Committee promoting gender-sensitive budgeting to the government of Manitoba.

Christina Vinters completed a Bachelor of Laws degree in 2009 at the University of Victoria, where she was awarded the Horne Coupar Prize in Family Law and the Borden Ladner Gervais Summer Legal Research Fellowship. Prior to attending law school, she studied sociology and women's studies at the University of Toronto, where she received the C.L. Burton Open Scholarship and the Irving Zeitlin Award. Her interests include family law, social and legal theory, and social justice issues.

Index

Note: "(f)" after a page number indicates a figure; "(t)" after a page number indicates a table

Stephen Clarkson and Stepan Wood
A Perilous Balance: The Globalization of Canadian Law and Governance (2009)

Amanda Glasbeek
Feminized Justice: The Toronto Women's Court, 1913-34 (2009)

Wayne V. McIntosh and Cynthia L. Cates
Multi-Party Litigation: The Strategic Context (2009)

Renisa Mawani
Colonial Proximities: Crossracial Encounters and Juridical Truths in British Columbia, 1871-1921 (2009)

James B. Kelly and Christopher P. Manfredi (eds.)
Contested Constitutionalism: Reflections on the Canadian Charter of Rights and Freedoms (2009)

Catherine E. Bell and Robert K. Paterson (eds.)
Protection of First Nations Cultural Heritage: Laws, Policy, and Reform (2008)

Hamar Foster, Benjamin L. Berger, and A.R. Buck (eds.)
The Grand Experiment: Law and Legal Culture in British Settler Societies (2008)

Richard J. Moon (ed.)
Law and Religious Pluralism in Canada (2008)

Catherine E. Bell and Val Napoleon (eds.)
First Nations Cultural Heritage and Law: Case Studies, Voices, and Perspectives (2008)

Douglas C. Harris
Landing Native Fisheries: Indian Reserves and Fishing Rights in British Columbia, 1849-1925 (2008)

Peggy J. Blair
Lament for a First Nation: The Williams Treaties in Southern Ontario (2008)

Lori G. Beaman
Defining Harm: Religious Freedom and the Limits of the Law (2007)

Stephen Tierney (ed.)
Multiculturalism and the Canadian Constitution (2007)

Julie Macfarlane
The New Lawyer: How Settlement Is Transforming the Practice of Law (2007)

Kimberley White
Negotiating Responsibility: Law, Murder, and States of Mind (2007)

Dawn Moore
Criminal Artefacts: Governing Drugs and Users (2007)

Hamar Foster, Heather Raven, and Jeremy Webber (eds.)
Let Right Be Done: Aboriginal Title, the Calder Case, and the Future of Indigenous Rights (2007)

Dorothy E. Chunn, Susan B. Boyd, and Hester Lessard (eds.)
Reaction and Resistance: Feminism, Law, and Social Change (2007)

Margot Young, Susan B. Boyd, Gwen Brodsky, and Shelagh Day (eds.)
Poverty: Rights, Social Citizenship, and Legal Activism (2007)

Rosanna L. Langer
Defining Rights and Wrongs: Bureaucracy, Human Rights, and Public Accountability (2007)

C.L. Ostberg and Matthew E. Wetstein
Attitudinal Decision Making in the Supreme Court of Canada (2007)

Chris Clarkson
Domestic Reforms: Political Visions and Family Regulation in British Columbia, 1862-1940 (2007)

Jean McKenzie Leiper
Bar Codes: Women in the Legal Profession (2006)

Gerald Baier
Courts and Federalism: Judicial Doctrine in the United States, Australia, and Canada (2006)

Avigail Eisenberg (ed.)
Diversity and Equality: The Changing Framework of Freedom in Canada (2006)

Randy K. Lippert
Sanctuary, Sovereignty, Sacrifice: Canadian Sanctuary Incidents, Power, and Law (2005)

James B. Kelly
Governing with the Charter: Legislative and Judicial Activism and Framers' Intent (2005)

Dianne Pothier and Richard Devlin (eds.)
Critical Disability Theory: Essays in Philosophy, Politics, Policy, and Law (2005)

Susan G. Drummond
Mapping Marriage Law in Spanish Gitano Communities (2005)

Louis A. Knafla and Jonathan Swainger (eds.)
Laws and Societies in the Canadian Prairie West, 1670-1940 (2005)

Ikechi Mgbeoji
Global Biopiracy: Patents, Plants, and Indigenous Knowledge (2005)

Florian Sauvageau, David Schneiderman, and David Taras, with Ruth Klinkhammer and Pierre Trudel
The Last Word: Media Coverage of the Supreme Court of Canada (2005)

Gerald Kernerman
Multicultural Nationalism: Civilizing Difference, Constituting Community (2005)

Pamela A. Jordan
Defending Rights in Russia: Lawyers, the State, and Legal Reform in the Post-Soviet Era (2005)

Anna Pratt
Securing Borders: Detention and Deportation in Canada (2005)

Kirsten Johnson Kramar
Unwilling Mothers, Unwanted Babies: Infanticide in Canada (2005)

W.A. Bogart
Good Government? Good Citizens? Courts, Politics, and Markets in a Changing Canada (2005)

Catherine Dauvergne
Humanitarianism, Identity, and Nation: Migration Laws in Canada and Australia (2005)

Michael Lee Ross
First Nations Sacred Sites in Canada's Courts (2005)

Andrew Woolford
Between Justice and Certainty: Treaty Making in British Columbia (2005)

John McLaren, Andrew Buck, and Nancy Wright (eds.)
Despotic Dominion: Property Rights in British Settler Societies (2004)

Georges Campeau
From UI to EI: Waging War on the Welfare State (2004)

Alvin J. Esau
The Courts and the Colonies: The Litigation of Hutterite Church Disputes (2004)

Christopher N. Kendall
Gay Male Pornography: An Issue of Sex Discrimination (2004)

Roy B. Flemming
Tournament of Appeals: Granting Judicial Review in Canada (2004)

Constance Backhouse and Nancy L. Backhouse
The Heiress vs the Establishment: Mrs. Campbell's Campaign for Legal Justice (2004)

Christopher P. Manfredi
Feminist Activism in the Supreme Court: Legal Mobilization and the Women's Legal Education and Action Fund (2004)

Annalise Acorn
Compulsory Compassion: A Critique of Restorative Justice (2004)

Jonathan Swainger and Constance Backhouse (eds.)
People and Place: Historical Influences on Legal Culture (2003)

Jim Phillips and Rosemary Gartner
Murdering Holiness: The Trials of Franz Creffield and George Mitchell (2003)

David R. Boyd
Unnatural Law: Rethinking Canadian Environmental Law and Policy (2003)

Ikechi Mgbeoji
Collective Insecurity: The Liberian Crisis, Unilateralism, and Global Order (2003)

Rebecca Johnson
Taxing Choices: The Intersection of Class, Gender, Parenthood, and the Law (2002)

John McLaren, Robert Menzies, and Dorothy E. Chunn (eds.)
Regulating Lives: Historical Essays on the State, Society, the Individual, and the Law (2002)

Joan Brockman
Gender in the Legal Profession: Fitting or Breaking the Mould (2001)